SIR JAMES MACKENZIE, M.D.
1853-1925
GENERAL PRACTITIONER

The Author

ALEX MAIR

M.D., F.R.C.P.(Edin.), F.F.C.M., D.P.H., D.I.H.

Department of Social and Occupational Medicine,
University of Dundee

Sir James Mackenzie (aged about 70).

SIR JAMES MACKENZIE, M.D.
1853–1925
GENERAL PRACTITIONER

by

ALEX MAIR

CHURCHILL LIVINGSTONE
EDINBURGH AND LONDON
1973

ISBN 0 443 01001 3

M4267
27/6/80

Printed in Great Britain

To
the memory
of
Miss Dorothy Mackenzie
whose
great love and admiration for her father
were such an inspiration

ACKNOWLEDGEMENTS

The writing of this biography has taken a very long time. The only excuse one can offer is that, over the years, it had to be fitted in during brief leisure moments, in train journeys and holidays in what is a very busy professional life. I hope, in the process, that the demands on my wife and family on the one hand, and my department on the other, have not been too exacting, and that neither has suffered unduly!

First, I would wish to express my indebtedness to the late Miss Dorothy Mackenzie to whom the work is dedicated and to whom I owe so much, for her encouragement and confidence that one day I would see it through. My one regret is that she did not live to share that moment.

Lord Amulree has throughout been a constant help, and has given generously of his time and made available to me so much that was intimate and personal between Sir James and his father.

In such a work as this, the collection and collation of facts and opinions relating to the subject of this biography have ranged over a wide field, and involved interviews and correspondence throughout the world with people far too numerous to mention. Failure of me to do so, one hopes, will not be taken as any mark of ingratitude or discourtesy.

Acknowledgement and thanks are due to a number of individuals to whom many requests for help and assistance, albeit persistent and tedious, never failed to be met with a courtesy and kindness which was, to me, almost embarrassing. Among these, I would like to mention the names of Dr John Linnell, M.C., London; Mrs Ruby Mackay, Burnley; the Reverend David Keir, Perth; and Dr Andrew Garvie, all of whom have died since I started to write this biography.

Tribute is also made to the help and assistance from Mr Richard Caul and Mr R. C. Burton of the Borough Library, Burnley. I am particularly indebted for personal impressions and recollections from Sir John Parkinson, Dr William Evans, Sir Alum Rowlands, Professors Emeriti Adam Patrick and David Dow of the University of St Andrews. Dr J. Mulligan, formerly of the Department of Anatomy, helped to interpret and decipher parts of the Wenckebach letters, while Dr A. C. McKerrow recalled vividly for me the excitement of the early days of the St Andrews Institute. I am indebted also to the Library staffs of the Universities of St Andrews, Dundee, Aberdeen, Edinburgh, Toronto, to the Wellcome Historical Medical Museum, and the Royal Colleges of Physicians in Edinburgh and London.

Acknowledgement is also made to the Court, University of Dundee, who so kindly granted me three months sabbatical leave in order to complete the biography.

Above all, I owe a deep debt of gratitude to Mrs Nancy Small who, in the earlier years, served not only as secretary and typist but as a colleague sharing with me the pleasure of discovery and exploration, of sifting masses of letters and papers, and drawing together the web of this story. Assistance in the typing of drafts fell to Miss S. Duncan, while the final draft was completed by Mrs P. McDonald. Thanks are also due to Miss G. Russell, Librarian, and Miss M. Laing.

Lastly, I wish to express my gratitude to my friend and former colleague, Emeritus Professor Sir Ian G. W. Hill, who was so kind as to read the manuscript.

Alex Mair

Dundee, 1970

PREFACE

The first edition of *The Beloved Physician*, by Dr R. McNair Wilson, appeared in October, 1926, eighteen months after the death of the subject of his biography of Sir James Mackenzie. With memory fresh, with the cadence of the great man's voice still ringing in his ears, with the aura of Mackenzie's influence ever present in the world of medicine, the author had an unrivalled opportunity to launch that great romantic story. For romance it was.

It was reprinted in the following month, again three months later and finally in April 1927. It was superbly written, and it was no small tribute when the author could say 'it represents the best of which I am capable . . . It is really very easy to write when you are given a great hero, and a great dramatic story . . . My other books seem so difficult and dull by comparison . . . I will never again write any book as I wrote that one . . .'

The key to the popularity of this first biography and the need for further reprints is illustrated by a further letter to Lady Mackenzie, in which the author writes, 'Perhaps you will think that I have written in too popular a way . . . and that I strove earnestly to make my hero live and to make his ideas comprehensible to ordinary men and women . . .' In this, Dr McNair Wilson saves me the need to offer an apology for the appearance of yet a second biography. Moreover, he wrote . . . 'I began in the kind of academic way I thought would be the right treatment. And then, curiously . . . I knew that this would never do . . . I had to write about *the man*.'

Whatever verdict posterity will proffer, medical history owes a great debt of gratitude to that author for rekindling a flame which might have dimmed or died with the death of Sir James Mackenzie in 1925. Instead the story lives on.

In the event, it has stirred the enthusiasm and imagination of countless people, of young medical students, aspiring doctors and lay people from all over the English speaking world. Above all, it has sustained the enduring belief that for the practice of medicine to survive, it must remain an endeavour which is essentially human and humane.

Dr McNair Wilson was Medical Correspondent of *The Times*. His association with Mackenzie was brief, extending from the autumn of 1916 to 1918 when Mackenzie left London for St Andrews.

Although McNair Wilson continued to practise from Harley Street, his heart was in journalism. ' It is the aim of my life to live, in the end, by my pen alone . . . I have always been " pen-struck " since I was a child. My people made me a doctor . . .'

I can make no such claims to the literary art, nor indeed can I claim to be a clinician in the true sense of the word. Suffice it to say that during World War II, I returned from Europe (actually on the eve of V.E. Day) on my very first visit to Burnley in order to marry a Lancashire lass. For me, Burnley became a second home. Small wonder then, that, as a young Scots doctor, I was soon to be made aware of how the memory of ' The Beloved Physician ' was still revered by the older generation. Years later, in 1954, fate was to decree that I should be appointed to be the second incumbent of the newly formed James Mackenzie Chair of Public Health and Social Medicine at St Andrews University.

Soon requests of all kinds, for letters, for books and relics of Mackenzie came from people in all quarters of the world and, in particular, from America. The medical records of the former James Mackenzie Institute of Clinical Research were in the safe keeping of one of the Trustees, who stored them in the basement of his draper's shop in Dundee. Were they worth keeping or should they finally be destroyed? It was impossible to avoid entanglement in this fascinating web of medical history which began and ended here in this north east corner of Scotland.

Later I was to learn that Sir James Mackenzie's daughter, Miss Dorothy Mackenzie, was still alive and had made her home in Liverpool. From her I learned that it had always been her wish, and that of her mother, the late Lady Mackenzie, that an official and more objective biography of Sir James should be written. On reflection, perhaps prudence should have persuaded me otherwise. The task proved more formidable than anything I had imagined, and I had few qualifications for undertaking such a daunting task. But I had fallen under the spell . . .

CONTENTS

Chapter 1

THE HEART

Mountains divide us and the waste of seas,
Yet still the blood is strong,
The heart is Highland
And we in dreams behold the Hebrides
                        Canadian Boat Song

The scene was the Albert Hall in London and the year 1925. The vast arena was packed, the atmosphere tense and expectant, for this was Burns Night. At this same moment, at similar gatherings all over the world, Scots, exiled from croft, from glen and sheiling, were gathering to pay homage to their national bard.

Among the bleak mountains and scattered villages of the Highlands, lack of opportunity had for generations, like some huge centrifugal pump, driven its young men to the farthest corners of the earth. It was Dr Johnson who said ' The noblest prospect which a Scotsman ever sees, is the highroad that leads him to England.'[1]

Two distinguished members of that band of exiles at the Albert Hall that January night of 1925 were Sir James Mackenzie and his brother Sir William (later Lord Amulree). Both had brought their families. Sir James, now 72, knew that his days were ebbing fast. The tablets of trinitrin seemed now to be losing their effect and could not dull the excruciating pain across his chest wall—the angina pectoris, to the study and understanding of which he had devoted so much of his professional life. He had not been well all day, but he so much wanted to attend what he perhaps knew would be the last Burns evening of his life.

Faintly at first, then louder and louder came the skirl of the pipes. The concert was about to start. The ' kilted warriors of the north ' were making their triumphant entry to the stage. Few there are among Scots who are not moved by scenes like these, reminded as they are of mist clad mountains, of rugged landscapes, the snow clad shoulder of Ben Nevis, the sombre shadows flitting across Coruisk, of Ben Hope and Stac Polly . . . reminded also of that great heritage which is theirs. Sir James was obviously moved. Suddenly

[1] Johnson's Remark to Mr Ogilvie, 1763.

1

his face paled, turning bluish-grey. He was ill, and would have to go home.

For the next 24 hours he lay gradually becoming weaker and weaker. He was, however, very composed, would wake now and again and then quietly on the 25th January he died in his sleep. But this was not the end . . .

'Mackenzie,' wrote Sir John Parkinson[2] 'took his anginal pain and physical restrictions in good part, for he arranged his life accordingly and otherwise took no notice. I never remember him being nervous or anxious. A few weeks before his death, he told me at his flat in London, that I had to do a " post-mortem " when the time came. I protested, but he smiled and said that his brother, the late Lord Amulree, would see that I did as he wished. At that period he would quietly chew a trinitrin tablet before leaving his study to enable him to walk into the lounge to greet one of his numerous visitors.'

And so it was, clinical research must prevail. Assisted by another of his former young promising assistants, Dr J. W. Linnell, Sir John carried out the post-mortem in the bathroom next door. ' He died undoubtedly from an attack of coronary occlusion . . .'

> Far may we search before we find
> A heart so manly and so kind.[3]

The meeting of the Senatus Academicus of St Andrews University had ended sooner than expected. It was mid afternoon on a grey November day in 1961, and my next train to Dundee was not due for another hour. Across the sky, menacing clouds were sweeping in from the east telling of storms far out in the North Sea. Should I repair to the common room and join my colleagues for tea? I ambled on, my steps echoing through a low ivy hung archway to the cloistered quietness beyond. Two girl students, red gowns billowing, were making their way towards the library. White fan-tailed pigeons, startled at my presence, took themselves up to join others on the eaves and windows of St Mary's. Five centuries and more seemed to bear lightly on this famous seat of learning. I recalled it was to this small town with its ancient University that Sir James came to carry out the last of his great researches in clinical medicine.

To the far end of this quadrangle lies the more modern Bute building, made, like its neighbours, of grey-yellow sandstone, but not

[2] (1954) *British Heart Journal*, **15**, 125.
[3] *Marmion,* Sir W. Scott, Canto 4, Introd.

yet mellowed by centuries of exposure to the salt sea air. Within this building is housed the Department of Anatomy, and it was towards this place I now slowly directed my steps for I had heard it whispered that here was preserved the actual heart of Sir James Mackenzie. How strange I thought, and yet how appropriate, that his heart should have been brought back home to that part of Scotland from whence he had started out nearly 50 years ago. Did not the Knights of old, in bygone days of chivalry, set out on their crusades against the Saracens, some to return with glory and some to die? Six centuries earlier Robert the Bruce fought another crusade against the English. Unable to fulfil his fondest hope, to be buried in the holy land, he asked that his heart be carried thence by the Black Douglas. Alas, his earlier crusade, like the journey of his heart were to remain unfulfilled. James Mackenzie was of a similar mould. Did not he set out from Edinburgh University on a similar crusade, armed with simple weapons of medical knowledge and skill, to seek battle with the giants of disease, of death and medical ignorance? No more fitting tribute could be paid to this modern Knight than that his heart should be brought back to rest here in St Andrews, where his last battle was to be fought.

Mr James Brown, the Chief Technician of the Department has given long and yeoman service to the University of St Andrews, a fact to which successive generations of medical students will testify. What is more, he had actually worked as a technician to the great man himself. When I explained the purpose of my visit, his joy was immediate, his face glowed and off he went. In a few moments, he returned with a huge perspex specimen case which he carefully and reverently placed on the bench before me. As if about to display the Crown Jewels, he whispered awesomely. ' This is his heart . . .'

And may I remind the reader that this heart, for well nigh 73 years, beat the rhythm of a remarkable story.

Chapter 2

SCONE AND DESTINY

' Behold the Tiber !' the vain Roman cried,
Viewing the ample Tay from Baiglie's side;
But where's the Scot that would the vaunt repay
And hail the puny Tiber for the Tay
SCOTT, The Fair Maid of Perth

Winding its leisurely way from beneath the shadow of Ben Lawers and Ben Bhreac onwards beyond Kenmore, past Aberfeldy and Dunkeld, the Tay meanders through Perth to meet the tidal waters of the Firth some sixty miles beyond. To the north, Kinnoull Hill stands sentinel over the river and wooded valley below, its tower reminiscent of the castles of the Rhine. Beyond Kinnoull and sloping gently towards the north, lie the fertile acres where this story begins.

It was on a cold day in early December, with winter's grip already hard and unrelenting on the frozen fields, that I came to the village of Scone, in Perthshire. My journey was in the nature of a pilgrimage, for here James Mackenzie was born—the farmer's son who, to use his own words, was ' steadfast to the bottom of his class ', but who nonetheless was to become one of the world's greatest pioneers in medicine.

He was born on the 4th of April, 1853, at Pictstonhill Farm, on the outskirts of Scone. This village is a place of singular beauty, rich in historical associations. Of the ' old city ' of Scone scarcely a stone now stands save the market cross, the burial ground and the ancient moothill. It is a ghost town . . . for towards the end of the eighteenth century the owner of Scone Palace, the royal residence, decreed that it must be removed further from his gates. In its ancient Abbey Scotland's Kings were crowned from the beginning of her history, upon the Stone of Destiny, until its removal to Westminster Abbey on the orders of King Edward I. As long ago as the year 910 Scone was a Royal City, Regalis Civitas according to ancient muniments. It stands on the north bank of the Tay about two miles above the city of Perth. The present village, known as New Scone, took its place, and the site of the ancient royal city now forms part of the policies of Scone Palace, home of the Earl of Mansfield. Throughout the course of history many a town must have lost its Cross, but the Cross of Scone is perhaps the only cross to lose its town!

The road winds steeply up from Scone to Pictstonhill. I passed the little stream which was called locally ' Mackenzie's Burn ', and on this December day it was edged with spicules of ice. Bare trees were wreathed in mist and around me there was a deep winter silence, a sense of timelessness. A hundred years ago the children of farmer Robert Mackenzie and his wife Jean had run laughing down this very path, their heels ringing on the icy ground, heedless of the high destiny to which two of them at least were to be called. The low single storey building which was their home stands on the crest of a hill, its squat lines contrasting strangely with its modern counterpart nearby, where now lives the present owner of Pictstonhill;[1] he uses the old building to house his office and garage. Looking at the old sandstone walls, testifying to the rigors of many years of Scottish wind and weather, and at the small room and low ceilings, it was impossible not to marvel that here, in this small holding and farm, the Mackenzie family, father, mother and seven children, had lived and been nurtured. Across the yellow waving corn the children had looked from their tiny windows south-westwards to the spires of Perth rising from the hanging mists below—Perth, the ' Fair City ' of Sir Walter Scott. Westwards their young eyes would have encompassed Ben More and Ben Vorlich, on a clear day even the distant heights of Argyll. A wider vista would have taken in the Grampians, ending in the broad shoulder of Schiehallion.

The Mackenzie family originated in Ross-shire, that part of Scotland to the north and west of Inverness. The name ' Mackenzie ' is an anglicized form of Mac Coinnich—' Son of Kenneth '—and the Clan Mackenzie is said to be of pure Scots-Gaelic descent. At one time a very powerful clan, it held sway over much land in the Kintail district on the southern shore of Lochalsh, across the narrows from the Isle of Skye. It is probable that James Mackenzie's ancestors came south into Perthshire after the Jacobite Rebellion in 1746, driven by the tide of poverty and eviction, a trend which was to become a feature of the ' clearances ' in the Highlands a hundred or so years later. The Mackenzie forebears settled at Stanley, a little town on the banks of the Tay about seven miles north of Scone, and it was here at Derrymill Farm that James' father, Robert Mackenzie, was born.

---

[1] Mr J. Reid has since died.

Little is known of his mother's family. She was born Jean Campbell Menzies, daughter of Basil Menzies whose family had farmed for several generations around the village of Amulree in the Strathbraan district of Perthshire. Jean, the mother, was born in the tiny hamlet of Inver, where the River Braan joins the Tay opposite Dunkeld. Inver has its own small claim to fame; it was once on the main coaching road from Perth to Inverness and was the home of Neil Gow, famous Scottish fiddler, and was well-known as a musical centre in the early eighteenth century. To-day it is a picturesque hamlet hiding in the shadow of Birnam Hill; readers of Shakespeare will recall the witches' warning to Macbeth: ' Fear not, till Birnam Wood do come to Dunsinane.' Dunsinane Hill lies roughly five miles east of Pictstonhill Farm.

It was to Pictstonhill, then, that Robert Mackenzie brought his bride in the year 1846. Its extent then was roughly 100 acres of arable farm land, leased, as were the other farms in the district, from the Earl of Mansfield. This was the fourth earl, whose life-span extended nearly the whole of the nineteenth century. Robert Mackenzie paid an annual rent of £500 for his hundred acres, surely a heavy burden at nineteenth-century values. Added to which was the requirement that any benefits resulting from improvements of building carried out by him automatically accrued to the landlord and no compensation was paid to the tenant. Robert Mackenzie was an enterprising and progressive farmer who was out to make two blades of grass grow where one grew before, and he made many improvements to his land, including the drainage of his fields. This task was so well done that the drains were functioning, and functioning well, some 50 years later. He had untiring zeal for order, for neat and tidy workmanship, and would never ' let a slack stitch pass.' 'Ae dae a thing snod ', he would say, and he would have been happy for all his sons to have followed him into farming. As it was, he had to be content that one, the eldest, did so, but each member of the family was expected to work in the field.

Four sons and three daughters were born to Mr and Mrs Mackenzie of Pictstonhill; James was their third child and second son. Their first-born, Maybelle, was born in 1848, followed by Basil two years later and James in 1853. Then came Robert in 1855 and William in 1860, and the family was rounded off in 1862 by the birth of twin daughters, Jane and Margaret.

Of the four boys born in that small farmhouse, two were destined to achieve greatness and a third also to make his mark in the world, though to a rather lesser degree. This was Robert, who became a

PLATE 1. Pictstonhill farm.

PLATE 2. Pictstonhill farm showing former gable window.

PLATE 3. The Mackenzie family.

From left to right
Standing behind: Maybelle, Basil.
In front: Robert, 'Auld Jockey', who worked on the farm, Jean, Mrs Robert Mackenzie (Mother), Margaret, Mr Robert Mackenzie (Father), William, James.

Minister of the Church, and wrote several books, the best-known being ' John Brown of Haddington ', a biography of the famous Scottish clergyman whose ' Self-Interpreting Bible ' had an immense circulation in Scotland and elsewhere. William, the youngest son, became an able and distinguished Barrister and filled several high Government positions; he was knighted in 1917, and created a baron. the first Lord Amulree, in 1929. The career of James as physician, cardiologist and clinician the following pages will enfold.

The education of the Mackenzie boys demanded considerable sacrifice on the part of their parents. James, Robert and William all attended Edinburgh University. There were no educational grants in those days. Times were very hard during the 1870s, when, to add to the pecuniary difficulties, there was a succession of bad harvests. and many tenant farmers in the district went bankrupt. That the Mackenzies survived, and survived so well, was due to three factors. the improved methods of agriculture, the sheer persistence and hard work of the father and, above all, the inspiration of the mother. If Mr Mackenzie was the solid, reliable yeoman of the soil with his feet firmly fixed on the ground, his wife was the abiding inspiration around whom the family revolved. She was the vivid personality upon whose encouragement they all relied and whose ambition for her sons captured their imagination and stirred them to do great things. Her ambitions and horizons extended far beyond the boun·· daries of the farm. William, later Lord Amulree, has written of her:

> She was the mainstay of the family. She had a strong, indomitable spirit, and when things were going badly on the farm it was her noble soul that rose above difficulties and trials. She was also the unostentatious and generous helper of the poor in the village, and all in distress came to her for assistance and comfort. James owed much to the example of his parents, and his mother's influence endured throughout his life.

With his brothers and sisters, James attended the village school in Scone, and progressed from there to Perth Academy at the age of twelve. James by this time was already beginning to show the distinct characteristics of the man. Lithe of limb, with long tapering fingers, not seemingly destined for either toil or soil, tall for his years, even in the family portrait he stands out as distinctive and apart. A proportionately large body supported shoulders tending to droop away from head and neck, which in turn seemed to display, even at this tender age, an attitude of simple courage and defiance. His eyes, grey-blue and piercing, were set wider apart and obviously

7

had all the liveliness and awareness of his mother. He had also inherited her wide mouth with narrow lips accentuating a chin which seemed to become more aggressive and purposeful as the years went on. From an unusually large brow, thick brownish black hair was swept firmly back partly hiding his large ears, to bestow on a young face that air of leadership and personality which was later to mark him out from the common herd. But inwardly he felt doubts —doubts about his future career, uncertain about his innate ability. In his early years at school he did not excel, probably for the reason that learning for the sake of learning did not appeal to him. One of his teachers once remarked to his mother: ' Mrs Mackenzie, your James is the most stupid boy in the school ', and James remembered this taunt when towards the end of his life, he presented the prizes at his old school, Perth Academy, in the summer of 1922. Addressing the pupils, he went on.

When you go out into the world, you will discover that those who did not get prizes, and whom you and your teachers thought were stupid dunces, turn out after all to be the really clever boys and girls. Everyone is surprised, and the boys and girls are delighted.

The reason for this disappointment which awaits the clever boy and girl, and the delight which awaits the dunces, is simply due to the fact that the manner in which prizes are gained is no evidence of real ability. If you inquire into the reason for this difference, you will find that there are two types of mind. There are boys who have got the power of memory highly developed, while other boys have a different quality of mind, by which they exercise their reason and they cannot remember a thing unless they have got a reason for remembering. The boy who can only remember 10 or a dozen lines learns them with understanding. He tries to see what is the reason of this con-glomeration of words, and he is therefore utterly unable to learn the 100 lines because he fails to perceive what they are all about, and moreover his type of mind prevents him from giving the words exactly as they follow one another. That is to say, he may understand the sense of the words although he may not be able to quote them exactly. Let me illustrate this. When I first came to this school, after being here a few months, I was extremely steadfast to the bottom of my class, and my mother called to see the teacher. This teacher informed my mother that there was no use of wasting any money on my education as I was hopelessly stupid. My mother didn't believe him, because mothers have a far better conception of a boy's capacity than a schoolmaster has, and the reason is very simple, for the mother sees the boy under natural circumstances and can tell whether he is a stupid boy or not, while the schoolmaster sees the boy under artificial circumstances when the boy is never himself, and therefore he can never get to know that boy. I place a mother's estimation of a schoolboy before that of a schoolmaster.

His was the second type of mind; he had to have a 'reason for remembering.' To a young mind, groping and uncertain, a verdict of stupidity delivered by a teacher may well be daunting and discouraging. But not to James Mackenzie, nor to that shrewd observer and discerning helpmate—his mother.

Chapter 3

PIETY AND PROSE

' I think you would have called him an agnostic '
—DOROTHY MACKENZIE.

In 1843, ten years before Mackenzie's birth, Scotland had been the scene of the Disruption, the break-away movement from the Evangelical Church. Approximately a third of the Evangelical ministers, followed by roughly the same proportion of the population, formed what came to be known as the Free Church. They gave up their manses, churches and stipends, and their faithful congregations had to find buildings for worship, and by various means to find the wherewithal for economic survival.

The previous tenant of Pictstonhill Farm at this time was Mr James Stewart, father of Rev James Stewart of Africa, better known as ' Stewart of Lovedale '. He was the great friend of David Livingstone and founded the Livingstonia Mission in Central Africa. One of the great Empire builders, he was the adviser in all native questions to General Gordon, to Cecil Rhodes, to Sir Bartle Frere and Lord Milner. It was fitting, then, that the barn at Pictstonhill was offered by Mr Stewart as the first meeting-place of the Free Church in Scone, and in these austere surroundings the first Sacrament of the new Church was held. An extract from Urquhart's ' Historical Sketches of Scone ' reads as follows:

> The first Sacrament was dispensed in the barn, an old-fashioned building without windows, the only light coming in by the doorway. When the Communion elements were placed on the table, which was opposite the door, the light falling upon the cups, aided by the effect of the assembled worshippers receding into the darkness, produced quite a Rembrandt picture . . .
>
> Meanwhile, the erection of a substantial church was proceeding. At first the stones from the nearest quarry were refused by the proprietor, and the Committee had to procure whinstone from Muirhall at considerable expense and labour. When it was seen that the congregation were determined to proceed in spite of all difficulties and opposition, the proprietor relented; but the lower band of blue whinstone round the church building is a

standing memorial of the animosity that then existed towards the Free Church.

The Mackenzies themselves belonged to the United Presbyterian Church, of which Robert Mackenzie, the father, was an elder, as the grandfather had been before him. Mackenzie's father was also treasurer of the Church for many years, and his grandson, the Rev David Keir, recalled him as a ' most methodical man, a formidable statistician '. When he presented his annual report he gave details of every single coin which had been placed in the offertory-plate during the previous year, recording the exact number of half-pennies, pennies, etc. The Mackenzie children grew up in an atmosphere which was strongly religious. Sundays were completely devoted to public worship and to private Bible instruction and discussion at home. During morning and afternoon the family filled two pews in the United Presbyterian Church, and all the children attended Sunday School as well. The great feature of these early Sundays, however, was the evening session when they gathered round the kitchen table, the father at one end and the mother at the other, the seven children taking their places in between, and joined by Jocky Menzies, the old ' orra-man ', who had served Mr Mackenzie for a lifetime.

Then the father would put his family to the test on the substance of the sermons they had heard at the morning and afternoon services. Discussions and interruptions were sometimes lively, as when James was asked what the minister had said under the third heading of his discourse, and James' version was challenged by everybody else: ' No, no, Jim, he didn't say that!' Whereupon James warmly re-torted: ' Well, if he didn't say that he ought to have done, then he wouldn't have landed up the tree where he did!' Unluckily, when his father began his weekly questions on the Shorter Catechism it was James who landed up the tree. He could not fit the questions and answers into anything he knew on earth; he could not remember the sequence of words that hung meaningless in the air, seemingly disconnected and irrelevant to the thoughts that absorbed his lively and restless mind during all his waking hours. His father sighed, and sometimes grumbled under his beard, for he was troubled by the boy's obvious inability to get ' inside ' the Catechism. To his own disciplined mind the whole orderly tenor of his life kept in unison with the precise clauses of accepted doctrine, and inability to recite the commandments jarred upon him as a false note will disturb the harmony of an orchestra. The rest of the family did not take it so seriously, and one of them said once : ' Jim always got fairly stuck in the Catechism, but if *he* hadn't been there, our Sunday evenings wouldn't have been the happy time that they were.' To James, faith and the blind acceptance of faith was one thing, but his was a quest for truth.

James told his own story of these evening meetings: another extract from his speech to the pupils of Perth Academy:

> There is nothing that showed a total want of knowledge of what education meant than when boys were forced to learn the Shorter Catechism. No boy should be asked to learn anything he does not understand. Boys in my day were compelled to learn the Shorter Catechism. My father was a worthy elder of the Kirk, and according to his lights, wished to bring us up in the way we should go, and on Sunday evenings he used to assemble his seven children and all the servants and ask them questions in the Shorter Catechism. Invariably, during this ordeal, I came in for severe reprimands, for I could never remember the words of any question except the very shortest. There was one of the servants who was word perfect; he could answer every question from beginning to end perfectly. Now this man was what we called on the farm an ' orra-man '. That is to say, he did odd jobs about the farm because he had not enough intelligence for any work that required the use of his brain. He had no power of reasoning; in other words, he was half-witted, but he had a most remarkable memory.

Despite the remembered discomfiture at his struggles with the Catechism, Mackenzie's mind must often have strayed back in time to those Sunday evenings at Pictstonhill. More important, his intellect was being moulded on the anvil of experience, that there were two kinds of brain, one the repetitive and the other the reasoning. Yet Mackenzie in his adolescence was groping, still uncertain and insecure, and convinced that in later years this need for reasoning and logical deduction based on observable facts was to become the keystone of his life's work.

James in his address, was both taunting and provocative towards things ecclesiastical and doctrinal. Perhaps he was being less than fair to the remarkable influence which this upbringing and environment has had not only on himself but on countless Scottish ' lads o' pairts ' who have gone forth into the wider world with no better equipment than an unswerving respect for right and wrong, for human integrity and morality and the abiding virtues of truth and righteousness.

There was found amongst his belongings at the time of his death a small pocket Scripture Atlas in which he had painstakingly written the details of his homework for Sunday School. The rounded, schoolboy hand records: ' May 27th: to learn Psalm 121. Scripture reading. Gidean, Baal, Midianites, Aprah, Joash.' That these early lessons and Bible readings stood James in good stead is borne out by reference to the letter he wrote.

He was a prolific correspondent all his life, and was never at a loss for an apt Biblical quotation. His nephew, Rev David Keir, told the story of what must have been one of the first of these apposite remarks:

> As a first-year student in Edinburgh, my father had written a friendly letter to James, who was still living at Scone. By way of a little showing-off, he quoted a sentence or two in Greek, and the Greek hadn't much bearing on anything else in the letter, it was just hauled in by the hair. James replied in due course, a long chatty letter which filled several pages. It ended like this: ' Now, David, next time you write to me, don't you be quoting Greek, I don't understand the language and don't need to. Besides, remember what St Paul says: " I had rather speak five words with my understanding than ten thousand words in an unknown tongue." (1 Corinthians 14, verse 19). My father, who told me of the incident, considered that rejoinder as almost unsurpassable in the circumstances.

The Mackenzies' minister of the United Free Church at this time was the Rev John McNeil, who was ordained at Scone in 1864, a young man of extraordinary energy and enthusiasm. Almost immediately on his settlement in Scone he stirred up the young men of his congregation to get together and run their own society, called the Association for Mutual Education and Improvement—or less formally the Scone Young Men's Association. Other groups came into being within other congregations, and they were soon led to meet fraternally in a larger and comprehensive society. The Mackenzie boys, one after another as they became old enough, joined the forty or so other lads from the village who became members of the Association. Meetings of a religious nature were held on Sunday mornings after the Church services, and on Monday evenings the discussions and lectures were more general, though mainly devoted to the subject of literature. Rev David Keir wrote vividly of the Association in Scone:

It dated from about 1864, and in 1873 joined up with the national and international Y.M.C.A. which had been initiated in London in 1844. The comprehensiveness which was an attractive feature of the Y.M.C.A. as founded by Sir George Williams was excellently illustrated in Scone, where the members of the Association, belonging as they did to one or other of the three village churches, collaborated in a lively unity and endeavoured to make the business of Christian living and working their first and outstanding business. Just because they were principally concerned about putting ' first things first ', an *esprit de corps* grew up among them and between them that persisted long after they had left their native fields. I have witnessed instances of this spontaneous and happy concord that grew up in the village Association where they gathered in from their different ecclesiastical affiliations. On one occasion I was present when two ' old boys ' of the Scone Association chanced to meet after thirty years or more. They had never glimpsed each other in the interval, and their lives had fallen far apart, but now when they were meeting again, the intervening years dropped away, and the two middle-aged men were back amid the explorings and literary adventures of those Monday evenings when they had talked their heads off and had built their flimsy bridges into the future.

James Mackenzie was an active member of the Scone Association, and it was in the various papers which he wrote, and presented, that his undoubted literary ability first showed itself. He became one of the first members of the literary branch of the Association, and kept up his membership all through his university career, although it was only during vacations that he was able to play an active part. The following letter referring to one of his papers is headed; ' Pictstonhill, February 14th, 1873 ' :

Dear David,

I am sorry that I have not found time until now in answering your last welcome epistle. I have been so busy of late in preparing a paper which I delivered before our Association on Monday last. The subject of the paper was ' Paul's Character and Travels '. In such a subject as this, you will easily see that it would be impossible to do proper justice, and to give in detail the various circumstances owing to the wide scope of the subject on hand. However, I managed to get through it. Although I received some small praise for it from the members of the

Association, yet I know better than to place any importance on the statements of the various members, as it is their invariable custom to do so, to every aspiring member. However, I was exceedingly glad when I resumed my seat after spouting for the space of half an hour. Had I had time I think I could have made a great deal better job of it than I did, especially of that part whereon I had to speak of Paul's character.

(' Dear David ', was, later, the Rev David Keir (1853-1933), minister at Dennyloanhead, Stirlingshire. In their early years James Mackenzie and he were close companions, and became related in 1879 when David married James' elder sister Maybelle. David Keir left school very early—in his case ' res angusta domi '—learned the bakery business, and, by the time he had reached the age of twenty, had acquired sufficient classics and mathematics to gain a bursary at Edinburgh University. He was ordained at Dennyloanhead in 1879 and remained there for forty-three years. His son, also Rev David Keir (one of eight children) has left on record many of his recollections of the famous uncle he loved and revered.)

James Mackenzie may have been doubtful about the success of his paper on St Paul, but apparently he had no need to be, for the records of the West Church in Perth show that it was also read there in the same year (1873). Mackenzie retained a deep veneration for the man Paul, and some fifty years later he sharply called to account a St Andrews student who was debunking the apostle.

Mackenzie and David Keir were in the habit of criticizing each other's efforts in the field of literature, and took the subject seriously, as this further extract from the same letter will show :

From D. Keir to J.M.   14th February, 1873.
    How is your paper progressing? When you have finished it, send it to me so that I will be able to form an opinion as to your literary capabilities. Of course, I will not set it down in my mind as a sample of your ability as that would be doing a great injustice to you, indeed for what do I, or any other one, know what will follow a ' first attempt '. Be sure, though, and send it for my inspection . . . You ask me to give you an idea of the defects in your composition, but I must see about my own being properly rectified first. I find that as regards composition yours is correct, or at least nearly so, as far as I am aware. The mistakes in spelling are only those that would be caused by one writing in a hurry. I need only, to substantiate this, quote one, and I think solitary one, in your last epistle.

It was ' competion '; of course you meant ' competition ', but as I said before the haste accounts for that. I shall be more able to give a minute review should you favour me with a look at your essay. Also tell me if my letters to you are lucid and if they are properly done, as it is a great dread to me that I should be falling off in composition.

This dread need not have troubled Mackenzie. He continued to write with ease and fluency all through his career, and owed a great deal to the experience gained at the Scone Association. Many years later, when he was in general practice in Burnley, he wrote to his brother William :

J.M. to Will :

My lecture about which you evince some curiosity was delivered before a Society in connection with one of the churches, and the members reminded me much of the Scone Young Men's Association. There was an equivalent for the Venerable Keir and another who resembled James Robb. Altogether there were forty working lads and men; I read them two pieces and used a lot of padding about the cultivation of the intellect . . .

After Mackenzie's death in 1925 there was found in his pocket-book a paper yellowed with age, the corner creased and torn, but the handwriting on it still clear and legible after more than fifty years. It was an interpretation of the thirty-seventh chapter of Genesis, the story of Joseph, and was written during these early years at Pictston-hill when James too would have been about seventeen years. Probably read at the Scone Association, it begins :

In these verses we have presented to us the commencement of the detailed account of Joseph's eventful life. Here—at the age of seventeen years—full of life and vigour, with all the buoyant spirits of youth developing into manhood; guileless, free, open-hearted, of a sound moral disposition, possessing in fact all these qualities which give promise of a future life to be directed into paths of virtue and rectitude. How sad must it have been for him at this most susceptible period of life, to be torn away from all old associations, from all whom he held dear and amongst whom it was expected that his latent qualities would have been developed. Sadder still to contemplate that he was forced away by his own brothers and barely escaping with his life from their hatred he is compelled to submit to a state of slavery and misery for thirteen years.

16

Mackenzie goes on to explore the reasons for the hatred shown to Joseph by his brethren; their own misdeeds reported in all innocence to their father Joseph; Jacob's deep and freely-expressed love for this younger son; above all Joseph's own character . . . ' Joseph's habitual good conduct and fine moral nature would not only endear him to his father, but would also engender a spirit of hatred in the hearts of the brethren. Such is always the case; that which is good and true is always hated by that which is bad and false, and any means are taken to thwart its increase.' The young Mackenzie had early realized this essential truth, and his summing up of Joseph's story shows an understanding of human nature beyond his years:

Why was it that Mackenzie carried this faded and tattered essay with him to the end of his life? Did he value it as a priceless gem of literary merit? Was it to remind him later of the ' severe and harassing experiences along life's way?' Or was it an eternal light which perchance would shine through these early biblical teachings to remind him ' that which is true and good is hated by that which is bad and false?' In any event, it is known that his early faith did not long survive, and that he himself deeply regretted its loss. His daughter Dorothy has illustrated this:

> I remember once somebody saying: ' Of course Mac, you're an atheist ', and Father was very angry; he said he was not an atheist, but he said ' I do not know.' I think you would have called him an agnostic. He had the greatest longing for Faith, that I do know, and I remember when I was reading Livingstone's Journals towards the end of our time in Burnley when I would be about seventeen, and I said: ' Oh, Father, how awful, the way he died ', and he said: ' He was one of the happiest men in this world—I envy him with all my heart; he had complete faith '.

His nephew Rev David Keir (son of D. Keir his teenage friend) wrote more recently:

> I never heard him crystallize in so many words his position towards institutional religion or any particular Christian creed, and can only offer a surmise of my own . . . He did appear to feel a wistful sense of detachment from the traditions of the Kirk that was dear to his mother and from the Catechism which his father treasured and taught to his family, and which Mackenzie confessed was always too high and too hard for him as a boy. Perhaps a mist *did* gradually intervene between the

17

questing man stretching onward towards new horizons and the Bethlehem of his early years. If that was so, he was still the last man in the world to cast any chilling reflection that would disturb the honest devotional life of the many sincere believers with whom he worked; and he would be first and foremost in his willingness to acknowledge the debt he owed to a godly heritage and upbringing.

Did Mackenzie find difficulty in resolving an inner conflict or perhaps was he like his great friend, Sir Arthur Keith, whose origins, background and training so closely resembled his own, and who wrote in *An Autobiography* (London, Wates & Co., 1950):

> I had no difficulty in accommodating in my mind my religion and my science in those study days. The story of the Creation was, of course, a myth, but what of that? The incompatibility of religion and science was a plant of later growth . . . My consciousness reminded me that if I did put on the garment of repentance, it was a mere pretence, for in my heart I did not believe it . . .

The year was 1885, and Darwin's *The Origin of Species* had reached its sixth edition. Science and religion were in conflict and the prevailing climate of opinion called for followers of a new doctrine to stand up and be counted. Mackenzie, unlike Keith, may not have stood up, but he was uncertain.

Chapter 4

BETWEEN SCHOOL AND UNIVERSITY

To seek the light of truth, while truth the while . . .
Light seeking light, doth light of light beguile
SHAKESPEARE, *Titus Andronicus*

James Mackenzie was fifteen when he managed to persuade his father to allow him to leave school. He was impatient for a change and had resigned himself to the fact that he was no scholar. Despite his anxiety to be quit of school life, he nevertheless retained happy memories of his years at Perth Academy, and in 1922 he wrote an article the ' Young Barbarian ', for the school magazine, in which he recalled with affection some of his former class-mates and paid tribute to his teachers:

I left the Academy in 1868 at the age of fifteen, and have not visited it since, so I expect many changes have occurred in its interior—structural as well as educational. As I early migrated South, I also lost contact with my old fellow-scholars, and there was little of interest to keep the Academy in my mind.

In after life I accidentally came across a few of my old school fellows. Pat Geddes, now the brilliant Professor Patrick Geddes, was a class-mate of mine. I did not come across him till many years after we had left school. As a boy he was a nice-looking, plucky little chap. I remember a great fight he had on the North Inch with another boy belonging to another school. In those days, when the snow lay on the ground, there were pitched battles on the Inch, when the other schools combined to fight the Academy. Occasionally during those snow-ball fights a personal encounter would arise, and it was in the centre of the ring that the future famous professor engaged in fisticuffs.

Another class-mate was Willie Archer, now the famed dramatic critic; a great traveller, and the translator of Ibsen. I had not seen him for over 40 years, when we met in London and talked over our school days. He then lived at Scone, and we went back and forward together. I have still a distinct recollection of my first introduction to the immortal Pickwick. Walking home one afternoon, just beyond Kincarrathie, I overtook Archer reading a book, but stopping every now and again to yell with laughter.

When I asked him what he was reading he told me it was Dickens' famous novel.

A few years ago we were lunching together in a famous London Club, and we fell to comparing the present meal with that of the spartan days of our youth. I said I thought I was allowed three half-pennies for my dinner. He said: 'You must have been a millionaire, I was only allowed one penny. When I spent this on two buns, about 12 o'clock, I felt starved before I got home between four and five, so I used to spend a halfpenny on a bun and a halfpenny on sweety bools. These latter I sucked on the way home, and they put off the craving for food . . .'

There was one experience which has stuck to me through life. For many years I have been engaged on an investigation into Pain, a subject which is of immense importance in the study of disease. The most bitter experience of this subject is linked in my mind with a sense of injustice and embitters the recollections of one of my teachers. No doubt I received and deserved many punishments, but they were forgotten, probably because the punishment 'fitted the crime', but there was one which remains in my memory because of its injustice and severity. I had to walk from Scone to school, and, once on one bitter cold windy day, the road slippery and covered with snow I was five minutes late. My hands were tingling with cold, and Bulldog Smith took up his cane and with all his strength gave me a 'palmy.' The cane hit right across the end of my half-frozen thumb, and the agony remains in my mind to this day as the severest pain I ever experienced.

I cherish a kindly regard for these old teachers, and although we called them by names of seeming disrespect—Horney, Poker, Ghosty and the like—yet we had a profound veneration for them, and in after life, a feeling of gratitude and affection. In place of handing the junior boys over to an inexperienced teacher, they did the elementary teaching themselves, for it is at the outset of learning that the most experienced teacher is wanted—' as the twig is bent', etc. But there, I have views on the psychology and physiology of education which are not orthodox.

One of the unorthodox views to which Mackenzie referred was that children should not be taught anything until they were ten years, when they should learn to write, read and add up with understanding, never being allowed to read one sentence more than was completely understood. They should never be taught to memorize multiplication tables and such, 'like parrots'. His own inability to learn 'by heart', was directly responsible for these views, and he found no reason to alter his opinion when later he went to Edinburgh University and met exactly the same difficulties which he had encountered in school. He wrote forcibly when telling of his personal experiences, on a theme which was to recur again and again:

> There are two very distinct qualities of the human mind, memory and the power of reasoning. The earliest to be developed is that of memorizing and this can be cultivated with great ease. The power of reasoning is quite different, although no doubt memory takes a part. When we look at a great number of students we will discover that this power of memory is greatly developed in a few, and all our educational methods are devoted to its cultivation. Examinations are specially contrived for the purpose of discriminating those with the best memory, and to them all the honours and prizes are given. Theirs are minds which have difficulty in remembering isolated facts, but if these facts are related in some consecutive manner, they can not only remember the facts but appreciate their relation the one to the other. But this type of mind is slow in acquiring knowledge, and in our present-day methods of education, less and less encouragement is given to this type of student. His peculiar powers are never developed and their presence is never suspected.

Mackenzie's was not to be the only voice crying in the wilderness on the subject of education and examinations. Patrick Geddes, to whom he referred in his article in *The Young Barbarian*, and who was destined to become botanist, biologist, sociologist, educational reformer and practical town-planner, was, like Mackenzie, a man born before his time. He was born at Ballater, on Royal Deeside, but from the age of three he spent his boyhood in a cottage on the slopes of Kinnoull, a few miles from Pictstonhill. Again, like Mackenzie, he was for a long time unsure of the path he was to tread, and on leaving school he spent a year in a Perth bank, followed by three years studying at home under tutors. Then he entered Edinburgh University in October 1874 (which was also when Mackenzie started his first term as a medical student) to study botany. He stayed a week, and decided it was not for him. The following year he became a student under Huxley at the Royal School of Mines

21

3

in London. Here he proved beyond any doubt the statement Mackenzie was to make that 'examinations are specially contrived for the purpose of discriminating those with the best memory, and to them all the honours and prizes are given.' Patrick Geddes boasted to his fellow-students that 'any fool can cram', and proceeded to wager each one of them half-a-crown that with a week's notice he could pass any examination the school had to offer. For a week he studied Metallurgy, and then sat for the official examination along with the engineering students. He passed, and received a certificate which entitled him to fill the position of government metallurgist. A week or so later he could remember next to nothing of the facts he had so hastily crammed . . . but he still had his certificate of 'knowledge and competence'. Writing in the *Scottish Review* in 1888, he said that a complete reversal of academic policy was needed, so that *teaching* would dominate mere routine *examining*, and if Mackenzie read those words of his one-time school-fellow he must have added a loud and heart-felt 'Hear, hear'. All his life Mackenzie was occupied with the subject of reasoning, of logical deduction, of learning for the sake of knowledge and not for the mere accumulation of unrelated facts. In 1922 he stayed at the home of his nephew David, the Minister, whilst he was in Perth for the Speech Day of his old school.

'Have you read *Kim*?' he suddenly barked at David, who had to confess that he had not, although he knew that Kipling had written a book of that name, an Indian story.

'Read it then, read it,' Mackenzie replied. 'There's a lot of good stuff in it, especially chapter nine.' And he lent David his own copy so that he would have no excuse for not reading it.

The ninth chapter tells how Kim, the young Anglo-Indian boy who is being prepared for the Secret Service, is sent to stay with one Lurgan Sahib in his shop at Simla for ten days' intensive instruction. One of his first tasks is to play the 'Jewel Game' in competition with a Hindu child, and Kim makes very heavy weather of this. A pile of jewels is heaped on to a tray, and after only one brief look the boys must tell each item on the tray. The native child is able to describe each gem in minutest detail and to judge its weight; he is equally successful with other articles. Even when his eyes are blindfolded and he is allowed only a single touch with his fingers he is still expert and unbeatable. Kim is angry and humiliated because he has been shown up in this fashion, and asks how it is done.

'By doing it many times over till it is done perfectly for it is worth doing', is Lurgan Sahib's answer.

PLATE 4. The young apprentice chemist, 1869.

The chapter goes on to relate how the two boys play the Jewel Game each morning, and how each afternoon they sit concealed in the shop where their task is to observe the many customers who come to see Lurgan Sahib. At the end of the day they must give a detailed account of all they have seen and heard, their view of each man's character and their notions of his real errand. The native child, so quick and clever with the Jewel Game, is slow and clumsy at this task, as he is also at the ' dressing-up ' game which follows, in which they must try to assume the identities and mannerisms of the people they have observed. Kipling wrote:

> The Hindu child played this game clumsily. That little mind, keen as an icicle where tally of jewels was concerned, could not temper itself to enter another's soul, but a demon in Kim woke up and sang with joy ...

At the age of sixty-nine Sir James Mackenzie recognized immediately his affinity with the child Kim, but the boy Jimmy Mackenzie at fifteen was only dimly aware of his latent faculties. He was discouraged by his lack of learning ability; he had as yet no sense of vocation, no calling to the profession in which he was destined to play so distinguished a role. He wanted a change, to earn his own living. The light still did not beckon.

He left school in the summer of 1868 and spent the golden harvest days in the fields with his father and brothers. During these long summer hours his thoughts strayed to Perth, to the chemist's shop in George Street, where he was to take up his apprenticeship with Messrs Reid & Donald. It happened like this. One wet Saturday he had passed the shop, and seen the window brightly lit, the large jars of coloured water sparkling and scintillating. Their jewelled brilliance contrasted vividly with the drabness of wet, grey streets and represented to the boy who stood there all the colour and glamour which his life seemed to lack. His imagination was fired, the colours beckoned him in some inimitable way, his mind was made up: he would be a druggist.

Poor Jimmy Mackenzie; he found that, contrary to the dreams of that Saturday night, there was little glamour attached to his new occupation. The work was humble and wearisome, the hours long; twelve hours each day from Monday to Friday, fifteen hours on Saturday and four on Sunday. It was a sadly disillusioned youth who trudged the mile and three-quarters between Perth and Pictstonhill each day, and he came to dislike his work at the shop more and more as time went on. It gave him a sense of claustrophobia. Nevertheless, he was to say in later years that he did not regret the time he had spent in the chemist's shop, because it taught him endurance. It brought him into social contact with the hardships and realities of life. As always his mother was his mainstay during the uncertainty of his apprenticeship; she it was who revived his often despondent spirits and encouraged him to stick to his chosen task. His father had not wanted him to leave school; the boy could not very well complain to him that things had not turned out as he had imagined they would, for fear of a sternly parental ' I told you so '. But Mrs Mackenzie knew her son, and her sustaining influence did much to brighten his days. On Saturdays it was often close on midnight when he trudged the last mile up the hill to the farm, and on these nights, before she went to bed herself, she placed the lamp in the gable window casting its beam down Mackenzie's brae, so that its tiny gleam would shine out to light him home on his last weary steps.

For his first year's toil Mackenzie received the princely sum of five pounds, the first instalment of £2.10. being paid over to him at the end of six months. One of his most vivid recollections was of the thrill of receiving that first wage packet and handing it over to his father. He must often have looked back and seen in his mind's eye the tall youth running breathlessly home through the February gloom; over the bridge with never a glance at the dark waters of the Tay, nor at the glimmering lights of Perth as he left them for the lonely road to Scone. There would be the last lap up the hill to the farm, the triumphant flinging open of the door, the flushed, excited cheeks, the thought that it had all been worth it for this moment alone. Mackenzie's three subsequent years as an apprentice were to bring in £7. 10., £10 and £15 respectively, and during his last year with Reid & Donald when he had reached the position of assistant, he earned between £30 and £40.

There was little spare time for James Mackenzie during those years at the Chemist's shop, but he devoted much of it to reading. He came under the spell of Dickens, and was attracted also to Scott, Smollett, Fielding, Thackeray and Wilkie Collins. It was at this time also that ' Jimmy's novel ' (to quote his mother) began to take form. His life in the shop in George Street had provided him with much raw material and he felt the need to write of his experiences. Little information is available about this first adventure into fiction, but the theme and setting of the book were not in Perth. His handling of the subject-matter was a source of pride and also of amusement to his mother: she would say to her eldest daughter: ' Come on, Maybelle, and we'll have a read of Jimmy's novel and see what he's making of it now.' The young man felt no shyness or embarrassment about his handiwork, for the special drawer where the manuscript was kept lay open for inspection by the whole household. Unfortunately, like *Edwin Drood*, which was undergoing incubation at about the same period, ' Jimmy's novel ' remained unfinished. What had been written disappeared suddenly, into what limbo the author himself knew and he alone. But here once again was that literary thread so noticeable in the Monday evening activities, beginning to show itself against the backcloth of the drab monotony of the chemist's shop. Beyond the narrow confines of the farm, new horizons were beginning to appear. James Mackenzie found a new interest, books and more books—their themes intermingling with the new social fabric of Perth. He could write. He could now express himself. Perhaps he was not stupid after all? Perhaps a university and professional education might yet unlock the pent-up stirrings of an inward ambition. He decided to be a doctor.

No one knows with any certainty just when it was that James Mackenzie decided that his life's work lay in medicine. During his years as a chemist he would have come into contact with many doctors, and it would not be surprising that one may have inspired him to take this decisive step. For undoubtedly, the cloak of glamour which now surrounds the hospital specialist today, lay appropriately on the family doctor eighty years ago. Life and death were then his frequent companions, hope and gratitude his daily reward. Small wonder that Mackenzie was drawn to a career in medicine. There has been a suggestion that he was attracted to the ministry at this stage of his life, but there is no real evidence for this. His brother Robert was a divinity student at Edinburgh University, as was his friend David Keir, and his youngest brother William was also taking the Arts course there. It was inevitable that he should ponder over University life and contrast it, favourably, with his own. His decision was taken by the time he was twenty, for he was then offered a partnership in the firm of Reid & Donald, which he refused. It must have been a tempting offer to a young man of his age, and was proof of his ability, but his face was by then turned towards the University and towards medicine.

Mackenzie knew that as he had been away from school for five years he would have great difficulty in passing the university entrance examination, and that Latin would be his greatest bugbear. Accordingly he sought out the Rev John McNeil, the minister, as the one most likely to help him, and asked him to give him lessons. John McNeil's Latin was rusty from disuse, and he stumbled through the first book of *Caesar's Gallic Wars* as lamentably as did his eager pupil. Then all at once Mr McNeil seemed to collect his ' second wind ', and became extraordinarily fluent, rattling off each day's ration of Caesar like newsprint. Young James was astounded. He began to wonder how this facility was achieved so quickly, and if similar illumination would awaken in himself. His curiosity remained unsatisfied until one day when the meaning suddenly became clear. Mr McNeil was called out of the study. James was left stretching his long legs from his chair, and his eyes fell upon his tutor's desk, where a little yellow book lay upside down. He read on the cover: *Dr Giles' Key to the Classics, Caesar, Book I.* Just so simply was the riddle solved. James had not known that there existed such aids to learning as those of the philanthropic Dr Giles. In the years to come the pupil was to solve many a dour and difficult problem, but never so easily and conclusively as on that day in Mr McNeil's study!

He did not go to Edinburgh immediately on leaving the shop in Perth. Instead he spent a year in Glasgow, taking a position with the firm of Glasgow Apothecaries Ltd. in Sauchiehall Street and using his spare time to continue his studies, preparatory to sitting his university entrance examination. The reason for his going to Glasgow is obscure; he may have meant it as a trial period in which his decision to take up medicine would be confirmed or otherwise, for he had made one mistake and would be anxious not to make another. It appears from a letter written to his friend David Keir in December, 1873, only a few months after he had left Scone, that there were no doubts in his mind as to his intentions:

J.M. to David Keir

Mrs Johnston's,
151 West Graham Street,
Glasgow

Dear David,

I was rather surprised on opening your letter tonight for the purpose of replying to it that it was so long since you had written me. My neglect, however, must be excused on the grounds that the statements contained in your letter always remained fresh and green in my memory; I never thought the time flew so quickly by. And again I must be excused because of the trouble I have been put to lately in regard to the matter of lodgings. As I found it necessary to remove my tent from 24 Cleveland Street, I had some trouble in looking about the other lodgings, and also in getting my things all ready for removal. On Friday last we hired a cab drawn by the ghost of a horse, and after loading the cab with our boxes, etc., we entered ourselves, and were driven over here. On the journey, all enjoyment of our honourable position was marred by the fact that we were in dire trepidation lest our ghostly and fleshless horse would capsize ere reaching our destination. However, our transmission was made with all safety, and so here we are.

Ere proceeding further, however, I must congratulate you on the success you obtained in the Bursary competition. It is exceedingly gratifying, and cannot but be pleasant for yourself, taking everything into consideration, to see you standing so high amongst your compeers—Scone may indeed feel itself flattered seeing that two of its natives hold such high and honourable positions in the affairs of the United Presbyterian Students' Society. You have apparently got plenty of irons in the fire, seeing you have so many studies in hand. I have no doubt that you will have plenty of work before you. As for myself, I am grinding up my Latin, and various other subjects . . .

Mackenzie sat the Preliminary Examination in General Education of Glasgow University on 3rd and 4th April, 1874, and his certificate reads as follows:

Sir,   15 . 4 . 74
I hereby intimate to you that you have passed the Preliminary Examination in General Education—namely in the subjects of English, Latin, Arithmetic, Euclid and Algebra, and Elements of Mechanics—for Medical Degrees at this University.

I am, Sir,
Your Obedient Servant,
T. Moir, Registrar.

No-one has been able to explain satisfactorily why it was that Mackenzie sat the preliminary examinations for Glasgow University and yet went to Edinburgh. In any event, the first hurdle was overcome, and he left Glasgow in the autumn of 1874 with a glowing reference from his employers, and with the blessing of his parents in his new venture. He entered Edinburgh University for the winter session 1874–75.

Chapter 5

EDINBURGH UNIVERSITY

I was only suited for . . . the lowest place in the medical profession.

Ipse dixit

James helped his mother to pack his 'kist', the wooden chest traditionally used by Scottish boys journeying away from home. Into it went enough linen to see him through his first term, and plentiful supplies of oatmeal and butter. His father instructed him to keep careful account of every penny he spent and warned him that these accounts would be inspected on his return. Explanations would be called for if there had been any unnecessary expenditure. Times were hard at Pictstonhill, and James had witnessed his father's minute scrutiny of the accounts brought home for his perusal by both Robert and William. He was going to share 'digs' with his brother Robert, who was in lodgings with a joiner, his wife and small son in a typical 'room and kitchen' home in one of Edinburgh's tall grey tenements. The family lived and slept in the kitchen; Robert had the box-bed in the parlour— or 'the room', as it was simply called. There he ate, studied and slept. Together, he and James practised a naughty deception on their landlady. 'I will *not*', this good soul had declared roundly, 'have another *medical* student in my house'. She had had enough of the rowdy goings-on of the medical fraternity, and, moreover, had not her last student literally kept a skeleton in his cupboard? So when Robert tentatively enquired whether his brother James might come to share the box-bed, he carefully omitted to mention the nature of James's studies; the unsuspecting lady of the house assumed, naturally enough, that the brother of quiet, well-behaved Mr Mackenzie would also be studying divinity . . . James was duly welcomed into the household, and his secret was not discovered. There was no money to spare for riotous living, so noisy parties were out of the question in any case, and if he did have a skeleton in his cupboard, the noise of its rattling did not penetrate as far as the kitchen. The late Sir Edward Appleton, Vice-Chancellor of Edinburgh University, once wrote in the *Scottish Field*—'Let's not forget the great contribution made to student life by the good old Edinburgh landlady—alas, there are not so many

28

PLATE 5. Student days at Edinburgh university.

of them now!' Sir Walter Elliott, himself a medical graduate, distinguished politician, made similar laudatory remarks about the Glasgow landlady. In parenthesis, may one ask, is there any evidence that university paternalism in the form of canteens, cafeterias, and halls of residence, make for better students or more balanced graduates?

James and Robert were fed plentifully but plainly. There was porridge for breakfast, made from the Pictstonhill oatmeal; mince or steak with potatoes for lunch (but no pudding); and for supper bread and butter, jam and tea. Their social life was confined to occasional visits to the Debating Society and to visiting a student friend of theirs, John Gellatly. John would return these, and it was a standing joke between them to count up how much had been spent on each other's tea. John, on his visits, would look the table over with a critical eye and say: 'Scones, 2d, jam, 1d, butter 3d.' etc. 'Oh, shame! You've only spent a shilling, and I spent one-and-six on you last week!'

So the term passed uneventfully, with daytime lectures, evening study and very occasional relaxation, and with Church on Sundays, for the brothers carried on the pattern of church attendance which had shaped their lives at home. They were members of the United Presbyterian Church, Queen Street. There were no diversions and entertainments which would to-day be considered essential for the mind and body of a healthy young man, but James and Robert, and many others like them, survived and were immensely happy.

Three years after Mackenzie's death, Dr W. A. MacNaughton, joint Editor of the *Caledonian Medical Journal*, to which Mackenzie contributed over many years, wrote to Lady Mackenzie recalling the day when James first entered the portals of Edinburgh University:

> We held the Jubilee meeting of the Caledonian Medical Society in February last in Edinburgh. The thing that is chiefly memorable to me in connection with the old college is my first interview with Sir James. During the Jubilee proceedings I stood on the spot where I was when Robert and James came up the steps just 54 years ago and when Robert handed the raw recruit over to me. It was James's absolutely first entrance to the University of which he was to be such a distinguished graduate. Having been an Arts student for the preceding four years, I was qualified to act as guide. Standing there, and the place was unchanged, I pictured the advent of the two brothers quite distinctly, but somehow it did not seem to be the same world . . .

Edinburgh is the youngest of the four ' old ' Scottish Universities.
(Aberdeen, Glasgow and St Andrews are the other three). It was
founded in 1582 under a Royal Charter from King James VI, though
medicine did not form part of its curriculum until many years later.
The first college was built at Kirk o' Field, which had been the scene
of the explosion in which Darnley, husband of Mary, Queen of
Scots, lost his life. In 1879 the foundation stone of a new university
building was laid on South Bridge, and the medical school attended
by Mackenzie is still one of the largest single medical schools in
Britain. Since World War II it has incorporated one of the first of
the general practice teaching units in Great Britain, and Mackenzie,
with his insistence on the primary importance of the general practitioner, would have rejoiced to know that its first Chair of General
Practice, established in 1964, was named after him. But the young
student of 1874 had no thought of future fame as he struggled to
keep up with his lecture notes. He was not classed as anything more
than average, and he found his first year or two a dour struggle,
encountering the same troubles which had faced him at Perth
Academy. He had great difficulty in keeping pace with the lecturer,
and new words which he did not understand were constantly bom-
barding him. All his concentration was required to keep pace with
note-taking so that there was no time to comprehend what the
lecture was actually about. The evening hours were spent in tran-
scribing these scribbled notes and in trying to find out the meaning
of the unknown words. Often this was not possible, and he had to
try to memorize instead of understanding. He found out later that
the subject matter of all the lectures was printed in advance, and
after this he took care to arm himself with these printed notes before
the lecture concerned was due to take place. He would read them
over in advance and then when he went to class the following day,
he found that it was a joy to listen to his lecturer and that now he
only needed to make notes on any new matter which was introduced. Once he had established this routine he was able to pass his
exams more easily. From the beginning, however, there was one
man whose lectures were a sheer delight to Mackenzie, because he
took the trouble to reason the facts with his students and taught
them how to observe the significance of these facts. This was
Professor Sanders, who lectured in general and practical pathology,
and to whom Mackenzie was to work as clinical clerk in the wards
of Edinburgh Royal Infirmary during his final year. The interest in
clinical medicine aroused in him by Professor Sanders was to endure
throughout the whole of his life.

In this year of 1874, great discoveries were shaking the medical world. Holding the Chair of Clinical Surgery in Edinburgh was Joseph Lister (1827–1912), preaching to his students his gospel of the germ theory of disease. Lister had returned to Edinburgh in 1869 from Glasgow; between 1854 and 1860 he had been surgeon to the Edinburgh Royal Infirmary and lecturer in surgery to the Edinburgh College of Surgeons. Lister was convinced that the suppuration of wounds, the gangrene and the blood-poisoning which were so alarmingly prevalent in surgical wards all over the world, were due to the presence of micro-organisms introduced into the wounds either by their very presence in the air, or by way of the hands or instruments of the surgeon himself. In France Louis Pasteur (1822–1895) inspired by his interest in the chemistry of life, had earlier by his researches on fermentation led to the discovery of germs and thus to the science of bacteriology. Mackenzie was entering medicine at a propitious and exciting moment of time. What is more, he was to study clinical surgery under Professor Lister, himself a disciple of Pasteur. Whilst he was in Glasgow, Lister had introduced the use of carbolic acid into his wards in the Royal Infirmary, with striking success. Wounds healed without suppuration, patients recovered who would otherwise have been condemned to painful death. Yet amongst his colleagues were many who disputed his claims and who refused to believe the evidence of their own eyes. In Edinburgh, there were Listerians and anti-Listerians, those who supported the germ theory and those who did not. It is not recorded to which school James Mackenzie belonged, though in general the students were ' for ' Lister and the older men, reluctant to relinquish their own ideas and jealous for their own reputations, were against him. Like most men with an over-riding interest in one particular subject, Lister returned again and again in his lectures to his germ theory. Yet despite the tremendous impact that Lister's epoch-making contributions on osepsis in wounds must have made on the medical world, there is no evidence that it kindled a spark in the young receptive mind of the student from Scone. Indeed, as if in despair, Mackenzie heads his notes on one of Professor Lister's lectures on bacteria with an elaborately-pencilled ' Germs again !' and one can imagine the half-humorous, half-resigned groan which greeted the Professor's return to his hobby-horse. That it was a humorous, tolerant groan cannot be doubted, for Lister was well loved by his students. An addendum to Mackenzie's lecture notes dated 22nd February, 1877, reads as follows:

31

J. B. Balfour, Esq., at this stage presented Professor Lister with a requisition signed by over 700 students of medicine to the effect that he might not accept an offer to fill the Chair of Clinical Surgery in Kings College, London, which some people thought he was going to be asked to take. J. B. B. in a neat speech referred to the interest which many people had in this University, the glory of which was centred in and around Professor Lister, etc. etc. Professor Lister replied that he was not aware of anything that would tempt him to leave Edinburgh for London, etc. etc. (deafening applause, etc. etc.)

In spite of his statement on this occasion, Lister did, in fact, accept the Chair of Clinical Surgery at King's College, London, shortly afterwards.

The paths of the two men crossed briefly in 1888 through a patient of Mackenzie's:

My dear Sir

Mrs Handsley brought her daughter to see me the other day and I gave her advice which she said corresponded with your own. The tonsils are really not very large, and Mrs Handsley is quite sure that they are gradually diminishing, and we have further her own experience of having outgrown completely a similar condition. I think therefore that her child may do without operation, and at all events wait to see whether the diminution already going on will continue. Occasional touching of the tonsils with lunar caustic would very likely expedite matters.

> Believe me,
> Very sincerely yours,
> Joseph Lister.

There is no record of any further correspondence between them.

Neither Mackenzie's lively mind nor his facile pen was idle during these years in Edinburgh. His need to write of his experiences was still in evidence, as is borne out by the following account of his not-very-happy association with a fellow-student of poetical turn of mind:

I was particularly struck during my attendance at one of the classes one winter session by the appearance of one of my fellow-students. In the matter of dress he was distinguishable by its decidedly foreign cut. He wore his hair long and shaved his face very closely. During the lecture he was either gazing abstractedly at the roof or vainly trying to keep pace in note-taking with the lecturer's remarks. Somehow or other I always felt as if I would know this stranger, but did not feel at all anxious for his acquaintance, nay rather I felt more inclined to avoid him.

During the vacation a lady visitor at our house told me she was going to bring out next week a fellow-student of mine to see me. He was a nephew of hers, and hailed from California. Immediately I divined who the nephew was. Nor was I in error, for next week my mysterious stranger appeared. I found him at first rather a nice fellow, and in the walk we had together rather wondered at my feeling of aversion. However, the cause for this aversion was soon found. As we entered by a footpath that wound by the side of a stream, the mystery was explained by his announcing that he was a poet. This beautiful place reminded him of another occasion when he had been accompanied by a young lady. He had stolen a kiss, to the young lady's indignation, and the result was a poem which he now recited to me, and one poem led to another . . . Next session in Edinburgh, as he had few friends, he sought my acquaintance, and I yielded to his pressing invitation to spend an evening with him. About 7 p.m. I sat down in his bedroom on a narrow, uncomfortable cane-bottomed chair . . . he sat down in front of me with a massive volume . . . Catching sight of my furtive yawns he asked with pained voice if he bored me. Unluckily I lacked moral courage and said not at all—never was more interested—proud to hear a poet declaim his own poetry, etc. etc.

The poet, looking up at about 12 o'clock, found his appreciative audience fast asleep . . . supperless and exhausted I left his lodging.

Several things spring to mind on reading this passage of a chance encounter. The first is Mackenzie's intuitive sense and foreknowledge; when he first observed the poet in the lecture-room, he felt ' as if he would know this stranger '. When the ' lady visitor ' came to Scone: ' Immediately I divined who the nephew would be '. It comes to many of us at some time or other, this momentary, disconcerting glimpse into the future, but to the Highlander it comes more often and it speaks with certainty. How often in later years was he to emphasize the importance and clinical significance of observation and prognosis? Secondly, Mackenzie's ability to express himself is

33

confirmed; the aptitude he had shown earlier for literary expression, for painting word pictures in writing his papers for the Scone Association and attempting a novel, is still there. Had he chosen this field, instead of medicine, the world might have gained a writer of considerable merit—but it would have lost far more. The third and most striking thing to emerge from the passage is the character of the young Mackenzie, gentle, kind-hearted, incapable of inflicting hurt. 'As he had few friends, he sought my acquaintance ', and despite his confessed aversion Mackenzie could not spurn him. Neither could he bring himself to plead fatigue, to make any sort of excuse, as the hours to midnight wore on and his cane-bottomed chair became increasingly uncomfortable. Mackenzie set out to tell of an encounter with a poet; he has told us much about himself.

Mackenzie may not have acquitted himself with much distinction, but his class certificates at University show that he was by no means the also-ran which he invariably considered himself to be. He was a diligent student, and his certificates of attendance at lectures show that he was very rarely absent; only eleven absences are, in fact, recorded between 1874 and 1878. His examination results show consistent improvement; up to 1875 the only first-class certificate of merit he received was for practical chemistry, but in 1877–78 he received four. In the class of Practical Physiology he ' acquitted himself with high distinction and obtained 84 per cent of the available marks and a Medal.' As a member of the class of Operative Midwifery and Practical Gynaecology he obtained 86 per cent of the available marks and the first prize, and for Medical Juris-prudence 1878 ' he obtained 88·5 per cent of marks in the com-petitive examinations, gaining thereby the First Bronze Medal of the University '.

By any criteria, this represents a very creditable performance. Assuming a class of 180 students, he must certainly have found a place in the upper quartile, if not in the first ten. McNair Wilson, in his earlier biography, errs in literary licence by over-emphasizing his lack of academic achievement in writing:[1]

> Following graduation he prepared himself for General Practice. In other words, for the second time in his life he wrote himself down as an academic failure—a ' dunce ' and for the second time in his life—but this time deliberately—turned from the weariness of schools to the solace of life. His humble spirit

[1] McNair Wilson, *The Beloved Physician*, page 29.

accepted the low estimate of his abilities, which some, at least, of his teachers appear to have formed. He comforted himself with the reflection that, in any case, he had secured his degree and achieved his purpose, in however undistinguished a fashion.

Mackenzie himself could be faulted for over-playing this theme. The facts tell a very different story. Among the 103 medical students, who graduated in 1878, were Matthew Hay[2] and G. Sims Woodhead.[3] Hay distinguished himself by graduating (with six others) with First Class Honours. There were no second class honours. Both Mackenzie and Woodhead were in the ordinary pass list. Matthew Hay fulfilled his early academic promise by becoming Professor of Public Health at Aberdeen University. Sims Woodhead became Professor of Pathology at Cambridge. On the assumption that there is some meaningful correlation between student academic performance and elevation to a chair in later life, a study has been made of the Class ratings at University of these three students, two of whom were to become Professors, the other a general practitioner. Results are as follows:

FIRST PROFESSIONAL EXAMINATION

	Botany	Natural history	Chemistry	Chemical testing
Mackenzie	S*	S	S+	B
Woodhead	SB	B+	SB	Passed
Hay	S+	B	B	B

* Class ratings, *assumed meaning*: B = bene—good; B+ = better than good; BB = bene bene—very good; S = Satisfactory; S+ = very satisfactory; SB = satisfactory—good.

SECOND PROFESSIONAL EXAMINATION

	Anatomy	Institutes of medicine	Materia Medica	Pathology
Mackenzie	BB	S+	S+	S+
Woodhead	S	S	S	S
Hay	S+	S+	S+	S

[2] Professor Matthew Hay, 1855-1932.
[3] Professor G. Sims Woodhead, 1855.

FINAL PROFESSIONAL EXAMINATION

	Surgery	Medicine	Practice of Physics	Juris-prudence	Clinical Surgery	Clinical Medicine
Mackenzie	S+	B	S+	S+	BB	S+
Woodhead	S+	B	S	S+	S+	B+
Hay	B	BB	B	B	BB	B

Mackenzie did less well than the others in his First Professional, better than both in the Second, and marginally above Woodhead in his Third Professional. The outstanding and consistent performance of Matthew Hay is self evident.

Mackenzie wrote thus of his years at University:

> In my career through college I always had the greatest difficulty in keeping pace with lecturers and seldom succeeded. Evidently the standard, if there is a standard, which guides a teacher, is to pour out facts at a rate a little beyond the capacity of the student who has the most retentive memory. The consequence is that no student is able to absorb the whole knowledge, and most of them only a very small part of the knowledge. The only subjects in which I seemed to achieve a little success were in those where time was given us to reason out the meaning of our teachers, such as in the different clinical fields. During my college career I felt a longing to devote myself to some of the branches of medicine concerned in research, but my very moderate attainments precluded me from obtaining any of the coveted posts about the University, and I quite clearly recognised that I was only suited for what is considered the lowest place in the medical profession.

Mackenzie's own assessment of his overall academic achievement was ' moderate '. While his early years in the basic sciences were adequate, albeit undistinguished, his performance in the clinical years was quite outstanding. Moreover it must be remembered that unlike his fellow students he had left school at fifteen, and had the tremendous handicap of having no extended secondary education in either physics or chemistry. He had been away from school and study for six years. To hold his own in competition with his fellow students and to avoid any failures in his first two years at University, is itself a creditable performance. Mackenzie seemed to be labouring under a marked inferiority complex. Granted that University teaching posts

36

in those days were few, but new horizons were appearing in Surgery, Bacteriology and Public Health. Was not Matthew Hay to shine brightly amongst the galaxy of public health pioneers, to discover Hay's Sulphur Test in Urine and in his Annual Report at Aberdeen in 1902 almost correctly to anticipate the vector of typhus some five years before its discovery by the Frenchman, Nicole in 1907? Academic promise is not always fulfilled in later life, but more often it is. Mackenzie seems rather to have been expressing the universal doubts and uncertainties that weigh heavily on medical students, near or after graduation. Academically, Mackenzie may not have been a star, but equally he was no ' dunce '. Clinical medicine was his forte, and in Practical (presumably Applied) Physiology, even as a student he was to find his real métier.

University status and research were complementary. It was unthinkable for anyone to envisage doing research in the community without all the equipment and paraphernalia of a laboratory.

He despaired. There was no alternative. He was resigned, then, to joining the ranks of that lesser breed in medicine, the general practitioners.

Whilst he was still in the throes of his final examinations, Mackenzie received a proposition from his friends and neighbours in Scone. The farmers of the district had approached his father with an offer to guarantee him £120 a year if he would return there when he had qualified and practise amongst them. Mackenzie was troubled; what would be the best thing for him to do? He went for advice to his friend, Dr John Brown, Professor Lister's demonstrator and dresser. Dr Brown was several years his senior and had taken the young man under his wing, recognizing from the first his many sterling qualities. He and his wife, Mary, a famous social worker of her day, were living out at Joppa, and to their small flat in Leven Terrace came James with his problem.

' I think I had better just accept it ', he said unhappily—for who knew, there might be no other chance for such a mediocre student as himself.

' You'll do no such thing ', was John Brown's positive rejoinder. ' There's a residential post vacant at the Infirmary, in fact there are two. You can try for one of those.'

' Me? Try for a residency? Incredulously James stared at his friend. ' I wouldn't stand a chance, you know that as well as I do. I haven't any influence with anyone who matters and—well, I'm just not good enough.' The appointments to these coveted posts were made through open competition, and his faith in his chance of obtaining one was nil. But Dr Brown would have none of it. ' Nonsense, absolute nonsense ', he said. ' Just you take my advice, and you'll see.'

James took his advice, perhaps for the first time, certainly not for the last, and to his complete amazement the good doctor's confidence had been fully justified; he was awarded one of the resident posts. The appointment did not take effect until November; this was July, and he had therefore to find some means of support for the intervening months and also to save something for his pocket, for although bed and board would be provided at the Infirmary, his new post carried no salary. He had also to bear in mind his considerable debt to his father, for it was his intention to pay it off in full and as soon as was humanly possible.

He went first as locum-tenens to a colliery practice in Spennymoor, County Durham, where he received £2 a week and his keep. Most of his patients were members of a club; the head of each family paid sixpence a week to the doctor. This contribution was to cover all medical eventualities, and, in token of this payment, there was an attempt on the part of many patients to get as much out of the doctor as possible. James Mackenzie received at Spennymoor his first lesson on the psychology of medicine; the faith of the Durham collier in a bottle of physic was powerful, and the physic had to be powerful too, both in colour and in taste. A small quantity of burnt sugar makes a very dark colour in solution, and a little ginger added to this gives a strong ' grip ' when it is swallowed. This mixture, Mackenzie found, was widely sought after and there was unbounded faith in its curative properties. His years as an apprentice druggist had not been in vain !

From Spennymoor he went to Crooke, also in County Durham, to spend a few weeks with Dr Joseph Keay, a friend of his boyhood days, and then returned to Edinburgh to take charge of another friend's practice. This brought him to November, 1878, when he entered upon his duties at the Royal Infirmary, spending the first six months there as House Physician to Professor Sanders. Dr John Brown, whose advice he sought once again had invited Mackenzie to follow his own footsteps and enter general practice in Burnley. Officially, his student days were over; in a sense they were to last for another forty-seven years !

Chapter 6

BURNLEY

Poverty, that great reproach,
Bids us do or suffer anything
HORACE, *Odes*, Book 3

It was in the month of August, 1879 that this uncertain Scotsman made south to cross the border.

From Edinburgh to Manchester, the train takes some four to five hours, first through pleasant open country, amongst heatherclad hills, through the undulating uplands of the Cheviots, on towards the fringe of the lovely Lake District, through Preston to Manchester. The remaining twenty four miles to Burnley can only be described as grim. At the end of a long journey, this last stretch of country would blunt even the most ardent hopes and the most lively anticipation, particularly of someone nurtured in the beauty of the Scottish Highlands. Mackenzie could have been no exception. Crumpsall, Bowken Vale, Heston Park, Besses-o'-the-Barn, Bury Summerseat, Ramsbottom, Studdins, Rawtenstall, Huncoat, Hapton, Accrington— only the startling and unpoetic jangle of these station names could have helped the tediousness of that railway journey which was to prove so auspicious. Through the carriage window, how different from the golden acres around Scone. For miles and miles, one town seemed to merge into the next, the tall chimneys belching brown-black smoke. For that was Lancashire. This was the grim forbidding environment which boasted ' where there's mook there's mooney!' Soot and riches, however, were by no means synonymous, and did little to describe a precarious economy built around coal and cotton at that time. In the centre of this cotton conurbation was the town of Burnley.

A warm welcome awaited him from Dr Briggs, the senior partner, who took him to his bedroom on the top-floor of his house at 68 Bank Parade. The household consisted of the doctor and his brother, Mr Whitham Briggs, and his sister, Miss Grace Briggs, who kept house for the family. At London University, Dr Briggs had been a fellow student of the famous Joseph Lister, with whom he had frequently competed for medals. For example he was awarded the Second Gold Medal for Surgery in the final professional examination, and also the Fellowes Gold Medal for Medicine in the summer session 1847-48; this medal is now in the possession of Dr Briggs great-nephew, Mr W. Appleyard, F.R.C.S. It will have been noted that Dr Briggs' partner was Dr John Brown, that same Dr Brown who had persuaded Mackenzie to try for a post as House Physician in Edinburgh. Dr Brown, Demonstrator in Anatomy, had come to Burnley through the good offices of Joseph Lister, who had recommended him to Henry[1] Briggs, his old friend.

Three months earlier, Mackenzie wrote to Dr Brown.

Royal Infirmary, Edinburgh
May 23/79.

Dear Dr Brown,

I was surprised tonight to see by your post-card that my letter had not reached you, as I wrote you immediately after sending the telegram. I gave it to a friend to post and I sincerely trust he did not forget it.

In answer to your letter I said that I was anxious to accept the office of assistant with you. After duly considering Sick Children, and Spence & Sanders *strongly* urged me to accept your offer, the details of our conversation I'll give you again, but that was the result, and now I would be proud if you'll have me for a twelve month and see how I'll get on.

The work you describe that I'll have to do, is the sort of work (but not so bad by a long way) that I was expecting to do some day. I think I could leave here at the end of June . . . I will write you again tomorrow night, and you might send a P.C. or anything to let me know if you have received this and also if I have a chance.

Believe me,
Yours sincerely,
James Mackenzie

Once again in asking for a twelve months' trial and wondering if he had a chance, Mackenzie was displaying great doubts about his own capabilities. Professor Spence did not share these uncertainties.

21A Ainslie Place, Edinburgh
May 27th, 1879

Mr James Mackenzie was one of the most industrious and successful students of the University, and distinguished himself in many departments of study. The appointment which he at

[1] Note Dr *Henry* and *not* Dr William Briggs as in *The Beloved Physician*.

present holds as one of the Residents in the University Clinical Wards is awarded by competition and that in itself should be a guarantee of his qualifications in medicine.

In the Surgical Department Mr Mackenzie acted as dresser and clinical clerk under me for a long period and discharged his duties with great care and skill. He was a most diligent pupil of my surgical classes, and my confidence in him may be judged by the fact that I had placed his name amongst those I had selected for resident surgeons in my wards.

I have a very high opinion of Mr Mackenzie's professional attainments and consider that he possesses all the qualities which go to form a successful medical practitioner.

(Sgd.) James Spence, F.R.S., F.R.C.S.,
Surgeon in Ordinary to H.M. the Queen of Scotland,
Professor of Surgery, University of Edinburgh.

A little should be said here about Dr Brown, a remarkable product from an even more remarkable Scots family. He was descended from John Brown, the ' honest weaver ' of Carpow[2] (so-called because he measured the cloth he sold on the far side of his thumb). The weaver's son, the Reverend John Brown of Haddington, author of the self-interpreting bible, taught himself Greek when still a shepherd boy, later to become a leading Scottish Divine. One of his sons, Samuel, originated the Village Circulating Libraries, the other, the Reverend John Brown of Whitburn, was grandfather of doctor John Brown, the author of *Rab and his Friends*. Dr John Brown of Burnley was a close friend of his distinguished namesake and cousin.

Dr John Brown of Burnley was born in Scotland, but spent much of his early life in South Africa. He came home to study medicine at Aberdeen University, and when twenty three years of age he sailed again for South Africa in 1867, practising at Wynberg, where he met his future wife, Mary Solomon. As Mary Brown she was to eclipse her husband in the public eye, for she was an indefatigable social worker, and her life story is told in the book *Mrs John Brown . . .*[3]

It was now evening and from his top-floor bedroom, the prospect facing Mackenzie was not encouraging. Bank Parade is terraced on one side by tall, solid but austere houses, of sandstone walls, dark and sooty with grime. Soot seemed to pervade everything, the pavement, the cobbled street, and even the gradually changing colours of the

[2] *John Brown of Haddington*, by Rev Robert Mackenzie (brother of James Mackenzie).
[3] *Mrs John Brown*. (1937) London : John Murray, Publishers.

leaves on the bank beyond. To the left stood the gaunt and simple architecture of the Parish Church, while around it had begun the stir and bustle of the streets beyond. For it was six o'clock and the mills were closing. The town had suddenly come alive with the sound of ironshod wooden clogs on cobbled streets. The day's work was over. Through the faint smoke and haze in seemingly endless rows, stretched the back-to-back houses, intermingling with more and more mills, until they disappeared in the rising contours of the hill beyond. For Burnley lies in a large cup or basin, sparse of trees and cover, which slopes gently down to form the junction of the Rivers Brun and Calder.

If this portrait of Burnley is unattractive and uninspiring, then how unlike the character and sterling quality of its people. Boom and slump, poverty and unemployment during the nineteenth century may have dimmed, but had certainly not extinguished their vitality and the ardour of their spirits. Kind, simple, blunt but transparently honest, they imparted to the stranger an immediate warmth and friendliness. Fate or fortune had brought a Scots doctor to their midst. Mackenzie was at home.

At the same time, so he had thought, the door was closed on his dreams. Not for him the flights of academic achievement and research. In general practice he was to join the humblest in the profession. So be it, but he was not the type of man to feel bitterness or regret. His daughter, Miss Dorothy Mackenzie, has said of him :

> He never regretted anything. Whatever he did, he gave most careful thought to. He said : ' Never look back. You've done what you believed to be the best, carry on '. He never regretted any of his moves.

Mackenzie by this time was aged twenty six. Six feet two inches tall, he was already a fine looking man, impressive with broad shoulders and massive frame. By now, his face had developed strength and character, and from a noble brow to short beard, it was long rather than round, rugged rather than soft. High cheek bones belied his Highland ancestry. His eyes, of a clear penetrating greyish blue, gave to his appearance a sternness through which shone a discerning warmth and sympathy which was later to colour his whole attitude to life and things. A moustache drooping at the sides, added firmness and determination to his chin. All in all, it was his ' bigness ', both in sheer physical size and the quality of his nature, which were to be his dominant characteristics, and it was this all-

PLATE 6. The surgery door in Bank House Street.

PLATE 7. Burnley Centre, *c.* 1890.

pervading strength of physique and character which was to grow and mark him out from the common run of men.

His secretary, Mrs Hilda Francis, now in Canada, recalls:

> While I was with him there was a project started somewhere in Europe—I think Germany—for a photo album of distinguished doctors and Sir James sent in a middle-aged one. I regretted this as he was much more picturesque as an older man with his height, massive shoulders, and slightly long hair. I asked him why he didn't send a present-day picture and he said: ' If I am going down to posterity I am not going down as an old man ' . . .

But posterity was yet a long way off!

Official records show that when Mackenzie went to Burnley it had a population of some 55,000 people, served by a part-time Medical Officer of Health who received a salary of £60 per annum. The Sanitary Inspector, who was also Inspector of the Fire Brigade, earned £150 per annum. By present-day standards the prevailing conditions were primitive. Sanitation was carried out mainly by means of ash-pits and privies, and months, even years, might elapse between one cleaning-out and the next. There are constant references in the Annual Reports of the Medical Officer and other town officials to the accumulation of night-soil close to houses, and the difficulties of emptying these closet tanks:

> The difficulty of ridding the increasing quantity of ash-pit and privy refuse, especially night-soil, has assumed increasing importance. The way . . . is to adopt a Water-Carriage system of some kind.

It is hardly surprising that under such conditions, infectious diseases were rife. Scarlet fever caused 56 deaths amongst the population in 1879, typhus and enteric fever 9, diarrhoea 53, and measles, still a lethal disease, accounted for another two. Even so, it was the high infant mortality rate which caused most concern to those in charge of Burnley's health. This rate stood at 54·6 per cent of total deaths, whereas in the so-called ' healthy areas ' it was only 11 per cent. Five years later in 1883, the infantile mortality rate (deaths in the first year of life) per 1000 live births was 205. There was little or no change in the situation between 1879 and 1886, when the Medical Officer's Annual Report included the following paragraph:

> Another cause governing the infant death rate in Burnley is the comparatively high rate of wages earned by women in shed

and factories. The strong desire in the feminine mind to earn high wages cause married women to work longer in the mill than is good for their offspring, in fact it is well known that a man who marries a six loom weaver may be a gentleman, a Burnley woman has no idle bones, but probably she has but little sense; in consequence of married women working in the mills, infants of the most tender days are put out to nurse, this leads to a train of consequences hurtful to children, particularly in winter when the infant is taken out of a warm bed into the cold morning air to be left with the nurse, whilst in summer infant food soon becomes sour and often causes diarrhoea . . .

' Premature birth and debility ' was the cause of 111 infant deaths in 1879; ' teething and convulsions ' caused a further 127.

Infectious diseases increased rather than decreased during the next ten years. On the subject of measles and scarlet fever, and their spread by careless nursing, the Medical Officer of Health wrote in 1883 :

There is no doubt considerable excuse for the medical man, he sees a case of measles, or scarlet fever, in a large family; the mother must nurse the child, there is no room for isolation, the healthy and sick must live together and intermingle, and the medical man, however bent on stopping the spread of the disease, must give it up in despair, it is the despair of helplessness and the number of such cases he meets which blunt his sanitary ardour . . .

Although in the 1870s the birth rate was high (it had to be) around 40 to 45 births per 1000 of the population, the Crude Death Rate was equally high, ranging from 29 to 34 per 1000 compared with 10 or so today. The truism that poverty and disease, disease and poverty, are part of the same vicious circle, is further illustrated by the number of persons in receipt of Poor Law.

RELIEF AT THAT TIME

Year	No. of Persons	£
1877	4376	6064
1878	6552	6810
1879	15701	11716

It would appear that Mackenzie's arrival had coincided with an economic slump in the cotton trade. Employees in order to provide for medical treatment during illness banded themselves into Friendly Societies to which they contributed a few pence per week. The same story is told from the following table:

FRIENDLY SOCIETIES

Year	No. of members	No. of members sick	%
1877	2481	417	16·8
1878	2682	432	16·0
1879	2591	454	17·5

In other words unemployment in 1879 is reflected in the fall off in membership while at the same time there was an increase in the number of those receiving sickness benefit.

This was a far cry from Scone and Pictstonhill. Struggle and hardship there was on a farm, but it was against nature herself in all her changing moods. Here in Burnley the struggle was different. Here man was pitted against man.

It was a struggle for survival; a battle against an enemy savage and relentless and seemingly determined to undermine health, to maim and kill. It was an environment of appalling housing and sanitation, of overcrowding and unemployment, of the all-pervading noise of machinery, of smoke and dirt . . . It was the Industrial Revolution.

Small wonder then, that as Mackenzie began his work amongst the Lancashire people he was possessed of an inward feeling of revulsion and revolt. But then, like them, had not he himself known hardship? Like had called unto like.

Chapter 7

BURNLEY HAS ASSIMILATED ME

No man's knowledge, here, can
go beyond his experience

JOHN LOCKE

Mackenzie could hardly have been more fortunate in his appointment to the Burnley practice, and that he fully recognized this in
later years is borne out by this extract from his *Personal Experiences*.

In the practice in which I became an assistant I was fortunate
to serve under two doctors with exceptional attainments, the
one being a shrewd general practitioner of many years' experience, and the other a surgeon of no mean ability. Our practice
comprised all classes, the bulk being of the working class. It was
an old-fashioned practice of many years' standing and we
followed the old custom of dispensing our own medicines. It
will be seen that the type of practice was not of a very elevated
order, but nevertheless, I am now thankful that it was of that
kind, for the simple reason that, having to assist in the dispensing of the drugs, I had an opportunity of judging the effects of
remedies which I otherwise would not have obtained, and having
that opportunity, I was able to make some observations on the
actions of drugs that physicians and pharmacologists with all
their magnificent opportunities had failed to achieve . . .

Through long experience, by trial and error, Briggs had acquired
intuitively that faculty which is referred to as ' a well developed
clinical sense '. All too often in medical circles, one hears reference
to the possessor of such ability, as a ' good doctor '. Seldom does
anyone try to define whether this quality is inherited or acquired!
In any case, Mackenzie, to his profound dismay, soon discovered that
he was quite unable to diagnose the complaints of the majority of
his patients, and characteristically he attributed this to his own
shortcomings. In this, Mackenzie was not alone. Countless medical
students must have felt this same utter inadequacy in trying to translate academic theory to clinical practice. He had come from Edinburgh reasonably confident that he could carry out any duty required
of him; now it seemed that he could not perform even the simplest

46

medical task, that of finding out what was wrong with his patients. He arrived in Burnley labouring under the misapprehension that every man, woman and child whom he saw would be suffering from some easily-identifiable ailment and that their signs and symptoms would fall neatly into separate categories. His teaching at medical school had over-emphasized the simplicity of differential diagnosis; that disease categories could be readily correlated with symptomatology. But this was not so. Would he have to spend years and years, like Dr Briggs, in acquiring this mystique of ' clinical judgement '? Perhaps it would never come to him. The uncertainties of his early school days returned. His unwarranted inadequacies again loomed large. Mackenzie suffered yet another blow to his self esteem. Would his plaintive request for a trial period of twelve months in practice end in ignominy and failure? Many a faint heart would have resigned at this point, content to accept the treadmill of monotony, which seemed to be general practice. But this would be to underestimate the qualities and character of the man. Several years were to pass before he began to perceive, dimly at first, but then with ever growing conviction, that the fault perhaps was not one which lay within himself but within the teaching of medicine.

He later wrote:

> The great majority of students of medicine become general practitioners, and in the teaching schools, with rare exceptions, there is not one teacher who has obtained a knowledge of many of the problems which will meet the general practitioner. Probably in this respect medical education is unique in that all other branches of knowledge, whether of trade or profession, the teachers or instructors have a practical acquaintance with the subjects they teach . . .
>
> I had not been long in the practice when I discovered how defective was my knowledge. I left college under the impression that every patient's condition could be diagnosed. For a long time I strove to make a diagnosis and assiduously studied my lectures and my textbooks, without avail. I finally invested in the ponderous volumes of Ziemssen's Encyclopaedia and studied them, but all in vain. For some years I thought that this inability to diagnose my patients' complaints was due to personal defects, but gradually, through consultations and other ways, I came to recognise that the kind of information I wanted did not exist . . .

In 1879, Mackenzie was young, reticent and, like so many of his countrymen somewhat shy, inhibited and inarticulate. He would

47

ponder over his deficiencies. His mind would revert once again to Dr Briggs and this intuitive clinical skill which he himself seemed to lack. Once again, he assumed the role of student which had been so fruitful under his master Professor Sanders at Edinburgh. Dr Briggs' ability had grown with years of experience, until now, his diagnostic ability was uncanny—intuitive. Signs and symptoms were certainly important, but they had to be interpreted against the wider back-cloth—of the patient as a person and his response to an environment of home and work, of climbing hills and stairs—the whole art and process of living. It was the whole man, then, in his response to effort, that had to be studied and to do so, time was all important. Time was thus needed to acquire experience. The other missing ingredient was knowledge.

At Edinburgh patients with marked symptoms and definitive signs of disease had been presented with knowledge and with authority to the students—impressive and convincing. Laboratory and pathological tests were presented as confirmatory and conclusive.

In Burnley, Dr Briggs, Dr Brumwell and the older practitioners in town had no such laboratory facilities, yet they could with their knowledge make diagnoses, and with equal confidence. What was more, they could with some certainty predict what was likely to happen to that patient. Not only did they possess clinical knowledge, they had this flair for prognosis, of foretelling the future course of events. How could one predict the outcome of an illness without knowledge of the disease process itself? The twin elements of diagnosis and prognosis, therefore, were complementary. But what Dr Briggs had committed to the recesses of his mind, to be brought forth by appropriate visual and tactile stimuli, through signs and symptoms, was not readily accessible to the eager novitiate. Mackenzie resorted to his lecture notes, to available text books, to Ziemssen's Encyclopaedia, but all to no avail. Time and knowledge were fundamental. Well might he say with Wordsworth:

> For as by discipline of Time made wise
> We learn . . .

Then like St Paul the great Biblical hero of his Sunday School days ' there shined about him a light . . .[1] go into Damascus and there it shall be told thee of all things which are appointed for thee to do[2]:' Mackenzie had suddenly seen a vision. If the knowledge did not exist, then he would set about to find it.

[1] *The Acts*, Chap. 9, Verse 3.
[2] *Ibid.*, Chap. 22, Verse 10.

By June, less than a year after taking up practice, he had been consulted by a young baker, aged thirty eight, complaining of retention of urine, sexual incompetence, loss of power in the left leg and numbness in the right. The care and meticulous way in which he studied this case, recorded signs and symptoms, physical examination, recourse to the literature, is preserved for posterity in a small school jotter of sixty six closely written pages—surely a classic of clinical observation and an example to every student of medicine about to set out on this same lonely road . . .

> While syphilis of the cord is far from being rare, all authorities testify to the rarity of the form which I have attributed to this case. Thus Henbuer of Ziemssen's Encyclopaedia, Vol XII, p. 338 throwing doubts says, ' etc. etc.'

How he must have pondered and puzzled about these neurological findings, but everything he did was done methodically. It is impossible to convey adequately to the reader the immense industry and application of this young doctor. These meticulous notes of careful observation were now to be the keynote of his professional life. This was but the beginning.

He must henceforward study his patients more closely. It was necessary to observe the workings of their minds as well as their bodies. Every sign and symptom must be recorded, even the most insignificant sensation of discomfort, pain or unease. This, he himself recalled, he began to do in 1883 or 1884, but he did, in fact, commence recording cases in minute detail from almost his first day in Burnley. The following extract portrays vividly the drama of a struggle to save the life of a young baby :

> Mrs W. was safely delivered of a male child on August 20/79 and was making a good recovery . . . On the 25th the child was doing quite well and nothing wrong was observed till about 3 p.m. when the mother (who was still in bed with the child beside her) heard it hiccup. Her attention being then called to the child she lifted it up and found that its lips were blue, as also its hands and feet. The breathing only occurred at intervals and was always accompanied by that sound. Her alarm was excited and she called on the nurse who, seeing the state the child was in, sent at once for a doctor. On arriving about 4.30 the child was found to be lying apparently comatose. The skin of the face was livid, the hands and lips blue. The whole body was jaundiced pretty deeply and the conjunctivae were of

49

greenish rather than yellow colour. The attempts at breathing were made at about 10 or 12 times a minute. They were spasmodic and often ineffectual. During the inspiration the chest walls contracted strongly . . . Generally with each attempt a vocal note was uttered—not a crowing but more guttural, and occasionally a loud sigh. The expiration was often accompanied and at times apparently stopped by a " hiccuping " sound. At all times a distinct vocal note was struck. During the respiratory acts a spasm of suffering crossed the child's face.

On auscultating the heart the sounds were loud and distinct but varied greatly in rate. During the latter part of the time that would follow the respiratory effort the sounds would gradually diminish in rapidity till they would number as few as 40 a minute. After the effort they would suddenly beat at least 100 per minute.

So far as could be made out no foreign mechanical obstruction existed and it was inferred that there was spasm of the glottis. The patient was immediately placed in a hot pack and allowed to inhale steam. For a very short time the breathing appeared to be a little relieved, but it soon lost its effect and the patient gradually got to be as bad as when first seen.

A note was sent to Dr B. asking him to come with the tracheotomy instruments. On his arrival about 5.30 the condition of the child was apparently hopeless. The respirations were fewer and the laryngeal sounds imitated those of a person who breathes and allows his vocal chords to emit a note during both inspiration and expiration. There was scarce any respiratory muscles now contracting save the diaphragm which did so in irregular convulsive manner. The heart sounds were also fewer, but of the same character before described.

The operation for opening the trachea was commenced and with a little difficulty and the loss of some blood the trachea was opened. The smallest tracheotomy tube could not be admitted with the shield in, which was consequently removed and the tube introduced, some blood having been previously sucked out of the trachea, and as the respiration had almost stopped, air was blown in and sucked out with our mouths, after which the patient began to breathe more freely. The tube being introduced the respirations became quite regular and in number normal. The lividity soon disappeared and signs of relief came to the pained countenance, the eyes opening and signs of returning animation established. The heart's regularity and rapidity were regained. This condition of affairs went on for about an hour, the air being warmed in the best manner that could be devised in a private house of moderate substance, viz, by keeping steamed blankets around the head. About this time the breathing suddenly became more difficult and spasmodic and the heart's action of the same irregular character as at first. Fearing that some blood had got into the trachea, the body of the child was raised and head lowered, the tube cleaned with a probe and sucked by the mouth. Forced respiration was kept up by blowing in air and sucking it out with the mouth over the wound. Again after a time the respirations were voluntarily performed and the little patient regained its former condition. After this the patient was so placed as to be protected from draughts and the steam from a kettle allowed to play over him, and the head was kept a little lower than the body. The tube and trachea were kept free from blood by passing a bent silver probe, round the end of which was rolled a little cotton wool, down the tube and into the trachea, this process being constantly repeated according as the wool was soaked with blood or not. At times the respirations were almost stopped, and over and over again it was found that by pushing the probe down to the bifurcation and sometimes into one or other bronchus, a spasmodic jerk of the chest wall would ensue, and the breathing again be established. This state of affairs continued and finding that the wool was no longer stained with blood, this process was discontinued. A vapour bath was prepared and the child was placed in a cradle and shielded by a blanket, a small quantity of the steam allowed to play about his head.

He continued to breathe freely till about 10.30 when again the breathing stopped and only occurred at intervals. All efforts at resuscitation failed and the heart ultimately stopped . . .

Any comment here would be superfluous, except perhaps to note once more the unmistakable touch of the born writer.

Not only could he write. He could recall every conceivable item and incident which could lend completeness to the clinical picture. What is more, he was already beginning to make the bricks which would provide, perhaps for the first time, an edifice, an epidemiology of general practice.

Mr Rawstron, in an extract from his *Reminiscences* recalls another small patient of Dr Mackenzie:

. . . I don't remember Dr Briggs myself, but I do remember his successors, Dr Mackenzie and Dr Brown, who both made names for themselves in the world of medicine outside the boundaries of Burnley and district. A younger brother of mine died before he was quite two years old. Dr Mackenzie and Dr Briggs differed as to the cause of his death. Dr Mackenzie asked if he could make a post-mortem examination to see if the exact cause could be made out. Permission was granted and it was found that Dr Mackenzie's diagnosis was right . . . that was in February, 1880 . . .

So there were occasions when Mackenzie could feel confidence in his own powers.

It must not be supposed that during these first few years in Burnley his mind was wholly occupied with medicine. On the contrary, he entered fully into a host of other activities, both mental and physical. In the 1880s, Burnley may have been somewhat backward as regards its public health standards, but educationally it was far ahead of many towns of comparable size and larger. One of its most successful ventures was the Mechanics' Institute, which held classes in a wide variety of subjects for students who wished to continue their education beyond night school standard.

It was possibly at the Mechanics' Institute that Mackenzie studied Greek during his first year at Burnley. He passed an examination in this subject and wrote triumphantly of his success to his cousin James Burnfield, a solicitor in Edinburgh. James Burnfield's mother was a sister of Mackenzie's father Robert, senior, and his people were also farmers, in the Stanley district of Perthshire.

68 Bank Parade,
Burnley
Oct. 22/80

My Dear Cousin,

I intended writing you when I got word of the result of the examination, but neglected doing so. Well, then, I have passed and passed too, with Distinction. I must confess it is no very hard job to get that honour—since coming back I have been cogitating on a subject for my thesis for the M.D., but I find as much difficulty in selecting a subject as I can expect from writing it.

Dr Briggs is still off work yet and I do not know how long it will last. He is practically well, but takes such care of himself that he scarce does more than get out of bed, and after accomplishing this heroic act regales me at the first opportunity with a long and minute account of the various sensations experienced, and his idea of the causes thereof . . .

Dr Briggs' great care of his person was a source of considerable amusement to Mackenzie, too young yet to worry about cold and draughts and the possible ill-effects of chill morning air. Dr McNair Wilson, in his book *The Beloved Physician*, told us that ' Dr Briggs was frankly terrified of draughts, and, indeed of all forms of air which had not been brought under domestic control ' !

After passing his examination in Greek, Mackenzie turned his attention to French and German, reporting this in another letter to James Burnfield:

> 68 Bank Parade,
> Burnley
> Feb. 20/81

My dear Cousin,

. . . I am getting along here pretty well; knowing a few more folks makes the place less irksome, yet I do not go out much at all. I still endeavour to do some work here. Have been getting up my French since passing the Greek, and lately have begun to tackle German—Dr Brown and I together. I also peg away at something that I suppose by this time next year may assume proportions sufficiently large to do for a Thesis . . .

The ' something ' duly reached the required proportions, and he wrote to Burnfield in June of the following year (1882) of his fears as to its fate:

. . . I expect to see you in Edinburgh about the end of July. I intend graduating M.D. on the 1st August, if the authorities accept my Thesis which I sent in some time ago, and the result was promised to be told me before this, and the silence is becoming painfully ominous. I am beginning to have grave doubts as to passing and I shall be made a fool of if I fail, as in my usual manner I have blabbed and everybody knows. I have written Woodhead[1] enquiring about it but he has not replied. Under certain circumstances this also would have been ominous, but I reflect that he is also recently married, and that neglecting friends may be considered to be an unfailing symptom in people suffering from that disorder . . .

Once again, with grave doubts, the spectre of inadequacy and failure in Mackenzie returned.

[1] G. Sims Woodhead.

Moreover, this slight sensitivity on the subject of marriage is beginning to become evident in many of Mackenzie's letters at this period. ' I am grateful,' he wrote to the newly-married Burnfield at the beginning of the letter quoted above, ' that there still remains a niche in your love-lorn heart for the memory of bygone friends.' Referring to John Gellatly, he had asked Burnfield in 1881 :

> Is it true that he is . . . going to sneak under the enfeebling influences of petticoat government? Somehow or other I have got the impression . . . that there is to be a change for the better or I am afraid the worse among my old cronies. And so he is to be first to go! Poor chap! . . .

Mackenzie's fears about his thesis proved to be groundless, and after his visit to Edinburgh for the graduation ceremony, he again wrote to Burnfield :

> On the Tuesday I left Edinburgh I dutifully made a pilgrimage to the bell handle superimposed over your name at 13 India Street, but received no response to two vigorous applications. I must say I missed you very much, for it appeared to me strange to be in Edinburgh without seeing you, an incident, mark you, almost unparallelled in the history of my peregrinations. Whether it was in consequence of this, or some other unintelligible cause, I did not enjoy myself nearly as well as I expected, and consequently I hurried off as soon as possible . . .
>
> . . . I still remain in that happy state of bachelordom in which awhile you and Baxter used to glory. Whether I may yet succumb to the alluring, but, I fear, temporary charms of t'other condition remains yet to be seen. In the meantime I am content to jog along . . . I regret not having had the benefit of studying the effects of married life, not so much on you, for you were always a comfortable stay-at-home chap, but upon that flightish man of levity J.G. I had only courage to call at his office, but found that he had gone to Glasgow. The Head Clerk gravely informed me that his partner was in the next room. I stayed not to enquire whether it was the domestic one of his bosom or that of his business, but sneaked off downstairs . . .

There is more than a hint of wistfulness underlying the fun Mackenzie poked at his friends, and a glimpse too of the rather shy and lonely young man usually safely hidden away beneath a cloak of gaiety and good humour. One senses that this visit to Edinburgh fell rather flat despite his graduation, and that is was a somewhat despondent Mackenzie who left there for a holiday in Scone when the ceremony was over. He had little further to say about it :

> . . . the Graduation as you can imagine went off all right. I got one star to my name which indicates ' Commended for the excellence of the Thesis ' . . . the rest of my holiday I lazed about at home and Blantyre . . .

The subject of the M.D. Thesis was 'A Case of Hemiparaplegia Spinalis ', the case being one of his earliest patients, the thirty eight year old baker whom he first saw in June 1880.

This was now August, 1882. Once again, the fears of his own academic and intellectual ability were proved to be unfounded.

Chapter 8

'MARY HELM'

How to cure it—there's the rub

It was inevitable that social conditions in Burnley should have a far-reaching effect on Mackenzie, and that as a result of his early experiences a certain amount of iron should enter into his soul. His daughter has said:

> . . . He saw so much injustice, so much dire poverty. These lock-outs were such terrible things and the men who owned the slum property were extremely comfortable, with plenty of money. He went to see the people who lived in these slums and it made a most deep impression . . .

This deep impression found voice in his second novel. Contrary to Dr McNair Wilson's statement in *The Beloved Physician*, that Mackenzie wrote only two or three chapters of the book, he did in fact complete it, although there is evidence to show that he brought it to a premature end. By that time he was completely absorbed in his work and everything else was of secondary importance. He wrote to Willie in 1890: *Only a Working Lass* proceeds slowly, an occasional chapter being added. But at the beginning his burning indignation at the social injustices he witnessed lent wings to his pen and fire to his words.

Only a Working Lass (he later called it, more simply, *Mary Helm*) is not merely the tragedy of a working-class family, it is essentially an account of life in Lancashire in the late nineteenth century, and it is deeply concerned with the growth and development of the Trade Unions. Today it might be called a ' dramatized documentary.'

In the 1880s, the Trade Union Movement was in its infancy, and Mackenzie betrays his concern for its future and his fear that men would prove unequal to the ideals for which they strove. The T.U.C. had been formed in 1868, but until the Act of 1871 the Unions were small local associations. Their position was legally defined in 1871, and the Second Trade Union Act of 1876 provided for the amalgamation of two or more unions. In *Mary Helm*, Mackenzie seeks to explore in the 1880s the reactions of ordinary men and women to this new force in their lives and to present to the reader a picture of the apparent hopelessness of the working classes.

PLATE 8. A view of Burnley from Slater's Clock. Sandygate. c. 1900.

Mary Helm is the long-suffering, patient wife of a drunken, ne'er-do-well husband, Sam Helm, who had married her because 'she possessed the great attraction of being a good six-loom weaver . . . He judiciously calculated that while it took nearly all his own earnings to meet his indulgences . . . the yield of six looms would materially assist in adding to his comfort.' Mary 'did not expect much loyal attachment from her husband—her surroundings had not taught her to indulge in such vain hopes.' Sam Helm soon relapsed into his old ways and was invariably out of work, leaving his wife to provide the money they needed:

> . . . At first work was good and money sufficiently plentiful, so that they were comfortably provided for. But when the first child was born . . . her whole life seemed altered. The need for more money and her inability to work made her feel the want of many little things she had hitherto looked upon as necessities. Habits of thrift and of laying up a store for future contingencies were things she could not comprehend and never practised. In this she but resembled many thousands of her class . . . Time wore on and with it more children came, and the mother's weary life became a burden. The day's work at the mill . . . was not the end of her labours, for the evening meal had to be cooked and the children and the house attended to. Besides, she had to spend many weary nights nursing restless children, always more or less ailing from being badly nurtured . . .

Things go from bad to worse for Mary Helm. Her husband rarely finds or attempts to find constant employment, and her eldest son leaves home as soon as he is old enough to contribute anything towards the household expenses. The youngest child, a boy to whom Mary is passionately devoted, is weak and ailing, and it grieves her to have to leave him in the care of her ten year old Alice whilst she goes to the mill each day with her elder daughter. Mackenzie's pen continues:

> As the afternoon wore on Alice was getting tired out walking up and down in her vain endeavours to soothe the child. At last she laid it in the cradle and gently rocking it she fell asleep herself. How long she slept she could not tell, but at last she woke with a start. A peaceful stillness reigned in the home, and it was a little time before she could gather her senses. At last it dawned upon her, the baby was asleep, and peeping into the cradle she saw him peaceful and quiet. With thankful heart she

sat down giving to the cradle meantime a gentle soothing motion . . . Shortly after . . . the latch of the door was gently raised and a curly black head of Harry Riley appeared . . . ' Be very quiet, Harry ', Alice said in a whisper, ' Little Johnnie is asleep and Mammy says he has scarce slept all night.'

Harry crept in and sat quietly on a stool by the fireside, gazing at Alice as she performed various little household duties. Harry was Alice's playfellow. He had come home from school and had come to have a quiet half hour's play before the mills would close. At last Alice had completed the arrangements necessary, and, peeping at the peaceful infant, sat herself down. The fire glinted and sparkled and the kettle began to hum, then to splutter and boil, and Alice, fearful lest the noise should awaken the child, arose to take it off. The door opened and her mother and sister entered.

' Oh, Mammy, Johnnie's having such a nice sleep ', she said in a joyful whisper. A pleased smile lit up the anxious mother's wan face and she went softly to the cradle. Stooping over, she gazed in the child's face, then a great fear seized her and she hurriedly lifted the child up, and clutching it in her arms sat down with a great cry. ' My Johnnie's dead, my Johnnie's dead ', and a violent outburst of crying followed.

The children looked affrighted and scared in the presence of the woman's passionate sorrow. Alice began to weep copiously, but in the silent way which had become habitual to her. May joined in more demonstratively, and Harry, with scared face, beat a quick though noiseless retreat. He went home and told his mother that ' Mrs Helm and Alice and May were all crying ower little Johnnie who were doin' nowt at all '.

Mrs Riley comprehended what had happened, hastened for Mrs Smith, and the two kindhearted neighbours went into Mrs Helm's house. They found the poor mother hugging the dead child with hysterical vehemence. They gently soothed her, and persuading her to give up the child, took it and tenderly performed the little offices necessary. They then helped to prepare the evening meal and withdrew, leaving the mother gazing with tearstained face into the fire . . .

In the following chapter of his novel Mackenzie introduces a character of truly Dickensian villainy in Joshua Buggins. This wholly unpleasant individual calls on Mrs Helm shortly after the child's death, dripping sympathy and Biblical phrases (a wonderful chance here for Mackenzie to make use of the storehouse of knowledge he had gathered during those early years at Scone), and offers to organise the funeral. Impressed with his good neighbourliness, Mrs Helm accepts, though begging him not to make it ' ower dear '. Buggins promises that he will ' temper the wind to the shorn lamb ' and takes his leave, to return under a different guise once the funeral is over. Now he is shrewd and businesslike, demanding payment of the account, and urging Mrs Helm to collect the insurance money if she cannot pay him otherwise. The interview which takes place between the unfortunate Mrs Helm and the corrupt officials of the insurance company displays much of the cruelty which Dickens sought to convey in his novels, an indictment against the evils of the time and of ' man's inhumanity to man '—a theme with which Mackenzie was always preoccupied.

There is no insurance money for Mary Helm; she is cheated out of this by the men who play on her ignorance and congratulate themselves afterwards on their cleverness. The rascally Buggins continues to line his own pockets at Mrs Helm's expense for the next three years, also counting on her ignorance of money matters. Finally, when her health deteriorates and she cannot keep up the payments, he sends in a ' bum bailiff ' to sell her out, a tragedy which is averted by her neighbour, John Smith. He investigates the position and soon sends Buggins about his business with warnings of possible legal proceedings. This, in effect, is the end of Mary's story; she slips quietly into the background, and the main theme is taken over by her daughter Alice, and by the boy Harry Riley. Harry was now a young man, a millworker.

It has been said that every novel is autobiographical in the sense that it must reveal something of the essential character of the author himself. In *Mary Helm*, James Mackenzie speaks through the voice of Harry Riley, the small playmate of Mary's daughter Alice. He grows up to become the first leader of a trade union of weavers; he ' dreams dreams and sees visions ', knowing that there is something terribly amiss with the society in which he lives, that the working people have barely enough of this world's goods to keep themselves alive. But the landlords, the builders, the merchants, all live by the principle of buying in the cheapest market and selling in the dearest:

> . . . they built up this great kingdom, and yet people worked, and people died, in order that the great principle might be carried out, and no-one could see that there was any fault. But how to cure it, there's the rub . . . At this time a movement of

restlessness occurred throughout the whole labour world. The workpeople were beginning to perceive dimly that they were a great power. But their efforts to utilise their power were not successful. They seemed like a giant who had lain in a long lethargy and whose first movements were irregular, spasmodic and ineffectual. There had been combinations which had appeared to succeed, but there were many others that had failed. The sense of wrong, and yet dimly the sense of power, affected the people of Lancashire . . .

Harry forms his Union, and for a time all goes well and his position is undisputed, but he ' had not counted on difficulties within the camp '. There were petty jealousies and disruptive elements, centred in the person of Silas Harker, an unpleasant, ambitious man who sows the seeds of mistrust amongst Harry's followers. Harry does not take this seriously at first and here, Mackenzie says, Harry was at fault :

In all his dreams and visions he had not pictured his fellow workman as he really was. Surrounded by men much of his own way of thinking he imagined that the thoughts of others ran in the same groove. He did not fully appreciate the condition of mind of those amongst whom he sought to work. These men had hard lives. Their education was very imperfect . . . The old idea that giving an education to a rising generation can rid that generation of the habits of vice of preceding generations has little foundation in fact. The race has gradually emerged from conditions of great backwardness. The process of improvement will be slow and the most that can be hoped for is that each succeeding generation will be more enlightened than its predecessor. Harry . . . in the full belief of the strength of their position . . . saw only the difficulties from enemies outside . . .

The ' enemies outside ' are the employers. Astounded and enraged by the effrontery of the weavers in forming a union, they retaliate by forming an organization of their own which, however, soon dies a natural death through lack of support. The first clash between the union and the employers results in victory for the union, a victory which brings fresh enthusiasm and increased membership. From this position of strength Harry feels that the time is ripe for the compulsion of mill workers to join the union, a decision which meets with some resistance. A strike is precipitated when one of the employers declares that *his* workers need not join the union, and this strike has

PLATE 9. Cotton Operatives, Springhill Mill, Burnley, c. 1890.

far-reaching effects on Harry Riley. Whilst the majority of workers come out on strike, there are those, nick-named ' knobsticks ' who for various reasons continue to work, enduring the jeers and cat-calls of their former work-mates. One of the knobsticks is Alice Helm, and Harry is in love with Alice . . .

> Each night when the knobsticks left their work they were surrounded by the strikers who hooted vigorously at them . . . There was a low wall surmounted by a palisade separating the street from the mill yard. On this Harry mounted and began exhorting the strikers to keep firm. Soon a considerable crowd gathered round them, and approving cheers encouraged Harry so that he became more and more vehement . . . While he was yet speaking the gate of the yard was thrown open and the work people commenced to issue forth . . . The crowd soon surrounded them and the few policemen were soon engulfed in the mob. The crowd slowly made its way down the street towards where Harry still stood, watching with no little interest and pride the results of his inciting speech . . . With ever increasing frenzy the strikers became more demonstrative and began to jostle and push the workers . . . Harry, from his elevated place . . . saw faces flushed with anger and excitement, eyes staring fiercely, mouths set hissing forth angry words . . . he saw cowering figures, terror-struck faces, shuddering and recoiling from blows directed at them. As they passed his attention was arrested by the slim form of a girl who was struggling hard to get in amongst the workers but the strikers surrounded her and retarded her progress. She struggled on and Harry saw one of the crowd push her violently, another kick her and one, laying hold of her shawl, dragged her and exposed her terror-stricken face. The face was turned towards Harry at the time and the sight of it haunted him for many a long day after . . .

Regardless of the ugly mood of the mob and forgetful of his own inciting speech a few moments earlier, Harry rushes in and knocks Alice's assailant to the ground and takes the girl home, persuading her that she must not go back to work whilst the strike is on. He discovers that she did not join the Union because she could not afford to pay the weekly subscriptions: her mother is failing fast and it takes all the money Alice earns to provide the necessities ordered by the doctor. For the same reason she could not come out on strike. Harry is bitterly upset and torn by doubts as to the wisdom and expediency of his actions. At a meeting held that night he explains his conduct:

> . . . that he had gone there and encouraged these men as he had already told them. Amongst the knobsticks was a girl whom he knew to be the sole support of an ailing mother. He saw her hustled, he saw her struck and he saw the girl terrified nearly out of her wits. He ran to help her and this fellow Spencer was pulling her shawl away and kicking at her at the same time—so Harry knocked him down and protected the girl to her home. ' If ' said Harry at the end very deliberately ' if you expect me to apologise I will apologise for my using in the heat of the moment language that might seem an incitement to the Unionists to assault, but to apologise for protecting that girl I won't . . .

Much of Harry's support is lost as a result of this incident, and even some of his staunchest supporters ' wavered in their loyalty towards him '. The strike comes to an end when the employer has to give in and accede to the Union's request that all his workers must be members. Alice, unaware of this ruling returns to work, and this gives Silas Harker the chance he has long awaited. At the next Union Meeting he is the instigator of a ruling ' that those who have worked in a shed against the Union, while the members of the Union were on strike, should not be admitted to the Union. And the Union demand that they should be dismissed '. Harry succeeds in adding a rider to the effect that the rule should be only temporary, but as the mood of the meeting is against him he has to agree that the rule be passed. This is the signal for one of Harker's men to bring up the case of Alice Helm, carefully omitting to mention her name:

> Mr Chairman, there's a lot o' trouble at our shed—a weaver was a knobstick and worked when t'Union were on strike. This 'ere weaver is working now and hastn't joined t'union—what should we do ? . . .
> Have you asked this man to join the Union ? asked Harry.
> ' The new rule, the new rule ' shouted the members.
> ' But it has hitherto been the custom to request that the offending member should join. Why has that not been done ?' again asked Harry . . .
> ' It was such a bad case we thought it should come before t'meeting.'
> ' Well, I think ', said Harry cautiously . . . ' I think you should still ask them to join.'

' I move the new rule be applied in this case ', shouted Silas . . . So Harry, in the face of the whole-hearted determination of the members, is forced to give in. The form requesting the dismissal of the knobsticks is passed to him for his signature.

. . . Harry took the form and dipping his pen into the ink, glanced carelessly over the paper. His eye was arrested at the name 'Alice Helm ' . . .

' In the name of the Weavers' Trade Union I request that you dismiss Alice Helm . . .

Bitterly Harry realizes that Alice has been made the tool to bring about his own downfall; he refuses to sign the paper and walks out of the meeting, his mind in a torment. He visits Alice's neighbour, his friend John Smith, hoping that he may see Alice there, but she does not appear and he begs John to make sure she does not go back to work at the same shed, offering too, to help her financially, if that can be arranged without her knowledge. Alice cannot believe that her presence at the shed can cause any trouble, and protests to John when he sees her later that ' they wouldn't have a strike all on account of me '. John replies :

> Well, there's summat some folks call a principle—a principle's a queer thing. When they want to do something that doesn't look altogether square and honest they say it's the principle, so they have a principle—I suppose which means they'll have their own way . . . When such-like folks have a bit of spite it doesn't matter how small the subject is they must vent their spite and uphold their principles . . .

Alice, submitting to John's and her mother's entreaties, does not go back to work. Silas Harker becomes temporary Chairman of the Union and is finally elected President, seeing to it that Harry loses even his place on the Committee. As the meeting passes this resolution Harry felt as if in a dream !

> . . . He made no further effort. He listened to the dispute as to whether he should continue as a member of the Committee with unconcern. He noted the look of triumph which Silas cast upon him when a large majority elected an opponent of his and supporter of Silas in his place, but it affected him not. His high hopes were gone. He knew with what fatal facility the structure he had laboured to raise would fall down. In the hands of an unprincipled man like Silas Harker the danger which he saw

63

and which his limited experience had already taught him to guard against would be sought for in place of avoided . . .

The story moves rapidly and somewhat hurriedly towards its close. Alice is forced to take casual employment, moving from mill to mill with crowds of other unfortunate people who cannot get regular work. Mrs Helm dies:

> . . . She had striven to do her duty, without knowing that there was anything creditable about it. She had slaved and sacrificed herself without being aware that it was commendable. She had found work to her hand and she had done it—because it had to be done. Principles of action there might be; of their existence she was not conscious. Martyrs to duty are numerous, and more numerous than this selfish world imagines, but there is a grand absence of consciousness amongst these most noble martyrs, and in them dwells the hope of rejuvenation of this world . . .

Silas Harker had found the affairs of the Union in good order. It was respected throughout the town because Harry had always made an honest attempt to be fair. Silas, however, is not content until he achieves the very pinnacle of his ambition, a whole-time salaried post as leader of the Union. From that moment on the organization into which Harry had put his heart and soul starts on the downward trend:

> . . . Amongst the manufacturers there were those who took the measure of the new management of the Union and who soon found that the condition of quiescence was not the peacefulness of conscious strength but the outcome of calculating selfishness. So they began imperceptibly to lower the weaver's earnings. When interference became necessary they had no difficulty in coming to arrangements with the paid President. This weakness of the President and of the Union became so obvious that at last the weavers began to be suspicious and distrustful. With most this took the form of simply refusing to subscribe to the weekly collection, and this action spread, so that the resources of the Union were becoming seriously imperilled . . .

The end comes for Silas and for the Union when ' with the weak man's despair which is often mistaken for courage ', he calls a strike and cannot back down, though he knows that the Union funds will not be sufficient to support it. The employers retaliate by enforcing a complete lock-out. In the chaos which ensues Silas disappears, taking his salary with him, and police and military have to disperse the angry mobs which roam the town . . .

> Detachments of soldiers and policemen patrolled the streets until far into the night. Whenever they saw a number collected they dispersed them. Next morning the rioters collected, but a detachment of cavalry from a neighbouring town had been brought over and these prevented any crowds forming. Amongst the body of the work people much anger was aroused. This was directed not so much against the masters as against their own Union and its officials. Naturally then when the weaving sheds were announced by placards to be open, the work people all returned to work and the Union that had looked so powerful became suddenly a thing of the past . . .

The final tragedy is reserved for Harry and Alice. Unable to get work at her old shed, Alice eventually finds employment in one which has a very bad reputation in the town. She is unaware of this for, as Mackenzie says: 'It is wonderful too, with what perfect safety innocence will walk daily in the midst of sin and be unaware of its presence.' Alice saw and heard nothing to alarm her, and when one of the other girls proposes herself as a lodger in Alice's home Alice is happy to agree. She has no suspicion of the girl Betsy's real character, for Betsy takes care to adapt herself, though she enjoys many a quiet laugh at Alice's ' greenness '. She takes the unsuspecting Alice to a dance-hall of ill-repute, where Alice, after being first entranced by the gaiety and the music, is shocked by Betsy's behaviour and that of the young men with whom she is obviously very friendly. One of these young men attaches himself to Alice, and when she insists on leaving, accompanies her home, much against her will. When Betsy follows with several young men in tow Alice refuses to let them in, and asks Betsy to find other lodgings.

Meantime, Harry has been offered a position abroad for three years. He had never found courage nor opportunity to speak to Alice of his feelings, but now he wants to discuss this with her. Unfortunately for them both, he chooses the night when Alice is out with Betsy, and once more the opportunity slips by. Joshua Buggins reappears to bring about the climax of the story. He has the contract to supply food and drink to the dance-hall, and he makes it his business to inform Harry's father of Alice's conduct:

'It is against my habit, brother, to carry talk but it would be unbrotherly if I did not warn you that you are about to take one into your family whose conduct is such that I would prevent her becoming one of our body' (meaning the religious sect to which both belonged.)

'What do you mean' asked Abraham.

'You have told me that your son Harry, before he goes away, wants to settle matters with a girl—let me see—Helm is her name?'

'Yes', assented Abraham, 'and a good lass she is too'.

'That may be' said Buggins, 'but I happen to know she visits a certain undesirable place . . . last night she went home with that dissolute young man, the eldest son of Alderman Bagstock . . .'

Harry, when he is told of this by his father, rushes out to tackle Alice:

'Alice, were you at the Dancing Hall last night?'

'Aye, Harry,'

'And did you come home with that dissolute fellow Bagstock?'

'Aye, Harry,'

'How could you?'

Alice simply hung her head and burst into a flood of tears. Harry gazed angrily at her, turned his head and banged the door after him as he went out . . .

We are left with the picture of Alice, miserable and lone, and Harry rushing off to tell John Smith he will take the job abroad and is leaving the following day. There is no happy ending, rather the note is one of hopelessness and despair, but this should not be taken as a reflection of Mackenzie's own state of mind.

We know that he was in a hurry to finish the story, and perhaps this was the easiest way.

Mary Helm may not be a good novel; the writing may be clumsy in parts and the sequence disjointed, but it remains a revealing commentary on the social conditions of Burnley at the time. It contains many truths in which Mackenzie firmly believed, and much of his penetrating insight into the ways of men. He brought his clinical mind to bear on a social problem, and diagnosed a sick society.

Chapter 9

PATER FAMILIAS

The thread of our life would be dark,
Heaven knows!
If it were not with friendship and love
intertwined

THOMAS MOORE

During Mackenzie's early years in Burnley, many changes were taking place within his family circle. Towards the end of 1880 his father retired, and his old parents left the farm in the safe hands of their eldest son and went to live at Langley Bank, a square-built stone house on the main road between Perth and Scone, not far from Pictstonhill. Here his father died from cardiac asthma in 1898. Basil Mackenzie, who is recalled as ' a popular, breezy character ', continued to farm Pictstonhill until 1892, when he went to Goukton, a farm on the Kinfauns Estate, six miles east of Perth. In February of 1880 the third son, Robert, was appointed minister of the newly formed Livingstone Memorial Church at Blantyre. It was a tough, mining community, predominantly Irish, and the young minister needed initiative and resourcefulness to build up his congregation. He possessed both these qualities in abundance, and when he moved from his Blantyre parish to Alloa in 1888 he left behind a virile and flourishing congregation.

Despite the overwhelming personal conflicts assailing Mackenzie in those early years in Burnley, he was already assuming the role of *pater familias* to his brothers and sisters at home.

William, the youngest son, who was always known as Willie within the family, went up to Glasgow University in 1880, attending the Arts Faculty while residing at Blantyre with Robert. He had finished his law apprenticeship with Thomas & McLeish of Perth, and after a year at Glasgow he transferred to Edinburgh University. Maybelle, the eldest daughter, married the Reverend David Keir in 1879 and left Scone for Dennyloanhead. Of the twins, Jane and Margaret, or more familiarly Jeannie and Maggie, Mackenzie wrote to James Burnfield in 1880; ' Jeannie is to remain this year at Langley Bank and Maggie is to go to Blantyre to take care of Robert.' He made no further comment, but he was not at all happy about the

67

education of his sisters. He undertook to pay for extra schooling for them, in addition to repaying his father the money spent on his own education. After his visit to Scone in 1882 he wrote to Burnfield:

> When I was north I was not at all satisfied with the progress that Jane and Maggie had made at their school, and on making enquiry I have been strongly recommended to put them to St George's Hall classes. Consequently, I expect they will be both in Edinburgh for this coming winter, where with Willie's help I hope for better things from them ...

The twins were twenty years old at this time, and Mackenzie from his meagre savings assumed full responsibility for them, as he later did for Willie, and financed all three.

His activities thus far described were all aimed at improving his knowledge in one way or another, but he had time to spare for leisure pursuits. He joined the Burnley Literary and Scientific Society, of which he soon became secretary, holding this position until 1884. The members of the Society met regularly and held discussions on a wide variety of topics, taking turns to deliver speeches to their fellows. Mackenzie had a sly dig at a section of the Society in a paper he called 'The Ubiquitous Member'. It is not clear whether he actually read this at a meeting of the society or wrote it for his own amusement; probably the latter!

> Occupying my modest place on a back seat I study with lively interest the members of greater importance who disport themselves on the front benches; Some are in the habit of entering the room at any time during the night, and with imposing mien stalking to a comfortable seat, serenely indifferent to the interruption caused by their entrance. For these worthy members I used to have great respect. The imposing mien I mistook for the calm dignity born of the consciousness of unlimited knowledge, and the selection of a prominent seat but the natural place for a superior mind. Watching weekly the proceedings of these members, I became impressed with the profundity of their learning, not so much from what they said but from the vast territories of knowledge which you caught but a glimpse of, when they condescended to speak on any subject ...
>
> . The ubiquitous one asserts his opinion as if it were as incontrovertible as an Euclidean axiom. Any hesitating objection ventured by a less confident man is at once put out of court by the contemptuous smile that radiates round the ubiquitous man's mouth. Literature and Science, Art and Manufac-

ture are equally patronised by him. He will talk equally glibly of the poetical merits of Chaucer and Henry Mutter and adorn his opinion with a mellifluous quotation from Tennyson or an acrid snarl from Carlyle. He is equally familiar with the steam engine and the three-dimensional space of Professor Cayley, with the geological formations of Jupiter and the Burnley Coal Basin. In high art he is particularly resplendent. Whenever the subject is introduced he assumes a dreamy, faraway abstract tone, as if it were his spirit from afar making a telephonic communication through his vile body. If some unpolished barbarian should venture a rough criticism, he becomes faint and looks pityingly upon him, and shakes his head with the languid air of one whose ineffable spirit cannot find words subtle enough to express the delicacy of his feelings . . .

. . . The individual herein described is a type of a class that is to be found more or less in all trades and professions. It may be that in his most perfect form he is found amongst the professions, as in the education for a profession there is much studied to which outsiders may little regard. Knowing then that there are subjects on which he knows more than his neighbour, he continually drops these into the conversation, and as he will loftily say : ' raising it in a medical (or legal, as the case may be) light—a layman cannot appreciate the important distinctions ' and so on. He glories in calling other people ' laymen ', and his habit of giving advice for fees grows upon him so that he is never at ease when any other person is talking, or when his own opinion is not deferentially accepted . . .

This passage, and more especially the last paragraph, is another illustration of Mackenzie's insight into human nature, remarkably well-developed in so young a man. It is easy to picture him in his back seat, saying little, but observing and absorbing all, his eyes alight with interest and humour. He wrote a series of verses depicting the members of the Society and the subjects they dealt with: Boswell, Thomas Carlyle, Charles Lamb, rambling in Devon, architecture in Belgium, the Aztec civilization, philosophy and sketching. Four lines sufficed for his own contribution :

> We expected fury and frenzy
> On the part of Dr Mackenzie,
> When with much ratiocination
> He lectured us on vaccination . . .

6

In addition to its indoor meetings, the Literary and Scientific Society organised outings to places of interest both in the vicinity of Burnley and further afield. Mackenzie spoke of one in June 1882:

> I intend going off for three days next week to south Durham. It is an excursion of the Lit. and Scient. Soc. to Teesdale which I hope to enjoy as there are some jolly fellows going . . .

Mackenzie played chess and billiards during his off-duty hours and was no mean performer at either. He also loved bridge, and was a good all-round sportsman. Golf was to become the main leisure interest of his life as he grew older, but as a young man he was wildly enthusiastic about tennis. His nephew David Keir commented on this:

> . . . His prowess at tennis was recognised among his friends. On the occasions when he returned to Scotland, his predilection for Blantyre was accounted for not only by his life-long affection for brother Robert, but also by the tennis court which Robert had fitted out in his garden . . .

Mackenzie himself wrote to Burnfield:

> . . . I lately discerned that a wealthy lawyer (in Burnley) had made a lawn tennis court in his garden, and I thereupon greatly regretted having refused an invitation to supper which he had made me last winter. However, I lay in wait for him and have so far cultivated his acquaintance that I have had one game with him and he is going to have me over every fine day. Unfortunately, it has rained continually ever since . . .

So passed James Mackenzie's first three years in Burnley, a judicious mixture of work, study and play. He had now been given a third share of the practice and had moved from 68 to 64 Bank Parade. He summed up these years as follows:

> . . . I feel cut off from the fellowship of Edinburgh now . . . I get on very well here, making new friends and finding more attractions about the place. Burnley—more aptly ' auld Reekie ' than the original bearer of the title—has assimilated me so that I now feel as of another kind . . .

Evidently, Mackenzie had now in perspective put aside the many drawbacks of Burnley, its smoke, its dirt and grime, and begun in medical and human terms to discover gold amongst its dust. The opportunities for medical research in this community were great. He was, in the event, to be equal to the challenge.

It will be seen there were strong bonds of affection between Mackenzie and all the members of his family, but he was particularly attached to his youngest brother Will (later the first Lord Amulree). His weekly letters to Will, first in Edinburgh and then in London, testify to this affection and to his sense of responsibility for his brother's success as a barrister. Will entered Gray's Inn in 1873, and in April of that year Mackenzie wrote to him:

> Make what arrangements you like about the Inn, I'll leave it entirely in your hands, and go and stay in London as long as you desire. Perhaps you had better get a complete suit of decent clothes that will exactly suit you as mine will do for wearing. Go to Senior's and tell him to put it to my account. *Go to London respectable.*

' Mine will do for wearing ' may defeat the English reader, but it will be obvious to the Scot that Will had fallen heir to one of James' old suits, which was now to be relegated to second-best. To the Scot, to be ' dressed ' indicates being dressed in one's best and a suit ' for wearing ' does not come into that category but is merely for every-day use.

Once Will was settled into Gray's Inn, Mackenzie began sending him regular monthly cheques, for varying amounts. He was deeply interested in Will's life in London, and begs again and again in his letters for yet more details of his doings, but Will was not, apparently, so prolific a correspondent as Mackenzie would have liked: ' I enclose a cheque for £10 and would send you more, but it looks as if you would never write unless you were hard up so I'll keep you short and thus get more letters.' His own letters were invariably long, and full of encouragement and advice :

Burnley, Nov. 1/83

My dear W.,

I was glad to get your letter, and was much interested in your account of your daily round. I cannot say, however, that it pleased me to observe the manner in which you perform your gastronomical operations. You may think it economical to gourmandise a 6d dinner, but I am of a totally different opinion. With the work before you that you have got and with the necessity for providing for a growing frame, that frame itself being none of the smallest, you will find out to your cost how ruinous your economy has become. In the first place this excessive brain work must have food, else the brain works ineffectually, and a failure on examination day will be the result. In the

71

second place your bodily health is bound to suffer. Now I shall not be content unless you spend 2/6d a day upon food alone. You need not necessarily spend it on luxuries although a modest allowance of the good things I would not object to. But I must insist upon your having a good dinner. Or if the dinners be not enough, an egg or two at night with your tea. I presume you get breakfast and tea at your lodgings. See to it that henceforth feeding time bulks more largely in the day's routine, and feeding expenses bulk more largely in the week's bill. I do not think 10/- at all too much . . .

Passing next to your dutiful forecast of the result of your studies and the drudgeries entailed, more particularly in the Dog Latin of the Roman Law, nowadays if we are to succeed in the world it must be in excelling in those things wherein others fail. Now the very fact that you find that Dog Latin such drudgery gives me hope for you. For this reason—that others have likely found it the same, and have therefore allowed their feelings to get the better of them and to neglect it with a bad result. Further drudgery is the thing that pays in the long run. Just consider for a moment what would be the result of your six months' successful drudgery. Not only would it pay you immediately in getting the prize for which you strain, but it will bring you prominently before the members of your Inn, and unless the system there is the antithesis of that in the medical profession, a successful student is always marked out for promotion. Who knows but that the success that can attend you in your coming exam may determine your future to be one of success, or one of struggling for existence? Keep these things in view, not so much as dreams to while away the time with but as legitimate objects for attainment of which is by carefully working through this mire of drudgery. Do not think that I am supposing more to be in you than there is. I know quite well that you have nothing particularly brilliant about you in the way of study, and know further that brilliant students can accomplish things with ease that other ordinarily-endowed mortals can do only at the expense of great labour. You have the gift of not being satisfied with your reading unless you fully understand and appreciate what you have read. Now I could never do this for a prolonged period. What successes I had were accomplished during the summer sessions when there were but three months' study instead of six. I remember once starting to read up with one of the most brilliant students I knew. I remember it was the very dry drudgery of learning all about the bones, and I was struck with the secret of success, which was the methodical way in which he made himself acquainted with each little fact as it arose and by never leaving a bone for another until he had mastered every point. He appeared to me to make but slow progress, yet at the end of the session his knowledge was complete. Thoroughness was evidently his chief characteristic and do not think I flatter you if I say I detect the same quality in you. Be systematic as well and I dare venture to wager that success will attend you. You have got all the abilities necessary to take a first class and you just drudge most painstakingly and I'll answer for the end.

I don't know whether my lecturing you will be of much avail, but it may cheer you up. Do not be afraid of the expense. When you get to make a tidy income you can repay me in full. Supposing you have an income of say £600 in ten years, would you not desire to have had some of it to spend now? Take any little relaxation you wish. I'll try and come and spend a few days with you next Xmas time . . .

Mackenzie's ' lecturing ' may have had its effect, for in March of 1883 Will won the Essay Prize given by Lord Rosebery, the then Rector of Edinburgh University. The fact of this essay brought about many an anxious query from Mackenzie: ' I suppose the Lord Rector's Prize will have gone elsewhere as I have never heard from you about it . . .' ' Have you ever written to see who were the successful essayists for the Lord Rector's Prize?' . . . ' Don't you think you should write to Edinburgh and ask for information about the Prize?' This last was on March 13th, 1883, and on the 18th he was able to despatch a telegram to Will at his lodgings in Islington: ' Burnley folks congratulate you on the Lord Rector's Prize success. Got a ' Scotsman ' this morning containing the announcement.' On March 23rd he wrote:

My dear W.,

I got your letter yesterday morning and was indeed wondering what had come over you. I thought that in the first flush of victory you had gone off on the spree. I hope that this success but augurs for what is going to happen in May. I trust too, that the result may be to awaken the desire for hearty and substantial meals . . . The first news I had of the subject was receiving a ' Scotsman '. Have you any idea who sent it? I fancy J. Burnfield though I could not detect his handwriting

. . . Let me have a look at Sir Alex. Grant's letter, will you ? . . .
Write soon . . .[1]

Both brothers were interested in writing for publication, whether
in newspaper or periodical, and frequent reference to their efforts
to break into print are made in Mackenzie's letters. He had hopefully
sent an article of Will's entitled ' Reminiscences ' to the Editor of a
magazine called *Leisure Hour*— ' as he is an M.D., thinking that I
might have some influence with him '. When the manuscript was
returned he instructed Will :

> . . . I would recommend you to try either Cassel's Magazine or
> People's Journal. Set about it at once and do not give in until you
> get published somewhere, even although you get nothing for it.
> What you want is a start and you must not be too particular
> where you begin. With your attendance in the Assemblies, etc.,
> you should try and send reports again to Daily News etc. or
> Standard. Try and get into the Assemblies on the strength
> of being a correspondent to Perth Advertiser and other papers.
> Now's your chance for picking up a connection and you really
> must not be backward in the applying . . .

No great success marked their literary aspirations. Will put forward a suggestion for a book on trials for murder by poison, which
Mackenzie received cautiously : ' it will do you no harm and may
do you a great deal of good.' This project was never even begun,
because the following week he wrote to Will :

> . . . Your idea of publishing a book on trials by poison is I
> fear too late for lo! in yesterday's British Medical Journal I
> observe a notice of a book ' Reports of Trial for Murder by
> Poison ' by Browne and Stewart . . .

Another scheme which was destined to come to nought was a
series of articles for a local paper in Burnley :

> . . . I was stopped the other day by the proprietor of the
> Burnley Gazette, and asked if I would contribute a series of
> articles upon the Social life of Burnley for a new weekly ½d
> paper that he is going to start. I said that I would consider the
> matter and that in all likelihood I would take it up. Would it be
> worth while for me to suggest that you should send him a

[1] Thought to be Sir Alex. Grant of Forres, and the firm of MacVitie & Price.
Biscuit Manufacturers.

short weekly letter of a gossiping nature for the time you stay in London?'

But two or three weeks later Mackenzie reported:

> ... In regard to the correspondence and the new newspaper you need not trouble about it. I asked the proprietor what he was to pay me for my trouble, he rejoined that he wanted me to do it for nothing! Remembering the remark that what was worth printing was worth paying for I declined to assist him. For the same reason I did not broach the London letter. It is a miserable rag and would have done little credit to write for ...

Will was apparently more successful with the Perth Advertiser, for Mackenzie enquires more than once if he has been paid for his work. His own sole accomplishment seems to have been a letter published in the *Spectator* on September 29th, 1883, to which he refers with studied nonchalance at the end of his weekly letter to London. Both brothers read extensively. ' Get a read of Bain's English Composition,' Mackenzie advised Will, ' it will be of invaluable service to you ' ... ' Have you been hearing Henry George?' ... ' I have read his speech and I am going to read his " Progress & P." (sic) after I have finished Fawcett's Manual of P.E. I must say so far as I know his ideas they occurred to me as I was studying Fawcett and I feel more inclined to him than F ' ... ' I observe that Nicholson has published a book on " Tenants' Gain not Landlords' Loss ", or some such subject ... I am reading an interesting book just now, viz, *The Intellectual Life*, by P. G. Hammerton. He is a native of this district and I have had the honour of shaking his hand at a levée we got up in his honour when he happened to visit this neighbourhood. He now lives in France, having married a Frenchwoman. He is also the editor of the *Portfolio*, an art journal. When a young man, he created a great sensation in this neighbourhood by building himself a hut in the most desolate part of the moors hereabout, in order to study lights and shades and patches of heather ...'

Will's first Christmas in London, that of 1883, was the occasion of a letter crammed with advice on etiquette from his older brother:

Burnley, Dec. 19/83

My dear W.,

I got your letter this morning and was glad to see that in all London you had the opportunity of going to at least one home. I hope you will enjoy yourself there very much ... Perhaps as this is your first dinner out, a few hints will not be out of place. First of all *you must go in evening dress*. You have my swallow-tailed coat, haven't you? It will do very well. Black open vest too you have got, but have you black trousers? If not, order a pair at once. I think you have also my old thin dress shoes? If not, order a pair at once. Have you a good white shirt? If not, order one at once, one buttoning behind you know. And studs? If not, get the plain pearl ones as they look much nicer and in much better taste than more garish ones are. You must get a white tie—not one that has been washed but a new one, as otherwise they never look clean. If you cannot make a good knot, get your landlady to make one or get one of the ties with knot already made. You must go in a cab or hansom, and if the night be wet order one to come for you at 10 o'clock. Take your leave about 10, if you do not find them *very* pressing, or if there be a large company and they do not show any signs of breaking up. When you enter you will be asked for your name. Give it to the waiter or servant, not in that meek voice of yours which sounds as if you were begging a favour, but in that tone which inspires due respect in the hearer. When ushered in, the lady of the house will come forward, and shake hands with her first, the gentleman afterwards. If you be introduced to anybody do not shake hands with them but make a bow, unless they protrude their hand. Mind this when introduced to a lady, for I well remember my feelings on a like occasion when my projected hand was politely left unnoticed by a lady. You feel small for a few seconds. I have never been caught again. Unless those you are introduced to take notice of you afterwards, be oblivious to their existence. At dinner, keep your eye on others and watch what they do. Remember never put your knife to your mouth. Fruit knives and forks have a close resemblance. Be sure you employ the correct article. When taking your departure only shake hands with the lady of the house and the gent. unless other hands are offered you . . .

No fond Victorian mamma, launching her daughter for the first time into society, could have evinced such an anxious solicitude. Mackenzie had had plenty of social experience during his first few years in Burnley. ' What do you say to my engagements for next week?' he asked Will in January of 1884; ' Monday a carpet dance, Tuesday a public dinner, Wednesday a Ball, Friday a Ball ' . . . and in February: ' I have been having what I presume to be the last Ball I'll attend for this season. It was a private dance and I took a frightful headache and did not enjoy it as I would have done. Altogether this has been rather a gay winter for me . . .'

With the end of this ' gay winter ' came the formation of a St John's Ambulance Association in Burnley . . . ' and I deliver lectures to the ladies in rendering first aid to the injured ', he reported to Will . . . 'Fancy talking for one and a half hours to forty ladies . . .'

Mackenzie visited America on three occasions. His first tour was made in 1885 when, as an obscure general practitioner, he would have had no inkling of the triumphal progress he was to make through the States in 1918, accompanied by Sir William Arbuthnot Lane and Colonel Bruce, of Toronto. This first visit, however, impressed him deeply, and some of the wonder he felt is conveyed in this letter he wrote to his parents from San Francisco in June 1885: when he was aged thirty-two, seven years after qualification.

Dear Father and Mother,

I do not suppose *you* ever supposed that you would have a son writing you from this distant land—7000 miles away. This is the further limit of my journey, and I will begin now to retrace my steps. I have travelled through immense tracts of land and although I have gone on at a great rate yet I have seen sufficient to make me marvel at the wondrous fertility of the soil, and how large a ground there is for future generations to cultivate. When I thought how you had to struggle and plough and manure and clean your soil, and compared that with the easy manner in which crops are raised here, I felt that if you had spent as much labour here the result would have been different. The great want is water, but the process of irrigation is carried on in many places to such an extent that its want is scarcely felt. Once water is supplied, the land that looked a few days back as a desert becomes a garden of wonderful fertility. I spoke to you in a previous letter about the primitive forms of ploughing that I had observed. These were chiefly amongst the Americans—the negroes—but one part of the country I passed through, in New Mexico, the Indians were ploughing, and their implements were more primitive still. Some indeed had little ploughs, and had oxen to drag them, others had not even a made implement to plough with but merely a crooked stick. And yet they manage to get wonderful crops. These Indians that I saw are wonderful people, being descended from a nation that a thousand years ago had acquired a civilisation of a peculiar nature. They were conquered by the

77

Spaniards, but the Spaniards did them no good, and the Spaniards that were left behind became little better than the Indians themselves. When I was at Santa Fé I saw their queer little muddy-looking huts. The oldest house in America is at Santa Fé. In bygone centuries it used to be the palace of the Spanish Governor; now it is occupied by the Governor of New Mexico. I wanted much to get in and see this old building but I could not devise a plan. Having some time to spare, I called upon a Dr who showed me over the Hospital, then drove me in his ' buggy ' down to the Governor's Palace and introduced me to no less a person than the Governor himself. The Governor appeared to be glad to get hold of a Briton, for he hitched his chair as far back as he could safely swing, and elevated his legs on to the desk and talked at me for nearly an hour. I was so glad to get away from him that I forgot all about the interior of the Palace. After leaving Santa Fé I passed along the banks of a stream, that were low-lying and very sandy. In many places the Indians had dug rude trenches and the water from the river running in these brought the sandy plain into fruitful fields. Bye and bye we got away from the river and out into the desert, where not even a blade of grass would grow. As we passed further west towards California, the desert presented a peculiar condition called a mirage. Looking out into the desert it would seem as if a broad lake of the clearest waters lay stretched out before us. Distant rocks were reflected in the bosom of this lake with mirror-like distinctness, and some of these rocks being of irregular shape you would have sworn them to be ships and boats. One man whom I talked to had crossed this desert very frequently and he believed all the time that it was actually water, and it was only after I got him to put his head out of the window and see that we had evidently passed over water where there was no water, and that we were approaching what appeared to be water and yet when we got there there was no water but white sand, that he realised his mistake. Gradually we got further into California, the plain became covered with a rough grass growing in bunches whereon the cattle fed. Peculiar shrubs began to show themselves, especially the cactus which assumes all kinds of queer shapes. Sometimes whole hill-sides would be covered by these strange and weird forms—tall and straight like a pillar sometimes, two or three small ones growing out of the tall one half-way up. Again the plant would be made up of pieces like plates stuck to one another. These varied from a few feet in height to twenty or thirty. One night we stopped at a small station and the frogs in a neighbouring pool made the most terrific noise that I ever heard. Positively it was impossible to hear anyone talk, so deafening was the noise. When we got into more fruitful parts of California we saw the wheat and barley being already ripe, and some of it was reaped —that was in the latter part of May. They do not make hay here as you do, but sow barley and cut it green.

Now I write in the train in Utah going to the Yellowstone Park on July 5. It is so difficult to find opportunities for writing that I am afraid you will wonder at my negligence and at my bad writing. I left San Francisco on Wednesday July 3rd, and I will have no rest now till Sunday July 14 which I hope to spend at church in Salt Lake City amongst the Mormons.

I stayed on Friday night, May 22nd, at Los Angeles in California, and while there I went and saw the orange groves. Great parks of trees neatly laid out and the oranges growing on them, and men amongst the trees choosing the good ones from large heaps as if they were potatoes. There are also many fields of grapes here, and they make wines too. I was too early in the year to see the grapes grow. The following day, Saturday, I left for the Yosemite Valley. We had a long drive of nigh 100 miles in a stage coach with six horses before we got to the valley. It is a wonderful place—a flat plain six miles long and from one to a quarter mile broad with great pine trees growing in it. It is surrounded with precipitous rocks, many perfectly perpendicular rising some nigh 5000 feet above the valley. The peaks vary in shape and are very grand. Numerous waterfalls come tumbling down their sides, some from an altitude of over 3000 feet, nearly the highest in the world, if not the highest. We made a few trips on horse-back to the summit of some of the mountains where the snow was still lying, and we saw away in the distance row upon row of high mountains, their snow-covered peaks glittering in the sun.

Leaving the Valley on Thursday we got to San Francisco on Saturday last. I met some very nice people there and one man whose sisters live near Burnley was very kind, driving me about the city and showing me the town. We lived in an hotel said to be the largest and finest in the world. It is built in a square and in the centre is a large courtyard covered in with glass, and at night lit up with the electric light. The luggage vans and carriages drive right into the yard. It is six storeys high and we never went upstairs, but up hoists which work by hydraulic power. There are about 30,000 Chinese in San Francisco, and they keep themselves aloof in their manner of living from the Americans. I went over their part of the town one night and was sickened at their depraved condition. We were taken to their ' Joss ' house—as their temple is called, and saw the numerous gods whom they worship and the incense they continually burn before these and the offerings they place at their feet. We were also taken to their dens—low miserable rooms, dirty and stuffy, deep underground, where they smoke opium until they are overpowered with sleep, and there they lie drunken from the fumes of the drug for many hours till its effect passes off. Their theatre was a very interesting sight.

The train is off, and I'll post this at a wayside station and write you when I can get rest and peace . . .

On his return to Burnley, Mackenzie gave a talk describing his tour to the Literary and Scientific Society. Most of this talk was devoted to three days spent in the Yellowstone Park, Wyoming, although he also described, with the aid of maps and drawings, the journey recounted in the letter to his parents. Part of his journey to the Yellowstone Park was made in what he describes as a ' primitive waggon,' and seems to have been the reverse of comfortable, as frequent snowstorms were encountered and ' much difficulty experienced from the many snowdrifts '. Mackenzie pointed out that the park itself is over 6000 feet above sea level, and some of the neighbouring mountains reach a height of 12,000 feet. He and his party spent three days in the Yellowstone Park :

. . . Among other objects of interest . . . we may mention 1500 hot springs, among which are at least fifty geysers of the first magnitude . . . Starting from the primitive log-house, that does duty for hotel in the Firehole Basin, for a few miles our road lay through marshy flats, and then we struck a bare patch whereon no vegetation would grow. There were several hot springs here . . . varying in size from a few feet or 30 or 40 yards in diameter —most of them being 20 to 30 feet and irregularly circular. The springs contract in irregular terraces until the deepest part is but a few feet in diameter, and looking through the blue translucent water it would appear as if vast caverns extended beyond. The walls seem constructed of the purest ivory. Arising from the surface are faint clouds of steam, while the waters of a few are gently bubbling and boiling. There are a few where the deposited salts exhibit a variety of colours and the walls then assume the appearance of choicest mosaic, while one huge ugly hole is filled with dark and gruesome fluid. Other places presented a more awesome and oppressive appearance, one place in particular which bears the felicitous title of ' Hell's Half-acre '. Here there is a hot spring of great size, and as it continually overflows the deposited salts have raised its mouth considerably above the neighbouring stream down whose banks the collected waters rush in brooks with beds and sides of garish yellow. But the character of this vast spring we cannot discern, as the water is very hot and the cloud of steam so dense that our view is limited to a few feet of its margin. Close beside this is a smaller but still more awful spring. We dare not approach to its edge, as what little the dense cloud permitted us to see showed that the cracked and seamed edges were hollowed under and its troubled waters seethed some six or seven feet below the brim. At last we reach the Upper Geyser Basin, and a weird looking place it is. The ground slopes backward to the hills and a portion about a mile square is barren and covered with a silicious deposit. Many of the trees that fringe this place have their stems bleached, while others lie uprooted, sodden and without their bark . . . None of the large geysers were in action when we arrived, but jets of steam at intervals were thrown out of the craters . . . One became active shortly after our arrival. Premonitory of the eruption there is a deep rumbling noise and the earth in the neighbourhood quivers, then with a loud roar a column of hot water is projected suddenly nigh 200 feet in the air. The temperature of the water being at or above boiling point, most of it is immediately dissipated into steam, which arises in a cloud from the whole length of the column, and as it is borne away on a breeze expanding and rising higher and higher it adds a most majestic and impressive grandeur to the scene . . .

No record remains as to why he undertook this trip to America. It has been suggested that it may have been to accompany a wealthy American patient and possibly at the suggestion of Dr Brown. It is evident, in any case that the journey was more in the nature of a sightseeing holiday. So much still remained to be done at home.

Chapter 10

A HEART IS, WHAT A HEART CAN DO

' A heart is, what a heart can do '
MACKENZIE

There are two kinds of human endeavour, the one medical and personal and the other social. In medical terms, one effort is directed solely towards the individual patient, while the other is concerned with stirring the public conscience in order to remedy the more evident social shortcomings of life at a particular point in history. Mackenzie was exposed to both these influences.

Dr Briggs, the Senior partner on the one hand, was concerned with patients as individuals and with their diseases. His was a tightly knit household. A bachelor, he was concerned with draughts and cold, a self interest which was fostered by a spinster sister and an unmarried brother. Nonetheless, in the role of clinical teacher (and student) he exerted a powerful influence on Mackenzie in those earlier years.

Dr Brown on the other hand, along with his wife, was interested in social reform. He was recommended to Dr Briggs by Lister ' as a gentlemanly agreeable person '. Mackenzie moved to the Brown household about this time. Compared with Briggs, Dr Brown was cast in a very different mould. His interest in Mackenzie was more that of a benevolent father to a well-loved son. Theirs was a mutually rewarding relationship and the warm regard in which they held each other was to last all their lives. If the Briggs' household was circumscribed, the Brown's was outward looking, alive and vibrant with a ferment of new ideas for social action and reform. Dr Brown, warm and benevolent, worshipped his wife Mary. But then, she was an unusual woman.[1] In their early married years at Fraserburg in South Africa, John Brown used to read aloud to his young wife, beginning with John Stuart Mill's *Liberty or the Subjection of Women*. There she was also to be influenced by Olive Schreiner, and her first controversial novel *The Story of an African Farm*. Christian leader, Temperance worker, Social Reformer, Moral Welfare worker amongst unmarried mothers, woman's franchise, friend of rich and poor alike, Mary Brown was irrepressible. Her varied interests were reflected in the visitors who came to Bank Parade; General Booth

[1] *The Life of Mrs John Brown.* (1957) London; John Murray.

and his son Bramwell, Keir Hardie and a Russian exile Volkowsky. Lord Shuttleworth maintained that together with Florence Nightingale, Octavia Hill and Lady Frederick Cavenish, Mrs John Brown made up a quartet of four of the most outstanding women he had ever known. It is claimed in Mrs Brown's biography that Mackenzie was one of her enthusiastic temperance supporters. Sympathetic though he may have been to remedy the social injustices of the time, he does not seem to have been caught up in the maelstrom of Mrs Brown's community service. Instead, his social or political activities appear to have been limited to stimulating public interest in purely medical matters. For example, he agitated for and helped establish two new hospitals, which were so badly needed.

' The Dispensary[2] was situated in a house in Prospect Terrace and was in operation until it closed for lack of funds in 1854. At frequent intervals and chiefly through the agitation of various ministers of religion, meetings were called in support of the erection of a hospital but it was not until 1882, and through the suggestion of Dr Brown that a Committee, consisting of the Rev R. H. Giles, Dr Mackenzie and others, succeeded in enlisting the financial interest of many wealthy men in the town and district . . . Building started on three acres in the Burnley Lane District and the Victoria Hospital was erected on the circular ward principle . . .' It was opened in 1886 by H.R.H. Prince Albert Victor. Mackenzie acted occasionally ' in a surgical capacity '. He also became known as a skilled obstetrician and continued as the Acting Honorary Medical Officer to the Hospital until 1901, when he became Honorary Consulting Medical Officer, a position he held until his death.

On March 5th, 1889, he gave a public lecture on ' The Necessity for a Hospital for Infectious Diseases in Burnley '. Again with vivid portraits, he described the infectivity of scarlet fever, then a dread disease and illustrated the impossibility of adequate nursing and isolation, the hopelessness of treatment in housing conditions then prevailing. In the previous year, he noted there were 27 cases of smallpox, 851 of scarlet fever, 21 of diphtheria, one of typhus and 74 of typhoid fever. Conditions for adequate successful treatment, he concluded, could only be fulfilled in a Hospital, but as stated, Mackenzie's métier was not in public exhortation nor in Committee work, but in overcrowded homes of the Burnley people.

His was a lone battle—the fight against disease and death—his only weapons, his university teaching and the meagre knowledge acquired from his brief experience in general practice.

[2] Sir James Mackenzie (1967) The Burnley Years Medical History XI 3.

No notes are available, but McNair Wilson in *The Beloved Physician* describes a scene which was later to shape Mackenzie's whole remarkable life.

He was summoned one night to help a young woman in the pains of childbirth. She was a patient of his own, a girl whom he had visited during the period of her expectancy and whom he had then examined.

There is a sameness about all birth scenes no matter in what setting, they are enacted. Let the reader imagine a room warm above average, and cosy with screens set over against the cheerful fire. Let him picture the anxious faces of old women, as a rule a midwife and a near relative of the young mother, and the less anxious but alert and eager face of the doctor. Let him see the prostrate figure on the bed, a poor little figure of sorrow alone in that struggle with most monstrous pain.

The doctor is seated beside his patient so that, from time to time he may feel her pulse and so that he may render all the help in his power at each stage of the conflict . . .

' Oh doctor, I can't stand any more . . . please doctor . . .'

A great silence falls in the room. The girl's hair is wet with perspiration, beads of perspiration gleam on her brow. The doctor bends over and wipes her brow, supporting her with faith, assurances and encouragement . . .

A gentle knock heralds the husband ' Is she alright Doctor?'

' Splendid.' The good fellow goes away comforted . . .

' Then the girl's hand tightens on his wrist . . . A dusky hue overspreads the glowing face beside him. A new instalment in the price of motherhood is about to be paid . . .

Suddenly the Doctor starts from his chair. All the blood has run away from his cheeks. A wild fear shudders in his eyes . . .

He seizes the girl, and lifts her in his arms . . . There is no colour now in the fair young face and the long eye lashes fall in exquisite tranquility on the cheeks . . .

' Oh God, can it be possible?'

The girl was dead. She died of sudden heart failure . . .

An hour later, in his consulting room, as he paced the floor in the deep silence of the small hours, the full horror of this calamity was revealed to him. The question sprang to his lips; ' Would this death have occurred if I had had a better knowledge of heart afflictions?' In other words had there been present, before the time of delivery, signs or symptoms which might have served as warnings and enabled him to take preventive measures? He could not answer these questions and the fact of his ignorance appalled him . . . There and then, beside that piteous deathbed, he resolved to obtain better knowledge and to make a beginning by studying, in women, the mechanism and history of the symptoms usually supposed to indicate heart trouble. It was thus, that Mackenzie became a heart specialist . . .

In April, 1920 he could look back with justifiable pride, when he wrote:

> About 40 years ago I attended a woman with heart disease, in labour, who died after 36 hours of great suffering and undelivered. Although this danger had been long recognised no one knew where the danger lay, with the result that many women became pregnant and died, or had their health permanently impaired. A great many were forbidden to marry or become pregnant because they were supposed to have a heart defect, when as a matter of fact, there was not the slightest danger.

Evidently he had acquired a new philosophy in the understanding of heart disease. In later years, he was to say to his assistant Dr John Linnell, no doubt with the voice of authority, ' a heart is, what a heart can do.'

These are simple words, yet down the years, despite the great advances in cardiology, they still have a significance which has undoubtedly influenced the lives of countless people with heart disease.

The moral to this story is clear. Public concern to remedy social evils calls for concerted action which, in turn, may help many people. History, however, will show that the pioneering work and observations of one man on a few patients, may be of equal benefit to mankind. Mackenzie was one of these men.

7

Chapter 11

THE CLINICAL POLYGRAPH

Medicine is a science . . . more
professed than laboured

BACON

The period from 1882 until 1890 saw the early stirrings of clinical observation and research which were to become such a remarkable attribute of this young general practitioner. With the uncertain steps of the amateur he ventured into print. His first publication[1] concerned a coal-miner who had sustained a crush injury in the lumbar region of the spinal cord. The feature of particular interest in this patient was the sustained shortening of certain leg muscles in response to stimulation, while at the same time the limbs were paralysed. The patient was unable to produce movement by orderly contraction of muscles.

Six years later began his life-long interest in neurological disease and the distribution of surface pain and sensitivity. In a second paper[2] ' On a case of Herpes Zoster ', he describes skin eruptions in the hand, ball of the thumb, along with others on the outer side of the arm. This in anatomical terms was unusual, confirming a nerve root distribution conforming to areas connected with the fifth and sixth cervical roots. A third publication in 1890/1, 'A case of multiple symmetrical herpes zoster '[3] gave a full description of the case without deduction or inference.

Encouraging though these incursions into medical literature must have been to him, they were as of nothing compared to the baffling clinical problems in his practice for which there appeared to be no easy solution of diagnosis or prognosis. His restless mind would return again and again to conditions of the heart, to cases as described in the previous chapter, where in his efforts to elucidate he felt so helpless and alone. He recorded :

> I studied the circulatory condition of women before preg-
> nancy, watched them during the time they were pregnant,
> observed them closely during labour and the puerperium and for

[1] Lancet (1883) II, 942.
[2] Manchester Medical Chronicle (1889) X, 288.
[3] Manchester Medical Chronicle (1890/1) XIII, 356.

months and years after. I studied not only cases with damaged hearts, but also many healthy women. After several years I had collected a large mass of material. I found, among other things, changes in the size and position of the heart, murmurs of different kinds, variations in rate and rhythm and other departures from what is usually considered the normal.

The nearest medical school and library, it must be remembered, were twenty four miles away. In the conditions of transport then, obtaining advice from Consultants in Manchester was theoretically possible but inconvenient. In any case, there was his practice to consider. Consultant's fees, based amongst other things on time and distance, were beyond the means of all but a tiny minority of his patients. He would set out alone on this journey of clinical exploration, his twin guiding principles being those of induction and deduction. He would study, observe and record.

> The difficulties[4] attending the recognition of the pulse *produced in the veins*[5] by the contraction of the heart, have prevented this pulse being as carefully studied as it deserves. Since Freidreich published his careful researches with his numerous tracings of the venous pulse, his views have been practically accepted and his descriptions universally quoted. By carefully watching the time of the venous pulse *in relation to the heart beat*[6] and from consideration of the various events that occur during a cardiac revolution, I felt convinced, however, that Freidreich's views were erroneous . . . After much labour I hit upon a plan almost ridiculous in its simplicity . . .

In his cases of herpes zoster, the signs were self-evident and immediately apparent. The heart on the other hand is a complex organ, the study of which, during life, was possible only by indirect methods of inference and deduction. Records of blood pressure, pulse rate, auscultation and percussion were not enough to reveal the complexity and state of this important structure hidden behind the chest wall. At that time there were no X-rays. Lesser men, hoping to devote their professional life to study one system of human physiology, would have selected an easier path—Mackenzie chose the heart.

> ' Freidreich ', he writes, ' describes the case of a woman aged twenty seven, and seven months pregnant, where the venous

---

[4] Pulsations in the veins with the description of a method for graphically recording them. *Journal of Pathology and Bacteriology* (1892)—*1*, 54 to 89.
[5] Author's italics.
[6] Author's italics.

pulse gives a tracing in every respect identical with the triple wave form I have described . . . Although for the past twelve months I have carefully examined the venous pulse in more than a hundred patients, I delayed publishing the results till I thought I had examined a sufficient number.'

The cases he examined were mainly instances of stenosis and/or incompetence of the mitral, tricuspid or aortic valves following rheumatic fever. Of these sufferers, Burnley in those days provided him with ample abundance and Mackenzie was indefatigable in making the most of this clinical harvest.

The conclusions to which he came in this early paper on the venous pulse may be summarized:

1. Pulsations of the veins arise in cases where, from any cause dilatation of the right heart and great veins, (with incompetence of the tricuspid and venous valves) takes place.

2. While the auricle can contract vigorously, there is a wave synchronous with, and caused by, auricular systole.

3. When the dilatation is moderate in amount the auricular wave is followed by a great depression synchronous with, and caused by, the auricular diastole.

4. In most cases there is a wave produced by, and synchronous with the latter portion of ventricular systole.

5. The greater the incompetence of the tricuspid valve, and the greater the distension of the auricle, the earlier does the ventricular wave appear.

6. The ventricular wave in extreme dilatation of the right side may occupy the whole period of ventricular systole. The depression caused by the auricular diastole is then replaced by the ventricular wave.

7. In such cases, the auricle has ceased to contract independently, or its contraction is represented by a very small wave immediately preceding the ventricular wave.

The story of the young woman who died in labour has been referred to. 'The usual descriptions . . . did not appear to me to be adequate', he wrote, with typical understatement on his discovery that once again the text books could not help him. Whilst they would 'describe a murmur with meticulous nicety, no attempt was made to assess its value'. It was the value of the various murmurs and irregularities which concerned him, and having failed with the text books, he appealed to the physiologists. He was at this time in touch with Sherrington[7] at Oxford and with Langley[8] and Roy[9] at Cambridge; Roy was helpful in arranging that Mackenzie should have access to any relevant books in the library there. However, the physiologists proved to be of no practical help, and he set about trying to interpret for himself the results he obtained from his study of the maternal heart. General practice then, as now, is not the most favourable environment for undertaking this kind of research.

> . . . It is impossible for those who have not undertaken this kind of research to understand its difficulties. Let me describe one phase of the subject. One object I had in mind was to understand where lay the danger of pregnancy in a woman with a damaged heart. This is a problem which confronts time and again every general practitioner, and it is one of very serious moment to those concerned . . . I had to study the changes in the circulation during pregnancy, during confinement, and during the puerperium which occurred in healthy women; I had to watch the changes that took place in women with different forms of heart disease, examining them before pregnancy, and at all the subsequent stages. This meant attending them during labour, taking careful observations during the pains and when free from the pains. These observations were not made in a comfortable ward with plenty of help, but often after a hard day's work, during the night in poor cottages, where I had to do the duties of the doctor and the nurse, give chloroform, apply the forceps, and wash the baby. Yet this work had to be done, and in no other way could the knowledge be acquired . . .

This knowledge was later put to use in several papers on heart failure and pregnancy, and ultimately in his great book *Heart Disease and Pregnancy*,[10] published in 1921. But his study had aroused his interest in the venous pulse, and for some time this interest predominated:

> . . . The venous pulse, however, offers to us a different kind of knowledge, inasmuch as it is itself a pathological manifestation which gives information regarding the condition of two cavities of the heart (the right auricle and ventricle), the arterial pulse affording direct knowledge of the left ventricle only. The

[7] Sir C. S. Sherrington 1857-1952. Physiologist—Oxford.
[8] John N. Langley 1852-1952. Physiologist—Cambridge.
[9] Charles S. Roy, M.B. C.M. Edin. 1875. M.D. Edin. 1878. Pathologist—Cambridge.
[10] *Heart Disease and Pregnancy* (1921) Oxford Medical Publications.

venous pulse, too, presents a greater variety of features, and is subject to influences so subtle that it may manifest variations with the changing condition of the patient, during which the arterial pulse reveals no appreciable alteration. Did we but fully comprehend the import of these variations, then would our knowledge enable us to understand and combat certain diseased conditions of the heart as yet very obscure and ill-defined . . .

Two factors, Mackenzie continued, had militated against the proper recognition of venous pulsations, one being a misconception as to their nature, and the other a lack of a convenient method for recording them. He said:

A prime necessity in such an instrument is the ability to register, at one and the same time as the venous pulse, some known movement of the heart as a standard (apex beat or arterial pulse).

He set himself to overcome this obstacle and to devise an instrument which would fulfil the conditions required. There was much trial and error, though in his various writings Mackenzie makes light of his prodigious efforts:

. . . I began to consider whether some simple means of registering the venous pulse might not be devised, whereby tracings of the heart or arteries might be taken at the same time, in order to determine the time of occurrence of the various events during a cardiac revolution. After much labour I hit upon a plan almost ridiculous in its simplicity. This method consists in placing a hollow lead cone or funnel (called a ' receiver ') over any pulsating part where the surface of the skin permits the cavity of the funnel to be hermetically closed. The base of the receiver I have mostly used has a diameter of one inch and a half. This receiver is connected by means of an indiarubber tube to a Mareys' tambour and lever, the latter of which can be made to write on the smoked paper of a Dudgeon's sphygmograph or revolving cylinder. The advantage of this method is enhanced by the fact that several such receivers can be used to take tracings, at one and the same time, of heart-beat, and of arterial, or venous pulse. In this manner the time of the occurrence of the various incidents in a cardiac revolution can be discerned with certainty even in a pulsation at some distance from the heart . . .

A further development, of what was essentially a Phlebograph, Mackenzie called his ' clinical Polygraph ', followed. Of this he wrote:

> . . . Inasmuch as the whole arrangement can be used for taking, at the same time and on the same recording surface, tracings of the radial pulse, with tracings of the apex beat, carotid, venous or liver pulse, or the respiratory movements, and as its size is such as to permit its being carried about with the greatest facility, and readily employed in general practice, I will refer to it as the ' clinical polygraph '.
>
> The instrument consists of a tambour . . . supporting the writing lever, the latter being six inches in length. From the under-surface of the tambour a pipe protrudes, which is connected by the indiarubber tubing with a receiver. Screwed tightly to the bottom of the tambour is a stem . . . six and a half inches in length, projecting outward, parallel to the under surface of the tambour. Half an inch of the other extremity of the stem is bent almost at right angles . . . and this portion fits into a slot in the upright stem that supports the movable lever of a Dudgeon's sphygmograph, and this supports the tambour. When the tambour arrangements are adjusted to the sphygmograph, the tambour rests with its movable surface vertically, so that the writing lever moves horizontally . . . the lever can be raised out of reach during the adjustment of the sphygmograph to the pulse, and brought back and allowed to touch the surface of the blackened paper with sufficient delicacy to permit its movements to be accurately recorded, but not restrained by too close pressure, by rotating the tambour at a joint formed where the stem is fixed to the under-surface of the tambour . . . Some difficulty may be experienced in the employment of the clinical polygraph, on account of the weight of the tambour tilting the sphygmograph off the radial pulse. If we employ the inelastic band usually supplied with the sphygmograph, this inconvenience may possibly be very serious. I have long ago abandoned the use of the inelastic band (placing no reliance on the pressure supposed to be required to obtain an idea of the arterial tension), and employ instead an elastic band, tying the instrument to the wrist by a knot. Should any slipping occur, the sphygmograph and tambour can readily be adjusted . . .

The first ' clinical polygraph ' was made for Mackenzie by a London firm of instrument-makers, Messrs Krohner & Seseman. Writing to Will in February, 1892, Mackenzie reported : 'My labours

FIG. 2. Dr Mackenzie's Ink Polygraph, description and management.

"DR. MACKENZIE'S INK POLYGRAPH."

MAKER - - MR. S. SHAW, WATCHMAKER, PADIHAM, LANCASHIRE.

Description and Management.

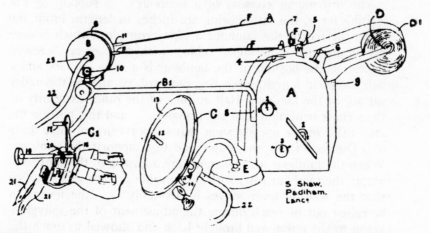

S Shaw.
Padiham.
Lancs

OBJECT.

The necessity for obtaining graphic records of the movements of the circulation is now universally recognised, but there has hitherto been a difficulty in obtaining a suitable instrument. Apart from the trouble of blackening and varnishing tracings, the present methods are not convenient, especially when long tracings are required. The ink-polygraph meets the necessary requirements as it enables tracings to be taken of any length, and after a little experience it is very easy to use. In investigating any movement caused by the circulation it is necessary to record at the same time some standard event whose position in the cardiac cycle is fixed and determined. Hence it is necessary that two events should be simultaneously recorded—the one to be investigated and the standard movement. The best and most reliable standard movement is the arterial pulse, radial and carotid, with the Ink Polygraph these movements can be recorded by one lever while the movement to be investigated is recorded by the other lever. Other movements, as those of the respiration, can also be recorded.

DESCRIPTION.

The most important parts of the " Polygraph " may be described as follows :—

The body A, containing the paper-rolling and time-marker movements. The writing tambours BB, with supporting bar B1. Wrist tambour C, with attachment C1, for strapping on to wrist. Paper roll bracket D. Paper roll D1. Cup receivers EE. Pens FFF.

92

The body A has also a few other details requiring description.—At the end of the machine are three keys. The large one (1) is for winding the paper-rolling movement. The top smaller stud-key (2) for winding the time-marker movement, and the bottom one (3) regulates the speed of the paper passing through the rollers, the direction required being indicated by the letters F and S (fast and slow). On the top are the writing table (4), friction rollers and tension spring (5) for passing along the paper.

Behind these, to the right, is the start-and-stop lever (6), and to the left the fork (7) carrying the time-marker pen F. This fork vibrates at the rate of 300 per minute, an equivalent to ⅕th of a second.

Attached to the case are two sockets.—The square one in front (8) for holding the writing tambours, whilst the other behind (9) supports the paper roll bracket.

The writing tambours with their pen levers (11) are fitted with friction joints (10) enabling the pens to be adjusted to any desired position on the paper or lifted entirely away when not writing.

The pen levers have each a small spring at the end which presses on and holds the pens in the grooves cut out to receive them.

The rubber membrane is held in position by the ring which encircles it. Both tambours have inlets (23) for attaching connecting tubes (22).

The wrist tambour C is in two parts.—1st the splint (16) which is strapped on the wrist, is fitted with spring tongue and button (19), that rises and falls with the action of the pulse. Also an eccentric (20) and regulating screw (18) for increasing the resistance on the artery.

2nd.—The tambour with supporting arm (14), rubber membrane (13), and compression disc and peg (12). *This portion is not placed in position until the artery has been correctly located and the maximum movement of the spring and pulse button obtained.* The two parts are held together by the clamping screw (15) in the supporting arm binding on to the pillar (17). The tambour itself is also secured by binding screw (17).

The paper roll bracket D has a roller running in slots at the ends of the bracket arms. This roller is kept in position by two springs fixed on the bracket arms having semi-circular notches engaging the rolling pivots. When putting on roll of paper, the roller should be drawn straight away from the brackets; which action causes the springs to be pressed under the pivots, thereby releasing the roller. After placing on the roll, press the roller back into position.

The receivers EE, are shallow, open cups with a nipple passing out of the roof to which an india-rubber tube is attached, the other end of the tube being attached to the tambour with the writing levers. When placed over any pulsating part in such a manner that no communication is made with the outer air, the movement within the receiver is conveyed to the tambour and writing lever.

The pens FFF have each small reservoirs and writing pins. These pins are grooved on each side to conduct writing fluid from reservoir to point of pin. The fluid used is a composition of 1 drachm of methyl blue to 16ozs. of water. Ordinary writing inks are objectionable owing to the corrosive action on the pens. These pens should be kept scrupulously clean, and the ink free from dust.

Each machine is sent out complete in plush-lined box, with two sets of pens, 1 dozen rolls of paper, bottle of writing fluid, brush for charging up pens, and rubber tubes for connections.

Price £10 10s. 0d. nett.

A FEW INSTRUCTIONS ON THE MANAGEMENT OF THE "POLYGRAPH."

TO ASSEMBLE MACHINE :

Place the body of machine on a table or stand, wind up both movements, then fix the tambour bar, which carries the writing tambours into the square socket attached to front of case. Next fit on the paper roll bracket into the socket at the back of the case. Draw out the roller and put on the paper roll. *Care must always be taken to have the paper unrolling from the top on to the machine, and not to come up from underneath.* Pass the end of paper through the friction rollers and let the clockwork take it forward until it overhangs the front edge of the writing table. Now place the pens in their respective positions, the writing pens in pen levers on the tambours and the small time-marker pen on the vibrating fork. The pens should be lifted away from the paper so as to observe the movement when adjusting for the maximum excursion. Charge up all the pens with fluid, and connect the cup receiver and tambour to the writing tambours with the rubber tubes. *The wrist tambour must always be connected up with the writing tambour nearest to the supporting bar.* The reason for this is that the pen lever on this tambour is allowed a greater leverage to amplify the small displacement of air imparted to the transmitting tambour by the radial pulse.

After full attention has been given to the foregoing, strap the splint firmly on to patient's wrist, locate the artery, and adjust the small eccentric on pulse button spring, until the best movement is obtained. Next attach the arm carrying wrist trambour on to the peg provided in the pillar fixed to the splint. Secure this arm with the binding screw, then drop the tambour until the compression peg on the rubber membrane rests upon the small plate above the pulse button ; then secure this also.

If these instructions have been properly carried out, a movement will be given to the pen. If the movement be not satisfactory, again adjust the regulating screw on the splint so as to get the greatest excursion. *Also take particular notice that the hand is thrown well back to bring the artery as prominent as possible.*

When the desired movement has been obtained, lay the patient's wrist across the arm of a chair or other support, to keep the hand in proper position, as the drooping of the wrist or closing the hand, has a deterimental effect on the action of the pen.

If a synchronous tracing be desired, the cup receiver must now be adjusted until the movement to be investigated transmits a suitable action to the other pen, after which the pens may be brought down to the slightest touch on paper, and machine started off.

A little experience will be necessary in the successful manipulation, but if these instructions be strictly adhered to a fairly decent result is absolutely certain.

A FEW OTHER IMPORTANT ITEMS ARE :

1st—Keep the pens well cleaned and avoid using ink which has become dirty and thick from exposure. If the pens fail to flow properly rinse them well with water at the same time brush out the grooves.

2nd—Pay strict attention to the tambours being perfectly airtight, as the slightest leakage causes loss of movement on the pens. To test for this, blow a little air into tambour, then stop up the rubber tube with the finger, when, if air-tight, the pen will maintain its position, otherwise it will gradually fall to its zero line owing to the escape of air. When this defect appears, a new membrane must be substituted. Should the faulty membrane be one of the writing tambours proceed to remedy in the following manner : Detach the pen lever bracket from the tambour by taking out the screw which holds it to the small block at the back of the tambour. Next draw off the ring encircling the membrane and flange of tambour. Now lay across a new piece of rubber—do not stretch it—and again push on the ring to its original position ; afterwards trim off all superflous rubber with a sharp knife, drawing it round the tambour edge behind the ring. Next replace the pen lever bracket, having previously removed all traces of old rubber ; then touch small disc with a little gum or secotine and bring down the lever gradually, allowing the disc to fall squarely on to the membrane, so as to find its proper working position. Test in the manner stated for leakage, and if airtight, it may now be again considered in working order.

The renewing of membrane on wrist tambour needs no description, as this is simply tied on to the groove, afterwards cementing the compression disc with the stud *perfectly central* as to ensure finding its proper place when dropped on to the pulse button.

3rd—When running the paper through very slow, the spring must be wound up to the top, as this method gives a more uniform speed. Turning the regulating screw too far in the slow direction stops the machine entirely, and it may sometimes happen that the machine fails to start to the response of the starting lever. Should this at any time be the case, turn the regulator in the direction of fast, when it will again commence to work.

on the pulse have had very good results, so much so that I am to give a demonstration before the Manchester Medical Society on March 16. I want to have a new instrument perfected by then and intend seeing a London instrument maker on Saturday.' The ink polygraph for which Mackenzie was to become famous, and which he devised with the help of the Padiham watch-maker Sebastian Shaw, was a much later development and did not appear until 1906, although it is possible that he had experimented with such an instrument before then. Dr, later Professor, John Hay of Liverpool, has stated that ' the greater part of his (Mackenzie's) heart work was carried out with the simpler instrument—the Dudgeon—and the small strips of smoked paper ', and this is undoubtedly true.

The first paper on venous pulsation appeared in the *Caledonian Medical Journal* in 1891, followed by ' Pulsations in the veins ' in the *Journal of Pathology and Bacteriology*[11] in 1892, and ' The venous and liver pulses '[12] in the same journal in 1894. Mackenzie was far from being the only man interested in the subject of the pulse, which had absorbed medical practitioners from the earliest times. Galen had written no less than eighteen books on the pulse: nearer to Mackenzie's time, in 1854, William Stokes of Dublin had been struck by the irregularity of pulsations in the veins of the neck. F. A. Mahomed, of Guy's Hospital, had carried out a long study of pulse tracings, and might have achieved much had he lived; he died of typhoid fever in 1884 aged only thirty-five.

In his paper ' The venous and liver pulses and the arrhythmic contraction of the cardiac cavities ', Mackenzie refers to the work of numerous writers on the venous pulse and prefaces his more detailed comments thus:

> . . . After noticing its forms I consulted such authorities as my limited opportunities at the time permitted me to have access to, and I found that the conclusions I had arrived at differed materially.[13] It seemed to me that if graphic records of the venous pulse, with a standard time, could be obtained, much light might be thrown upon the subject. Being myself devoid of all mechanical skill, my attempts were crude and tediously prolonged; and when at last I did succeed, it was found, as was to be expected, that both the method and the results had been already described. But it was fortunate that I was ignorant of the work that had been done, for had I been aware of what so

[11] *Journal of Path. & Bact.* (1892) *i*, 53–89.
[12] *Journal of Path. & Bact.* (1894) *ii*. 84 and 273.
[13] From those arrived at by the authors whose works I was able to consult.

many skilled observers, with the advantage of experimental research, had accomplished, I should have been deterred from attempting, at such great disadvantage, to follow them, and should have accepted their interpretations without question. As it was, in my numerous attempts to get a graphic record I acquired an intimate knowledge of the strength, the variations, and the situation of the pulsations in the veins. When at last I did get sufficient results, unfettered by any prejudiced notion of what should happen, or what others had explained, I evolved the interpretation given in the following pages. Here likewise, to a great extent, I had been anticipated, but my opinion still is that the most salient features of the more commonly occurring venous pulse had been entirely misunderstood by both clinical observers and experimental investigators. The subject, so far, has been involved in the greatest confusion, and has given rise to endless contradictory assertions and observations . . .

With growing confidence, born of his clinical observations and clinical polygraph, Mackenzie published his first full length article in the *Journal of Pathology and Bacteriology.*

The manuscript of this paper and Mackenzie's tracings reached the hands of Dr Charles Roy,[14] Professor of the Pathological Laboratory at Cambridge University. In conjunction with Adami he had published a paper ' Heart Beat and Pulse Wave ' in 1890. Writing to a Dr MacKendrick, through whom he appears to have received the manuscript, Roy stated :

Cambridge, Oct. 28, 1892.

. . . I have examined Dr Mackenzie's tracings with some care, comparing them with some of my own which I took by another method when I was in G. W. Balfour's wards in Edinburgh. I must say I am surprised that Dr McK. has got such decent looking curves with the method he employed—he has evidently been very clever in adjusting his lever so it should press just hard enough on the drum to prevent much inertia vibration without pressing so hard as to spoil the tracing. He has got good curves but I believe he would be wise to choose a more trustworthy method than that of air transmission to a Marey's tambour. I admit that his method has many advantages and evidently in his hands can give good curves, e.g. the ones you sent me seem all right while some of the others . . . do not

[14] Prize for M.D. Thesis Edin. 1878 ' The Influences governing the Work of the Heart.'

seem to me free from the suspicion of inertia vibrations of the recording lever. As to the interpretation of the tracings I am afraid I cannot agree with Dr Mackenzie. He seems to me to have overlooked the fact that a venous pulse necessarily travels along from the heart more slowly than the arterial pulse owing to the much greater tension of the arterial wall . . . It seems to me that Dr Mackenzie has got hold of something which will well repay further work. From the venous pulse can be learned something about the strength of the auricular contractions and as much about the condition of the right ventricle as can be learned by a *proper* sphygmograph from the arterial pulse tracing concerning the left ventricle. If I may take the liberty of advising Dr Mackenzie I should recommend him strongly not to trust to his present method alone. I think he should have another instrument on an entirely different principle and that for a time at least he should use both methods. If the tracings from his present arrangement agree with those taken by a quite different instrument then he may trust his tracings and can draw conclusions from them which could not safely be based on curves with an uncertain margin of error . . .

Will you kindly congratulate Dr Mackenzie from me on having hit on what I am convinced is a promising field. If he comes anywhere near Cambridge I should be glad to compare notes with him. I return the original tracings, with best thanks for the copy of the paper . . .

When the paper was published in 1894 Mackenzie referred to both points raised by Roy :

. . . It is assumed that the time occupied by the pulse wave in the veins will take the same time to travel from the heart to the jugulars as the arterial wave from the heart to the carotids. Possibly the difference in the structure of the walls, and the resistance offered to the wave, may make a difference in the rate of propagation, but if so it is so slight that it need not be considered. In employing the radial pulse to time the events of the jugular pulse, a distinct loss of time must be allowed for on account of the radial pulse appearing later than that of the carotid. But this difference is readily estimated by taking, immediately after the venous pulse has been recorded, a tracing of a few beats of the carotid pulse, and in calculating the time of the different events in the jugular pulse by the standard of the radial pulse, allow for the difference between the carotid and radial. It will be found that very little time is lost by air transmission as compared with the lapse of time between the carotid and radial pulses . . .

. . . I may here explain, with regard to certain imperfections, both in carotid pulse and apex beat tracings, which may be detected in the tracings, that these were frequently obtained under somewhat disadvantageous circumstances. Thus, most of the observations have been made on patients in their own homes, and with no assistance except what the patient could afford. While I held the receiver over the venous pulse with one hand, I had to manipulate the levers and the instrument with the other. The patient then had to hold the receiver or cardiograph to the carotid or apex beat; naturally under these conditions, I could not expect perfect tracings. I have not used any of the tracings where any doubt existed as to the interpretation, without employing various devices to guarantee the accuracy of the deductions. Since I have devised the clinical polygraph, I have been able to obtain, with great facility, more satisfactory results, as the patient's or other help is dispensed with. I have, however, in numerous instances, employed both the clinical and Knoll's polygraph in order to guard against any error . . .

Early work on his original phlebograph involved the use of a clumsy smoke drum, the recordings of which were limited in time. Each recording had to be varnished for preservation as subsequent records.

In his ' clinical polygraph ', Mackenzie devised a mechanism whereby a narrow strip of paper was fed at standard speed on which a lever and ink pen gave an immediate and continuous tracing. Moreover, it was portable and could be applied with simplicity in the homes of patients.

The tentative communication between Roy and Mackenzie through a third party, MacKendrick, became more personal, intimate and rewarding. Roy continued to be critical, although helpful and constructive.

Cambridge, Feb. 10, 1893.

My dear Mackenzie,

. . . I wish you clinicians would work out the exact acceleration of the heart for each degree rise of the thermometer scale so as to enable us to distinguish between acceleration due to fever and that due to anaemia . . . In a venous pulse with tricuspid regurgitation I should expect (1) a positive wave with the auricular contraction (2) etc., etc . . .

I am President of the Pathology Section of the B.M.A. Newcastle Meeting, and if you can come and read a paper I shall be very glad.

and again

June 28, 1893

I cannot grasp very clearly viz. your explanation of the negative wave curve which accompanies the ventricular contraction. The reasons you give . . . do not appeal to me . . .

Your curves are very good indeed, and put the whole question of the venous pulse on a decent footing . . .

Most revealing of all is the short reply in an earlier letter of Roy to Mackenzie who obviously was making a plea for access to text books of Clinical Medicine.

and again

Cambridge, Feb. 10, 1892

Dear Dr Mackenzie,

I should think you would find at Cambridge most of the medical books you want to consult but, of course, I don't know. We have plenty books on Physiology and Pathology, but are rather incomplete on medicine proper. I will give you what help I can in getting you access to books.

Yours sincerely,
CHARLES ROY.

Was this not significant? The pathologist/physiologist was content to study and teach physiology on experimental animals in the laboratory, without the necessity of applying it in a clinical setting. Mackenzie was essentially a physician but, not content with this, he was also becoming, perhaps unwittingly, a pathologist and an applied physiologist in his own right.

Mackenzie frankly admits that he later discovered in his work on the venous pulse that others had trod the same path before him. However, as he remarked ' unfettered by any prejudiced notion ' he applied these principles, placed upon them different interpretations, removed misunderstandings and confusion, and gave a new meaning to them because his findings were based on vast numbers of clinical observations in health and disease. A new confidence was beginning to replace the uncertainties of his student days at Edinburgh.

Chapter 12

LOVE AND TRAGEDY

The old order changeth, giving
place to new

TENNYSON

There is no record to show exactly when Mackenzie met his future
wife, but we know of the circumstances of their meeting. Frances
Bellamy Jackson was the daughter of a Lincolnshire farmer, and
when he died leaving seven young children, Frances and two of her
sisters were taken to London to be brought up by a step-uncle, Mr
Frederick Jackson, a lawyer and friend of George Bernard Shaw.
Frances was not very happy with Mr Jackson, and, after her formal
education and a year spent in Germany studying music and German,
she determined to take a position which would enable her to be
independent. So she came to Burnley as companion and governess
to the children of Mr and Mrs Handsley of Reedley Lodge. Mr
Handsley was a Solicitor and J.P. and also the principal agent to the
colliery owners and Executors of Colonel John Hargreaves. Dr
Mackenzie was the family doctor, and it was natural enough that
they should meet when he came to attend the children. Frances was
twenty two and Mackenzie was thirty four when he renounced
the ' happy state of bachelordom ' with which he had professed to
be content. They were married on 13th September, 1887, at Shotter-
mill, near Haslemere. Will was best man, and the honeymoon was
spent in Europe.

> Grand Hotel,
> Bellagio, nr, Lake Como, Italy.
> Sept. 28/87.

My dear W.,
    The honeymoon has proceeded so far without mishap,
rather it has been accompanied with all things that tend to make
it enjoyable—beautiful weather and glorious scenes. Do you
know your geography sufficiently well to be able intelligently
to follow our route? I fear not. We have viewed from afar the
wonderful snow-clad peaks rising high in the heavens and look
unearthly, almost of celestial origin. Leaving these we have
crossed into Italy by the mighty Simplon Pass where in times

gone by the Napoleonic hordes swept victoriously to other conquests.

From here we go tomorrow to Verona. We get to Paris on the 7th October. We want you to engage rooms at a hotel, say the Metropole, and places at some theatre. Francie joins with me in sending much love . . .

To this letter the new Mrs Mackenzie appended a postscript:

Mistress Mackenzie particularly requests that you write to her and not to her husband at Paris. As she writes most of the letters she thinks she deserves the answers, especially such a charming answer as will come from her dear brother-in-law. It will be more appreciated by the wife!!!

This gay little postscript illustrates delightfully the sense of fun which was one of Frances Mackenzie's chief characteristics. Miss Margaret Lorraine-Smith, whose father Professor Lorraine-Smith, was a great friend of Mackenzie's, writes of her thus:

. . . She had humour, and a capacity for making people happy; she was fond of a joke, and we used to laugh, and love her gentle teasing. I think that she had a great capacity for seeing life in proportion, and a great understanding and sympathy for all human beings. She had a very real influence on all who had the good fortune to know her—she made us richer, better people . . . she bestowed upon us some of her natural goodness. She was a very unaffected, natural woman, delicately made and gentle in manner, with bright, expressive eyes. On looking back, I think that she was probably much cleverer than she allowed herself to appear . . .

Mackenzie himself had anticipated this astute piece of deduction by declaring forthrightly that his wife had more wisdom and knowledge in her little finger than many of the so-called 'clever' women he met during the course of his professional life. He deferred to her judgement in everything, seeking her advice and approval and receiving always wise and gentle counsel. She was twelve years his junior, yet the protective nature of her affection was always apparent, as was Mackenzie's own essential simplicity.

Mackenzie was already collaborating in joint studies with Dr James Ross of Manchester. Forwarding a wedding present via Mrs Brown, he wrote:

8

Manchester,
Sept. 7, 1887

> . . . although the fact of writing to yourself places me under
> restraint, I do not see why I should hesitate to say I believe
> your future wife will find, or rather has found, you to be as
> warm and tender hearted as you are admittedly strong and
> constant . . .

The regard between Ross and Mackenzie was mutual. With his marriage Mackenzie had entered the happiest period of his life, and one of the secrets of his massive output of work during these Burnley years must have been the serenity and contentment in his home. In sharp contrast to his friend Sir Arthur Keith, who remarked in his autobiography that " I could never give myself to close study with anyone sitting by me ", Mackenzie did almost all of his work within the family circle. He wrote up his notes and pored over his tracings in the evenings, whilst his wife played the piano softly in the background. " It could have been the same tune over and over again for all he knew ", his daughter remembers, " but he was perfectly content just with the music going on ". He possessed to a remarkable degree the power of withdrawal and concentration; he would be oblivious of his surroundings, his mind focused entirely on the problem with which he was occupied at that moment, yet he could instantly bring himself back to full awareness of what was going on around him, switching his mind from one thing to another as cleanly and completely as an electric light switch is turned on and off. It was this faculty, developed to a remarkable degree, which enabled him to accomplish, with apparent ease, an amount of sheer hard work which lesser men would regard as impossible. The life of a general practitioner was no less busy then than now, and Dr Margaret Brotherston,[1] who spent some months in general practice in Burnley early in 1902, recalls that they saw on an average 60 to 70 patients daily at the surgeries or at home, and it can safely be assumed that the picture at Bank Parade would be similar. In addition there were night calls, and emergencies; Dr Wood,[2] estimates that there would be an average of three confinements each week. It was necessary for a man to be physically fit as well as temperamentally well-equipped, and Mackenzie's robust constitution stood him in good stead. He had succumbed to a mild attack of typhoid fever during his first year in Burnley, when he was nursed back to health by Mrs

[1] Personal communication.
[2] Personal communication.

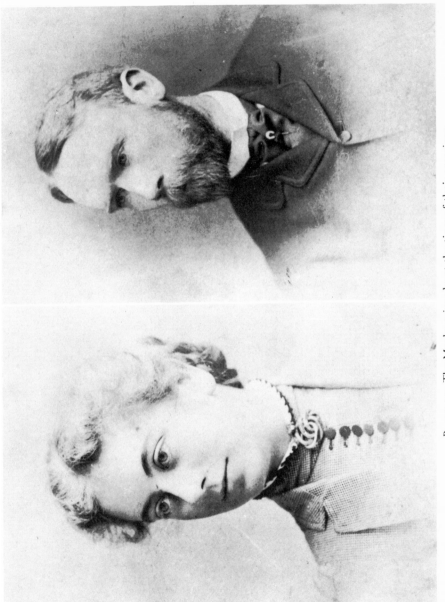

PLATE 10. The Mackenzies about the time of their marriage.

PLATE 11. The Mackenzies with Dorothy and Jean, 1900.

Brown, who afterwards declared that much of the credit for his achievements must go to her!

Dr Brown wrote of this from South Africa in 1906:

> By a process of reasoning I cannot quite follow, my dear good wife lays claim to a share of all your honours and discoveries and future benefits to the human race; she says you would have died of typhoid fever in the very first year of your coming to Burnley, had she not taken you north to your native air, on a memorable journey on the details of which she fondly dwells. This gives her a sort of motherly pride in your achievements, and added gratification . . .

This illness left Mackenzie's health unimpaired, and his only physical complaint was his susceptibility to migraine. It was out of his own experience that he wrote a paper on this distressing condition for Allbutt's book *System of Medicine* in 1899.[3]

What must be emphasized is Mackenzie's capacity for work. Dr Brown recognized this and referred to it many years later when he wrote: ' . . . the *primary* cause of your great success in life has been your hard work all your life through.' Equal emphasis, however, must be given to the motivating influence which lay behind this insatiable appetite for work. What drove him on? Perhaps the answer lay in a single word: Compassion. Mackenzie cared about his patients and suffered with them; his own ignorance and his inability to help many of them had distressed him beyond words, and this distress now impelled him forward. His own words were: 'To me, this research was but a means to an end, not the end itself —the end being the prognostic significance . . .' The prognostic significance, the need to know how to help: this deep humanity was the essence of the man—his only goal the relief of suffering.[4]

Many honours were to come his way; they were not to change him. An extract from *The Trader*, published in Burnley in 1927, reads as follows:

> . . . Had the whole alphabet been put behind his name ten times over it would not alter by a single jot the quality of the man himself or the value of his contribution to knowledge.
>
> Yet Dr Mackenzie was ours, of Burnley, in a sense more true than if he had been born in the Borough. Amongst us he made

---

[3] Thomas Clifford Allbutt, *System of Medicine*, Macmillan, 1899.
[4] Sir John Parkinson said of him 'I never knew how far it was love of truth or how far love of humanity that quickened his spirit.

his mental growth and formulated the concepts which are in essence his life work . . .

A daughter, Dorothy, was born to Dr and Mrs Mackenzie in December, 1888. Will was the first to hear the news:

Dear W.,

Just a line to tell you that next time you come here there will be a NIECE to welcome you—what think you of that, man? The wee lassie came shortly after noon to-day, and mother and daughter are doing well . . .

' Dorothy flourishes more than ever ', Mackenzie was able to report happily in a further letter to Will in January 1890, illustrating his remark with a comical sketch of himself and Mrs Mackenzie, and Dorothy between them taking her first uncertain steps. They were unaware of the tragedy which lay in wait for them only a few short months away, for in May of that year when she was seventeen months old, Mackenzie's daughter became a victim of poliomyelitis, or the ' essential paralysis of children ', as it was known then. It was a cruel blow which these young parents had to face, and there is a poignancy in Mackenzie's notes on his child's illness.

With surprising detachment and aware of his own helplessness, he writes again with that great clarity and simplicity:

. . . On Monday, May 19th, 1890, Dorothy (17 months) was lively, active and in good health and had trotted about more briskly than usual. During that night and next day she was feverish, temperature 102° and restless. Her sleep on Monday and Tuesday was disturbed, and she started at frequent intervals, in such a manner as often precedes convulsions. She had no convulsions. On the morning of the 21st she appeared better, but was rather afraid of walking, and when she did venture a few steps she fell. After this she did not attempt to walk, but preferred to be nursed, being somewhat fretful yet easily soothed. Her temperature never reached above 101° sometimes falling under 100°. On Thursday (22nd) she was sitting up in her chair when she began to cry and stretched her arms out to be taken up. From that time she would never sit up again, but cried when an attempt was made to place her in a sitting posture. This evening her canine teeth were lanced as they were felt and the only ones that were not through. On Friday (23rd) I observed her left leg hang limp when in her mother's arms, and playfully tickled the sole. There was no reflex action.

Being alarmed, I made a scratch on the sole with the point of a pin. The child cried from pain but did not move the leg. I fetched Dr Brown who confirmed the view that the leg was paralysed. I took her at once to Manchester where she was seen by Drs Ross and Ashley. They also confirmed the diagnosis as being the essential paralysis of children. During the previous four days she had been fretful and thirsty. After the Friday her sleep at night gradually became more composed till the Tuesday (27th) when she slept very soundly. After the 24th she became bright and cheerful, playing contentedly with her toys and evincing no pain, unless when attempts were made to move her. She cannot sit up and does not like to be propped up. She can move the toes of her right foot freely, less freely the foot at ankle and very slightly the leg at the knee and hip joints. The left leg she can make the slightest movement—by contraction of the thigh muscles—unable to flex the leg at the knee or move the foot or toes either in response to her will (which she tried in obedience to our urgent request) or by cutaneous stimulation. The left leg was found on the 27th to be much colder than the right and on the 28th the right was also colder than natural . . .

On June 6th Mackenzie reported that the child's left leg was still helpless but that she was able to sit in a semi-recumbent position; by August 25th she could sit upright and move her right leg freely in all directions, and could assume a crawling position ' but does not crawl '. When supported, she would try to walk, moving her right leg naturally but swinging the helpless left one forward. Her father ended his notes: ' General health good, and spirits merry and bright '. In that last phrase he used, all unconsciously, words which were to set the pattern of his daughter's life. With indomitable courage, and with gaiety and humour, she proceeded to ignore her paralysed leg and wasted no time on regret or bitterness. Inevitably her disability brought her a special measure of love and affection, but wise parenthood saw to it that she developed a sturdy independence. As a very young child she accompanied her father on his rounds, and was on occasions made responsible for the list of patients to be seen. Miss Mackenzie recalls one such episode . . . ' I always remember one day when I suddenly remembered I hadn't got the list—I had to meet him at a certain house in the hansom cab, and when he came out I said: " Daddy, I haven't got the list, I've forgotten it ", and he just said " Tut tut " and he frowned very much

—but he remembered every single place; he found when we got home that he'd got the whole list done.'

A great love and hero-worship for her father characterized Dorothy's early years; she stood a little in awe of him, but he was in no way the unapproachable Victorian father. Only once does she remember that he administered any physical punishment : ' Once I was smacked . . . and he was more upset than I was, if possible.' She was to become an accomplished artist, and probably one of the proudest moments of Mackenzie's life came when in October 1917 he reported to Will that ' Dorothy has just had notice that her two pictures have been accepted by the Royal Society of Portrait Painters for their autumn exhibition in the Grafton Galleries . . . It will soon be Sir J.M., the father of the artist '.

How he must have joyed to see his daughter begin to express herself in this way and to compensate to some extent for her inability to walk and live like other children. In such tragic circumstances, how easy for the practitioner, bombarded constantly by all the anxieties and ills of his patients, to think of his own and to turn away, perhaps even momentarily, to cynicism and revolt. But not Mackenzie.

Chapter 13

PAIN AND PLAGIARISM

Inter silvas Academi quaerere verum.

HORACE, Ep. 2.2.45.

At the time of his marriage in 1887 Mackenzie was fully established in Burnley. In addition to his work throughout his large and scattered practice, he spent an increasing amount of time at Burnley's new Victoria Hospital, opened in 1886.

Mackenzie never intended to specialize. He believed wholeheartedly that the future of medicine lay in the hands of the general practitioner, and as Lister had seized every opportunity to expound his 'germ theory', so Mackenzie never tired of reiterating his beliefs as to the unequalled importance and opportunity of the so-called 'ordinary doctor'. Dr J. A. Pottinger, of Invercargill, New Zealand, who knew Mackenzie at the Burnley Victoria Hospital, recalls that Mackenzie once told him: 'I fear the day may come when a "heart specialist" will no longer be a physician looking at the body as a whole, but one with more and more complicated instruments working in a narrow and restricted area of the body— that was never my idea.' It *had* been his idea to record all his cases, to follow them over the years, but he soon came to realize the enormity of the task he had set himself, and he decided with regret that, while maintaining his competence as a general practitioner, his observations and research must be restricted to no more than two fields:

> . . . [1] It is one thing to desire an object and another thing to know how to attain it. A great number of symptoms presented themselves to me and at first I did not know which to select. Finally I decided to attack two kinds of symptoms which were the most common, viz. pain and irregular action of the heart . . . As a general practitioner seeking for an explanation of the nature of the phenomena with which he is brought in contact, the symptom of pain was bound to arrest my attention. Here again, at the outset, however willing, I found no plan to follow, and I was groping about, spending a great deal of time with not the slightest progress being made, dividing and classifying

[1] *Personal Experiences*, Sir James Mackenzie.

pains upon their superficial resemblances. I had been making these observations in a seemingly purposeless manner. I tried to locate the pain accurately, and in doing this I had used a diagram representing the divisions of the abdomen into regions, and I was accustomed, in making notes, to draw the lines rapidly with the pen, representing those divisions. A mark was made where the pain was felt. Amongst the work people indigestion was extremely common and a good many suffered from pain. One day, after looking over a large collection of observations, my attention was arrested by the frequency with which these diagrams showed that the pain was felt in definite regions. The suggestion arose that there must be some connection between the diseased states and the pain, and that the location of pain had some definite relation to the diseased organ. At that time Gaskell had just described the distribution of the sympathetic nerves, but his discoveries had not been applied in the practice of medicine. In 1888 Dr James Ross[2] of Manchester, an extremely capable and observant physician with whom I was acquainted, published an article upon visceral pain and its relation to the sympathetic nervous system and drew attention to Gaskell's work and showed that herein lay the explanation of pain arising from the disturbances of the internal organs. Hilton and others had recognized referred pain, the most typical example being that of the pain felt in the region of the knee from disease of the hip joint. Ross described this referred pain in various affections and it was to him we owe the first true conception of the mechanism of visceral pain.

When I read this article I was very greatly excited, for it put into my hands the key for the explanations to a great many phenomena that had hitherto baffled me . . .

Ross's paper was published in *Brain* in January of 1888, and five years later Mackenzie's article ' sensory Disorders and Visceral Disease '[3] appeared in the same journal, further explaining his interest in Ross's work:

The Pain in Visceral Disease is a Referred Pain.

When I had for some time, in systematically examining patients, employed the site of pain as an important aid to diagnosis, I gradually became impressed with the apparent fact that there was little or no evidence pointing to the situation

[2] On the segmental distribution of sensory disorders, James Ross, *Brain* (1888).
[3] Sensory disorders and visceral disease. *Brain* 1893, XVI, 321–354.

of the pain in disease of the viscera, being situated in the organ affected. This view was strengthened by the results of post-mortem examinations in two cases of gastric ulcer, where the sites of the ulcers bore no relation whatever to the seat of pain during life. When Ross published his highly suggestive paper, I was greatly helped in obtaining an explanation of many of my observations. In conversation with Dr Ross I dissented from his view of the so-called splanchnic pain, maintaining that there was no evidence whatever in support of it. He stoutly main-tained the contrary opinion, and used as an illustration a case of gastric ulcer that he had then under observation, in whom there was a pain of great severity localized in a limited area. He said he felt convinced that, were he to push a long needle into this painful spot, the needle would inevitably pierce the ulcer. In opposition to this view (which is very widely held) I urged the fact that whilst the site of pain was absolutely station-ary, the stomach (and its ulcer) executed movements of a considerable excursion, both by reason of the musculature of the stomach itself, as well as by the mechanical movements of respiration.

My attention being somewhat accidentally called to the presence of hyperaesthesia in a patient recovering from an attack of gall-stone colic, I made careful search for this pheno-menon in other cases, and collected a large number of illus-trative cases, intending in the first instance to submit them to Dr Ross as evidence in favour of the somatic origin of his splanchnic pain. But this was never done, on account of his painful illness and deeply regretted death . . .

Ross had divided visceral pain into two kinds, splanchnic and somatic; Mackenzie stuck to his view that all visceral pain was somatic: 'when the[4] so-called splanchnic pains are critically examined they will be found to be of the same nature as somatic pain.' One of his illustrative cases was the oft-quoted one of bowel resection:

> . . . I had[4] occasion to resect a portion of the small intestine in a conscious subject whose abdominal cavity had been laid open. There were numerous peritoneal adhesions, and while I cut and tore these the patient was unconscious of any sensa-tion. I cut and stitched the serous surfaces of parietal and visceral peritoneum; I tore adhesions from the liver; I cut and

[4] The meaning and mechanism of visceral pain. *B.M.J.* 1906, i, 1449–1454, 1523.

sutured the bowel and mesentery, and no sensation was felt. After preparing the upper part of the bowel it was wrapped in a warm cloth and laid on one side. During the subsequent steps the patient frequently moaned. I asked him if he felt pain, and he replied that he did.

I asked him where he felt the pain, and he indicated with his hand that it was across the middle line at the level of the umbilicus. I at first felt that it might be due to the part that I was manipulating, but the pain was intermittent. Chancing to look at the prepared upper part of the bowel that lay on the left side of the abdomen, I observed that every few minutes a peristaltic wave passed over the lower portion of it, and when this occurred the patient moaned in pain. I made certain that the pain was connected with the peristaltic wave, and also made sure the patient had no doubt as to the place in which it was felt, with the result that here before my eyes was the cause of the pain which the patient felt, and yet the patient referred the site of the pain with precision to an area 10 inches or 12 inches away from the contracting bowel . . .

On another occasion Mackenzie wrote:

. . . Although the great physiologist[5] Heller had demonstrated 150 years before the insensitiveness of the viscera to mechanical stimulation, yet this fact had never been appreciated by clinical observers, and at the time that I began this investigation the belief was universal that the viscera were supplied with sensory nerves just like the skin, and the proof for this seemed incontestable, because on pressure over the different organs, pain was frequently experienced, so that in those days physicians and surgeons spoke of a tender stomach, a tender spleen, a tender liver, a tender gall bladder, as if such statements were beyond dispute. With this conception of Ross's I obtained a definite guide in my investigations. I seized the opportunity of noting carefully all the features of pain . . .

Mackenzie now occupied himself in endeavouring to discover the connection between visceral and sensory symptoms: '. . . and in the course of my observations[6] I was struck by the similarity of the nature and distribution of the sensory symptoms of herpes zoster, with those of visceral disease . . .' His first two papers on

[5] *Personal Experiences*, J.M.
[6] Herpes zoster and the limb plexuses of nerves. *Journal of Pathology and Bacteriology*, 1893, *I*, 332–348.

herpes zoster were published in the Manchester Medical Chronicle in 1889 and 1890, and the third in the Journal of Pathology and Bacteriology in 1893. His work on this subject anticipated by several years that of Henry Head, whose 'Herpes zoster' appeared in Allbutt's *System of Medicine*[7] in 1899.

It is necessary at this point to say a little about Henry Head.[8] At the time of Mackenzie's first investigations into the pathology of herpes zoster, Head was studying medicine at University College Hospital, having previously studied anatomy and physiology, botany and chemistry at Cambridge under Gaskell, Langley, Frank Balfour and Michael Foster. He had also studied in Prague for two years, under Hering. He qualified in 1890, and pursued with vigour his own investigations into the origin and nature of pain, selecting, as Mackenzie had done before him, the disease of herpes zoster.

Mackenzie wrote in 1895:

> ...[9] I was struck by the resemblance of the situation occupied by the eruption in herpes zoster to the situation of the pain and hyper-aesthesia in certain cases of visceral disease. As a rule the eruption in herpes zoster has hitherto been described only in relation to the peripheral nerves; but, inasmuch as these nerves are usually composed of fibres from more than one nerve root no very satisfactory information has resulted. Recognizing the fact that herpes zoster is usually due to an affection of the root of the nerve (probably the ganglion on the posterior root), the areas in which the eruption etc. occur become intelligible and instructive. Frequently there is evidence that more roots than one are affected, but these are generally neighbouring roots. It is difficult to say when one nerve root only is affected . . .

He wrote further in 1906:[10]

> . . . It was because of the resemblance of the area of distribution of the eruption in herpes zoster to the anaesthetic areas observed by Ross and Thorburn in affections of the spinal cord, and to the fields mapped out by Sherrington, that led me . . . to suggest that herpes zoster was an affection of the ganglia

---

[7] Thomas Clifford Allbutt (1899) *System of Medicine*, Macmillan.
[8] Sir Henry Head 1861–1940, Neurologist, London.
[9] Heart pain and sensory disorders associated with heart failure, *Lancet*, 1895, i, 16–22.
[10] The meaning and mechanism of visceral pain. *B.M.J.* 1906, i, 1449–1454, 1523.

of the posterior spinal roots—a suggestion I found afterwards had already been put forward on other grounds by von Bahrensprung. The subsequent researches of Head and Campbell have fully confirmed this view . . .

Head, however, had maintained that one ganglion only was affected, and there were other issues between the two men, as the following letter from Mackenzie to Arthur Keith indicates. This was written in 1906. Mackenzie had sent Keith an advance copy of his paper ' The meaning and mechanism of visceral pain ', and Keith apparently felt that not enough credit had been given to the prior work of Head on the subject. He wrote to Mackenzie:

> . . . I think you deal hardly with Head. Admitting that every observation you have made and every deduction you have drawn was drawn before Head ever felt a pulse or tested a reflex yet now when you publish there are many of Head's observations which do amplify those you make . . .

Mackenzie's only references to Head in his paper were:

> If I seem to pay scant attention to the results of other workers in this field of observation, it is not for lack of appreciation of such writers as Hilton, Ross and Head, but simply because space prevents me dealing with any matter other than that essential to my argument ' and his remark that ' the subsequent researches of Head and Campbell have fully confirmed this view ', quoted above.

To Keith he wrote at length and with feeling:

> Burnley, 27th March, 1906.
> . . . I should be sorry if you thought that I am taking his (Head's) ideas and not acknowledging them, and that I ignore any new fact that he has established. Head's name is so associated with this line of work that when any suggestion is made concerning these matters everyone at once says ' That's Head's idea '. Now will you bear with me while I refer to some aspects connected with this line of investigation? I had been working at the subject several years before I discovered the hyperaesthesia in visceral disease, which I showed then was due to reflex stimulation of the cord. Nobody would listen to me, no paper would publish any observations, until an editor friend, for want of material, buried them in the *Manchester Medical*

Chronicle.[11] Head got the idea from that paper, but save a passing reference in his first communication, he never alludes to my work in this connection in the many articles he has written. So that it is no wonder that text-books refer to ' Head's great discovery of cutaneous hyperaesthesia in visceral disease, sometimes adding that Mackenzie has confirmed Head. My original paper was very crude; Head's, on the contrary, was very precise and included a very profound reference to the visceral nerve supply, so that there is no comparison between the brilliancy of the two papers. But as a matter of fact Head's study of the cutaneous hyperaesthesia was extremely imperfect, and I pointed out in subsequent communications that no visceral disease can give rise to a ' segmental ' hyperaesthetic area, that cutaneous hyperaesthesia is extremely variable at its edges, that there is a deep and superficial hyperaesthesia of the skin and a deeper hyperaesthesia affecting more particularly the muscle. But all these facts Head has studiously ignored, and has gone on maintaining that the cutaneous hyperaesthesia is segmental and that these areas do not overlap, or but slightly, and so has imposed ' Head's areas ' on the world, which will be found to be wrong in many respects.

In this matter I had studied Herpes Zoster[12] and had come to the conclusion that it was an affection of the posterior spinal root ganglia, and published a paper demonstrating that in 1893. I told Head that the areas of hyperaesthesia had a central origin in the cord, and that Herpes was an affection of the root and that therefore there could only be a general and not an exact relationship. He pooh-poohed my idea and would listen to no argument, but asserted that Herpes was a central affection. Later, as you know, in his truly remarkable work he demonstrated the origin of Herpes. Before writing this paper he wrote to me for a copy of my paper published in 1893 in which, after spending much time and money, I had given a description of a large number of papers in many obscure journals. He employed all this research in his article without acknowledgement and never even referred to the work I had done on the subject, although he referred to all the foreigners—in fact he ignored my research as he had ignored my researches on hyperaesthesia.

[11] Contribution to the study of sensory symptoms associated with visceral disease. *Manchester Medical Chronicle*, 1892, XVI, 293–322.
[12] Herpes zoster and the limb plexuses of nerves. *Journal of Pathology and Bacteriology*, 1893, I, 332–48.

In 1895[13] I published an article on Heart Pain, in which I called attention to the muscular hyperaesthesia. When he subsequently published his article on the heart, again he ignored the very patent symptom of muscular hyperaesthesia and all my work on the subject.

When I read my paper on Pain[14] before the Neurological Society, I detailed my experiences of the insensitiveness of the viscera, and described in detail the viscero-motor reflex, and wished to discuss with him the meaning of these phenomena, but he waved me aside and said he had discovered the solution of the whole question and he would demonstrate the true nature of visceral pain bye and bye. He has done so recently, and ascribed visceral pain to an evidence of protopathic sensation. Again he ignored all the clinical facts and new observations I had brought to light. If there were any justification for this assertion that visceral pain is protopathic, I would have considered his views in this paper, but there is not one single fact to support his contention. As you know, the characteristic of protopathic sensation is sensibility to prick, recognition of two points of the compass, etc., all of which are totally absent in the viscera. When I started to write these papers I contemplated giving a summary of Head's views, pointing out where they were in conflict with clinical facts, but I found it would lead me too far afield, so I give only the fact, and interpretations I have myself worked out. The 'segments' in regard to the kidney which you say are Head's are not his. So far as cutaneous hyperaesthesia goes, I described these areas in my original paper and I really here only quote myself, having discovered in the meantime the muscular hyperalgesia and the viscero-motor reflex.

I write all this dispassionately and with no feeling against Head. He has his method of writing his papers, and if he chooses to ignore me it is no business of mine. Head is undoubtedly a genius, and like all geniuses he is not equally balanced. Like Gladstone, when he takes up a theory he can only see the facts that favour his theory, and shuts his eyes resolutely against every objection. I shall defy you or any other body to map out all of Head's segmental areas of the cutaneous hyperaesthesia of visceral disease, and I bet that if you take five cases of Herpes

[13] Heart pain and sensory disorders associated with heart failure. *Lancet* 1895. i, 16–22.
[14] 'Pain', read before the Neurological Society, 1902, 99.

Zoster, in three you will find that the distribution extends considerably beyond Head's areas.

One reason I do not enter into controversy is that Head's views are so widely accepted that it would look like jealousy on my part. Another is that I know the truth will prevail, and when I am wrong my views will be forgotten, and if I am right, time will vindicate them.

Towards Head himself I have the highest personal regard and in no way begrudge him the eminent position to which his great talents have raised him. I am sorry to have troubled you with this rigmarole, but I felt I did not like you of all people to fancy me a plagiarist . . .

In his reply to this somewhat uncharacteristic outburst, Keith regretted ' that the note I sent you was written hurriedly . . . and has evidently conveyed to you a conception that never was and never will be in my head. You made flames fizz round your pen-point when you wrote it, but all the same I am very glad to have it. I knew you had worked and wrought at the distribution of nerve areas before Head had touched the subject: I knew also that Head is a selfish forward who wants to kick all the goals and use the rest of the team as anonymous feeders, but I did not know he had gone about the matter so malignantly.'

Referring to the distribution of nerve areas, Mackenzie stated :

> . . . [15] The exact delimitation of the cutaneous distribution of an individual nerve can scarcely be obtained, on account of the overlapping of neighbouring nerves at the periphery of their areas of distribution . . . This overlapping of the nerve supply can be made out by careful dissection. Some years ago I was struck by this fact in some dissections I was making with respect to the nerve supply of the epigastrium. I then adopted the method of preserving the skin intact, and following the nerve twigs to their termination in the skin by carefully removing all the other subcutaneous tissues. I found that the terminal branches from neighbouring intercostal nerves frequently crossed each other. By a similar method, and under water, St John Brooks has made careful dissections of the nerves of the hand, and has demonstrated that this overlapping takes place to a considerable extent.

[15] Herpes zoster and the limb plexuses of nerves (1893) *Journal of Pathology and Bacteriology*, *i*, 332–348.

Head's paper,[16] ' On the disturbance of sensation with especial reference to the pain of visceral disease ', appeared in three parts in the journal *Brain*, the first part published in 1893. William Thorburn,[17] in an article published in the following issue, stated that Dr Head had demonstrated:

> 1. There are associated with various visceral diseases certain definite and constant areas of cutaneous tenderness, each having a ' maximal ' region where there is pain.
>
> 2. These maximal areas coincide with the areas which Mackenzie, Head himself, and to a lesser extent, other writers, have shown to be the areas marked out by attacks of herpes zoster . . .
>
> Contrasting Head's areas with those obtained by clinical observation of anaesthesia, or with Sherrington's experimentally determined areas, we are at once struck by their sharp delimitation, and by the total absence of fading margins, and consequently of overlapping of adjacent regions in the series . . .

Referring to areas of cutaneous hyperaesthesia, Mackenzie wrote:[18]

> . . . In very few cases could the field of hyperaesthesia be delimited with certainty. Parts at the border would be hyperaesthetic at one time, and when one would return there would be some doubt, or a distinct assertion that the part was not hyperaesthetic . . . When Dr Head published his extremely exact delimitation of the fields I imagined I had not been sufficiently accurate in delimiting my fields. I therefore made another series of careful observations, and although in a few cases I appeared to get results that partly supported his views, I must confess to having utterly failed in the great majority of cases. Even in my study of a few cases of herpes zoster I could not get them to fit into any one of his fields . . .

Mackenzie went on to describe several of his cases of herpes to illustrate ' the disagreement of my observations with those of Dr Head in this exact delimitation of the field of supply by individual nerve roots '. This was in 1893, and he had found no reason to change his mind when he read his paper on ' Pain ' before the Neurological Society in 1902, and stated:

[16] Head (1893) On the disturbance of sensation etc. *Brain*.
[17] William Thorburn (1893) The sensory distribution of spinal nerves. *Brain*.
[18] Sensory disorders and visceral disease. *Brain* 1893, XVI, 321–354.

. . . The borders of the hyperaesthesia are always ill-defined. The patient cannot accurately state where the skin becomes hyperaesthetic, and portions of skin evidently hyperaesthetic at one time, when tested a few minutes later are found not to be hyperaesthetic. This indefinite border is of importance, as it verifies Sherrington's observations of the overlap in the distribution of spinal nerves . . .

About this time, Keith wrote:

Dec. 10, 1903

. . . I wish I had seen your paper on Pain when it appeared. I had the matter loosely in my head: but with neither grasp nor perception; now thanks to you I have moved your conception of visceral pain into the field of working and teaching consciousness.

Remember making a reputation is the same thing as weighing a pound of sugar—the scale tilts all at once when the full measure of weight is reached. You will find you have done the rarest of things—bent and bending the minds of a younger generation from a position (i.e. Burnley) that 99,999 out of 100,000 people would have said was a cul-de-sac as far as reputation making was concerned. Your scale has tilted, I can assure you.

Mackenzie was not tilting sugar or even at windmills! He was trying to establish the originality of his early work and its variance with that subsequently attributed to Head. But as late as 1907[19] Herbert J. Parsons, giving two lectures on lesions of the trigeminal nerve at the Royal London (Moorfields) Ophthalmic Hospital, said:

As long ago as 1862 herpes zoster was attributed to lesions of the posterior root ganglia . . . The subject was attacked and exhaustively investigated by Cambpell and Head in 1900 . . .

Head has previously shown that there is a close correspondence between the distribution of the tenderness caused by irritation through visceral disease of the segments within the cord and the areas marked out on the skin by the eruption of herpes zoster.

. . . In conclusion I may perhaps be permitted to express the admiration which we must feel for the brilliant results which have been obtained by Dr Head and his fellow workers from their extremely laborious researches.

[19] *Lancet* 1907, *i*, 1412–1415.

9

Henry Head died in 1940. His obituary published in *Brain*, which he had edited for 15 years, included the following:

> His investigations . . . demonstrated the cutaneous distribution in man of each afferent root, a matter of considerable value in the localisation of disease of the spinal cord and of its roots, and they revealed the mechanism of the referred pains so often associated with visceral disease. Throughout his paper Head assumed that in herpes zoster one ganglion only is involved, but later investigations have shown that several may be affected at the same time, though the eruption is usually limited to the peripheral distribution of the fibres that take origin from that most severely damaged. Frequently, however, the eruption extends onto the areas of the neighbouring but less affected roots, and consequently Head's map of the cutaneous distribution of the roots has been modified by later workers using other methods . . .

In view of this correction, *post hoc, ergo propter hoc*, it may be permissible to give Mackenzie the last word. Professor J. A. Fraser Roberts,[20] of Guy's Hospital, Paediatric Research Unit, adds a postscript: ' I met him a number of times when he was an old man . . . he said that when he was in practice at Burnley he was sitting at the bedside of a patient who had marked erythematous patches on his skin. Mackenzie marked them with his pencil and then noted that after an interval the areas previously red were now blanched, and vice versa. He said: " I knew at that moment that Head and Rivers were wrong " . . . '

No more fitting tribute could be made to Mackenzie than to end by recalling his letter to Keith:

> . . . I know the truth will prevail, when, if I am wrong my views will be forgotten, and if I am right, time will vindicate them.

[20] Personal communication, 1966.

Chapter 14

MANCHESTER OR EDINBURGH—
TO BE OR NOT TO BE

To everything there is a season
and a time to every purpose under
the heaven ... a time to plant and
a time to pluck up that which is
planted

ECCLESIASTES, Ch. 3, V. 1. 2.

The first thirteen years of general practice in Burnley had been a time of trial, of exploration, and of discovery for Mackenzie. Not only had he gained confidence in his own professional skills, but he had succeeded beyond his wildest expectations. He had, by dint of his researches, established himself as a leader in one system of medicine. He was constantly in communication, and on equal terms, with leading physiologists and physicians—Graham Steele and Ross in Manchester, Sims Woodhead and Roy in Cambridge, Hay of Liverpool and Gibson of Edinburgh. He was about to begin a profitable correspondence with Arthur Keith. If he was to make further strides along the road of research and clinical medicine, then it was clear he would have to think seriously about his future and the possibility of uprooting himself to move on to new pastures.

As early as 1892, Mackenzie was contemplating leaving Burnley. At this time his thoughts strayed no further afield than Manchester, which was the natural choice, housing as it did the nearest University and Medical School, and providing his main source and supply of medical literature. In December 1892 he outlined his plan to Will:

Burnley, Dec. 8/92

My dear W.,

I am rather sorry that you are not coming down this time, as I wanted to lay a very serious matter before you, and your mature opinion may be of value in the ultimate decision at which I may arrive.

Since my return from London I have been more than ever impressed with the impossibility of doing the work I have set my hand to with any effect here, surrounded as I am with

119

continuous interruptions and my time taken up with petty affairs and the lack of opportunity of easy and ready references. I had a long talk with Dr Sinclair, one of the Owen College Professors, on Tuesday, and he strongly advised upon my going into Manchester and starting as a consultant. He says that I am sure to get in. Of that I am not altogether confident. I said that if I could see my way of making £150 to £200 to start with I would not hesitate long. He pointed out that there was some possibility of obtaining such things and that if I was on the spot I might get them. I feel certain that if I had better opportunities I could develop the work I have in hand into something of importance and I have been seriously considering the advisability of a migration to Manchester. Did I once decide then would I begin to make preparation. I would not remove at once, but wait a couple of years or so. By that time I might make good arrangements with Dr Brown in respect of the doctor succeeding me, and by rigid economy I might be able to tide over the years of struggle in Manchester. Thus I would sell off my conveyance and save the money to meet the Manchester expenses —which would be a considerable sum for that object. I would hope to leave Burnley with 3 or £4000 and would be prepared to spend a couple of thousand in the endeavour and if the worst came to the worst buy a practice elsewhere in a nicer place. Such are the ideas that pass through my mind and of which at present I am full. I thought I would cogitate the matter over till the end of December then broach it to Dr Brown and see how he would take it.

I am sometimes afraid that the small mole-hill I have erected from the proximity of my gaze might have developed into mountainous dimensions, but when I saw the wondrous effect produced by Head's work amongst the leaders of the science of neurology, while to me the defects of his work were so patent, I feel certain that with time and opportunity I could make a good deal out of that subject, whereas the venous pulse is fast developing into a subject of great importance. You might have a serious talk with Woodhead on the matter, not telling him however that I meditate going to Manchester, but rather asking if it were advisable I should . . .

Will was apparently quick to voice his doubts as to the wisdom of his idea. His reply must have reached Mackenzie almost by return of post, for on December 13th Mackenzie was writing again to Will:

Chapter 15

VENTRICULAR EXTRA-SYSTOLES

By mutual confidence and mutual aid
Great deeds are done and great discoveries made

POPE

Karl Frederick Wenckebach (1864–1940) was Mackenzie's junior by eleven years. Born at the Hague in 1864—a Dutchman, not a German as Mackenzie had supposed—he graduated at the University of Utrecht in 1888[1] and was for a time an assistant at the Zoological Institute there. After a period in a country practice he was appointed Professor of Internal Medicine at Groningen in Northern Holland, taking up his appointment there in 1901. Called to Strasbourg in 1911, then to Vienna in 1914, he is remembered as a great clinical research worker and teacher. He had, like Mackenzie, carried out a considerable amount of research whilst he was in general practice, and it was the results of this research which led to his appointment at Groningen. He was also stimulated and encouraged by Professor Engelmann[2] at Leipzig, who had been his professor of physiology at Utrecht, and whose experiments in connection with the frog's heart beat had roused Wenckebach's interest in irregularities of the heart. Supervision of a home for elderly patients gave him ample opportunity for the study of cardiovascular conditions. Thus, with a common background of general practice, the two had already much in common. Forthright and frank, they were to form a most fruitful combination.

As Mackenzie had reported to Gibson, Wenckebach began to publish his work on extra-systoles and irregularities of the pulse in 1898, and in 1902 his happy association with Mackenzie began, an association which soon was to include Arthur Keith. Wenckebach early developed a very high regard for Keith as he did for Mackenzie, whom he called 'The Lord High Justice of the Venous Pulse.' An outspoken critic of his contemporaries in medicine, Wenckebach peppered his letters to Mackenzie with caustic comments on such men as Hering: ' a very mediocre experimentist, a very bad scientist, an impolite and inconsiderate critic '; Einthoven: ' he is writing

[1] *Triangle* 1964, III, 6.
[2] Theodor Wilhelm Engelmann, 1843–1909. Physiologist, Utrecht, Berlin.

123

nonsense about the extra-systole. He is . . . not able to grasp the significance of what he sees '; Gibson (of whom Mackenzie thought so much): ' he gives himself a great deal of trouble to be an eminent man, but the stuff for eminence just isn't there.' Gossage was ' this pig-headed man, well satisfied with his own theories ', and Gaskell ' still standing on his stand-point of 15–20 years ago.' Keith, Osler and Allbutt were notable exceptions from this list, as well as his friend Engelmann. Wenckebach said of Keith ' You may cut 20 Aschoffs out of one Keith, and the rest will be still Keith—I like him very much, not only as a friend, but as an excellent scientific man too. He is, I believe, one of the best and most original anatomists we have just now. He has a sharp intellect, a great deal of intuition and is educated on broad lines, so that he has got a view of many subjects and their individual associations.' Allbutt he considered ' a splendid fellow ', and Osler ' a great advantage for the British medical world.'

Despite the outspoken nature of his comments and the severity of some of his criticisms, the over-riding impression given by Wenckebach's many letters (53 extant) to Mackenzie is one of a likeable, lively personality with a puckish sense of fun and a totally disarming candour. It is obvious that he and Mackenzie ' hit it off ' from the start; they had their differences of opinion but these never interfered with their comradeship, rather adding to its interest. As Wenckebach neatly put it : ' The little differences between us are just the relish, the " pickles ", to our meal!' In view of this close ' rapport ' between them, it is sad to realise that when they met for the last time in London shortly after the First World War, each found the other considerably changed, and moreover their expressed opinions of each other were startlingly similar. ' Wenckebach is a great man ', Mackenzie said to Dr Pottinger when the latter was about to leave for Vienna in 1924, ' but now very much the German professor. He came to see me in London and we had a talk together —I was telling him about the work we were doing at the Heart Hospital, but I could see that he was not interested. He walked to the window and said " You have quite a pleasant outlook here, Sir James ". But a great man; go to see him and convey to him my kind regards.' Pottinger did so, spending a day at Wenckebach's famous clinic in Vienna. Wenckebach expressed his admiration for Mackenzie and his work, and added : ' I saw him in London and enjoyed my visit there; he has, however, become very opinionated and I found it difficult to discuss some matters with him—but a great man . . .' Later, in 1933 at Cobanzal while entertaining a young Scottish cardiologist to luncheon, Wenckebach exclaimed ' Herr Doktor, you could not argue with Mackenzie!'

Back in 1902, however, the mood was one of mutual esteem soon to deepen into affection. Wenckebach had written to Mackenzie on the publication of ' The Study of the Pulse ', asking for copies of the book, and when these arrived at Groningen he wrote to Mackenzie thus:

University of Groningen.

2 . 2 . 03.

. . . I thank you very much for your kind letter and for sending me your book and the separate copies I asked you for.

Your kind offer to send me the cliches for the figures of your article in Brit. Med. Journal I accept with great pleasure. These cases are of the greatest interest for my way of explanation of some irregularities.

With regard to the figures in your remarkable book, I should like to reproduce in my book the figures 91 and 92, and 290, 291, 292, 295. When permission of the publisher in Frankfurt is needed I hope and believe you will obtain it from him in my favour. But I am inclined to believe that you are and always will be the owner of your tracings and may permit the reproduction of them. Numerous tracings from my papers are reproduced by Sahli, Hoffmann and others, without asking me . . . I think it will take some months before my manuscript will be ready, my time being extremely occupied. So I am not able to say when the editors will need the cliches.[3] After all, I think copying the tracings from your book will be the simplest way to get them reproduced in my paper. But the cliches from your paper on influenza heart I will accept with very much pleasure . . .

I should like very much to talk with you a long time on the phenomena which have interested us so much. Perhaps we may meet one day. I never was in England and should like immensely to see your country; perhaps I will try one year or another to take part in the annual meeting of the B.M.A. I have seen in the papers that foreign guests are very welcome at these meetings . . .

The paper on ' influenza heart ' referred to by Wenckebach was Mackenzie's ' The cause of heart irregularity in influenza with a

[3] Cliches—cuttings or tracings.

demonstration of the clinical polygraph.'[4] The cuttings were sent to Wenckebach, who acknowledged their receipt as follows:

> Dear Sir,
> The cliches from your paper on the influenza irregularity came in a good condition into my hands. I thank you very much for your kindness.
> I will be delighted to see you in Groningen. Visiting the north of Germany it would be easy enough to pass to Groningen. Perhaps the new large clinics would interest you, and please tell your friend that a new pathological institute of large dimensions will be opened in September; perhaps he would be interested to come and see it.
> I did as you asked me and sent off a copy of my paper to Dr Gibson . . .

The somewhat official ' Dear Sir ' was soon to progress, through ' Dear Dr Mackenzie ', to ' My dear Mack!' It is almost a tragedy to have to record that not one of Mackenzie's letters to Wenckebach was preserved, though it is obvious that they were lengthy and detailed and always friendly. When Wenckebach's book *Die Arrhythmie*—a collection of his former papers—was published in 1903, he sent a copy to Mackenzie with the following letter:

> . . . I send you herewith my book on arrhythmia, a physiological and clinical study. I hope you will be so kind to read it and to let me know your opinion of my explanations, especially on the interpretations of the curves you published in your book, and in the *Br. Med. Jl.*
> You should very much oblige me by giving me your opinion whether it might be good or advisable to prepare an English translation of my work. I think it would find a large public in English-speaking countries and the subject is still a norm in English literature, excepting the papers from Cushny. I hope you will, after reading my book, say your opinion quite truly, and advise me on this subject you better understand than I.
> It is my opinion to visit the next meeting of the British Medical Association and I hope to see you there and to visit you at Burnley. I think you will show me your instruments and your collection of cases.
> I have declined my nomination at the Amsterdam University; the institutes there are very insufficient; here I have now a fine

---

[4] *British Medical Journal* 1902, II. 1411.

new clinic and very sufficient clinical laboratory. When you visit Holland I hope you will not forget Groningen.

With kind regards . . .

Mackenzie took up with enthusiasm Wenckebach's suggestion of the publication in English of *Die Arrhythmie*. A postcard from Wenckebach less than a month later reads as follows: ' I received your very kind and complimentary letter and will not wait to express my thanks for the trouble you imposed upon yourself for the translation of my book. I received a letter from Mr W. Green and am now writing to my publisher at Leipzig . . .' William Green was the publisher of the English edition, which was translated, at Mackenzie's request, by a friend Dr Thomas Snowball. There now began a profitable arrangement between Mackenzie and Wenckebach whereby each translated the other's papers for publication in the journals foreign to each.

It should be noted that although Wenckebach was a Dutchman, his translations were from English into German, both of which languages he spoke fluently. ' hope you will be able to read these lines of a very elementary English ', he wrote to Mackenzie in November of 1903; his written English was to improve tremendously with the years of their association.

He did on one occasion become a little irritated that English people did not take the trouble to learn German: ' To-day there came a young man from Liverpool, a Dr Moore, with an introduction from Dr John Hay. I was sorry to have no time to give him full information. Why the deuce do these young men not learn the German language? There is Hay who doesn't understand it, and this Dr Moore too, doesn't understand two words of German! I have to explain all sorts of things they might read in my last paper. That is a curious lack in the education of English people . . .' Arthur Keith was to remark in 1904: 'Among the good things you have done me one of the best is making me acquainted with Wenckebach. Aren't these Dutchmen linguistic geniuses? We Scotsmen are not in the same class with them . . .'

Sir Arthur Keith (1866-1925), a Scot, like Mackenzie was a product of the soil. Like Mackenzie they were both to enter University later in life without advanced secondary school education. But there the similarity ends. Keith's sojourn in hospital and general practice was brief, and undistinguished. His subsequent career gives one the impression that he lacked the humanity which characterized so much of Mackenzie's life and work. Rather plaintively, he mentioned in a

letter to Mackenzie ' Yours is the only Xmas Card I have received.'
His interest in human hearts was more anatomical, embryological
and evolutionary than clinical. To unlock these doors of empiricism,
Mackenzie held the keys. Keith and Mackenzie were opposite sides
of the same coin—they were complementary to each other.

Keith came into Mackenzie's life at the same time as did Wenckebach. He was the sixth child born into a farming family in Aberdeen-
shire and was not particularly clever at school. Two attempts at
high education failed because of his lack of aptitude, and he was
working on his father's farm when he met an undergraduate of
Aberdeen University and became fascinated with the idea of University life. He drifted into medicine because he knew he would be no
good at Arts, and in medicine he found his métier, taking his degree
with the highest honours. He held a post in the Murray Royal
Mental Hospital in Perthshire, followed by a year in general practice
in Mansfield, before going out to Siam as Medical Officer to an
English mining company. It was here that he began his anatomical
studies of monkeys and gibbons, and developed his over-riding
interest in Darwinian evolution and the origin of *Homo sapiens*.
After three years he returned home to work on this subject, studying
fish, tortoises and monkeys at University College, London. In 1895
he was appointed Senior Demonstrator of Anatomy at the School
attached to the London Hospital, and he held this post, together with
that of Joint Lecturer and Curator of the Museum (of the London
Hosp.) when he came to know Mackenzie. Keith describes the beginning of their association in his autobiography :

> . . . At this time (1903) there were appearing in the *British
> Medical Journal* articles on disorders of the heart, written by a
> medical practitioner of Burnley. His name was Dr James
> Mackenzie. He had invented an instrument—a ' polygraph '—
> for registering the pulse in the veins at the root of the neck.
> His articles were illustrated by tracings of the ' jugular pulse.'
> Dr Mackenzie was clearly the man to help me to answer the
> question : 'Are the caval openings closed when the right auricle
> contracts?' So I wrote to him, and received from him this reply:
> ' You are the man I have been looking for; I have hearts which
> I observed in patients over a long series of years and now I want
> someone to examine them. Will you do it?' Such is the brief
> summary of a long letter in which he informed me of the ends
> he had in view. Of course I jumped at his offer. His first batch
> of hearts arrived at the museum of the London Hospital in

December 1903. Some of them illustrated forms of irregular action, of arrhythmia, two were cases in which he had made the daring diagnosis of ' paralysis of the auricles ' . . . For the moment the competency of the caval orifices went into the background. My chief business now was to find a pathological basis for the irregularities of action manifested by the Burnley hearts . . .

Keith set to work, drawing, measuring and dissecting with his usual meticulous skill, assisted by his museum attendant, Chesterman. ' I hope you are not expecting your hearts returned quite yet ', he wrote to Mackenzie in January of 1904; ' they have opened up a great number of points concerning what is normal and what pathological that I have to go again to fresh material. Will you let me show them at my Hunterian lectures which come off on the third week of February ? They are the only specimens extant, so far as I know, that have full pre-mortem records . . .' Thus were the long years of record-keeping vindicated for Mackenzie. He acceded to Keith's request, and in March Keith wrote : ' I shall send you a copy of my Hunterian Lectures and if you come across things anatomical in which I am wrong or in which you cannot follow my meaning— please give me a chance of showing you what I mean by sending specimens illustrating the points in question . . .'

Wenckebach, writing to Mackenzie during the same week, said :

> . . . With much pleasure I am following the Hunterian Lectures of Keith. It seems to me that here may be a method for well establishing the real movements of the heart and the origin of the waves in venegram and cardiogram. I will at once write to Prof. Keith and ask him for a copy of his interesting paper. Dr Gibson wrote to me, announcing that he proposed me as a corresponding member of the Ed. Med. Chir. Society, and that you sustained this proposition. I am very much honoured by this proposition, and am very glad that, when I will come to England, I may find there many friends . . .

The work continued in close conjunction with Wenckebach, whose book was proving to be as much of a success as *The Study of the Pulse*. A steady flow of correspondence was now established between Burnley and Groningen :

Groningen, 13 . 11 . 03.

Dear Dr Mackenzie,

My last copy of *Die Arrhythmie* I will send to Prof. Clifford Allbutt, whose name is so well known and some of whose

129

articles I have read with much interest. I thank you for your kind advice and for your interest in the success of my work . . . I have written directly to my dear elder friend Engelmann to send you such copies as he may happen to have still in his possession. I think he will be delighted to receive your book: it will be the best way for him to make your acquaintance.

When you will study the physiological basis for the interpretation of the arrhythmia of the heart, you will have to be very suspicious with the work of Hering . . . He seems to me to be very angry because I did anticipate his explanation of the pulsus bigeminus; his critic of my earlier work is very insipid, and it has given me much trouble to answer him as courteous(ly) as I did in my book. So far as I know there is at present only one physiologist who can be trusted in this matter, and this man is Engelmann himself. You will be astonished by reading his successive articles on the physiologic actions of the heart.

I will set at work on the subject of the pulse and venous pulse a young student who has to write his ' doctor dissertation ', and will buy a polygraph for his use. It seems to be a very handy instrument . . .

This professional and personal venom which characterized so many of Wenckebach's letters was completely alien to Mackenzie. With one doubtful and notable exception, he never once referred disparagingly to any of his professional colleagues in the voluminous correspondence which is on file.

Groningen, 19 . 11 . 03.

My dear Dr Mackenzie,

I have not doubted that you would be interested by the explanation of all these curious arrhythmias and I think you understand how I was pleased as I made acquaintance with the so carefully recorded cases you give in your book. Your cases on " Hertzblock "[5], that I quoted and interpreted in my book, gave me the conviction of the rightness of my explanation of Störung der Reizleitung[6]: and the most enjoying thing is, that here, and now in your recent case again, not only the Herzblock is demonstrated, but also the retardation of the conduction, the increasing of the interval A_s–V_s. The most inefficient critic of Hering is now reduced to its real value, and this rejoices me,

[5] Herzblock = heart block.
[6] Störung der Reizleitung = disturbances of conduction.

not because I am so desirous to see me right in my presumptions but because it is a pity to see progress hindered by unscientific work from physiologists.

As to your recent case, the tracings of which you so kindly sent me, there is no doubt that you have rightly explained it and I think it valuable enough to publish this case. When you will write an article on it in English, I will be glad to translate it into German and to send it to the *Deutsche Medicinische Wochenschrift* or any other Journal you desire. Of course it will be necessary to give the curves with your explanations also.

There is one point worth noting expressly in your future paper, that is the Reizleitungsstörung occurred after the administration of digitalis. As you will have seen in my book, I said in my first article that digitalis should be contra-indicated in cases of Leitungsstörung. Hering criticised this point and in my later work I came back to this point and said it was still to be proved, whenever there were many facts that made probable that my view would be the right one. Your case is well apted to give a proof that digitalis may be the cause of decrease of the conductive power of the heart muscle and that, for anyone who is not a homeopath, digitalis therefore should not be given in cases where decrease of conductive power may be presumed.

I received a charming letter from Prof. Cl. Allbutt. I will be very glad to make his acquaintance when I pay my first visit to England. It will be quite impossible to me to come to the assembly of the British Medical Association . . .

There is some confusion as to the date of Mackenzie's discovery of extra-systoles. McNair Wilson gives it as 1890; Mackenzie himself said it was in 1900:

. . . The first success was in detecting an irregularity in which the auricle continued its normal rhythm, while the ventricle contracted prematurely. This was in 1900, and I can remember yet the excitement which filled me when I fully appreciated this discovery. Of course, today, the idea of being excited over the discovery of an extra-systole will seem absurd, but it must be borne in mind that at that time no one had the remotest idea of how this common form of irregularity was produced . . .

In one of Mackenzie's numerous notebooks, he records the case of a Mrs Ashworth:[7]

[7] See Appendix.

. . . I saw her in May 1892 and found her complaining of weakness and shortness of breath . . . The heart was irregular due to the frequent occurrence of ventricular extra-systoles (this was the case in which I was first able to demonstrate that these extra-systoles were due to the contraction of the ventricle before the auricle) . . .

Mackenzie's notes on this patient continued until 1904, and although he does not make it clear that the extra-systoles were discovered during the examination of the patient on this particular occasion in 1892, the inference is there. It must have been a rewarding moment, and his delight in it was only slightly marred by the fact that he could persuade no-one to take it seriously. Arthur Cushny in America was able later to prove the existence of extra-systoles in the mammalian heart, but until then Mackenzie's contentions were ignored. He was not unduly dismayed: ' notwithstanding the complete indifference with which my work was viewed, I knew that I was getting at the truth.'

There is sound evidence that this case was that of Mrs Ashworth and Mackenzie had to wait fifteen years for his answer. The post-mortem report from Keith (see Appendix) referred to the great dilatation and atrophy of the auricles . . . ' The central fibrous body (node) is atheromatous and at the point of perforation the bundle is affected and fibrous . . . with a certain cellular change. This is also seen in the node at the commencement of the bundle . . . Thus . . . I should expect conduction to be delayed.'

Mackenzie's series of pulse and jugular tracings, his meticulous and continuous clinical records were extant. The jig-saw was complete.

One of Mackenzie's ' future papers ' was the controversial ' Inception of the rhythm of the heart by the ventricle as the cause of continuous irregularity of the heart ', published in the B.M.J.[8] of 5th March, 1904. Keith, when informed by Mackenzie of this proposed paper, wrote in December of 1903: ' I should like to see your M.S. and will send it you back at once. The ventricle as leader in the cardiac cycle will waken the old foggies up, yet the work of Gaskell[9] etc. prepares the way for you does it not! . . .' Mackenzie did acknowledge the work of Gaskell when he wrote this paper, mentioning also the contributions made by Hering, Engelmann and MacWilliam.[10]

[8] British Medical Journal, 1904, I 509.
[9] Walter Holbrook Gaskell, 1847–1914, Professor of Physiology, Cambridge.
[10] J. MacWilliam, Professor of Physiology at Aberdeen.

. . . This paper seeks to explain that most puzzling of all forms of irregularity of the heart, where the heart is never regular in its action, where seldom or never two beats of the same character follow one another. Many names have been applied to this condition, such as delirium cordis, the mitral pulse, pulsus irregularis perpetuus, a heart irregular through loss of vagus control, etc. As the result of a study of a large number of cases where a jugular pulse was present I have been able to establish the fact that the cause of the irregularity is due to the rhythm of the heart proceeding from the ventricles, and not, as normally, from the great veins as they debouch into the auricles. I am also convinced that in all other cases of continued irregularity where there is no jugular pulse to explain matters (as in old people and others who suffer from attacks of palpitation with irregular action of the heart) the same cause is at work, not only because of similarity in type, but because in such people there is a great tendency to extra-systole of the ventricles—a condition which, as will be seen, often precedes the continuous irregularity . . . There is not space here to note the investigations of many observers, both experimental and clinical, to explain what the extra-systole is. The salient facts are as follows: during the contraction of the muscular fibres of the heart and for a short time after, the heart muscle cannot be stimulated to further contraction—that is, it is ' refractory '; hence it is impossible to set up a tetanic contraction of the heart muscle. The stimulus that normally produces contraction originates periodically at the mouths of the great veins and passes from thence downwards to auricle and ventricle. The auricle or ventricle may be stimulated to contract by some extra stimulation before the normal periodic stimulus is due, so that there arises a premature contraction of the auricle or ventricle—an extra-systole. When the periodic stimulation arrives from the great veins it finds the auricle or ventricle in a refractory state; they do not respond but remain quiescent until the next periodic physiological stimulus arrives. Hence, as Engelmann has explained there is a long pause—the so-called compensatory pause —after the extra-systole, and hence also the fact that the period occupied by the extra-systole and the preceding beat equals that of two pulse periods . . . From what has been said in regard to the extra-systole, it will be seen that the starting point of the heart's contraction may not necessarily be at the great veins as they debouch into the auricles, but the stimulus may originate in either the auricle or ventricle. So far, the evidence has only shown that the ventricle can start the rhythm in isolated beats. The question arises; Can it be shown to affect the heart in a series of beats? I have proof that the ventricle can take on the inception of the rhythm of the heart and when it does the rhythm is almost invariably irregular—the heart staggers, so to speak . . .

Mackenzie goes on to discuss the cases he has studied, all in considerable detail and illustrated with tracings. The paper continues:

. . . when the rhythm of the heart originates at the auricles, or at the auricular mouths of the veins, it is always regular. When, however, the ventricle takes on the inception of the rhythm the heart is always irregular.

The explanation for this is to be sought for in the nature of the functions of the muscular fibres of the heart. Independent of any nervous connexion, as Engelmann has shown, the muscular fibres possess, amongst other attributes, the power of creating a stimulus and the power of conducting a stimulus arises with greater rapidity in the region where the great veins open into the auricle. From hence the muscular fibres convey the stimulus from auricle to ventricle. One great characteristic of the stimulus-production of the veins is its periodicity—that is to say, the production of the stimulus is carried on with great regularity, and hence the continuous and equal rhythm in the regular pulse . . . as all the muscular fibres possess this power of originating the stimulus, certain abnormal conditions may affect the muscle fibres of the ventricle, so that the stimulus-production arises prematurely, not only at rare intervals producing the occasional extra-systole, but continuously so that the origin of the stimulus-production is in the ventricle, and not in the veins. Such indeed, is the conclusion drawn from the study of these tracings, and from their study it can be asserted that when the ventricle gives the rhythm to the heart movement it is an irregular one—the only exception being, so far as my observations have gone, when the heart beats with great rapidity as in paroxysmal tachycardia and for periods of rapid regularity . . . Not only can one demonstrate in these tracings the power of creating the stimulus by the ventricle, but one can also show that the conduction of the stimulus takes place in a manner the reverse of what happens in the normal rhythm . . .

There is no lack of observations in experiments on animals confirming the above interpretation. Gaskell says: ' The ease with which a reversal of the beats of the heart can be observed is well exemplified in the hearts of the skate and tortoise, and in both cases it is clearly seen that the only factor requisite is to start a rhythm with a rate quicker than that of the natural sinus rhythm; that as might be expected the heart beat starts from the place where the rate of the spontaneous contraction is quickest . . . '

After mentioning the experiments of MacWilliam and Hering, Mackenzie concludes:

. . . The cause of the continuous irregularity is to be sought for in the exalted irritability of the heart muscle and not in the stimulation of the heart through the nervous system. So far as I know no experiment has demonstrated that stimulation of a cardiac nerve can produce a continuous cardiac rhythm where the contraction begins with the ventricle. Hering's experiments were carried out in hearts isolated from their nervous connexions . . .

As I have had several opportunities of noting the beginning of the symptoms associated with attacks of continuous irregularity, I am convinced that the dilatation and ineffective action of the heart is secondary to the irregularity . . . I suggest that it is the irregularity that is the cause of the inefficient heart action, and not the dilatation that causes the irregularity . . .

Keith, although admitting that it was ' rather forward ' on his part, had some criticisms to offer on the interpretation of the tracings used by Mackenzie in this paper; ' If your interpretations are right then I must seek quite another interpretation of the manner in which the musculature of the auricles and ventricles (sic)—for mine must be wrong and yet under my theory I can give an interpretation of your records which differs in some detail from yours. I shall take up the tracings in your paper one by one and give my interpretations . . .' He did so in some detail, and concluded his lengthy letter: ' Well, it is getting very late. I feel I am writing stuff . . .' When Wenckebach read the paper he commented: ' It is a most remarkable work. I am not yet *wholly* convinced that your view is the right one, but I hope to discuss the matter with you and expect that you will really convince me. I do not doubt that you *may* be right and that the ventricle may start the rhythm . . .' He also wrote, on a postcard to Mackenzie in January of 1904: 'Did you see the last paper from Engelmann on the own and independent rhythm of the ventricle in the *Archiv. J. Anat. and Physiology*? It has a great value to support your view of the possibility of an independent action of the ventricle . . .'

Keith was not the only person to query the interpretations of ventricular extra-systoles which Mackenzie put on his tracings. The leading article appeared in the same issue of the *B.M.J.*[11] The review was critical, cautious but sympathetic.

> . . . Yet it is by physicians that scientific discoveries are to be turned into service in dealing with the perversions of disease and the frailties of decay and to a few physicians who, like Dr James Mackenzie, are skilled in physical methods, we look and do not look in vain, for transitional studies by which a bridge may be built between the researches into the science and the practice of the art of medicine.
>
> Tracings of the pulses of the heart and vessels are often difficult to obtain by any instrument. Many are published which signify nothing except the inability of the instrument to record the movements to which it is vainly applied. Still more frequently the movements are such as the instrument might in skilled hands have recorded; but most hands are unskilled. A sphygmograph needs as many dexterities as a cricket bat. In the best hands the records differ not only on different persons but also on successive applications to the same person. In his article on another page Dr Mackenzie shows that in this technical part of his equipment there is nothing lacking. His curves tell us as much as in this way can be told. But here is the rub! What is to be the interpretation of these fragmentary registers? Dr Mackenzie knows better than most of us that if his curves are correct his interpretations may be fallible. For example, for true interpretation we must have a *point de repère* . . . Now Dr Mackenzie will admit that in many of his curves the instrument gives him no benchmark, so he has to make one—arbitrarily. He has to set down his *a* or his *v* as seems to him best, and he takes off from this: and small blame to him. But his readers must have a like benefit, and as arbitrarily fix their own benchmarks, it may be at other loci in the heart's circuit . . . We recommend to Dr Mackenzie two experiments: If a striated muscular fibre be made taut and then

[11] *British Medical Journal* 1904, 1, 560. Leading Article.

stimulated it will be seen that even in this state it can propagate stimulus to a free fibre; and, again, if a right auricle be forged with fluid by means of a syringe till, even by the tonometer, no contraction can be detected, and now the auricle be stimulated, it can and does propagate stimulus to the ventricle. Let it not be said that herein we are begging the question that the ventricle may have started an independent rhythm . . . Dr Mackenzie admits that the behaviour of the heart in tachycardia is difficult to bring into accord with his views; but into this we have not space to enter. In such papers as we publish today, as in his book on the pulse, Dr Mackenzie has proved himself a laborious, able and ingenious worker; he opens new problems and excites us to test his propositions to the utmost. We are far from asserting that his propositions are wrong, and in any case we help each other to tease out these perplexities . . .

Extra-systoles arose in the ventricular fibres and independently of auricular stimulus. The message was clear and unequivocal. This was Mackenzie at his best. Had he not examined, carried out pulse tracings and followed carefully for ten to twenty years the Holdens, the Ashworths, the Tattersalls and hundreds of other patients with heart disease? Had the post-mortem reports of their hearts from Keith not confirmed his clinical impressions? He was absolutely confident and he spoke with the voice of authority.

Keith wrote to Mackenzie on March 14th: ' Like you I rubbed my eyes when I read the physiologist's remarks on your paper in the *B.M.J.* It will take him a ' bit more sweat ' to catch up with you : he may then begin to understand. I had gone as far as to indite a reply when I concluded you were more than able to hold your own with those beggars. Curious isn't it how London and its Press drags along in the rear? . . .'

Mackenzie was indeed more than able to hold his own, as these extracts from his reply, published in the issue of *B.M.J.*[12] of March 12th, will show:

Sir,

In last week's *British Medical Journal* a writer criticizes a paper of mine on continued irregularity of the heart, which appears in the same number. The objection that the writer takes to my interpretation of the tracings is that I have arbitrarily asserted that certain waves are due to auricle or ventricle

[12] *British Medical Journal* 1904, 1, 637.

without affording material for proving whether such an interpretation is right, suggesting that I give no standard ('bench-
mark', *point de repère*), by which the movements of the heart
can be ascertained. When I read this statement I rubbed my
eyes in astonishment and re-read the article several times to see
if I really understood his drift.

Before sending my paper to the Journal I submitted it to one
of the ablest authorities on the heart [was this Keith?] and he
remarked that the value of my tracings was greatly enhanced
by the fact that I invariably gave with scrupulous care a
standard by which all the events could be referred to their
proper place in the cardiac cycle with certainty.

When I began taking observations of the movements of the
circulation, now many years ago, I was struck by the great
amount of work that had been done by other observers which
was rendered valueless, because they gave no standard by which
their observations could be rightly interpreted. In my earlier
work I employed the carotid pulse, the apex-beat, and the radial
pulse as standard times; but I soon found, for many reasons,
that the radial was by far the most reliable. Its causation is so
well understood and its relation to the ventricular systole is so
readily ascertained, that all events that happen during a
cardiac cycle can be easily allotted to their proper place by
considering their relationship to the time of the occurrence of
the radial pulse. Hence in every tracing I give a radial tracing
which is taken simultaneously with the jugular, and I also give
ordinates at the beginning or end of each tracing, from which
the various events can be easily recognized by measuring with
a pair of compasses. This oversight on the part of my critic
deprives his suggestion of the nature of the waves of any
value . . .

The writer suggests for my consideration two experiments
showing that conductivity is a function of muscle apart from
contractability. I think my critic might have given me credit for
knowing this. As a matter of fact I have for many months been
carrying on a very prolonged inquiry into disturbances of conductivity, for which inquiry my method of observation is
peculiarly adapted. In the human subject the conductivity is
judged by the interval of time between the auricular and
ventricular systoles. If my critic would pay me a visit I would
show him a number of cases where the interval between the
auricular and ventricular systole is doubled, trebled and quad-

rupled, and two cases where the ventricular systole only responds to every second or third auricular systole. I could also demonstrate to him how conductivity in the human subject is modified by exertion, fever, digitalis and chloroform. I mention these matters so that I can satisfy him that the question of conductivity has not been overlooked in analysing these ' fragments ' . . .

The writer further states : ' Dr Mackenzie admits that the behaviour of the heart in tachycardia is difficult to bring into accord with his views.' What I said was : ' I am inclined to believe from the evidence that I have at hand that in paroxysmal tachycardia the ventricle also takes on the inception of the rhythm . . .'

In a footnote to this letter from Mackenzie, the *B.M.J.* stated :

We have spoken in the highest terms of Dr Mackenzie's graphic work, and we fully recognize that he gave scrupulous comparative measurements. We are still of the opinion that on the interpretation of the curves there may be a difference of opinion; and Dr Mackenzie ought not to resent the expression of it . . .

Lest the reader be constrained to think Mackenzie depended entirely on the interpretations of his tracings, it must be explained that this was but part, although an important part, of his physical examination of the patient. Signs and symptoms were paramount, and using a wooden monaural stethoscope, he could, according to Dr Brown, discern the faintest of heart sounds when everyone else failed.

Dr Mackenzie made no further comment in the correspondence columns of the *B.M.J.*, at least not on this particular subject. He had been quick to jump to the defence of his friend Wenckebach, whose *Die Arrhythmie* had been reviewed, on the whole favourably, in the same issue in which his paper on ventricular inception appeared. Criticism had been meted out to Wenckebach thus :

. . . In reviewing Professor Wenckebach's book we have kept for this more formal place a remonstrance which it is our duty to make on behalf of English observers. German observers in this field, because they have been behind us, have not recognised the priority of English work on the functions of the heart, and their neighbour Professor Wenckebach does not correct them.

He too, attributes to Professor Engelmann work done in England twenty years ago by Dr Gaskell and his school, and we may add by Porter also. Engelmann has elaborated the detail and has invented some large technical terms for those several elements of cardiac function analysed by Wenckebach and Mackenzie, but previously discriminated by Gaskell; yet to the essential solutions of the problem Engelmann has contributed but little.

Mackenzie replied:

. . . I am sorry that my critic should have written the last paragraph . . . where he refers to the work of Gaskell, Engelmann and Wenckebach. Surely it is not necessary, in rendering Gaskell a due mead of praise, to disparage the work of Engelmann. Gaskell's position in the scientific world is so high and so assured that if any writer chooses to neglect his work he only exposes his own ingorance and incapacity. In his book Wenckebach repeatedly acknowledges in terms of highest praise the pioneer work of Gaskell, but he utilizes Engelmann's work, as it indicates with more detail the various arrhythmias resulting from interference with the separate functions of the heart. Engelmann continually in his writings alludes to the work of Gaskell with appreciation.

The *B.M.J.*[13] had the last word here also, and in a footnote stated:

. . . We disagree moreover with Dr Mackenzie in his assertion that 'Engelmann continually alludes to the work of Gaskell with appreciation. From the time of Stokes and Latham down to this of Dr Mackenzie himself and his contemporaries the English school has been in advance of the German, if the Germans do not recognize this, there is the less reason for our own observers to quote German work incessantly in place of that of themselves and their own countrymen. Many recall, for instance, the work of Roy on ventricular rhythm.

Wenckebach himself was a little nonplussed at the attitude taken up by the *B.M.J.* After thanking Mackenzie for his review of *Die Arrhythmie* (published in *The Lancet*): ' you have very clearly exposed the contents and the aims of my book and I feel greatly obliged to you for this introduction to the English public !' he went on :

[13] *British Medical Jounnal* 1904, 1, 638.

. . . The " animus " of the editorial note has greatly wondered (puzzled) me; the remarks on your tracings are, as you say, trivial, and the remarks on my account and Engelmann's are, so it seems to me, really unjust. I half intended to write myself a short reply in a very mild and civil form, now that you have taken this task on your shoulders, I will wait, whether there should be any necessity of answering myself. The writer has not at all understood the significance of Engelmann's work, and when I should have given all the names of the men that gave worthful contributions to the knowledge of the heart, I should have produced an unintelligible work for most readers. Where I deal with my own work I have really corrected some German observers, and fully appreciated the work of Cushny and Matthews, Webster and Dr Mackenzie. But I will add that such remarks and controversies do not harm me : Allen gefallen ist schlimm[14]

But despite this professed imperviousness, Wenckebach had been hurt by what was apparently a most destructive review of his book by Hering, and the fact that this hurt rankled is borne out by the number of times it is mentioned in his letters to Mackenzie. He first reported it thus (20 . 3 . 04).

. . . I was very glad to receive your kind letter for I was somewhat depressed by the most destructive critic from Hering. What you received and what he sent me, are a second fruit of his ingenium; the first one, to which I alluded, I send you here, that you may see what sort of man H. really is . . . Of course, I cannot answer such sort of critic : it is more destructive of H. as to me, at least in the opinion of self-thinking men. When I should further publish more articles on arrhythmia I will not mention his critic but only the facts that he may publish. Have you seen that H. is now also aware that there are really Leitungsstörung, and a real Pulsus alternans? He will manage so, that *he* may claim himself the discoverer of these disturbances . . .

Clearly, not much love was lost between Professor Wenckebach of Groningen and Professor Hering of Prague!

In this spring of 1904, Mackenzie may well have been contemplating his own future with an increasing degree of confidence. He was now well and truly caught up in the flood tide of the affairs of

[14] To please all is a bad thing.

medicine, and events were crowding in on him thick and fast. His immediate plans included a trip to Groningen, a visit to Bad Nauheim where he had arranged to meet Dr and Mrs Brown and in particular to see for himself the effects of the famous baths at this German health resort. He was already beginning to organize a return visit to this country for Professor Wenckebach. He originated a vigorous correspondence in the *British Medical Journal* on the efficiency—or otherwise—of the blood pressure instruments of Oliver, Hill and Barnard. At home, his practice continued to thrive. He was the possessor of one of the first motor cars to be seen in the streets of Burnley, and indeed had proudly driven his family from Lancashire to London in 1902 to see the Coronation of King Edward VII. In London, the leaders of his profession were uneasily aware of his potential challenge to their complacency. Perhaps most important of all, he had his champions. His friendship with Keith was firmly established, and the hearts continued to travel regularly between Burnley and the laboratories of the London Hospital. In Wenckebach he knew he had found a staunch ally, a stimulating colleague and a most useful contact on the continent of Europe. Wenckebach wrote:

> I am glad to see that now your work is so well appreciated; I may add that also in Holland the value of your book is generally recognised. I send a short announcement of your book to our ' Tijdschrift ' . . . I saw that the German translation of your book has appeared and I know it is already in the hands of several clinicists, Dr Gerhardt and others. I recommended it also in Italy, to Prof. Salaghi in Bologna, who has written some most uninteresting articles on the arrhythmic action of the heart . . .

London apart, international recognition was now becoming a reality for this general practitioner in Burnley.

Chapter 16

IRREGULAR ACTION OF THE HEART

Tam Marte quam Minerva
(As much by fighting as by wisdom)

Roman proverbial expression

Among the important events of his contributions to medical science was the commencement of his first text book which was about to be published.

On December 5th, 1895, he began his notes on the book, heading them 'Scheme and notes on a book on "The Pulse, Arterial, Venous and Hepatic".' He used only the right-hand pages of his note-books for the proposed text, keeping the left-hand side for corrections, suggestions, references, etc, such as 'sphygmograph had better come in here'... 'can I ascertain this from tracings?..' and once, when the right-hand page contained a reference to an increased pulse rate, the memo: 'Get Francie to run upstairs.'

Mackenzie seemed to write easily: the text contains some insertions and alterations but on the whole the impression is of a fluent, fluid style and of a lucid and concise mind. His handwriting is another matter; thin and scrawling, especially when hurried, it must often have defeated his wife's attempts to decipher it, for hers was the self-imposed task of preparing the manuscript for publication. Frances Mackenzie taught herself to type in order that she could perform this service, and Mackenzie's instructions to her adorn his left-hand pages: 'Francie—take here the sentence enclosed in lines on next page', and so on.

The Study of the Pulse[1] was not finally published until six years later, in 1902, six years of untiring effort.

The book had only a small sale in Britain and America.[2] Nonetheless, it was translated into Danish, Russian and German, suggesting a great demand in these countries. It is tempting to conjecture that, indirectly, countless unknown patients had in those days obtained benefit and succour from the teachings of this one general practitioner in Burnley. As Joseph Pratt says, 'this book was considered by some as his greatest and most original work. It contained reproduc-

[1] *The Study of the Pulse.* Pentland, Edinburgh and London. 1902.
[2] Recollections and letters of Sir James Mackenzie. *New England Journal of Medicine* 1941, 1–10, 224.

143

tions of over three hundred carefully analysed tracings that he had made in cases observed in his practice . . . Nothing to compare with this collection had ever been published.' Yet in Britain, the leaders of medicine were unmoved. How could a general practitioner have any original contribution to make to medicine?

Excerpts from the preface are revealing and show the man in all his sincerity, idealism and humility:

> In the following pages I give the results . . . of the circulation which has engaged my attention for the past twenty years . . .
>
> I have been wishful to show where our information fails us . . .
>
> It (the sphygmograph) should be far more used in teaching, and thus students, accustomed to use the instrument, would become more familiar with the variations in the pulse . . . Did they (teachers) use graphic records to verify their observations their teaching would gain in accuracy though it might lose in piquancy . . .
>
> The usefulness of the instrument in general practice will, I trust, be fully demonstrated . . .

and finally

> I have seldom been able to give an uninterrupted hour's study to the subject. While working out some argument, interruptions have often been fatal to its completion, as it has been days and even weeks before I have been able to resume it. While the working out of these problems has been a source of interest and of pleasure, the labours of writing them out has been a weariness to the flesh. This I do not offer as an excuse, but as an explanation . . .

The book he dedicated to ' My Old Friend Dr John Brown ', but in the inset page of his own copy he wrote:

> To my dear wife, whose loving help lightened the labour of writing this volume.
>
> Burnley
> 2/4/1922.   J. Mackenzie

Mackenzie continued with a description of his discovery of the condition he named auricular paralysis:

> . . . The greatest discovery I made at this period was the recognition of the sudden onset of auricular paralysis. I had, early in my investigation on the venous pulse, recognised that in some patients there was no evidence of auricular contraction.

As is now well-known, during the systole of the ventricle, there is, in most healthy people, a great fall in the tracings, whereas in some other people with damaged hearts, there is a great rise during the contraction of the ventricle. This has been recognised by Friederick and Riegal and others, and they had called the former a negative venous pulse, and the latter a positive venous pulse. I had obtained records of these pulses, but their meaning did not become clear until 1898. I had been watching a patient with mitral stenosis since 1880, as I was trying to find out when mitral stenosis appeared, and the changes that occurred in its development. This patient had shown for many years a presystolic murmur, pulsation in the jugular vein and in the liver, due to the systole of the auricle. The heart had always been regular with the exception of an occasional extra-systole. In 1898 she suddenly became very ill with breathlessness, cyanosis and a weak, rapid, irregular pulse. After some weeks the heart slowed down, and the records taken showed a complete disappearance of all signs of auricular activity, and in place of a negative venous pulse there was now a positive venous pulse, and on auscultation the presystolic murmur had disappeared and the pulse had now become persistently irregular.

The reason now became clear for this difference in the venous pulse, and this is the reason that I changed the nomenclature and called the one form of pulse auricular, and the other ventricular. But I was convinced at the same time that something far more important had happened, and according to the conception of paralysis which is held today, I considered that the disappearance of all evidence of auricular activity indicated that the auricle was paralysed . . .

Some years later, probably about 1902, Mackenzie had cause to alter his definition of ' auricular paralysis ':

. . . I had a post-mortem examination of a patient whom I had attended when the heart was normal and I witnessed the onset of this auricular ' paralysis ', and watched her progress seven years afterwards till she died. At the post-mortem examination the auricles were not dilated and atrophied, but seemed to be somewhat hypertrophied. I therefore concluded that if the auricle were hypertrophied it could not have been paralysed. This altered my conception, and I reasoned that the heart's contraction may have started at the auriculo-ventricular node, and that both auricle and ventricle had contracted together, and so called the condition ' nodal rhythm '.

He wrote to Keith :

Burnley,
31st Oct., 1907.

. . . I am actually writing the chapter on the ' nodal rhythm ', and after weighing all the facts, have come to the conclusion that ' paralysis of the auricles' does not account for the rhythm in the vast majority of cases, if in any . . . Take the case of Mrs Still who gave to me first the notion of auricular paralysis in 1897 (?1898). You say ' on the endocardium under the aortic orifice and situated on the pars membrane septi right over the bundle there is a large mass of endocardial thickening . . . and involves a great part of the bundle. The stretching of the bundle is extreme. In view of these findings I came to the conclusion that the nodal rhythm is the result of undue excitability, a con-clusion which accords best with pathol. and clinical data. Now you say my original hypothesis is correct.

While I am leaving the final decision . . . Of course I am treating the matter almost entirely from the clinical and general practitioner's view of the matter . . .

The hypothesis of ' nodal rhythm ' was abandoned when the work of Cushny and Edmunds and that of Lewis placed it beyond doubt that the condition of the heart in these cases corresponded entirely to that of the experimentally produced auricular fibrillation in the dog, and in the third edition of Diseases of the Heart (first published in 1908) Mackenzie adopted the term ' auricular fibrillation '[3] to de-scribe the condition.

Mackenzie did not know, and freely admitted that he did not know, what was the mechanism which resulted in the phenomenon he christened ' auricular paralysis.' Many years later he suggested it to Thomas Lewis as a suitable subject for investigation and Lewis, stimulated and encouraged by Mackenzie, pursued his own re-searches, researches which showed beyond any reasonable doubt that the condition was one in which the muscular fibres of the auricle contracted rapidly and independently of each other : ' the auricle stands still while its walls quiver with the fibrillary contraction, and auricular systole never takes place.'[4] Mackenzie accepted this ex-

[3] Present nomenclature refers to it as ' atrial fibrillation '.
[4] Schronstein Lecture 1911, London Hospital.

planation and also Lewis's term ' auricular fibrillation ', but he was unable to agree with many of Lewis's methods of research and similarly unable to agree with Lewis's theory, put forward in 1920, that the cause of auricular fibrillation was a circus movement, a wave travelling continuously around the base of the great veins. This theory, nevertheless, persisted until 1952, when Prinzmetal[5] and others using high-speed cinematograph and the cathode-ray oscillograph, concluded that auricular fibrillation originated from and was perpetuated by a single rapidly discharging ectopic focus, and these workers were unable to obtain evidence of a complete circle of movement around the great veins.[6] Thus it seems that Mackenzie was nearer to the truth than was Lewis, for he stated that there *was* a structure ' which has not yet been detected anatomically '[7] which took up the function of starting the auricle—the ectopic focus.

Throughout all these years in which he studied, recorded, analysed and investigated, Mackenzie was conscious of one thing; his lack of what he called a guiding principle. It has already been stated that his motive force was prognosis; what was going to happen to his patients? It was all very well being able to differentiate between this murmur and that murmur, to say that this symptom was due to one thing and that to another, but was he any nearer to saying this is the dangerous sign, the other can be disregarded? There were times when he felt he had made no progress at all :

> . . . I spent a long time noting with great particularity the murmurs and modified sounds, and the rate of the heart when at rest and on effort. But the results were so unilluminating that I found I was getting no further. I got a sphygmograph and took records of the pulse, and spent much time measuring the height and breadth of the waves, the depth of the notches, seeking in these signs for light upon the subject of prognosis.
>
> In efforts of this kind I spent several years, and felt inclined to give up in despair. My experience at this stage may be of some service to others who undertake similar forms of medical research. Pausing to reflect. I was struck with the resemblance of myself to one of the characters depicted by Bunyan in his *Pilgrim's Progress*. He describes a man earnestly engaged in raking the mud in search of something he was not quite clear about, while above his head shines the crown of glory which was the real object of his research.

[5] *Canadian Medical Association Journal* 1952, 66, 535.
[6] *British Medical Journal* 1960, i, 1379.
[7] Mackenzie, J. *The Basis of Vital Activity*. Faber & Gwyer. London. 1926.

There is a mistaken belief widely held in general practice today (and fostered all too often by published and authoritative statements) that worthwhile research is possible only in hospital and laboratory. The future of medical research in Britain may well reflect on the analogy of the *Pilgrim's Progress*. Mackenzie continued:

> I felt like the man with the ' muck rake ' . . . I saw I must have some clearer guide in my work . . . I continued the study of affections on the heart. The methods necessary to differentiate symptoms and study their mechanism were comparatively easy to discover, but it was a long time before it became clear how to proceed with the inquiry into prognosis. At last I put to myself the question: 'What are you afraid of?' The reply was ' Heart Failure '. The next question then arose: ' What is heart failure, and what are the symptoms by which it can be recognised?' Were murmurs and irregularities signs of heart failure? I had to confess that, except in certain forms of heart failure where dropsy and dyspnoea occurred, I had no idea of the signs of heart failure . . . so I set about to acquire this knowledge. After many years I was able to differentiate the irregularities. I had also to study with care the sensations of the patient, for, as I ultimately found, this was the key which brought the solution of the problem. I thus found out the sensations that indicated heart failure. I found, among other things, that the first signs of heart failure were not to be detected in the heart itself, but were shown in the disturbed function of organs remote from the heart. Then I had to see people before the heart was affected; I had to watch the circumstances which weakened the heart; I had to see the effects of hard work, of pregnancy, of intercurrent diseases, and I had to detect the onset of the earliest sign and watch the progress till death.

There has been speculation whether Mackenzie was actually a Cardiologist or Specialist or Consultant. His concern for the background of his patient, the whole man in his total environment, gives the answer. He was a general practitioner, with a special interest in heart disease.

> I had to find out the mechanism by which the various symptoms were produced, and to do this I had frequently to resort to the physiologist for help. By the knowledge thus acquired I was able to distinguish those signs which were of significance from those which were of no significance. . . . It was necessary

not only to seize the opportunity and make a note of symptoms, but to have a clear guiding principle. I want you to grasp this point, for it was the want of this principle that caused me to spend years in ' muck-raking '. I remember examining repeatedly a man suffering from angina pectoris and failing to detect any physical sign of disease, yet he could not walk two hundred yards without being pulled up by an excruciating pain. When he died I found the myocardium extremely atrophied and the coronary arteries blocked. I saw that this condition must have been coming on for many years, and this caused me to reflect on the effects of the damaged muscle. When the man was at rest he was quite well, mentally active, and complained of nothing, but when he made an effort he was pulled up. So I dimly conceived that the symptoms were only produced in response to effort. Then I considered the nature of the heart's functions, and recognised that the muscle force of the heart could be considered as being of two kinds, one to maintain the circulation when the body was at rest, and the other a reserve force, called into play when an effort was made. On reflection I recognised that the first sign of heart failure was found to be a diminution of this reserve force, and that the earliest symptoms of heart failure would be shown in a response to effort. I therefore made a long investigation into this response to effort, . . . and, for a time being under the delusion that instruments were the most scientific method, I spent much time in recording the rate of the heart, and studying the changes in the character of the pulse by graphic records and blood pressure instruments. These did not help. Then it occurred to me to ask of the individual, healthy and ailing, ' Why have you to stop? ' and they all replied, ' Because of a feeling of distress '. This gave a new turn to my inquiry, and I then investigated this sensation of distress. At first it was difficult to get a clear conception, for I was too ignorant to ask the suitable questions and too ignorant to interpret the answer. After a time I got a little understanding, and gradually the nature of the distress became perfectly clear. The reason why I failed . . . to understand the symptoms of heart failure is because of their extreme simplicity. When we search for the recondite and the obscure we fail to recognise the simple and the obvious. . . .

The temptation to ' give up in despair ' must at times have been very strong. It would have been so easy to leave all these vexed questions to those with time and opportunity to pursue them, but

Mackenzie could not do that: he could not content himself because he was beginning to realize *he* was the man who was to carry out this work and that there was no one else who was even remotely near to the truth of the interpretation of the living heart. There was no sense of vanity in this realization: all who knew Mackenzie are agreed that vanity and personal ambition had no part in his make-up; but he had begun to realize instinctively the validity of his work, and that humanity had need of him.

These discoveries and the interpretation of atrial fibrillation, came to him after long study and observation of patients. It is all the more remarkable that he was able to do so, and so convincingly with the few mechanical aids to diagnosis which existed at that time. Indeed, all Mackenzie's work must be viewed in this light. Not only did he lack hospital and laboratory facilities, which are considered a pre-requisite to the practice of medicine and research today, he did it all despite the demands of a busy general practice in Burnley. Today the problems of morbidity of general practice may differ but they still exist and for their elucidation await a modern Mackenzie armed not with expensive and electronic equipment but with intuitive and instinctive powers of observation, capacity for hard work and determination to succeed.

Chapter 17

NAUHEIM—'TINSEL AND TRAPPINGS'

New opinion are always suspected,
and usually opposed, without any
other reason but because they are
not already common

JOHN LOCKE

It was largely at the request of Dr Brown that Mackenzie visited the German spa of Bad Nauheim in 1904. Nauheim, situated near Frankfurt and about 500 feet above sea level, was at this time a popular health resort, where the brothers Schott had, according to the *British Medical Journal*,[1] 'been instrumental in elaborating Beneke's (1850) treatment of disorders of the heart and circulation with such conspicuous success that Nauheim has become the most renowned heart cure in Europe'. There were five classes of bath, including brine baths, thermal steam baths and sprudel baths; as well as taking these as recommended by one of the numerous physicians in attendance, the patient visiting Nauheim might also be required to undergo 'resistive gymnastic exercises'. These consisted of 'voluntary movements with resistance', the resistance being against the hands of the person supervising the exercises. A full course at Nauheim, including baths and gymnastic treatment, lasted from five to six weeks. The most satisfactory results, reported the *B.M.J.*, occurred in cases of dilated heart, 'the superficial area of cardiac dullness being diminished.'

In view of the claims made for Nauheim, Mackenzie would undoubtedly welcome the opportunity of visiting the spa to see for himself the effect of Dr Schott's treatment on someone who had formerly been one of his own patients. Mrs Brown, at this time (1904) in her 57th year, was suffering from Osteitis Deformans,[2] a progressive bone disease which was eventually to cripple her completely and to rob her of both sight and hearing, but it was the condition of her heart which caused Dr Brown most concern. He wrote to

[1] *British Medical Journal* 1904, I, 1203.
[2] Paget's disease of bone—first described by Paget in 1876.

Mackenzie from Bordighera, where he and his wife were enjoying a prolonged holiday, towards the end of 1903:

> ... That good fellow Willie Mackenzie sent me the *Edinburgh Monthly Medical Journal* for June and July 1901, with a long paper on Nauheim by J. McGregor Robertson of Glasgow ... Do you know the paper and can you get it? The effects on the pulse rate and cardiac dullness are marvellous and if, as I think, her case is a suitable one, it seems quite unfair to her and foolish for all of us not to give it a trial. 'Muscular weakness of the heart—cases of dilatation without hypertrophy and without heart-lesion. This without doubt is the case that exhibits the benefits of the bath treatment in the highest degree. It is the most suitable case for treatment by the baths and the results can be as certainly predicted as those of any other therapeutic agent.' I take it, old chap, that in your opinion that is the exact description of the state of Mary's heart ...

In his next letter, written in February of 1904, Dr Brown wrote:

> ... Thanks for yours of Jan. 24th. I am very glad to say that we see our way pretty clearly to give Nauheim a trial on leaving here and both look forward with much pleasure to meeting Mrs Mackenzie and you there on or about June 1st ... who knows, we may have one of our old rubbers together, you and I ... I think for Mrs Brown's sake I would very much prefer that you should see her before she commences the course. You could judge of the improvement already secured through rest and her stay here, and you could see the first effects of the treatment, with every opportunity of seeing how long the physical change induced by the bath or the movements lasted, and could judge much better of the good results or otherwise of the course by seeing them ' *ab initio* ' ... I tried the movements with I think some success the last couple of days, and shall persevere and report if there is anything good to report. I am rather favourably struck with McGregor Robertson's papers. I do not gather from your letter that you have read them. He devotes his remarks and reasoning solely to the action of the waters which naturally affect the circulation in the skin and superficial tissues, and gives but scanty notice to the movements. The movements, however, through the muscles being called into play, affect, it seems to me, a still larger vascular area ...

Mrs Brown added a postscript to this letter: ' It is hope of " cyc-ling[3] on the flat " and being more companionable to the old man and burning my boat (that is my bath chair) that induces me to postpone Durban for Nauheim . . .'

Dr Brown's anxiety to have the benefit of Mackenzie's experience and advice at Neuheim is betrayed in his succeeding letters from Bordighera. ' I should like very much, if such a thing were possible ', he wrote in March, ' that you should see her before she begins the course of treatment . . . you would see what our seven and a half months' stay here has done, and what is of most importance you could give the doctor who undertakes her care the benefit of your knowledge of it and her . . .' He goes on :

> . . . I do not know whether you have made out your itinerary yet. You had very kindly proposed to meet us there on June 1st and let us all have a week together. If you have time I would ask you, some time in the first half of May, to write out for the doctor fully your opinion of Mrs Brown's condition. The ques-tion of a doctor will be decided later on, when you have got all the information you can . . . If your itinerary is not yet fixed, and if without much inconvenience you could take Nauheim a fort-night earlier than you thought of doing I shall be very glad . . . We have Keir Hardie[4] here just now in a bedroom in the same house, and coming to meals with us sometimes; he is recovering after an appendicitis operation some five months ago, and we both find him a very pleasant guest and interesting man . . .

His letter dated 7th May begins ' Dear old Kennie :

> . . . Many grateful thanks for your very kind letter of May 2nd. I shall be selfish and allude to our affairs first. Seeing what you think of Mrs Brown's case my first feeling is strongly in favour of consulting Schott . . . Do please give me a letter with your opinion as to Mrs Brown's case—stating the murmurs you find and have found and your view of their cause, and what you have seen of the physical condition of the heart. I would very much like Schott (or whoever the man may be) to see this before

---

[3] Mrs Brown had been given a bicycle by her husband on her forty-eighth birthday, and was the first woman in Burnley to own and ride one. She wrote an article ' The joys of cycling' which appeared in the *Manchester Guardian* of 21st August, 1895; the local Conservative newspaper condemned cycling for women as disgraceful and unwomanly.

[4] Scotsman and pioneer of the Labour Movement, J. Keir Hardie, 1921, Inde-pendent Labour Party, London.

he sees her, and then after his first examination to have a consultation with you ere he begins his course of treatment. So I would like to have your letter here before we leave . . .

Mackenzie travelled to Nauheim from Groningen, where he spent five days with Professor Wenckebach, his journey taking him through Arnhem, Utrecht and Cologne. He met Dr Schott, and saw Mrs Brown started on her course of treatment, returning home by way of Brussels where he and Mrs Mackenzie spent a short time. Dr Brown's next letter is dated 7th June:

Dear Old Kennie,

You will be home, I suppose, tomorrow, back to work again and the continental trip fast becoming a pleasant memory . . . Schott is as kind and attentive as ever, he has sent us his very best masseuse or movement operator—a very nice German, speaking perfect English, to whom Mrs Brown has taken . . . Saturday she was weighed . . . and had gained 3 lbs which I think was remarkable. She gets more ' Mitterlange '—two pints in the baths now, the reaction is more marked; the pulse generally falls at first, but very little, and then is usually higher—but quite apart from rate the volume of the pulse varies visibly, first smaller then fuller and better. The apex beat and dullness are usually half an inch nearer the middle line and this persists always for an hour sometimes for two. The rate of pulse neither after baths or movements gets down to 76 which it is in the mornings in bed on wakening; but the other changes—the size of the heart that is and character of the pulse, must be accompanied by great alterations in the circulation . . . The curious thing about the movements is the constant marked diminution of the dullness, nearly one inch one night . . . I can get no inkling as to when we leave but am doing my best to persuade the patient to stay till July 20th, in which case we would probably come south together from Scotland via Burnley during the last week in August . . .

A postcard dated two days later reveals that Mackenzie must have written to Schott before he got back to Burnley:

. . . Schott was very pleased at getting your letter—and asked me last night to tell you so, and that he wished all his medical friends to see for themselves the results—the facts. He said they all made theories—that he had done so too, and that so far he was still obliged to hold to his own theories, but he hoped to hear from you again when you had had time to consider what you had seen . . .

Dr Schott did hear from Mackenzie again, just two months later. This letter is dated 7th August, 1904:

Burnley, England.

Dear Dr Schott,

I saw Mrs Collinge (a patient who had been at Nauheim at the same time as the Browns) yesterday before she got out of bed. I did not detect any improvement in her heart condition. The pulse rate was 112, the dullness a finger's breadth outside the left nipple and the murmurs still present at apex and base. These were also the conditions present when I saw her in Brussels on the way to Nauheim after a long journey—the rate of the pulse being then only 100.

I have twice examined Mrs Brown since she came back and found her heart also exactly as it was when I saw her in Nauheim before beginning the treatment—only the pulse was usually much more frequent.

I must confess being disappointed with the results in both cases. I had expected at the least the size of the heart to be diminished and the rate to be slower.

Since I came back I have been at times carefully testing the movements, and find that in real heart failure with dilatation I cannot slow the pulse. Thinking that I did not do the movements properly I got Dr Brown to do them in half a dozen cases. To make certain I had tracings taken with a time marker, and in not a single case was he able to slow the pulse. One possible cause for error I noticed. In one patient, before Dr Brown came into the room the pulse was registered at 100 beats per minute. When he entered the pulse immediately rose to 115, and remained there till he began the movements. After the movements the pulse rate fell to 100. Now if he had counted just before he began he would have imagined he had slowed the pulse 15 beats, whereas the pulse just returned to the normal. When the operator was wont to say to Mrs Collinge that her pulse rate fell 8 or 10 beats after the movements, I should be inclined to suspect that his entrance had first quickened the pulse, because her heart is very excitable.

I have been carefully studying your tracings and those of Dr Thorne, and I find that there is not much evidence of slowing. It is presumed that the sphygmograph paper always travelled at

155

uniform speed and therefore a given space would represent a given time. If I measure the duration of the cardiac cycle in the sphygmogram in the two tracings on page 30 of your paper *Zur. Path. Therap. der Ang. Pectoris*, Berlin 1888, I find that the pulse is quickened after the movements. On page 35 the rate is exactly the same after as before, so also the first two tracings on page 39. In Dr Thorne's book an increase of rate is to be seen on page 51. In a number of others of Thorne's tracings the same evidence of increased rapidity is to be found both after movements, after baths and even after treatment (see pages 68 and 69).

Also the claims of Thorne that he has reduced the size of the right heart are not substantiated for these diagrams of his are manifestly unreliable to anyone accustomed to map out the heart or to examine the heart by X-rays—as I am now constantly doing.

I am sorry to have to write like this, but before I can be perfectly convinced much more reliable evidence and of a more critical nature will have to be produced. That the movements may temporarily slow a pulse in special instance I do not deny. Thus I have a patient whose pulse will slow from 72 to 64 beats after a few movements, but sometimes I find this patient's pulse at 60, without the movements. In Mrs Brown's case she was liable to extra-systoles and when perfectly quiet her pulse would become as slow as it would after movements. Had these movements been of the use you claim, would they not in the course of six weeks have permanently slowed Mrs Brown's pulse and Mrs Collinge's, and should these hearts not have been diminished in size?

I am still open and willing to be converted, and write you thus to let you know the stage at which I have arrived. The cases you kindly showed me at Nauheim did not impress me much as none of them showed actual signs of heart failure except Mr Henkel. I have large numbers of the other kinds of cases under my care and can show as good results. Also cases like Mr Henkel I am constantly treating with success. Records of cases like Dr Thorne gives are not convincing for recovery from extreme danger in heart failure is such a common incident that no special form of treatment can claim a superiority.

I think it more candid to write like this that you may perceive the difficulties which meet the ordinary medical man. I have a high opinion of Nauheim and of you for certain cases that need removal from all worries etc., and if I can be given a method to treat my patients more satisfactorily I shall rejoice exceedingly. I shall continue to study the effects of your treatment, and shall come to no hasty conclusion respecting it. I shall endeavour to persuade Mrs Collinge to return to Nauheim in order that your method should have a fair trial. In any practice the larger number of heart cases have to be treated while they are performing other duties. Your method as I understand it needs complete rest and freedom from worry and work. The vast majority of doctors have to combat heart affections in people who cannot afford to rest. How can your method help in these cases?

I would have preferred to have written you a letter enthusiastically supporting your views. But if I write you candidly the results of my experience you can appreciate my difficulties. I am conscious that my experience is far too limited to enable me to pronounce a final judgement, and I shall not do so until I have studied the matter much more fully . . .

Mrs Brown's hopes of ' cycling on the flat ' were not to be realized, and it seems fairly clear that any improvement effected by the Nauheim treatment proved to be of a temporary nature only. Writing to Mackenzie at Dr Brown's request to ' tell Kennie all about myself ' in February of 1905, Mrs Brown stated :

. . . but I can't walk 100 yards without panting and feeling done, and getting (they tell me) grey-blue! What troubles me most is after the least exertion my heart beats so irregularly as to make me feel sickish sometimes, and unfortunately as I can always count my own pulse in my head, I am very conscious of the irregularity. If I walk up from the garden gate to the verandah, a distance of 60 yards, or go about the house for five minutes or less without sitting down my pulse will run up from 84, its normal beat, to 96–104, but it slows down at once as soon as I sit still—I *think* it's the exertion of walking owing to my stiff limbs more than the condition of my heart—I mean I don't think it is actually worse, and I have the sort of feeling that the less I am worried about it the better. To live in the perpetual atmosphere of a Dr and two trained nurses is like being in a hospital, only I can still rebel against too much discipline, which shows I keep up the character you gave me long ago when you were a bit cross with me—' half saint, half devil '.

Goodbye, dear, good old friend . . .

(In July 1906 Mrs Brown aged fifty nine was considerably worse and her husband was told by Dr Saunders of Edinburgh that ' if there was not a great change for the better she would not last six months longer '. Despite this, and various other ups and downs, she lived to be eighty seven years of age, surviving her husband by over five years.)

Mackenzie kept his word and came to ' no hasty conclusion ' about the merits or demerits of Nauheim, for his paper ' The spa treatment of heart affections '[5] was not published until 1908.

It seems from the following extract from one of Dr Brown's letters, however, that he had intended to express his opinions in no uncertain terms. Dr Brown wrote in August of 1907 :

. . . I doubt you are in for a long letter this time for I want if I can to make you very careful in your proposed strong masterful manner of dealing with Nauheim and the Poly-clinic . . . I just want to recall to you the justice of giving the devil his due, and the wisdom of seeing as far as possible that no link in a chain of evidence is weak and that the exactly proper logical conclusion is drawn from the premises. Thus the facts that neurotics benefit by a stay at Nauheim, and that impaired heart action owing to physical organic changes of the structure of the heart do not justify logically the conclusion that none but neurotics will benefit by a stay there. However careful your statements are you cannot prevent their being misrepresented, but you can and must be careful not to give adverse critics the opportunity of showing that a minor state-ment is wrong, or even probably incorrect, or a little too strongly put. Then too in reasoning about such very variable factors as men and their diseases much must be a matter of inference, little of demonstration, and the truth of the old saw ' there's aye some water where the stirkie droons '[6] is one to be borne in mind.

As far as possible give the facts by themselves—all of them—altogether. Then apart also by itself give your deductions, and let others draw their own. If all are mixed up and one little fact, perhaps of minor importance, is shown to be doubtful or incorrect—so many draw the false conclusion that all the argu-ment is floored.

It is quite true that when you saw Mary in Burnley her heart beat as quickly as when you saw her at Nauheim, and her apex

[5] *The Practitioner* 1908, 81, 34.

[6] Stirk = young cow or yearling ox, Scots phrase for ' Where there's smoke there's fire '.

beat was in the same position. You are probably right, there was no permanent improvement . . . however useless the temporary relief given by resisted movements or baths in regard to permanent relief, do not deny that baths (or the alteration of temperature they produce) and resisted movements temporarily affect the amount of fluid in circulation and the rate of the pulse.

My failure and your bad heart cases were probably due to physical alterations—organic changes in the structure of valves or cardiac muscular fibres. Such cases are few compared to those of functional impairment, surely. Neurotic cases may I suppose be made up chiefly of those with healthy hearts, but may include some of those cases of functional impairment. Considering the kind of disbelief, disappointment, disgust and almost disgrace a patient feels at being told she or he is hysterical, neurotic or neurasthenic, it may be prudent to allow that besides neurotics some cases of functionally impaired hearts may get benefit. You must not alienate every patient who thinks he or she gets benefit at Nauheim, nor every one of the many physicians who send their patients there.

Again, even grant Professor Dr Schott to be an ignorant, self-conceited quack as many think, he is not the only doctor there. Even if they were all quacks, and their patients all fools, don't go and say so, to the great delight of all the young London physicians who would welcome you to a position in their own hospitals above them if only you would not practice . . . 'Ca' canny, lad, Ca' canny ' . . . Looking over your letter I must add as to Mary at Nauheim—the records are made day by day to the best of my ability—the care and attention she got in the baths and out of them were all I could give, and more than almost any other patient had or could have. You saw her before and as soon after as I could and you have known her all your medical life; and as you say Schott was glad to send her to you. The temporary alleviations could not affect the permanent condition of the over-distended heart, even if for the time they were of some infinitesimal use. Spite of all our pleasant experiences I doubt if I shall ever go again, or recommend a patient . . .

Mackenzie's conclusions,[7] published in 1908, were perhaps milder in tone and couched in more general terms as a result of Dr Brown's timely advice, but he made it plain nevertheless that he had no faith

[7] British Medical Journal 1908, II, 1683.

in the baths and movements of Nauheim and their unmerited reputation so widely held by the medical profession at that time.

> . . . If we carefully read the records of heart cases by spa physicians, particularly those who employ some special form of treatment, we shall almost invariably find that the writer attributes the recovery of his patient to that particular form of treatment . . . The antecedent circumstances are rarely taken into account, and the spa physicians have often not enough experience of what can be done by other means. Therefore their account of the benefits of the ' cure ' lacks that comprehensiveness of knowledge which should enable them to estimate rightly and dispassionately the causes of the recoveries recorded . . .
>
> A very powerful influence can be exercised on the circulation by the immersion of the body in water; this may act in several ways, perhaps mainly by the action of the temperature. Great therapeutic efficacy is claimed for certain waters, but it is very doubtful if their ingredients have any effect upon the heart except from stimulation of the skin. In observing the results in patients who have returned from the various spas, I have seen nothing of their good effects to lead me to place hydrotherapy very high as a means of treating affections of the heart. The best results I have seen have been from bathing in the open sea. Where I have had patients with heart trouble who were fond of sea bathing I have allowed them to indulge in it, warning them to be honest with themselves and to refrain if it brought on any sense of discomfort. In many cases the result has been extremely satisfactory . . . Doubtless many patients obtain great benefit from visiting the various spas, the supporters of each of which claim for its waters some special virtue. In order to assess the value of these claims, it is well to bear in mind by what process this benefit is obtained . . . When patients are sent there it is often because the individual has been busy with his affairs and his heart complaint has been thereby aggravated; or again a patient is convalescent and a change of air, scenery and mode of life is found beneficial . . . it is but human nature to attribute whatever improvement has accrued to the factors that most appeal to the imagination such as the hot gaseous waters from the bowels of the earth.
>
> Every practitioner of experience will agree with me that a large proportion of heart cases return from their holiday greatly improved, and this is not limited to those who went to some

particular spa but also to all sorts of places . . . it is manifest that the result thus obtained cannot be ascribed to the peculiar constituents of the waters of any particular spa. If anyone wishes to investigate the Nauheim waters, he will have the greatest difficulty in finding wherein the healing quality lies. If he visits Nauheim and enquires into the properties, he will learn that every practitioner there resorts to accessory means; nor is there any agreement as to which of these means is of use . . . Upon enquiring into the manner in which these baths act, it will be found that ten or twenty years ago, when the notion was prevalent that to have a good heart you must have a strong pulse, these baths had a remarkable effect in strengthening the pulse, raising the arterial pressure 20, 30 or 40 mm.Hg. Nowadays, the fashion being to soften a strong pulse, the waters are found to have a remarkable effect in lowering the arterial pressure. So wonderful are their virtues that it is claimed they can increase the pressure where it is low and lower the pressure where it is high! Patients with low blood pressure and high will be found indulging in exactly the same kind of bath. When the patients are examined it will be found that those who improve are just of the kind who would do so under similar treatment at any other spa with the water peculiar to the place.

In order to appreciate the manner in which spa treatment proves beneficial, it is best to consider what is the real nature of heart failure and what are the principles essential to the restoration of the heart. The class of case which concerns us here is the chronic—as I have said, acute cases rarely experience spa treatment. In chronic affections of the heart, whether valvular or muscular, the weakness has been brought about because the heart muscle has become exhausted . . . the essential requisite in recovery in these cases is *rest*. The exhausted heart has to have its load made easier. With suitable rest, it begins to acquire gradually a greater and greater reserve force, and with the accumulation of the reserve force, recovery takes place. The agencies employed during the process of recovery may be of the most varied description—drugs, baths, exercises, etc. The cure is attributed to these, whereas, if the actual circumstances are considered, they are but the tinsel and trappings—the real cure has been effected by rest . . .

There is an element which should be taken into consideration in every case, and that is the mental factor. The majority of people when told there is something wrong with the heart become oppressed by the consciousness of their ailment. Unfortunately little has been done by the profession to ascertain the prognostic significance of many cardiac abnormalities. Such patients will be found in great numbers at spas reputed for the healing virtues of their waters. The beliefs in these waters being shared by the doctors resident there, they encourage the patients by telling what remarkable cures have been effected. The appeal to the mental factor goes a long way to cure the patient. Another factor . . . is a quiet and contented mind. An individual who is restless, worried and sleepless will never recover. If he can be freed from cares, then recovery will follow, if recovery is possible. Spa treatment is very beneficial in these cases . . .

It is interesting to note the differing opinions of the two leading British journals on this subject. The *B.M.J.* of 21st May 1904[8], held different views and stated:

. . . The benefit derived from Nauheim may be attributed mainly to the tonic effect of the gaseous baths on the circulation, the reflex stimulation of the vagi and the increased elimination of waste products of metabolism, which have accumulated owing to defective circulation . . . it (Nauheim) is perhaps the one spa where the majority of patients treated are genuinely ill—some sick unto death—many of them being sent there when their physicians are at their wits' ends, and dying even before they leave the train or soon after arrival. The treatment should be recommended before the evil becomes too serious; and indeed, the patient should be sent there after the first symptoms are discovered, on the doctrine that prevention is better than cure.

The *Lancet*[9], after commenting on the paper read before the Hunterian Society by Dr Paul C. Franze on the physiological action of the Nauheim springs and the indications for their use chiefly in circulatory disorders, reached a similar conclusion to that held by Mackenzie:

. . . We venture to suggest, however, that the good results often obtained at Nauheim in patients suffering from chronic cardiac affections cannot altogether be assigned to the virtue of its waters . . . the patient is subjected to a régime which is highly beneficial . . . The hour of rising, the time, quality and quantity of meals, the journey to and from the bathhouse, and particularly the

[8].*British Medical Journal* 1904, I, 1204
[9] *Lancet* 1904, I, 1140.

amount and nature of exercise are most carefully regulated. Cases of ' cardio-vascular neurosis ' are especially favourable cases for treatment at Nauheim and doubtless the strict régime under which they are placed has much to do with their recovery. It is exceedingly difficult, if not impossible, to impose the same restrictions upon these patients in their own homes; they are therefore sent to Nauheim for a special purpose and devote all their energies to ' getting well.'

History has shown how right Mackenzie was. Of course, some cardiac patients would benefit, but some would not. Improvement could occur if they went to Nauheim *or other places* because the benefit derived from rest, controlled exercises and removal from anxieties and worries at home. The restorative and invigorating affects of Nauheim and similar watering places in Germany had, when medicine had so little to offer, an important place in the therapeutics of heart disease at that time. Mackenzie as a student was not exposed to the teaching of psychology or psychiatry, and it called for courage and determination to swim against the tide. But despite the persuasive Dr Brown, Nauheim to Mackenzie was mere ' tinsel and trappings.'

CHAPTER 18

WENCKEBACH AND 'LIEBER MACK'

What went we forth to see? . . .

Mackenzie's ' tremendously erudite ' papers commenced publication in the *British Medical Journal* in March of 1905, under the general title ' New methods of studying affections of the heart.' He prefaced the series thus :

> I propose to endeavour to apply some of the results of recent experimental and clinical discoveries to the explanation of certain phenomena observed in the clinical examination of the human heart. Although, in the main, these papers are explanatory and indicate how certain signs may be recognized, I have accumulated sufficient evidence to show how these signs may profoundly modify our conception of many affections of the heart, and how these views here set forth may have a very practical bearing on the treatment of a great variety of cases of heart disease.

The first paper, 'Affections of the functions of conductivity ', was divided into ten sections. The first dealt briefly with the functions of the heart muscle fibres :

> The muscle fibres of the heart possess the power of rhythmically creating a stimulus, of being able to receive a stimulus, of responding to the stimulus by contracting, of conveying the stimulus, from muscle fibre to muscle fibre, and of maintaining a certain ill-defined condition called " tone ".

The second section, dealing with arrhythmias due to affections of the muscle fibres, afforded Mackenzie the opportunity of mentioning Wenckebach's work on the subject. Mackenzie's own study of heart irregularities had been pursued ' by a different and more complicated method ', by which he was able to confirm Wenckebach's interpretations. The third section of this first paper dealt with the muscle fibres connecting auricle and ventricle. Mackenzie was much concerned with the ' nature of the conducting power ', and believed that the wave of contraction began in these fibres. The next section, illustrated by tracings demonstrated the fact that the function of conductivity could be recognized by the time which elapsed between the auricular and ventricular systoles. Simultaneous tracings of radial and jugular pulses, stated Mackenzie, afforded an ' exceedingly simple and readily demonstrable method ' for observing conductivity in man. Further sections dealt with the intersystolic period, depression of the conductivity without arrhythmia, the influence of rest upon conductivity, and arrhythmias due to depression of conductivity, where the stimulus failed to cross the auriculo-ventricular junction. Here Mackenzie again put paid tribute to the work of Wenckebach :

> This form of arrhythmia has been described by Wenckebach, and its cause inferred from the manner in which the radial pulse varied. His proof rested on similar variations in the movement of the frog's heart described by Engelmann, and it affords me much pleasure to be able to verify the interpretations of this shrewd observer.

The final section of this first paper described bradycardia due to depression of conductivity, and independent ventricular rhythm due to heart block.

The next three successive articles of the series dealt with the action of digitalis on the human heart. Once again, Mackenzie acknowledged his debt to Wenckebach, stating :

> The second event which enabled me to get a clearer insight into the mode of action of digitalis was the perusal of Prof. Wenckebach's book on arrhythmia of the heart.

> This author, who had made himself familiar with the most minute details of the action of the individual functions of the heart muscle fibres, drew my attention to the exact meaning of many forms of arrhythmia which I had found resulted from the administration of digitalis.

(The first of the events referred to by Mackenzie was the observation that in a large class of patients for whom digitalis was frequently prescribed, the rhythm of the heart did not proceed from the auricle to the ventricle, but originated in the fibres joining auricle and ventricle, (the remains of the canalis auricularis) or in the ventricle itself).

Mackenzie was, he stated, ' concerned mainly with certain modifications of the heart's action produced by digitalis.' He discussed first the action of digitalis on the normal rhythm; on stimulus production and excitability, illustrating his remarks by tracings from his own

12

cases; and the action of digitalis where the inception of the rhythm was due to the ventricle. 'The inception of the rhythm of the heart by the ventricle' was the subject for the fourth paper. Mackenzie considered that this form of arrhythmia was due to 'an over-excitability of the muscular fibres joining the auricle and ventricle.'

He added this rider :

> I am aware that the evidence I shall give is not absolutely conclusive; still I shall adduce sufficient presumptive proof in favour of this suggestion, and in doing so try to indicate the lines on which investigation into this difficult problem may profitably be pursued.

He recalled that at the Nottingham meeting of the B.M.A. in 1892 he had demonstrated the fact that when the pulse seemed to miss a beat in cases of irregularity, this was due to the contraction of the ventricle prior to and independent of the auricle, and was called by him the ventricular extra-systole. 'I published the proofs for this statement in the *Journal of Pathology* in 1894', declared Mackenzie, and continued :

> Though this statement passed unnoticed by clinicians and physiologists, I was convinced that in it lay the key to many of the mysteries of the heart's varied action, and I have never ceased to enquire deeper into the true meaning of this observation. Subsequently Engelmann published the results of his experimental observations on the extra-systole in man, and Cushny and Matthews and Hering demonstrated experimentally this ventricular extra-systole in the mammalian heart, and subsequently these observers describing the same irregularity in man, depending, however, for their proof only on the fact that the irregular period, including the extra-systole, occupied two pulse periods, whereas in my original paper I showed the actual relationship of the auricular systole to the ventricular . . .

Mackenzie had anticipated that these papers would cause comment, but he was not prepared for the extraordinary interest they aroused. Writing to Will on 17th May, 1905 he said :

> The 'pamphlet' is the herald of the greatest revolution to be made in Heart study in this generation and it is inconclusive, as its object was to excite the attention of the British medical public. I has done so in a degree I scarcely expected as my correspondence with many eminent people shows.

Wenckebach had been grateful for Mackenzie's tributes. On 26th March he wrote:

> Your articles in B.M. Journal are *very* good indeed, and very flattering for your most obedient servant! Can you conceive what a pleasure it is to me to see my views so completely and so eloquently and in such a convincing manner verified? . . .

and again on 15th April:

> My dear Mack,
>
> I saw your fifth article yesterday evening. I readily understand that your articles are giving origin to some ' sensation ', at least among thinking people. They are really very good, and instructive, and suggestive, and I am very glad that you are so very careful to point out the weaker points of your argumentation. I assure you, that I find your method of dealing with this very tough and difficult matter admirable, and I will take it as an example for my next publications, just as I got my models for my book from the other side of the Channel!
>
> You expect that we would part company after your IV and V articles. Well, I cannot follow you in some of your explanations, but I am not prepared to give a conclusive explanation, so I have no right whatever to blame! . . . (here follow details of points on which Wenckebach disagrees with Mackenzie in interpreting tracings) . . . I know that I do not tell you anything new; we talked and corresponded about the matter, but as you expected that we should part company after your articles I would point out my objections only to give proof of my being much interested in your work and of my happiness in having found such an admirable worker on arrhythmia. Indeed I am quite delighted by your work and thankful for all the good words you said about my work. The little differences between us are just the relish, the ' pickles ' to our meal! . . . I could scarcely read your last letters . . . There are many words that I was not able to read . . . !

The year 1905 was proving to be a very busy one for Mackenzie. Besides his researches into the heart it must be remembered that he was also engaged in an intensive study which resulted in his paper published in the *B.M.J.* the following year. He was also preparing a paper which he and Wenckebach were to publish jointly early in 1905. This had been Wenckebach's idea and the following extracts from Wenckebach's letters will illustrate the progress made from the inception of the idea to the publication of the paper:

Groningen, 15.11.04.

... And now another question. Brandenburg has written five articles on digitalis in the heart and found an inception of the rhythm by the ventricle, I think we should *now* publish a paper on the subject. Shall we put together our experiences, tell them about your " ventricular rhythm ", about my doubts on the subject, there being no compensatory pause, and about the solution of the problem by assuming that the muscle cells in the atrio-ventricular part of the heart start the rhythm. I think we have made up our mind on that subject; we may call attention to this explanation and point out that the question is important, because the cause of these extra-systoles may be an increase of excitability as well as of automatic stimulus-production.! and the relation with the digitalis! Why should other men ' eat us the cheese from our bread ' and point out the fact, where *we* are able to do so? Please tell me at once, what you think about a paper, published by M. & W. on the subject, in some German paper (*Zeitschrift für Klinische Medicin* ?) I got a splendid tracing of a case of outfalling ventricular systoles with regularly beating auricle, *without disturbance of the conduction, caused by loss of excitability of the ventricle.* Off goes Hering! ...

Groningen, 30.11.04.

... As to our work, I think you should first publish your work on digitalis poisoning and lack of conductions. I would be glad to have the ' Preneur ' of it, but it is *your* work and I would not for the world put my name at the head of it. When you tell in a few words the manner in which I analysed the lack of conductivity from the radial pulse and afterwards from your tracings of the venous pulse in your beautiful cases, I will be quite contented! Where our co-operation should come in is in the extra-systole matter. I agree fully with your scheme: I am now taking tracings of ordinary extra-systoles: you do the same thing, we exchange our tracings and remarks. The article should tell (1) about the ventricular extra-systole, coming at different intervals, and followed by a complete comp. (compensatory) pause; (2) the auricular extra-systole, with its shortened comp. pause, as it is experimentally found in mammalian heart by Cushny and Matthews, pointed out in man by myself and

Cushny, but detected and rightly described in man by you in 1894, and after all, described by Hering, and explained in its variations by me (in the paper which I send you today in English translation, not translated by me!) We let go the question of the extra-systole of the veins without any comp. pause, as being not yet quite clear and connected with the heart-bigeminy question. (3) We point out that there is a third sort of extra or premature systoles of a ventricular type, but: *a* not having a complete pause, *b* coming in series of beats, *c*, often playing a so predominating part that the original rhythm disappears totally, *d* giving a curious phlebogram, in which a certain Dr Mackenzie detected quite cleverly, that auricle and ventricle contracted at the same time, so as to give rise to a wave, being a composition of an auricular, a regurgitation and carotid wave. (4) We point out that the difficulty of these waves, not being true ventricular extra-systoles, has to be solved by the newer physiological investigations. They arise from the second 'automatic centre' in the atrio-ventricular contraction and a recurrent auricular wave, being able to affect the rhythm at the veins, it being shorter in or above the connecting fibres, just as in Harrison's ligature and similar experiments. If I should write this last arguing, you might give your explanation of the wave as in your papers on ventricular rhythm. Does this plan suit you? . . . In reading your letter over again I see that you are bound to the editor of the *Br. Med. J.* so far as your conduction work is concerned. Well, I don't see why you should not publish it there. As to the journal for our joint work on the ventricular rhythm, we may publish it as well in England as in Germany: only I think it will be more-regarded in German . . .

Groningen, 30.12.04.

. . . I don't know whether you are reading the *A. of Anat. and Physiologie* and other Journals? I think not. Now there are very interesting articles on the inception of the rhythm by the A-V muscle fibres: these researches open a wide view on clinical diagnosis, so that our mutual work will take a great deal of time, years perhaps. But there is *periculum in mora*. If we don't say now at once that we know that such A-V extra-systoles are occurring in man, any other may say it. Therefore my proposition is that I should write a short notice for Engelmann's *Archiv für Physiologie*, to be published in the next volume, containing that what *you* call the ventricular rhythm, that which I tried to

analyse without success, what Volkard and Hering called Rück-
läufige Wellen (recurrent waves) and indeed A-V extra-systoles.
We may point out the great significance of this statement as
well for physiological as for clinical medicine and refer to a later
paper that will deal with the facts more thoroughly. I am
writing Engelmann to reserve a little space for us. After having
written the paper I will send it you, to see whether you
agree with it or will add something to it. Please answer me at
once, whether you agree or not. I am very anxious to have this
fact published, regarding my further publications which I should
like to begin at once, and regarding a clinical lecture that I am
asked to write on arrhythmia for a new German journal. I have
to mention these A-V systoles.

Have you seen the silly articles of Hering and his pupils on
the venous pulse and extra-systoles: he published this in his
own journal, a new one, which I certainly will not buy . . .

Groningen, 4.1.05.

. . . I understand from your letter that you agree with my
sending a short paper on ventricular rhythm for Engelmann's
Archiv. He writes that he will accept it at once. I will send it
you as soon as possible, if you agree, it has to be published with
both our names . . .

Groningen, 6.1.05.

Lieber Mack!,

I send you with the same post as this letter the short article
for which I asked the hospitality in Engelmann's Archiv. Please
read it, improve and correct what you think should be altered,
and send it back to me so that I may write a new and clean copy
for the press. In publishing this article we lay hands on our
discovery (!) and apply a stimulus to the *good* experimentators
in Engelmann's laboratory, for which Engelmann himself will
be very grateful, and what may be a cause to further analysis of
this curious phenomenon. At the same time we gain time for
quietly working out your problem of the ventricular rhythm
. . . I have marvellous cases of your ventricular rhythm, and
found them under very remarkable circumstances! . . . Please
send back the papers as soon as possible with your remarks. I
will improve the German language of it.

Groningen, 11.1.05.

Dear Mack,

This afternoon I received your kind and interesting letter. First of all, I agree *fully* with your views on co-operation and I would not have to do with joint-work if you did not make *all* remarks you have to make! The order of our names is the alphabetical one. I am nearly always behind with my *W*, it is the same thing in publishing joint-work with one of my assistants: so please let it be so!

Now as to your remarks: 1) many thanks for your hint regarding dear Gaskell[1]. He *has* been the first indeed in many observations: why did he not stick to it and get all *out* of it, that there was *in* it?

I will put his name in my short account of the history: only I refer only in a superficial way to physiological work done on A-V extra-systoles: it will be our duty to deal fully with the history of the matter in our big work . . . 2) I remember very well your clever deduction from the a-c interval, and I made the objection you mention in your letter . . . I have thought over this question and am sorry not to agree with you. I am pretty sure that we will find this difference in our tracings: only it will be necessary to get widely-written tracings with a good time-marker . . . I think you have no right to put your diagram as you do: there is no reason why the auricle should not be affected by an A-V extra-systole: there should be added a recurrent auricular contraction to your diagram! As I said, this is just the *causa questionis* of the A-V extra-systoles, that they give simultaneous contractions of auricle and ventricle and affect the rhythm of the veins . . . You are quite right; as soon as the A-V stops for a moment, the normal rhythm sets in. It is a battle of the two centres! I hope I have been clear enough, so that you may understand my argumentations. If not so, please argue at once! . . .

Under these circumstances I cannot put my name under this statement, I think it is opposite to our further demonstrations. I have now several cases of ventricular rhythm, and without a shade of flattery, I am astonished at your correct observations of these cases. This afternoon I had a patient (a high judge from The Hague!), who has most typical attacks of *irregular* ventricular rhythm. Today he had one ordinary ventricular extra- systole

[1] It is worth noting the generosity of Mackenzie in recognizing the earlier work of Gaskell.

only. But, he said, this is not what makes me anxious: it is the *other* form of *continuous* irregularity! I hope to see such an attack. He has a high blood pressure! I have another case that first came with a high blood pressure and heartblock *without disturbance of conductivity*! I gave him nitrites, and lo! the heartblock disappeared and occasionally there came ordinary ventricular systoles: *now* the nitrites did their work far too well, he has a too low blood pressure and . . . he has the ventricular rhythm varying with normal contractions! So there is certainly no direct connection between blood pressure and ventricular rhythm. Off goes Barr! So you see I am now keeping my eyes open to the rhythm in question and there is a lot to do on this matter! And so you see the true key to me was your inference about the auricle and the ventricle contracting simultaneously . . .

Groningen, 17.1.05.

Dear M.,

I will write our paper this evening and send it to Engelmann at once . . . I am really interested in your sensory matters and astonished my students lately in detecting beautiful cutaneous and muscular hyperaesthesia . . .

Groningen, 24.1.05.

. . . You ask me about heartblock without loss of conductivity. Well, the name is perhaps not quite the right one, but it is so; as you say in your paper I said that a ventricular systole might fail by loss of contractility as well as by loss of conductivity and I am very glad that you are able to point out the rightness of this supposition of mine . . .

Groningen, 12.2.05.

Dear Mack,

I really should have written earlier, but I am very, very, much occupied; my laboratory is now going full speed, so does my clinic and my teaching and I have taken so many tracings of high interest in these last weeks, that I have scarcely time for breathing! I have had no time to study thoroughly the matter of the A-V rhythm, but that I am not sitting quietly but working hard I hope to prove to you in a few days. I have made a new analysis of the venous pulse, in correspondence to the cardio-gram, as I have been corresonding with Keith about this matter

I will, as soon as lantern-slides will be made of my tracings, send them to Keith, with an explanation, and will ask him to make his remarks and to send the whole lot to you, with explanation and remarks and all . . . perhaps I am too strongly speaking for the ventricular extra-systoles arising *in* the ventricle, not at the A-V. As a matter of fact, I do not yet *know* how things happen: therefore, do as if I had said nothing : you might be right at the end; only I do not yet believe so . . .

Groningen, 3.4.05.

Dear M.,

I received forty copies of the first article[2] of Mackenzie, Wenckebach & Co. I send you your part at the same time as this card. Should you have received forty copies too, please return me these 20. If you will send copies to our mutual English friends, I will send copies to Volkard, etc. Please send one to Hering, if you like; I can't do so.

Have you any time to do things ? . . .

The answer to this last question must have been ' yes.' Mackenzie always had time to ' do things.' His correspondence alone must have entailed hours of work each week, as he was in constant communication with Wenckebach, Arthur Keith, John Hay of Liverpool and Gibson of Edinburgh, and passing tracings back and forth between them. He was consumed with a vital interest in all they did, and was always completely up to date with medical progress on the Continent, more so that was Arthur Keith himself, a fact which will be illustrated later. There was the Neurological Society's meeting in London to attend— and he was, even amidst this welter of activity, first and foremost a general practitioner.

He was still sending hearts to Arthur Keith. Keith's letters of this period show just how close was the co-operation between them :

40 Leigh Road,
Highbury Park, N.
Feb. 23, 1905.

My dear Mackenzie,

I send you herewith a parcel of tracings after your own heart and just enough of discrepancy of interpretation of fact to make

[2] Mackenzie, J. & Wenckebach, K. F. (1905). Ueber an der Atrioventricular-grenze ausgelöste Systolen beim Menschen. *Archiv für Anatomie und Physiol.* Edited by Engelmann. *Physiol. Abteil. Jahrgang* 1905, 235–238.

you pugilistic. I feel I'm threshing straw until I have the living heart beating in as nearly normal conditions as may be. I'm laid up with the ' flu '—been so for a week but am nearly better.

Wonder what Herman has got to say ! ...

Chapter 19

THE GALILEE OF BURNLEY

Domus et placens uxor

Horace. Book 2. 16

Mackenzie's home life was one of idyllic happiness. His second daughter, Jean, was born in 1892; she was a gay, fun-loving child who early assumed a touching air of protection towards her elder sister. Miss Mackenzie recalls an incident from their childhood:

> . . . When Father went to a funeral he always had his top hat, very well got up, and Jean was always so proud of him then. On one occasion we were going out just to enjoy ourselves, and I think he had on his old suit, and she said: ' Oh, Daddy, you do *humiliate* me when you've not got your top hat on !' . . .

The two girls were taught at home by a governess until Dorothy was twelve, when both attended Burnley Grammar School. It was during her years there that Dorothy discovered that her father was the author of the serial currently appearing in a popular children's magazine. ' I have an idea ', she says, ' that he sort of tried to find out from me whether the children liked it . . .' It is incredible to think that he found the time for such an engaging pursuit, but find it he did, and also for reading on a mammoth scale. Besides the British medical journals, he eagerly devoured every French and German one on which he could lay his hands, and also managed to fit in most of the popular novels of the day, particularly those of Sir Walter Scott and Charles Dickens. ' Uncle Will didn't like Dickens ', Miss Mackenzie recalls, ' but Father read him with great appreciation and great joy, and was delighted when I took to these authors. Jane Austen and all the Brontes—all these books he loved to read, and he quite deliberately chose to read them to take his mind off his actual work at times. On holiday he read anything including the most frightful who-dunits or Westerns and then he never looked at them for the rest of the year . . .' He was not fond of Thomas Hardy's novels, although they found a place on his book shelves, along with the works of such diverse authors as Tolstoy, Mark Twain, Rabelais, H. A. Vachell, Kipling and Jerome K. Jerome. There were biographies

175

and historical works in abundance, books on chess, travel and religion and many books of verse. He was not a great lover of poetry, however, except for the works of Robert Burns which, as a true Scotsman, he enjoyed and appreciated. Walt Whitman's 'Hound of Heaven' was a great favourite.

Doctors Wales and Shafar in 'The Burnley Years[1]' refer to his daily routine. Awake at 6 a.m. he would write consistently until 8 a.m. He found this early morning interval his most productive. Seated in a high-backed chair in the corner of the lounge, a small folding desk on his knees, he would apply himself with amazing concentration. Even in the evenings, he would return to his notes, unperturbed by the antics of two young and lively children. Between 9 a.m. and 10 a.m. he would attend to morning surgery held in a contiguous building running at right-angles to Bank Parade.

Then to his rounds with his coachman Ralph Lofthouse who remained with him even after Mackenzie resorted to a motor car, the first to be seen in Burnley. Prompt as always he returned for lunch at 1 p.m. to the warm greeting of his wife. Indeed, on the one or two occasions when the door was opened by Dorothy, he would ask peremptorily 'Where's your mother?'. He ate hurriedly, but never seemed to suffer indigestion. He would look quickly at the *Manchester Guardian* and have a brief nap until 2 p.m.

> On two afternoons in the week he played golf with his friends the Grimshaws at Hapton, but on other afternoons he ran a special surgery, to which he invited local medical men and those who were staying with him as guests.
>
> After his clinics he made his afternoon round to return for his evening meal at 6.30 p.m. precisely.

There is no evidence that the Mackenzie family ever took part in the social life of Burnley, such as it was. Unlike the Browns, who counted among their close friends such diverse personalities as Lord and Lady Shuttleworth and two temperance and religious fellows, Harry Gibson and Charlie Bray, the Mackenzie household revolved round the many medical visitors, many perhaps less distinguished than Osler, Keith, Wenckebach, Cushny, Graham Steele and John Hay, who made frequent visits to Bank Parade. Chess and billiards were frequent sources of pleasure, while of an evening he enjoyed the occasional game of bridge in company with the Browns. In all these games MacKenzie showed great skill and in some excelled.

[1] *Medical History* 1947, XI. 3.

PLATE 13. One of the first cars in Burnley. Mackenzie on his rounds.

Robert Holden was first his dispenser then coachman, assistant at laboratory experiments, collector of debts and surgery attendant. Obviously great affection existed between the two men, in their long association, broken only when the Mackenzie family moved to London. In January 1908 in thanking them for two small gifts, Holden writes . . . ' all your past kindness to me in so many ways, I shall never forget . . .'

It was thus a homely, closely knit family which revolved around Mackenzie during those 28 years in Burnley.

Despite the ever-increasing demands on his time, Mackenzie kept in constant touch with the various members of his family, and in particular he continued to encourage his brother Will :

" . . . There are three stages in the career of a successful barrister ", he wrote, " the first is when he gazes vacantly abroad amongst the world of solicitors and wonders when and how an opening in their serried ranks will be made in order to let his power be known. Then secondly when his reputation is being spoken of and he is looked upon as a likely man but no-one dares venture to trust him. And thirdly when the serried ranks aforesaid break into a crowd and surround him with much clamour to gain his services. It would appear as if you were at stage number two . . . let us hope the third stage is getting within measurable distance . . ."

and again :

. . . I read your letter in Saturday's *Speaker* with much interest. It is the first ' Letter to the Editor ' and it may be an interesting fact to remember . . . the letter itself I liked, and especially the first half, where you evidently let yourself have full swing, and are not hampered by the thoughts of taking up too much space. The latter part only falls short of the first in having to be too much condensed . . . I would lie in wait watching for another and yet another effective opportunity for letter writing. Ere you make your application be assured that your request may be listened to. It might be feasible to ask that your name be held in remembrance if any vacancy arose, and in the meantime cultivate the opportunity you possess of making that name as valuable as you can . . .

' You keep the £800 minimum in your eye ', he wrote to Will on another occasion, ' but live not for lucre alone.' There were affairs at

Scone which also demanded his attention, and he reported one domestic difficulty to Will:

> ... I have had a wailer from Margaret wanting help, or rather to help her to a post as companion. You know as well as I do she is eminently unfitted for such a post, and I can only tell her so and repeat the advice already given, i.e. to secure a suitable house for summer lodgers, and that you and I would engage to pay her rent for two or three years, or to get some better business and be independent. What do you think? Would you support me in this ...?

Robert Mackenzie, the father, died in 1889 at the age of 81.

It seems to have been to James that the family turned for advice and help; whether he voluntarily assumed the role or had it thrust upon him is a matter for conjecture, but whichever in fact was the case he never once shirked his responsibility. Margaret eventually went to South Africa where she had obtained a post as companion-housekeeper; her passage was paid by her brothers, and she stayed abroad for some years before returning to Scone to make her home with her twin sister Jane and Jane's husband. During the decade 1890–1900 there occurred the marriages of both Basil, the eldest of the Mackenzie brothers, and Will, the youngest. Basil's marriage was childless, but a son and a daughter were born to the William Mackenzies.

Dr and Mrs Mackenzie and their daughters spent several holidays at St. Anne's-on-Sea (where there was a good golf course. Mackenzie won a tournament on one such holiday). There were also visits to Hindhead in Surrey, where Mrs Mackenzie's uncle and her sisters still lived, and one family photograph was taken in Broughty Ferry, near Dundee, perhaps on a sea-side visit from a longer holiday at Scone.

The friendship between the Mackenzies and Dr and Mrs Brown prospered. Mrs Brown was always busy, deeply involved as she was in the social work in Burnley district, notably in connection with the British Women's Temperance Association, the Women's Co-operative Guild, and with the formation of a 'House of Help' for homeless and friendless girls. In this last work she received much valuable assistance from her husband. It is interesting to reflect the different attitude of the two. Mrs Mackenzie, gentle, kind and domesticated, assumed a supportive role dedicated to the work of her more dominant but devoted husband. Mrs Brown, on the other hand, abounded with restless energy, directed outwardly to community affairs and to the causes of social injustice—shared by her husband. Mackenzie was concerned with individuals, Brown with the Poor Law and the Board of Guardians. Although so different in outlook, their esteem and regard for each other was mutual, and the relationship more like father and son, master and student.

Dr Brown took Dorothy with him on his rounds, whiling away the time with stories of Uncle Remus and Brer Rabbit, and a strong bond grew between the kindly man and the young cripple, a bond which was not broken when the Browns went to South Africa in 1898. ' Tell Dorothy I'll have more stories to tell on my return when she comes to see me ', Dr Brown wrote, ' and say I have not yet forgotten " Billy my boy " and all the rest of them ', and there were similar messages in most of his long letters.

The Browns returned briefly to Burnley the following year and then spent some time in London and in Bordoghera, Italy, before settling in Rondebosch, Cape of Good Hope. A prolific correspondence ensued between Mackenzie and Dr Brown; they never lost touch and valued each other's friendship immensely. Brown edited with meticulous care the manuscripts of the various books. Even when he retired to South Africa, the editing continued with long letters, ' Dear Mac ', ' Dear Jimmie ', ' Dear Kenny ', etc. Rather pathetically, in his later years he would write ' What are endocrines?' ' Who was Marey?' ' Our whole long intercourse since 1876 ', Dr Brown wrote in 1915, ' has been a very great and profitable thing for me and mine, but I feel I've got much more than I gave in all those long years . . .' Mackenzie would not have agreed; he had a deep affection and respect for his old friend. That Dr Brown was a wholly lovable, wholly selfless man is inherent in his letters and is borne out by his granddaughters, Mrs MacGregor and Miss Dick, who have vivid memories of months spent in Capetown with their grandparents:

In February of 1901 Mackenzie was able to report to Will the completion of his book on the Pulse:

Dear W.,
The opus is finished all but the preface, Dr Brown's scathing criticism and a chapter to be typewritten.

Now I am certain I'll have to publish at my own cost, and I have a notion the book will ' go ' here in America. There are 335 illustrations. As these will cost about 10/- each, I thought I would communicate with sundry people to see what I could get them done for. There's Dr Crump's folks-in-law. (Dr Crump had succeeded Dr Briggs.) . . . Strange is a printer and I would get him to get an estimate for me. Also Krohne & Sesemann who will make any instrument without royalty may also be likely to help me in the matter.

When furnished with the price at which these tracings could be made I could then communicate with a publisher. My feelings lean towards Pentland of Edinburgh. I think though that he would likely charge me pretty heavily for the engravings. But I said that the publishers, not being medical, would not be able to push the sale of the books so much as a purely medical publisher. This view almost gives me into the hands of a medical publisher, for what boots it if we save £10 or £15 and yet miss a sale of 100 or so? Woodhead wished me to write him before opening negotiations, as he had much experience of Pentland. After hearing from you, I'll write him . . .

Pentland of Edinburgh published it the following year under its full title: *The Study of the Pulse, Arterial, Venous and Hepatic, and of the Movements of the Heart.*[2] Meantime he wrote to Dr G. A. Gibson of Edinburgh University with whom he was in constant correspondence and whom, incidentally, he invariably addressed as ' My dear Master ', saying on one occasion: ' I look upon you as my Master in heart affairs '. Mackenzie's letter to Gibson, dated March 24th, 1901, is impish and provocative.

. . . There is a point of view connected with the ap. that I do not think is properly realised. . . . How delighted I would be to get you to review my book. I only sent it to the publishers five days ago, and as there are over 300 illustrations it will take a long time to get it printed. I remember your scathing remark on Samson's tracings—in your review of his book, and I have taken it to heart. Thus each tracing represents something definite, and I give what seems to me the clear interpretation of every particular. I deal with the every-day pulse. Thus in pulse irregularity I enter very fully. By the by, a German, Wenckebach, and an American, Cushny, have been making wonderful discoveries in pulse irregularities and have been felicitating one another, while in sundry Journals their discoveries are hailed as epoch-making! Would you believe it that all their discoveries were known to me 10 years ago, that I sent a short paper describing them in 1893 to the B.M.J., that the learned editor put my MS and valuable tracings in the waste-paper basket, but that last year he published Cushny's discovery at length!

[2] Mackenzie, J. *The Study of the Pulse, Arterial, Venous and Hepatic, and of the Movements of the Heart*. Edinburgh and London: Pentland, 1902.

Since then I have travelled far, and I am able to describe and elucidate facts that neither of these two have as yet any conception of. I think I can show facts in this respect that neither experimental physiologists nor clinical observers have dreamed of. It is simply wonderful what curious and interesting facts can be demonstrated by the means I employ. It is likely that my facts will fall flat, and for that I am prepared, but this I do know—that 30 years hence it will be found that what I preach today to heedless ears will be accepted as gospel, for my views are based on true, undeniable, demonstrable facts . . .

To this letter Mackenzie added a postscript:

When I get my heart work finished I shall set about to convince you that there is no pain in an internal organ. I have some beautiful illustrating *facts*.

It was in this letter also that he made known his intention of writing a book on heart disease and pregnancy:

Take your paper on the maternal circulation in pregnancy. I have a large number of carefully observed facts, whose significance I saw as through a glass darkly, but when I read your paper the whole mass of facts became illuminated. If my pulse book makes any success I intend to write a book on heart disease and pregnancy, and your paper is the foundation on which my explanations will be laid . . .

It was Clifford Allbutt who finally wrote the review of Mackenzie's book in the *British Medical Journal* and Mackenzie wrote to Will in May of 1902:

Dear W.,

I should have sent the agreement with the publisher to you, but we have none! I was so bothered with the final stages of the book that the agreement escaped my memory and as he never mentioned it, neither did I. When I saw him last the understanding was that I paid for the publication, which I have done, then I receive all the sales less booksellers' and publishers' discount and advertisements. I insisted in our correspondence that I should have at least 10/- per volume, and as near as he could tell the 8/- would cover the deductions—the nett price is 18/-. But if it does not sell then there would be only the advertisements to pay for. I know nothing of the sales, but I have authentic information that at least two copies are sold. There

13

have been no reviews yet. The chief one in the *Brit. Med. Journal* will not appear till June. Clifford Allbutt is reviewing it there and he told me he could not do it till after May 24th . . .

The review appeared in the issue of July 26th, 1902, and was couched in terms of unqualified approval. After referring to the study of pulse variations by other physicians in earlier times, the reviewer continued:

But today, from the Galilee of Burnley in Lancashire, comes a new teacher to prove to us that our content was shallow enough; and in an important work he has lifted the whole subject into a fresh light and into a larger aspect. This complete work is just issued, but those who busy themselves with these matters know something already of Dr Mackenzie's researches, both as regard the circulation of the blood and in the sphere of referred visceral pain, and these readers will find their high expectations fully justified in the present volume. To the eye of one familiar with the records of the sphygmograph the first glimpse of these profusely illustrated pages is reassuring . . . So far as we are aware, this collection of 335 tracings, nearly all of them perfectly taken by the author and as carefully reproduced, is unrivalled. We often hear that in the bustle of general practice scientific work is impossible; if Dr Mackenzie had done no more than dispel this error he would have done good service . . . To read this book through, and to study, as we have done, every one of these admirable tracings in connection with the text, is even for the reader no light effort; and this effort of appreciation may give him some notion of the labour which it has cost the author . . . the work must take a permanent place in the standard records of the subject. In conclusion we must not omit to give high commendation to the style in which the treatise is written. The author is rather too much afraid of a long sentence, so that some pages read a little jerkily, but in the simplicity of the language, the modesty of the propositions, the scientific caution which never fails, and the avoidance of the fine words, such as the task of reading a tough piece of argument is made as easy as the subject permits. If the pulse be quick or slow he does not hesitate to prefer these terms to more imposing polysyllables . . .

Dr Cotton expressed the view that Mackenzie could *not* write effectively, but it was this very simplicity of style referred to by Albutt which was the hallmark of his work. Although clinical interpretation of his tracings often gave rise (in correspondence) to controversy, there was never any confusion about what he wrote. A German reviewer referred to the book as a 'splendid example of worthy clinical investigation'. Its publication opened many doors to Mackenzie, paving the way for his association with Arthur Keith and Professor Wenckebach. In London, despite Clifford Allbutt's glowing remarks, it made little impression.

Chapter 20

LONDON BECKONS

The die is cast, the deed is done
Caesar has crossed the Rubicon

IPSE DIXIT

' We very often speak of your kind and pleasant visit; for a week
we were in a really English kind of mood ', Wenckebach wrote to
Mackenzie in June of 1904. He continued :

> I was much interested and also amused by your kind letter;
> what you write about Schott and Nauheim is exactly my
> opinion. Only in Germany they don't share your favourable
> impression about Schott personally . . . I saw your paper in the
> *D.M.W.* and saw that little sentence about digitalis inhibiting
> the *Reizleitung* by means of vagus stimulation . . . I am anxious
> to see what Kraus and other great men will say to your observa-
> tion. I think they will be silent and are ' no' comin' oot to the
> fishin' wi' me ', as Wee MacGregor would say. This Wee
> MacGregor is delightful. I do understand it pretty well and will
> try to get hold of a fine Scottish accent before ' comin' to
> England ' . . .

One Englishman whom Wenckebach was particularly anxious to
see during his projected visit to this country was Dr George Oliver
of Harrogate. Oliver had perfected a blood-pressure instrument and
had crossed swords, though in a gentlemanly manner, with Mackenzie
on the subject through the columns of the *British Medical Journal*.
Mackenzie initiated the correspondence in a letter dated 23rd April,
1904 :

> Sir,
>
> The question of accurately measuring the arterial pressure
> in patients is one to which I devoted a considerable time some
> years ago. The result of my observations was to convince me of
> the total unreliability of the methods employed. The instru-
> ments I used were those of Oliver and Hill and Barnard, and,
> from a consideration of the constitution of others, the following
> objections are also applicable to them. To begin with, I had
> considerable difficulty in telling when the levers of these instru-

ments attained the maximum swing which was supposed to represent the mean arterial pressure. This, of course, may have been due to a lack of perceptive power on my part. I also found that the readings in mm of Hg from these instruments when applied to the same patient were at such variance that one was forced to conclude that some grave error existed in one or both instruments. When I reflected on the manner in which they were supposed to act, it soon appeared to me how utterly unreliable they were for practical purposes . . . (a detailed description follows of the instruments of both Oliver and Hill & Barnard) . . . Supposing one did get an accurate record of the pressure within an artery, what is its significance? Is it supposed to be a record of a pressure within the whole arterial system? An idea seems to be prevalent that if pressure within one artery, whatever its size may be, is obtained, the pressure within all the other arteries of the body must be the same. This notion is evidently based on the idea that as a variation of pressure in a fluid contained within a vessel is reflected at once to all parts of a vessel, so variations of pressure within the arteries is at once reflected to all parts of the arteral system. That this is not the case is evident from a little consideration. The arterial system is not like a closed vessel; the blood is a flowing stream escaping at one extremity. As the stream flows towards the periphery there is a great loss of pressure on account of the friction of the blood against the walls of the arteries. The smaller the artery the greater the resistance and hence the greater the fall of arterial pressure. It takes a light pressure to obliterate the digital artery, a greater to obliterate the radial and a still greater to obliterate the brachial. What the actual loss of pressure is from the aorta to the radial or digital arteries we have no means of calculating but it is a factor to be reckoned with and not to be ignored as inventors appear to have done.

I do not want to decry efforts towards the solution of this question. I think the ingenious inventors of these instruments have rendered a great service by their attempts, and if perfection is still far off, nevertheless by their endeavours they bring us nearer to the accomplishment of a very necessary requirement.

Wenckebach commented some days later:

I read with much pleasure your remark on the instruments for gauging arterial pressure in the last *Br. Med. Journal*, I have read the book of Oliver on this subject and did so with great pleasure. You Englishmen are excellent writers.! What a difference with our dear German cousins! But I was very little pleased with Oliver's instruments. I can not well handle them, and when I come to England I intend to pay a visit to Dr Oliver and to learn how he makes his sharp observations! . . .

Dr Oliver, quick to jump to the defence of his instrument, replied to Mackenzie with some magnanimity :

My attention has just been drawn to Dr Mackenzie's letter . . . It is quite obvious to me that Dr Mackenzie's heart was too much enamoured by the sphygmograph when he made his blood pressure observations to be open to the allurements of a new love; but that is doubtless fortunate for us, for we are now all the richer for the valuable work he has done on the circulation. Nearly all the points he mentions have been in my mind for years, and I have done my best to show how they can be met but it is difficult to get others to realise as one does oneself the importance of particular points of technique. Each one requires to be trained in the details of a method, just as Dr Mackenzie has trained himself in the sphygmographic line. We do not expect absolute perfection in blood pressure instruments, nor in anything else . . . I am satisfied of one thing, that the clinical observation of the arterial pressure is one requiring the greatest care and tact. The influence of the nerves needs to be sedulously excluded as much as possible, and physiologists and physicians have not yet grasped the great importance of the physiological variations which form the very ground work of the clinical study of blood pressure. As will be shown from some recent work, the time for accurate comparative observation during the day is quite limited. At present we are jumbling up normal with abnormal pressures, utterly disregarding a normal base line which does exist.

Exercising tact and caution I know nothing more valuable or more important in clinical observation than a well-recorded arterial pressure and a little experience of the right kind would soon assure Dr Mackenzie of this fact. I am quite sure if he could be at my side during the coming season at Harrogate, the practical aspect of this matter would dawn upon him, and perhaps he might glance with more favour on my first love.

George Oliver.

This letter of Oliver's brought forth the following ironic comment from Arthur Keith in a postscript to his letter to Mackenzie[1]: ' Be sure to go to Harrogate when the great " I am " is there for the season ...'

Dr Leonard Hill also replied, in unequivocal terms, to Mackenzie's attack. After describing the testing of the Hill-Barnard sphygmometer, he continued :

> ... These are the experimental observations on which we based the accuracy of the instruments. Our experiments may have been wrong, and if so Dr Mackenzie can repeat them and correct us, but I am not willing at present to accept his condemnation which is largely based on physical misconceptions. In the clinical use of sphygmometers I have had no experience, but I can predict that in certain cases the instruments must fail to give accurate readings ...
>
> As to the significance of the arterial pressure, I must refer Dr Mackenzie to the text-books of physiology ...

Dr Mackenzie had found the text books of physiology wanting on several previous occasions; he did not continue the correspondence.

Arrangements for Wenckebach's visit continued : he was to spend several days in Burnley. ' Would it suit you if I came on Thursday 13th October ?' he wrote (4.8.04). He planned to go from Burnley to Manchester and Liverpool, and thence to Edinburgh. ' Then I will go to London and make an appointment with Oliver, who, by your kind suggestion to him, invited me to stay some days with him at his home at Farnham. I am very glad that you have introduced me to Head and Keith. I think it is most necessary to have such an introduction in a city as London . . . Prof. Clifford Allbutt wrote to me that he will be back in Cambridge from his American trip . . . so I think it will be best to visit Cambridge on the last days of my sojourn in England, and leave via Harwich . . .' All went according to plan, and in November Wenckebach wrote to Mackenzie in full about his experiences in England and Scotland :

> I had a splendid time in England, good weather, nice men, interesting things ! But my best time was in Burnley. I enjoyed immensely to see you at home, to meet Mrs Mackenzie again and to make acquaintance with your nice children, and I am very grateful indeed for all you and Mrs M. did to make my

[1] 2nd May, 1904.

Burnley-days most enjoyable! My wife sends her best compliments and the children were very much amused by my tales from the home of that strange ' mynheer and mevrouw '[2] from England!

But now I will give you an account of my doings and the impressions I got. Edinburgh is the most beautiful and the loveliest of all towns I ever saw; I am quite charmed by the place and felt quite at home there from the very beginning. My homely feelings were greatly due to the sort of men the Scotsmen are. Gibson did his best and was very kind to me. What sort of man is he? Well, my first impression was decidedly an unfavourable one; I revised my first impression several times, seeing that he was very industrious, very anxious to give all he could afford to his students, gathering beautiful books (reading them?) etc., but the end impression was ' poor Gibson ' . . .

I lunched on Sunday with Dr Nicholson, a splendid man and co-admirer of Dr Mackenzie, and with Chalmers Watson, who is somewhat enthusiastic about gout and thyroid but a nice man, who showed me his preparations next day. . . Schäfer is an admirable man; he gave me a long afternoon in his laboratory, and I had a good talk with him . . . He told me the principle of Oliver's instruments as well as the instruments themselves were all right and perfectly genially constructed and worked admirably . . . Of course Gibson introduced me to Sir William Gairdner, fine case of heartblock with perceptible auricular systoles . . . And now my two days in Oliver's beautiful home! They were both very kind and genial; he is a good little man, somewhat particular, somewhat narrow-sighted about his blood-pressure and nothing else, and only in the mechanical way; she is not at all sympathetic but she was very kind to me, always correcting my bad English pronunciation, but to a somewhat exaggerated extent, so that conversation became somewhat difficult at some moments. But I will not tell nasty things about my most friendly hostess! . . . As to his blood pressure, I am still in a doubt, or rather I have to verify myself all he told and showed me, but I am very much inclined to think that he is *all right* and that his work has a very great value, scientific and clinical. He lowered and raised my blood pressure, widened and contracted my vessels in a most admirable manner and told me with great liberality all he could tell me about his researches, so that I will start at once to see if he is right. The matter is

2 Mynheer and mevrouw=gentleman and lady (Dutch).

extremely complicated and as I said before, he sees only the
mechanical side of the question but it is really very interesting,
and I think you agree with me that thorough knowledge of the
blood-pressure in patients would be of a very great importance.
As to Oliver's methods, I believe he is the only man in England
(to say nothing of the continent) who applies his instruments
with intelligence. The first thing Gibson told me was: Well,
what *I* say, Mackenzie is all right, just only that he is too indifferent about blood-pressure. In one of the lectures I attended,
he applied . . . Hill-Barnard's instrument and he got a beautiful
reading. But he did not take it into account. I asked in so innocent a manner, whether he had *ever* got *any* valuable information from the instrument, so as to change his former opinion
on a patient or to give an indication for treatment he did not
see before. Well, he said, I think *no*!! Well I said, perhaps
Mackenzie is all right, after all!

My London days were not so profitable as the other days; Dr
Salaman was so kind as to show me London Hospital and bored
me somewhat about his otherwise very interesting liver-things.
Head was absent, that day, and next day I did not find him in
London Hospital. I was very sorry. Keith is a very nice and
clever man, but was somewhat ill from a chronic tropical
malaria. London is a big place, with splendid but also with very
ugly parts . . . I met at dinner with Dr Ewart, a very clever jolly
little man, who had read my book with great care, and asked
a thousand clever questions and whom I could give scientific
information for some very clever practical questions of treatment he had thought about. It was a very good evening indeed.
In Oxford I missed Prof. Thompson, but had a very good
guide in the shape of Dr W. Collier, well acquainted with
Oxford's history. And Cambridge too proved to be a success.
Clifford Allbutt asked me to stay with him on Tuesday and
Wednesday. He was very kind to me, in the beginning somewhat high-professional, but from the first moment we talked
on Dutch pictures we went on splendidly, and *in* came Mrs
C. A. with a high and horrid voice, very much pleased by
finding the 'herr Professor' talking English much better than
in Burnley after these weeks of training, and I told some funny
things, and my impressions from England, and then the ice was
broken (or practically there was no ice), and we had a good
dinner with Langley and some other less prominent men, and
we became very good friends indeed . . . He (Allbutt) is a

splendid fellow, but in his own way, not in our way. He doesn't understand anything of our department . . . I told a great deal of good about Dr Mackenzie and told him so by and by what was your merit about the venous pulse, and that you just put an end to all the nonsense talked about the subject by men who did not care to *measure* . . . I had a long discussion with Gaskell. Well, it is just as I thought. Gaskell is still standing on his standpoint from twenty or fifteen years ago and did not follow the movement on heart-physiology. I first baffled him completely on heart-block and then got out my right-auricle tracing. At first he treated it ' en bagatelle ', but I got compasses[3] and our voices raised and in came one gentleman, and then another gentleman, and then there gathered seven or eight doctors round the table and looked over my shoulders and I checked him completely; most to the satisfaction of the gathered gentlemen, as one of them, who showed me some of the splendid colleges told me afterwards. Gaskell has become a ' non valeur ' in physiology and seems to be the same thing in embryology now (but we had a good lunch together ! !). Not only I *thought* so, but I told Clifford Allbutt so, who was somewhat disappointed by this statement but did *not* contradict . . .

I am delighted with my English experiences and certainly will return to do a great deal of sight-seeing in your wonderful country. Please *do* go to Edinburgh, if it were only for *our* sake, because it will be an excellent excuse for us to cross the channel and to see *you* there. I gathered that you will be welcomed in Edinburgh in a most hearty way by your admirers (they are many) and I believe there are some authorities there who are rather afraid of your coming there ! . . .

Perhaps Mackenzie did under-estimate the clinical importance of blood pressure. Wenckebach's comments on Edinburgh confirmed Mackenzie in his decision to leave Burnley and to return to his University city. In high spirits, he wrote confidently of his plans to Will on December 4th, 1904 :

Dear W.,

> ' The die is cast, the deed is done
> Caesar has crossed the Rubicon '.

So sang our poetic brother-in-law. Well, I have announced to Dr Crump that I want to leave Burnley as soon as he can get a partner and let me off, and he has consented and we are looking

[3] Dividers.

out for a man to take my place. The final decision was taken after mature consideration, depending on the nature of my work. My discoveries on the Heart are turning out to be more valuable than I dared hope for, and not only themselves interesting but of great practical significance. Joined with the work of Professor Wenckebach, our views worked a small revolution in the study of heart disease. As I cannot find time here to thoroughly expound all my views, the leisure afforded me in Edinburgh will be utilized in teaching these views if I can find or create a suitable opportunity. I am given to understand that I will not have much difficulty in earning a living in Edinburgh.

Professor Wenckebach's visit to this country finally decided me. He got to know the ' strong ' men in Edinburgh and found them very feeble—a view that I held, so I do not fear the quality of the opposition. Another thing that decided me was this. I can see that you, with your industry and ability, could if you had courage take a higher position in the world's affairs, and I considered it a pity that you should not leave the drudgery and aim at higher things. I applied the same test to myself and having made the resolve considered that as time is getting on the sooner I did it the better.

Even if after a few years I am a failure I will have something left to start anew. Of course the matter is kept quiet . . .

But Mackenzie's enthusiasm was not shared by his brother, as is shown by this further letter, dated 13th December :

. . . I knew you would not feel enthusiastic over the proposed exodus, but I feel now absolutely convinced that the sooner I go the better it will be for my future. You perhaps can't realize the prospect before me, the apostle of a new doctrine practically, which men fail to comprehend because they are not brought into actual contact with the method for recognizing it, but when found, so striking and convincing that they will wonder at their previous blindness. Being of practical application it will appeal all the more to the hoi-polloi of the profession. I shall start lecturing and demonstrating as soon as I can make arrangements, and I am in hopes of surrounding myself with a few disciples who will not only carry the blessed word but may stimulate the powers that be to enquire if these things are so. If I manage rightly, I should really take the leading place in heart speciality in the Kingdom ! I've not got a swelled head, but I am certain that no-one can interpret the living heart with anything like the power possessed by Professor Wenckebach and myself. Even the language we write is incomprehensible to the most erudite English physician and the strength of our position is not appreciated simply because they have not yet learnt the new alphabet. There is a drug digitalis or foxglove that has been empirically employed in the treatment of heart affections for centuries. Tens of thousands of experiments and observations have been made to find out the nature of its action on the heart. Cartloads of articles have been written about it, and yet our knowledge of its activities is practically a minus quality. Well, it has been reserved for me to demonstrate in the simplest manner the great part of the whole secret!

Regarding the financial question, it has been the main obstacle, and which I think I may now venture to put on one side. I have from my investments at present £220 per annum. I shall get £2000 for the sale of the practice, and at least £1500 for next year's work and the debts due to me when I leave. So that would leave me with about £350 per annum. I propose to put £500 aside to pay for rent and taxes and live upon the interest. If in the course of a few years that £500 is exhausted without any prospect, then I shall remove to some quiet place and do a little practice and serenely spend the declining years of this life. I even contemplate this termination of my scheme with content, and my family are of the same mind.

I am hoping to leave this time next year, but it may be the following June . . .

' I am glad to hear that your future lies in Edinburgh . . . you will be quite at your right place there ', wrote Wenckebach in February of the following year (1905), and Dr Brown wrote from South Africa at the same time : ' I think the Edinburgh move is quite right and safe. Your pleasure and profit is in your work, the field of which will be larger and more congenial and in infinitely better environment there than at Burnley.' But Mackenzie was in a quandary. Far from feeling convinced in his own mind about the rightness of a move to Edinburgh, he was now beginning to perceive that his success might be far greater than he had ever dared to imagine. London began to beckon him. This letter to his brother Will is dated 2nd April, 1905:

. . . Having determined to leave Burnley I am not quite sure Edinburgh is big enough to contain me. It might seem that I have a much greater reputation than ever I dared hope for and my notions are beginning to take on. I am publishing in the

British Medical Journal a series of papers which are coming out weekly on ' New methods of studying affections of the heart '. They are tremendously erudite, so much so that the medical public can only say ' wonderful ', but the fact that the *B.M.J.* should publish them in this form is so unprecedented that they call for enquiry. However, higher authority are impressed with them and honestly know that they predict a revolution in the conception of many forms of heart disease. On Friday a Dr from Cheshire brought me a patient. Tomorrow a Dr from Bristol is sending me another. This Dr has a heart trouble and he hunted me up in Oxford to examine him, and curiously in a postscript to his letter he says ' I wish you were in London '— a sentiment which has been bothering me the last week or two. I had a letter from an able physiologist in Amsterdam who wants to come to Burnley to see me. At a meeting in Liverpool last week my notions were expounded by a disciple amid general admiration . . . I went to Edinburgh a month ago and took part in a discussion on the heart, and without vanity not a soul knew anything really valuable on the subject but myself— so as I say I am feeling too big for Edinburgh and want to fly at higher game . . . Turn the matter over in your mind. I shall be coming up to London about June 23rd when the Neurological Society entertain us to a feast of reason and other viands . . . When in London I intend to have a talk with Head. Sir Lauder Brunton[4], Dr Ewart and perhaps some others. By that time they will have had time to digest by ' epoch-making ' paper . . .

In fact Mackenzie saw Dr Ewart in April, when he spent a night in London on his way back from a visit to Rome (there is no evidence as to the reason for this visit). ' I have just telephoned Dr Ewart (Curzon St and Mayfair!) ' he scribbled hurriedly to Will from the Charing Cross Hotel on 21st April . . . ' He is coming for me at nine and I intend to present my case of London and Edinburgh for his consideration. He is one of the leading men in London and is the one who has shown most appreciation of my work in writing to me from time to time . . .' ' Dr Ewart ', Mackenzie reported later, ' spoke confidently of my success ', but his approach to Henry Head did not meet with similar encouragement, as he told Will on 17th May :

> . . . Head wrote me a long letter pointing out very clearly the difficulties ahead if I settled in London . . . the cold logic of Head's facts appealed to my common sense, and so I have almost

[4] Sir Thomas Lauder Brunton, 1844-1916.

abandoned the London idea. I shall not finally decide until our visit to London next month . . . The ' pamphlet ' is the herald of the greatest revolution to be made in Heart study in this generation and it is inconclusive, as its object was to excite the attention of the British medical public. It has done so in a degree I scarcely expected as my correspondence with many eminent people shows . . .

It is tempting here to ascribe Head's motives for discouraging Mackenzie's move to London to the old scores on the segmental distribution of nerves. If he did harbour any dislike, then certainly Mackenzie did not hold any such rancour. Indeed it has been said that in such matters Mackenzie's attitude was simplicity and sincerity to the point of being naïve. The quality of research was his only concern, not personalities.

Mackenzie had also presented the problem to Dr Brown, who wrote on 10th May, 1905 :

> . . . All this morning and more or less ever since I got your letter I have been revolving this London plan in my mind. It will cost more money, but success if it comes will be greater . . . post-graduate teaching is the very ideal for you. I am inclined to think favourably of the idea . . . Continental patients might be sent to you there, who would never come elsewhere . . .

His thoughts moved once again to Edinburgh. Whatever criticism is used to determine the relative merits or demerits of consultants and consultant practice, the discerning general practitioner is, as consumer and user, the ultimate judge. Thus he wrote to a fellow graduate now in general practice and who replied :

> Linlithgow.
> 16th June, 1905.

> . . . With regard to the important matter mentioned in your letter I am, frankly speaking, not sure that I am competent to express an opinion because I don't care to mingle much with others and, therefore I don't know their thoughts. Moreover, I confirm to being prejudiced and therefore my testimony would be biased. But curiously, I met yesterday a much, very much, abler man than I am, who was a country doctor and who now lives in town, and whom I knew I could thoroughly trust. He said ' I think Dr Mackenzie would certainly do well in Edinburgh.' Needless to say, I heartily agree.

However, in regard to a Hospital Appointment and how you

would fare and whether you could extend your work without such an appointment, I just do not know.

In a place like Edinburgh there is often such conversation that seniority is preferred to real merit.

I fear you won't think my opinion is worth having, but I give it such as it is.

With ever kind regards,
Yours most truly,
James Hunter.

Despite an element of encouragement, this advice was tempered with caution, and the message was clear. Mackenzie could only succeed on his own merits. For the moment he would stay in Burnley.

But he was to return to the Edinburgh proposal, as we shall later see.

No record remains to show just when Mackenzie finally resolved this ding-dong battle between Edinburgh and London. His letters contain no further reference to Edinburgh, and one assumes that gradually his belief in himself hardened into the resolve that it must be London or nothing. Writing in July of 1906 Dr Brown refers to ' the postponement of the great move.' It is interesting to record that in September of 1905 Dr Brown met Sir Lauder Brunton, and put in a good word for his friend :

> . . . Some weeks ago while daundering on the heights of Wagon Hill at Ladysmith, I bore down on Sir Lauder Brunton and claimed acquaintanceship . . . he had forgotten my introduction to him in 1878 and his nice little dinner he gave me, but we got on nicely and had a good long interesting talk on various subjects. Among other things of course your name cropped up. I said ' you know my late partner Dr James Mackenzie '; ' Oh yes, I have his book with me, I intend to read it on the way home.' He had Wenckebach too . . . I further got Mary to copy out parts of your last letter, and took this to him on board the S.S. *Armadale Castle* as he was leaving : and told him in confidence you were thinking of coming up to London to work for a couple of years, and I asked if he would help you when you came up to spy out the land . . . he said he would be very glad to see you when you came up . . . Let us hope for a good voyage for the *Armadale* and plenty of time and energy on his part to master Wenckebach, The Pulse and the excerpts . . .

195

Further encouragement came from Arthur Keith. Keith to Mackenzie:

Kent,
April 30, 1905.

. . . I think London must be the centre of your choice. You will find your reputation has reached the point at which rapid expansion takes place. You could have a bench in a number of ' labs ' but you will find there is no one to help you but yourself. You have to be your own physiologist. Probably the Lister Institute will prove the place where you can pursue your work best untrammelled. Hill is a curious man; very honest, very able but his work follows his fancy; yet of all the men in London, he is the one from which you may best expect to get good. The ' London ' (Hospital) in some ways would suit you . . . Cushny has now come to University College. He would give you a place in his ' lab ' I have no doubt with great goodwill . .

and later, 20th September, 1905, he ends his letter :

come to London when you will be more than welcome . . .

Sometime in 1905, then, Mackenzie made his final decision : It was to be London. Two years elapsed before the move was made, two years in which his work continued to bring him recognition at home and abroad, and deep personal satisfaction.

Chapter 21

DIGITALIS—THE ETERNAL RIDDLE

Temporis ars medicina fere est
(The art of medicine is generally a question of time)

OVID. *Rem. Amor*

The University of Edinburgh can justly claim a high place in the role of honour of physicians who have gone forth to add lustre to its name and to the reputation of its Medical School. One such was Dr William Withering[1]. In the scientific climate of the 18th century his reputation as a botanist[2], chemist, analyst, research worker, was equalled only by his standing as a learned and successful physician in provincial England. His treatise on the foxglove and its extract digitalis[3] is a classic of clinical insight and therapeutic wisdom.

Completing a four years' apprenticeship, he matriculated at the age of 21 in 1762 and graduated at Edinburgh University four years later. ' His memory during adolescence ' it is recorded, ' was defective and proved an impediment to that progress which might have been expected from assiduity.' Withering apparently was most exact, a typical careful notetaker who kept details of every kind, rain, sunshine, snow, as well as the most careful notes on his practice—shades of Mackenzie!

Born in Wellington, Salop, the son of an apothecary, it is difficult to say precisely when and where his interest in botany originated. The holders of the first three Chairs of Botany until 1738 were apparently undistinguished. Then in 1838 came the publication in Latin of Linnean's famous book *Genera Plantarum*.

The year before Withering's arrival in Edinburgh in 1761, Dr John Hope, outstanding botanist, Fellow of the Royal Society and of the Linnean Society, was appointed Regius Professor of Botany. Other teachers who must have influenced him at Edinburgh were Professors Alexander Munro, Alexander Munro Junior and William Cullen.

In his second year at University, Withering was already making his mark and had instituted a Society for increasing knowledge of

---

[1] Dr William Withering, 1741–1799.
[2] William Withering of Birmingham, Bristol and London, Wright, 1949.
[3] Withering, W. *An Account of the Foxglove, and Some of its Medical Uses, with Practical Remarks on Dropsy and Other Diseases*. Birmingham, Robinson, 1785.

Latin, then the language in which all scientific publications appeared. Even so, Withering wrote home to say that he had formed disagreeable ideas of botany and did not feel that the challenge of a gold medal for the most industrious student, would make it attractive.

Dr Withering chose to settle in Stafford, but for some nine years, until he left, he did very little practice. In 1775 he moved to Birmingham, and a few months later published *The Botanical Arrangement of all the Vegetables naturally growing in Great Britain.*

This was followed by the publication of *Botanical Arrangement.* Limited to essential botanical facts, it did not discuss medicinal properties in any great detail. It did, however, provide useful information and directions for the drying and preserving of speciments, which was to prove so fundamental to the subsequent use and value of digitalis in medicine. Withering was impressed with the diuretic properties of digitalis and attributed improvement to its action on the kidneys.

> ' In the year 1775 ', Withering said, ' my opinion was asked concerning a family receipt (recipe) for the cure of dropsy. I was told it had long been kept a secret by an old woman in Shropshire, who had sometimes made cures after the more regular practitioners had failed. I was informed also, that the effects produced were violent vomiting and purging for the diuretic effects seem to have been overlooked. This medicine was composed of twenty or more herbs, but it was not very difficult for one conversant in these subjects to perceive that the active herb could be no other than the foxglove.'

It is important to repeat that digitalis was introduced as a diuretic, for the treatment of dropsy, ascites, anasarca and sometimes even pleural effusion, ovarian cysts and hydrocephalus. Withering recognized those cases of dropsy which were particularly likely to respond to digitalis. But it was not then recognized that the aetiological factor was heart failure. Withering often noted the presence of a slow pulse, but its real significance was obviously not understood. He had listed this feature amongst the many other varied and undesirable side effects.

In a section entitled ' Effects, Rules and Cautions ', Withering stated,

> Foxglove (*digitalis*) when given in large and quickly repeated doses, occasions sickness, vomiting, purging, confused vision, objects appearing green or yellow, increased secretion of urine with frequent motions to part with it, and sometimes inability

to retain it; slow pulse, even as slow as 35 in a minute, cold sweats, convulsions, syncope, death.

In smaller doses, the side effects were less. The sickness had characteristics which differed from that occasioned by other forms of medicine. It benefited some patients, and not others. Varying dosage was given, so that experience, trial and error, helped him to throw some light on the proper use of this remarkable substance. But all was empirical. Confusion and controversy raged in the medical profession. Some were sceptical, others hostile. One of his contemporaries was a physician named Dr Erasmus Darwin, grandfather of the famous Charles, who had never used digitalis and fought a long rearguard action with Withering. Another contemporary was Dr John Ferrier[4] who first concluded that the essential quality of the plant was exerted on the heart.

Nonetheless, for nearly a century or more, real understanding of the therapeutic place of digitalis in heart disease was to be a slow and uncertain process. Doctors who followed in the wake of Withering had no confidence in its efficacy. With its unpredictable side effects it was distrusted. Many actually feared digitalis and preferred instead to prescribe vinegar of squills in the treatment of heart failure.

Steggal[5] in 1858 wrote that the most remarkable property of digitalis was its influence on the heart, but added that it might be useful in inflammatory diseases generally. It was most used in pleuritis, phthisis, mania, epilepsy and pertussis.

Ten years later, Wunderlich[6] refers to the antipyretic effect of digitalis in enteric or ' typhus ' fever.

It would be unprofitable, indeed tiresome, to attempt here to catalogue all the events in our understanding of the pharmacological and therapeutic action of digitalis in the interval between Withering and Mackenzie. Suffice it to say that confusion and uncertainty in its use was still widespread. In a recent and thoughtful article on Medical History, Keele[7] asks how did digitalis ever escape from this web of misconception?

He holds that it was through the work of physiologists like Ludwig and Cushny; partly too through Nativelle's isolation of ' digitalin '

[4] Ferrier, J. An Essay on the Medical Properties of Digitalis purpurea, or Foxglove. Manchester: Sower and Russell. 1799.
[5] Steggal, J. A Medical Manual for Apothecaries Hall. London: Churchill. 1858.
[6] Wunderlich, C. R. A. Temperature in Diseases, a Manual of Medical Thermometry. London: New Sydenham Society. 1868.
[7] Keele, K. D. British Medical Journal 2, 1251. 1966.

in 1872. But by far the greatest elucidation came from revelations in medicine apparently unconcerned with digitalis:

> Through Bright's description of the renal form of oedema, in separating it from the cardiac form; later through clinicians like Watson noting that digitalis produced its most effective diuresis in cases of cardiac oedema. Then digitalis was noted to be particularly effective in cases with mitral disease in contrast to those with aortic valve disease. In the final stage, after Keith and Flack had identified the sino-auricular node, Mackenzie described auricular paralysis . . .

> It will be seen that progress in the knowledge of the value of digitalis was in fact due more to the lifting of veils of ignorance from oedema, mitral disease and cardiac arrhythmias than to work on digitalis itself.

Mackenzie pointed out that ' the action of a drug is modified by the disease which is present ' and that hearts that showed little or no response to digitalis when the rhythm was normal became extremely sensitive to the drug after the onset of fibrillation.

In retrospect Mackenzie wrote:

> I then proceeded to watch these cases to see what happened, and I found that on the onset of this abnormal rhythm the heart failure set in with such severity that some died within a few days, others within a few weeks, others led a crippled existence for months or a few years, and in a few the onset was not accompanied by any limitation of the heart power. Seeing these very diverse results I set about a long enquiry into the reasons. I found that in those who did well after the onset, though the heart rhythm became irregular the rate did not alter. On the other hand, in those who did badly the rate became increased, sometimes greatly. In watching them I found that if the rate slowed the patient improved, so I looked for means for slowing the rate, and naturally turned to digitalis. I gave the digitalis at first timorously, as we were brought up to look upon it as a dangerous though useful drug, and then more and more boldly, till I found the quantity that would slow the heart. When I had acquired a knowledge of the drug and how to administer it, I was able to give speedily the greatest relief to many patients who were apparently *in extremis*. But I found that as soon as the drug was stopped the patient relapsed, so I set about discovering how to give the drug so as to keep the pulse at a moderate rate, and at last devised a method by which many people who

were apparently hopelessly broken down were enabled to resume their occupations.

In some, the digitalis or other drugs would not slow the rate, and these invariably drifted and died. In others in whom the heart slowed, the symptoms of heart failure were not relieved— these speedily sank and died. The post-mortem examination in these cases invariably revealed such extensive damage of the heart muscle that one could infer that such hearts, embarrassed by the abnormal rhythm, were inconsistent with life. I need not go into the numerous interesting points that arose from this enquiry. One I may mention was that the particular kind of rapid heart for which digitalis is the remedy, stood now clearly revealed . . .

In his opening address to his new colleagues at the St Andrews Institute in 1919, Mackenzie said: ' The discovery of a new fact or a new method must not be the end of the enquiry which had revealed it. Rather must it be looked upon as a means to an end, a stepping stone to help a further advance . . .' This was his conception of research, that one thing must inevitably lead to another and that there is virtually no limit to the opportunities for research which await the enquiring mind.

In the light of present day clinical practice, even Mackenzie's views have been superseded. Of the two concepts of the action of digitalis on the heart, one holds that the restoration of cardiac compensation is an indirect effect and mediated through a reduction in heart rate and the consequent improvement in stroke volume which this implies. The other attributes its effect to a direct action on the myocardium. Mackenzie[8] and later Sir Thomas Lewis[9] attributed the benefits to depression of the A.V. conduction system and to vagal slowing of the heart. Digitalis therapy was thus restricted to patients with atrial fibrillation and a rapid ventricular response. In consequence, a large proportion of patients whose failure was accompanied by regular rhythm, were not treated with digitalis. Such was common practice in England, dominated by the teaching of Lewis and Mackenzie, but in continental Europe, U.S.A. and in Edinburgh the value of digitalis in heart failure with normal rhythm was recognized. This assessment is borne out by modern clinical views.[10]

[8] Mackenzie, J. Principles of Diagnosis and Treatment in Heart Affections. London: Oxford Medical Publications. 1916.
[9] Lewis, T. Diseases of the Heart Described for Practitioners and Students. London: Macmillan. 1933.
[10] Lown, B. and Levine, S. A. Current Concepts in Digitalis Therapy. London: Churchill. 1955.

This is not to decry Mackenzie's fundamental contribution to our better understanding of the place of digitalis in cardiology. After all, it is only in comparatively recent times in the resort to controlled clinical trials that medicine, and particularly clinical medicine, began to emerge from the age of empiricism and of trial and error. Well may Wenckebach explain (see next chapter) ' By Jove, I believe this may be the solution of the eternal riddle of digitalis.'

Terence East[11] has said ' It was really James Mackenzie who revived the rational and practical use of digitalis and raised it from the cloud of disrepute under which it had fallen.' Mackenzie's study of the effects of digitalis continued for many years after his arrival in London and notably in collaboration with Professor Cushny. His painstaking observations were finally published in the *British Medical Journal* in 1905,[12] in the *Proceedings of the Royal Society of Medicine*[13] in 1907-8 and in *Heart* in 1911.[14] In this, as in so much else, Mackenzie added yet another stone to the mounting cairn of medical knowledge.

Unmistakably, there is a surprising affinity and similarity in the careers, character, determination and originality of these two men, Withering and Mackenzie. Both in their early years were influenced by a background of the chemist or apothecary, both went to Edinburgh University, both had seeming difficulty in assimilating facts. Withering excelled in Latin in order to broaden his scientific interest. Mackenzie likewise pursued German. In the meticulous note-taking of case records, they both excelled. To what extent did Withering's methods influence Mackenzie? Certainly in their clinical work, they both gave meaning to the duality of pharmacology and therapeutics. Resolute in the confidence of their own clinical ability, they were impatient of the hesitancy and inadequacy of lesser men. Understandably, they had often to fight in public to justify their views and maintain their professional integrity. Like the prophets, they may in their own generation have been without honour, but time has vindicated their fundamental contributions to the history of cardiology, and of medicine.

---

[11] East, T. *The Story of Heart Disease*. London : William Dawson & Sons. 1958.
[12] A new method of studying affections of the heart—2. The action of digitalis on the human heart. *B.M.J.* 1905, i, 587; A new method of studying affections of the heart—3. The action of digitalis. *B.M.J.* 1905, i, 702; A new method of studying affections of the heart—4. The acion of digitalis on the human heart. *B.M.J.* 1905, i, 759.
[13] The action of digitalis on the human subject. *Proceedings of the Royal Society of Medicine, Therapeutical and Pharmacological Section,* 1907-8, i, 29-32.
[14] Digitalis. *Heart* 1911, ii, 273.

Chapter 22

KEITH AND OSLER

I will not cease from mental fight,
Nor shall my sword sleep in my hand

WILLIAM BLAKE

Sir Arthur Keith[1] in his autobiography writes:

At this time (1903) there were appearing in the *British Medical Journal*, articles on disorders of the heart, written by a medical practitioner of Burnley. His name was Dr James Mackenzie. He had invented an instrument, a ' polygraph '—for registering the pulse in the veins of the root of the neck. His articles were illustrated by tracings of the ' Jugular pulse '. Dr Mackenzie was clearly the man to help me answer the question : 'Are the caval openings closed, when the right auricle contracts?' So I wrote to him and received from him this reply: ' You are the man I have been looking for; I have hearts which I observed in patients over a long series of years and now I want someone to examine them. Will you do it?'

And so began a long and fascinating association by these two great men, so similar and yet so unlike. Of indifferent scholastic achievement, lacking formal secondary school education, Mackenzie went up to university at 21 and Keith at 18. Both men were cradled in the poverty of a Scottish farm, but despite all these handicaps, they did not seem to be impeded in their progress to success and international recognition. Far from the corn fields of Pictstonhill and Kinnermit, destiny was to unite them in a common purpose. They had work to do.

Keith to Mackenzie :

15th March, 1905.

My Dear Mackenzie,

It is long since I got your kind letter; I should feel grateful for the loan of your polygraph; I want to work out one or two things during Easter down in Kent.

As to your invitation[2] : that I intend to avail myself of in the

---

[1] Keith, Sir Arthur. *An autobiography*. London : Watts. 1950.
[2] This visit was actually postponed until the following year. Keith visited the Mackenzies en route from Belfast. Their co-operation developed into a warm friendship.

autumn—about the end of August if that is convenient for you (for Mrs Mackenzie I ought to have said)—or any date between July and October . . .

I am wrong about tricuspid regurgitation—about the time it should appear in the venous tracing.

I read your contribution[3] in the *B.M.J.* last week : it was clear to me but I dare say to some unaccustomed to tracings it may appear difficult.

Just now I accept your dictum that the a.c. interval varies according to the delay at the aur-ventricular junction—but I should like to do some experiments to see what effect overloading of the right ventricle has on this interval.

There are lots of things I should like to discuss with you about Wenckebach's tracings but leave that over now . . .

April 30th, 1905.

You will let me examine that heart won't you ? I will try and get one of my men to microscope the auriculo-ventricular junction and compare with normal heart. I will deal with it gently so that anyone coming after us can verify and also re-investigate. Do put some formalin in the spirit to keep it in shape . . . I have all the hearts you sent me; they are in the Museum of the London Hospital and described in the M.S. Catalogue . . . Try and keep an evening for us—a dinner of two courses and as much talk afterwards as you like—after the Neurological visit . . .

In 1903, having moved to Bredgar in Kent, Keith persuaded a young Oxford student, Martin Flack, to join him at the 'London' for his clinical studies, and this began a most useful partnership, in particular into the study of the heart.[4] Mackenzie provided the hearts.

June 2nd, 1905.

My dear Mackenzie,

Specimens received safely. Two days ago I set about sections of the last and famous specimen. I am to work it out side by side with a heart which is approximately normal.

I have proved a dead failure as a tambour physiologist. I'm sure the cardio-pneumatic tracings given by most physiologists are simply pulmonary venous tracings but I and my students cannot obtain them—we only get pure arterial tracings from our respiratory tracts.

[3] 'Affections of the functions of conductivity', *B.M.J.* March 1905. Vol I, 519.
[4] 'The auriculo-ventricular bundle of the human heart'. *Lancet* 1906, 2, 359.

I have made up my mind to bring out at my own expense a small text book on the ' Morphology and Malformation of the Human Heart ' this autumn. Any material you come across will be most thankfully received.

I'll have sections of the heart ready for your inspection on June 26th . . .

Writing of his comparatively brief career as a mining doctor in malaria infested Siam, Keith relates, ' I did not neglect my patients, but my heart was in Anatomy '. Mackenzie was involved in humanity, with *Homo sapiens*, Keith with *Semnopithicus albocinerus*, a monkey of Siam. ' My old longing to seek for further proof of man's origin awoke within me . . . By Christmas, I made and recorded six dissections.'

In their search for truth, each of a different kind, these two minds were to come closer and closer.

September 20th, 1905.

My dear Mackenzie,

I waited and expected a regular ' blowing up ' from you. Do you know Huxley said of Kitchen Parker ' That he was in his work like a dog on his way home—distracted by every smell that turned up by the road-side.' The Pygmies turned up in early summer; I was put on a Commission to examine and report on the little beggars and wasted three months on them and haven't finished yet. I got into a scrape over ancient Egyptians and lost weeks on that; I went to Switzerland to an anatomical International Congress and had simply a ripping time and at odd times had a turn at my abnormal hearts and the Mackenzie specimens . . . I write the article on visceral ptosis—pathology and mechanism of the condition—for Clifford Allbutt's System (New Ed.) and that will take up some of my time. I have got fine tracings with your instrument and with a manometer of the pressure inside my stomach—under all conditions. Now remember me in this matter; tell me of literature you see and of facts you know and have found out.

Now as to Tonicity : I did as you asked and looked over the specimens in our museum :

(1) Cases in which there is rupture of the heart (always due to atheroma of coronaries I think) there is no dilation of the left ventricle.

(2) There are examples of marked dilation of the left ventricle with mitral stenosis but where there was no aortic disease.

(3) There are cases of so-called atrophied hearts—from old-standing cases of cancer of stomach, liver, etc. and in those who die of wasting diseases: in these cases the left ventricle after death is commonly in a condition of systole (contracted or is it tone?). It is well known that the heart contracts in size in cases of gastric cancer is it not? Is that tone?

Tonicity in the heart (I agree to it being a separate entity) cannot be very different from tonicity in muscle—Sherrington ought to know more about it than most people.

You will see I have too much on hand to take an active part in collaboration. But if you put questions to me and ask for observations on material I am your obedient servant and willing. I must get to know the microscopic structure of the normal heart from top to bottom as soon as I can.

My dear Mackenzie; you much over-estimate my work: I simply feel my way for an explanation of the structure of the heart—which is only to be found in a complete knowledge of its mechanism. We both want the same thing for different purposes, but you lead and I follow . . .

Mackenzie must have been happy to receive such a tribute from a man in Keith's position. At much the same time—September of 1905—he received another, from no less a person than Dr William Osler. Osler had taken up his appointment as Regius Professor of Medicine at Oxford the previous May and had quickly become involved in everything that was happening in the profession in this country. Accordingly, he went to Burnley to see Mackenzie, accompanied by Dr Gibson of Edinburgh, Mackenzie's old friend. Writing to Gibson on September 24th, Mackenzie betrayed a little of the feelings he had about this visit. Obviously, he had been extremely anxious to give Osler a good impression of his work; one suspects he may even have been a little nervous. When the visitors had gone he was dispirited: had he done himself credit? :

. . . I have an uneasy feeling that you and Osler may be asking one another ' What went we forth to see—a reed shaken with the vain imagination of an imperfect observer? ' The time was so brief and I did not sufficiently explain what I wanted to do that I felt that I did not sufficiently expound the doctrine of ventricular rhythm to convince you. However you will live to find out the vitality of that doctrine . . .

Whether he had expounded it sufficiently or not, he was firmly, entirely convinced—committed to the ' doctrine of the ventricular rhythm '. His misgivings about Osler's reactions cannot have lasted long, although it was fully a year later that he received a letter from Dr Joseph Pratt of Boston, Mass., in which Dr Pratt stated:

> I had a letter from Dr Osler yesterday. He spoke of the splendid work you have been able to do at Burnley without assistance and without a hospital.

Osler kept in touch with Mackenzie although their correspondence was limited to essentials. The following letter written by Mackenzie to Osler is dated 17th December, 1905:

Dear Dr Osler,

I must thank you for yr. 2 papers.[5] I want to do this not in the usual formal method of acknowledgement for the Student Life has touched me very deeply and I feel that I shd. write and tell you so. As a literary effort I read it with that pleasure which I read one of Charles Lamb's & I consider it is quite fit to rank with one of his best in its quaint humour and its pleasant pungency. There is also a peculiar transatlantic flavour which adds to its relish, and in no way detracts from the literary grace. But above all this it is so full of good things & so inspiring. I wish I had it given me when I left college. What little I have done has been done exactly on the lines you suggest, & had I followed yr. suggestions more fully, I wd. have been a more competent man. It was twelve years after my degree before I ever thought of ' dusting my brain ' by a visit to Vienna, and the stimulus derived from that visit has remained with me ever since.

I had a few weeks ago a visit from that precious soul John Thomson of Edinburgh and our one sad refrain was why did Osler not go to Edinburgh? I tell you honestly had you gone to Edinburgh I wd. have been there too in all probability. How fortunate your students have been in having such a teacher! I am almost ashamed to tell of the discouragement with which I was met when I began in a very humble way to try and think for myself, from my old teachers. I would like all the students to read regularly this most wonderful essay every six months after they have left college . . . I have stated my opinion that this essay will rank with the best of C. Lamb's as a *prophecy* & I am prepared to say that after you have been interred a decent time it will become an English (or American!) classic . . .

[5] Aequanimitas with other Addresses to Medical Students.

It is not difficult to discern that on this occasion Mackenzie wrote straight from his heart; he did not often reveal so much of himself. Nor is it difficult to see what it was in Osler's writings which called forth this spontaneous response: ' The student needs more time for quiet study,[6] fewer classes, fewer lectures, and above all, he needs the incubus of examinations lifted from his soul . . .' ' Medicine is a most difficult art to acquire. All the college can do is to teach the student principles, based on facts in science, and give him good methods of work. These simply start him in the right direction; they do not make him a good practitioner—that is his own affair ' . . . ' I would speak of the general practitioner's failure to realize first the need of a lifelong progressive personal training, and secondly, the danger lest in the stress of practice he sacrifice that most precious of all possessions, his mental independence ' . . . Here was a man after Mackenzie's own heart, and he retained all his life the highest regard for William Osler. When his own days were numbered he wrote this letter to Harvey Cushing, then preparing his massive biography:

3rd August, 1925.

Dear Dr Cushing,

One of the great charms of Sir William Osler was the kindly interest he took in obscure workers in any field of Medicine. In 1905, I think it was, when I was a general practitioner in a remote town in Lancashire he paid me a visit to see the work that I was doing. Although my work was not one in which he was directly interested yet his appreciation was in itself a very great encouragement. I am very glad that you are writing his life. I am certain that such an account will be not only of very deep interest to all the members of our profession but it will serve as a stimulus to every earnest student, and may encourage the distinguished members of our profession to give that friendly consideration and help which was such a distinctive character-istic of Osler's interesting personality . . .

It was a biography Mackenzie did not live to read. Although the lives of the two men touched only superficially, there was neverthe-less a very real bond between them.

As Harley Williams[7] wrote:

Osler was proud of what medicine had achieved, while Mackenzie was haunted by what medicine has still to learn.

[6] The Student Life—A Farewell Address to Canadian & American Medical Students.
[7] Williams, Harley. *Doctors differ*. London: Jonathan Cape. 1947.

In early 1900[8] colleagues in Edinburgh were trying to persuade Osler

> to be a candidate for the chair of Medicine there vacant by the death of Sir Granger Stewart—' Tis a great temptation and if it is offered me I may accept. . .

Had Osler come to Edinburgh instead of Oxford, the influence of Boerhaeve on medical teaching (leavened no doubt by innovations and stimulus from North America) would have come full cycle. More exciting still, would have been the spectacle of these two complementary, yet contrasting giants of Osler and Mackenzie walking the wards of Edinburgh Royal Infirmary!

Suave, cultured, displaying an easy charm, Osler with his brilliance, inspired awe, respect, even reverence. He was a philosopher. In a sense he was also a painter, adding colour on the wider canvas, of men, of medicine, of literature and the good life.

Not so Mackenzie, gruff but kindly he lacked these finer graces. A couthy Scot, his was a lonely furrow. Recognizing each other's different qualities, their respect was mutual. Their bond was clinical medicine.

[8] Cushing, H. *The life of Sir William Osler.* Oxford: Clarendon Press. 1925.

Chapter 23

KEITH AND THE BUNDLE OF HIS

You must look where it is not
As well as where it is

Proverb. Fuller's Gnomolagia 1732

One of the first letters to reach Mackenzie in the year 1906 was
from Arthur Keith. ' I read with enlightenment your article in the
B.M.J. on tonicity ', he wrote, adding somewhat reproachfully: ' it
was the only Xmas message you sent me . . .' It will be recalled from
the previous chapter that some discussion in tonicity had already
taken place between Keith and Mackenzie. It had also featured in
the correspondence between Mackenzie and Wenchebach. ' Tonicity
has captured my heart.' Wenckebach had written the previous
August (1905) when he was on holiday at Nunspeit. He continued :

> My first thought was—digitalis! I had planned since a long
> time to talk to Engelmann about this matter. As you know,
> digitalis arrests the heart ' in systole '. This arrest in systole is
> nonsense, it must be so at least; there is no tetanus in heart
> muscle, and a prolonged contraction is a sign of life, not of
> death. There are investigations made on this arrest in systole
> (I do not know who made the experiments and have no library
> here, but I see before me tracings so they are published in the
> *Archiv. für Experimental Pathologie und Pharmacologie,* the old
> one, not Hering's) . . . As I said, I wanted to speak to Engelmann
> on this thing. This is not an arrest in systole but a want of
> diastole by enormously exaggerated tonicity. By Jove, I believe
> this may be the solution of the eternal riddle of digitalis. Please
> work out your idea very very carefully and put down the thing
> with all your clinical experiences and observations! . . .

In his paper[1] Mackenzie touched only briefly on ' digitalis and the
function of tonicity '. He dealt first with the cause of dilation of
the heart, which he considered to be due to the depression in the
function of tonicity and not to any mechanical cause. The symptoms
of the depression of tonicity were listed, and Mackenzie acknowledged the help of Keith in explaining apparent anomalies in these

[1] *B.M.J.* 1905, ii, 1689.

symptoms, especially the 'regurgitation from the heart into the veins'. 'The view of Keith is so rational', wrote Mackenzie, 'and based upon such convincing evidence that I have no hesitation in accepting it.' He (Keith) says:

> How are the caval orifices closed during auricular systole? The current teaching is that they are closed by the contraction of muscular fibres which surround the termination of the great veins. The largest vein of all, the inferior vena cava, has no circular fibres surrounding its termination, those round the superior vena cava are weak and do not seem strong enough to act as a common sphincter. The coronary sinus, on the other hand, is covered by circular and longitudinal layers of muscle, and is provided with competent valves as well. Thus, the explanation usually given of the manner in which the venous orifices are closed breaks down under anatomical examination, and the true explanation is still too weak.

He (Keith) then enters into a minute study of the evolution of the structures that prevent regurgitation in primitive hearts, and finally shows that the caval orifices are closed during auricular systole by the contraction of bands of muscle fibres in the auricular wall specially adapted for this purpose.

> Just as I have been struck by the want of relationship between the size of the heart and the presence of regurgitant murmurs, so in the past I have been greatly puzzled by the seeming anomaly of an absence of the venous pulse in some cases of extreme engorgement of the right heart. On the other hand, I have seen large forcible waves of blood sent back into the veins during auricular systole with no perceptible increase in the size of the right heart. It might, therefore, seem that in the former case the muscle bands that close the caval orifices acted efficiently, while in the latter case the tonicity of these bands had become so depressed that they failed to close the orifices efficiently, and thus permitted regurgitant waves during the contraction of the auricle . . .

Passing to the cause of this depression of tonicity, Mackenzie suggested that in certain cases 'a poisoning of the function occurs', describing the effect on a heavy drinker of arsenic in beer, and instancing anaemia as a poisoning agent. He demonstrated with tracings the fact that the marked jugular pulse disappeared when the patient's anaemic condition was cured. On digitalis and the function of tonicity, Mackenzie had this to say :

> In cases of heart failure where there is dilation of the chambers the contraction of the heart takes place at a disadvantage, for presumably efficiency of contraction will depend on a certain normal distension of the chambers, and an overdistension or dilation will interfere with the efficiency of contraction. In such cases the digitalis, by restoring the tonicity, will reduce the cavity to a size more fitted for the effective accomplishment of its contraction. Herein, probably, lies part of the explanation of why it is that the heart's condition is improved with a depression of certain functions manifestly due to the digitalis.

Keith gave his comment on this paper in another letter to Mackenzie :

> Your article is a preliminary canter to make men think and get away from the personal mechanical view of the heart—it has served that purpose as far as I am concerned and there is no word for me to add or take away except that rupture of the heart in a very large percentage of cases is due to a more or less extensive thrombosis of a coronary artery, but that fact does not interfere with your argument . . . Every letter you open certain windows and ask me to gaze out into my ignorance and tell you what I see . . . I enclose you a tracing from a puzzling case of bradycardia in the hospital which I tried to work out. Man about sixty. Pulse 22 to the minute, jug. tracing from ext. jug. vein. Auricle seems to have a rhythm of its own—now and again the *ventricle and it* fit in. Now, father of jugular pulses, read me this riddle ! . . .

At this time Mackenzie was deeply interested in the auriculo-ventricular bundle, the so-called ' bundle of His ', and enlisted Keith's help in trying to discover the bundle in the human heart. On January 15th Keith wrote somewhat irascibly to Mackenzie :

> . . . I have been working at hearts at intervals between other things and have given up the search for His' bundle—having come to the conclusion that there is not and never was any such thing—at least not in the position described as His' bundle. If it were so, then allorhythmia might occur in all cases of mitral stenosis—for in that condition the area in which His' bundle is

situated is reduced to a filmy cicatricial scar . . . I send Hering's monograph[2] back with thanks . . .

On February 4th Keith wrote again:

> . . . What I took my pen in hand for was this: to tell you that I have just finished a short note to the *Lancet* saying that I have failed to find the bundle of His—has anyone found it? A leading article in the *Lancet*[3] a fortnight ago accepted it as a basis of Stokes-Adams—I say it will be well to verify its existence first . . . I have been working at the matter again and from an anatomical point of view I have completely failed to get *any* muscular connection between the auricles and ventricles: nay, if you ask me, I would say this: that nature has put itself to a great trouble to make certain that there will be *no muscular* connection between the auricular and ventricular parts of the heart . . .

Thus it will be seen that Keith was absolutely certain that the bundle of His did not exist, at least in the human heart. He had a preconceived idea that a muscular connection in this position was highly unlikely, also he was not in close contact with work being done on the continent. It is significant that it fell to Mackenzie to supply him with the published work of Tamara, Hering and later of Aschoff.

Keith's letter to the editors of the *Lancet* appeared in the correspondence columns of the issue dated 3rd March, 1906:

> . . . In July of last year Dr James Mackenzie of Burnley sent me the heart of a patient in whom there had been observed a marked disturbance of the auriculo-ventricular rhythm. He wished me to examine minutely the auriculo-ventricular bundle of His which is now regarded by many as the muscular path by which the auricular wave of contraction passes to the ventricle. In answer to a note asking for some details of this muscular bundle, of which I was at that time in total ignorance, Dr Mackenzie sent me a paper which had quite recently appeared, by Professor H. E. Hering of Prague . . .
>
> Professor Hering gives minute directions as to the situation of His' bundle . . . having studied rather minutely the arrange-

---

[2] Nachweis dass der His' sche Uebergangsbündel Vorhof und Kammer des Säugethhiereherzens functionell verbindet. *Archiv. für die Gesammte Physiologie*, Band cviii, 1905.

[3] Stokes-Adams disease due to a lesion of the auriculo-ventricular bundle of His. *Lancet* 1906, i, 238.

15

ment of the heart musculature for some year and searched for a definite muscular path between auricles and ventricles, I was surprised that I had missed such an extensive muscular connexion . . . I renewed my search in the human heart, for it is inconceivable that the cardiac impulse should cross the auriculo-ventricular junction by a pathway in man which is different from that of other mammals. With the naked eye I completely failed to find the bundle of His in fresh or in formalin-hardened hearts . . .

With the co-operation of Mr W. Chesterman[4] a series of vertical sections of the auriculo-ventricular part of the septum were made of three human hearts from the pars membranacea in front to the posterior base of the heart, but in not one of over 100 sections was any direct union between the auricular and ventricular musculature observed . . . The septal site in which the bundle of His is said to lie is the last part of all the auriculo-ventricular union in which an embryologist or comparative anatomist would expect to find a muscular connexion between auricle and ventricle . . .

Still the fact remains that His, Humblet, Erlanger and Hering found that the situation of the bundle of His was the only point in the mammalian heart which gave a definite disassociation of the auricular and ventricular rhythm when a limited section was made. What is the explanation? I have none to offer except to point out that the part of the auricular septum just behind the position of the bundle of His represents morphologically the junctional wall of the tortoise's heart and by that wall, as Gaskell[5] demonstrated long ago, the cardiac nerves reach the ventricle. Are, then, the effects obtained by section of the cardiac septa due to the division of a band of musculature?

There may be an error in my observation or in my technique. I simply draw attention to the fact that I have failed to find a muscular bundle in the position described by His and Hering and that before it is accepted as the anatomical basis of Stokes-Adams disease its constancy must be proved . . .

A postcard addressed to Mackenzie by Keith and dated 17th February 1906 read as follows:

> . . . I am very greatly indebted to you for sending me Tawara's account of the bundle—I found it almost in the position and condition he describes.

[4] Mr W. Chesterman was Keith's museum attendant.
[5] *Text-book of Physiology*, edited by E. A. Schafer.

The *Lancet* letter continues as follows:

> ... Some days after writing the part of this letter given above, Dr Mackenzie sent me a cutting from the *Munchener Medizinische Wochenschrift* of Sept. 26th, 1905, p. 1904, in which Dr L. Aschoff gave an account 'Ueber die Untersuchungen des Herrn Dr Tawara, die Brückenfasern betreffend und Demonstration der zugehörigen mikroskopischen Präparate'. From Aschoff's account I learned that the bundle of His arose from the musculature of the coronary sinus and passed forwards in the inter-auricular septum to the central fibrous body of the heart, on which it formed a plexus of fibres. From this plexus a distinct bundle breaks through the fibrous body into the interventricular septum and after a very short course divides, to be distributed as a subendocardial muscular plexus on the right and left sides of the interventricular septum. The auricular part of the bundle is made of very fine richly nucleated fibres and the fibres of the ventricular part belong to the Purkinje type of fibres. With this account to guide me I renewed my search with success ...
>
> An investigation into the development of the bundle of His and into its comparative anatomy will probably help us better to understand its nature. The fibrous tissue between the mitral and tricuspid valves, which is perforated by the bundle, is believed to be formed from the endocardial cushions; if this belief is rightly founded then the bundle of His would appear to be developed by the formation of a new muscular connexion between auricle and ventricle.

This was a complete *volte-face* on Keith's part; only a few short weeks previously he had been adamant that 'no muscular connexion' existed between the auricular and ventricular parts of the heart. It is greatly to his credit that with a quite delightful honesty he explained the process of his change of view. He describes the episode thus in his autobiography[6]:

> ... Late in 1905 Mackenzie asked me to look into the state of a muscular connection between auricles and ventricles—a connection spoken of at that time as the 'bundle of His' or as the a-v bundle. Hering, the physiologist in Prague, had just published an account of it. To guide me, Mackenzie sent me Hering's paper. In all my dissections of the human heart I had never come across the 'bundle of His'. Indeed, I was sceptical of its existence.

---

[6] *Autobiography of Sir Arthur Keith*, chapter 14, p. 253.

With Hering's description to guide me I again set to work, but failed to find it. By January my scepticism reached a measure that made me sit down and write a letter to the *Lancet* telling of my failure and my doubt as to the existence of such a connection. By the time the *Lancet* had returned a proof of this letter, Mackenzie had sent me a paper by Professor Aschoff, then of Marburg. Aschoff's account was based on a research carried out in his laboratory by Dr S. Tawara, a Japanese. Again applying myself to the dissections of fresh hearts, with Tawara's description and figures to guide me, I was able in heart after heart to verify the existence of Tawara's system. The auricles, I found, were joined to the ventricles by an elaborate system which, beginning in a root like structure in the auricular septum, ended as an arborescence in the ventricles. The ' bundle of His ' was but a small segment of the Tawara system. When I received my proof from the *Lancet*, I had to eat humble pie. To my original letter I added an account of the circumstances which had compelled me to renew my investigations and the success which had attended them. I was then in a position to examine the a-v system in Mackenzie's specimens and to report definite lesions of the bundle in several of them. With the discovery of the conducting system of Tawara, heart research entered a new epoch ...

Keith's letter to Mackenzie dated 11th March, 1906, adds a suitable footnote :

> . . . I am to send you tomorrow a heart with the bundle of His worked out in it—a well-developed specimen and I am sure when you see it you will say I must be a great duffer not to have seen it before—let alone question its existence . . .

In August of the same year (1906) Keith further redeemed the position with the publication in the *Lancet* of a paper written in co-operation with Martin Flack of the London Hospital[7] :

> . . . In a letter contributed to the *Lancet* one of us described the initial difficulty in finding and displaying the muscular bundle which unites the auricles and ventricles and which is now regarded as the sole pathway for the passage of the auricular wave of contraction to the ventricles. Since that letter was written we have examined over 130 human hearts and although

[7] The auricular-ventricular bundle of the human heart. Arthur Keith, M.D.Aberd., F.R.C.S. Eng. lecturer on Anatomy, London Hosp. Med. Coll., and Martin W. Flack, B.A.Oxon., London Hospital. *Lancet* 1906, i, 359.

we failed to find the bundle in some of these earlier specimens we are now confident that our failure was due to our ignorance of certain variations which may occur in its position and relationships. We are now convinced that it is an absolutely constant structure . . . much of our pathological material we owe to Dr J Mackenzie of Burnley; in two of the hearts sent by him, in which there was an irregularity in the auriculo-ventricular rhythm, we found the connecting muscular bundle largely replaced by fibrous tissue. In short, all the evidence that we have been able to collect from human and comparative anatomy, from embryology, physiology, and pathology, substantiates the theory that the muscular bundle, which perforates the central fibrous body of the heart and connects together its auricular and ventricular parts, is the sole path by which the auricular wave of contraction passes to, and is distributed within, the ventricles. We take this opportunity of clearly stating that although some of our observations are new, our work is in the main but a verification of the accurate and complete monograph published recently by Tawara,[8] a Japanese working in the laboratory of Professor Aschoff of Marburg . . .

With regard to the clinical importance of the bundle much has been published recently, especially in connexion with cases of Stokes-Adams disease. From the interpretations placed by Wenchebach and Mackenzie upon tracings obtained in such and similar cases it has been apparent that in most of them there exist irregularities between the auricular and ventricular rhythm. The important question is, what is the cause of such irregularity? W. His, Jnr., writing in 1899[9] upon a case of the disease, opined that a lesion of the auriculo-ventricular bundle might be the cause. Recently both Hering and Erlanger have entered much more fully into the subject. Both believe that lesion of the fibres of the bundle of His can in itself account for the syndrome of events in Stokes-Adams disease . . . Evidence has recently been forthcoming in support of the conclusion of Hering and Erlanger[10] . . . Whether, of course, a lesion of these fibres exists in every case of Stokes-Adams disease is still open to question. His, Junr., thinks that in some cases the same phenomena can be produced by lesions of the vagi. In any case

[8] S. Tawara, *Das Reizleitungssystem des Saugetierherzens*, 1906, p. 198. Jena: Gustav Fisher.
[9] W. His, Jun.: *Deutsches Archiv für Klinische Medicin*, Band, lxiv, p. 329.
[10] Report of Congress for Internal Medicine, Munich. *Semaine Medicale*, May 19th, 1906, p. 223.

sufficient has been written here to show the great importance clinically of the auriculo-ventricular bundle.

Various opinions had been expressed in the medical journals[11] on the question of a lesion of the bundle being the cause of Stokes-Adams disease. At the meeting of the Medical Society of London held on 12th February, 1906, Dr Alexander Morison ' discussed the various theories suggested to explain the symptoms, and expressed the view that a disorder of the auriculo-ventricular Bundles of His hardly explained all the facts.'

Dr A. R. Short of Bristol General Hospital reported a case of Stokes-Adam syndrome in the *Lancet*[12] :

> The necropsy showed no adequate cause of death. The fibrosis of the heart wall was but slight, the patches in the endocardium being quite superficial. The coronary arteries were quite free throughout from any trace of thrombosis or atheroma. Not having at that time realised the importance of the auriculo-ventricular band of His in these cases I unfortunately did not submit it to microscopical examination . . .

The German Congress of Internal Medicine, meeting at Munich on April 23rd–26th, 1906, also discussed the pathogenesis of Stokes-Adams disease. Professor Snyers of Liege, as reported in the *Lancet*[13] said :

> that the principal theories proposed in explanation of this condition were three in number. One of them regarded degeneration of the heart muscle as the cause of the symptoms; the second held that the medulla oblongata was at fault; while in the third place pathological changes in the coronary vessels or in the vessels of the medulla oblongata or of the vagus nerves were supposed to be the essential lesions. It must, however, be admitted that the *pulsus lentus permanens* was a symptom occurring in a variety of pathological conditions in which the vagus nerve was irritated. Stokes-Adams disease was therefore to be regarded not as a distinct disease in either an anatomical or a pathological sense but rather as a symptom.

Dr John Hay of Liverpool, a great friend and colleague of Mackenzie's, in conjunction with Dr S. A. Moore[14] contributed to

[11] Erlanger; *loc. cit.* Also *Journal of Experimenal Medicine*, vii, 676.
[12] *Lancet* 1906, i, 30.
[13] *Lancet* 1906, i, 1777 The pathogenesis of Stokes-Adams Disease.
[14] *Lancet* 1906, ii, 1271 Stokes-Adams disease and cardiac arrhythmia. John Hay, M.D., M.R.C.P. and Stuart A. Moore.

the *Lancet* a paper on 'Stokes-Adams disease and cardiac arrhythmia.' This appeared in November: on September 16th Hay had written to Mackenzie:

> ... I wonder what you think of the chart showing variations in the conductivity. I have sent up the MSS of this case in full to the *Lancet* and hope that they will publish it because it is the best thing in bradycardia that I have done. I made another chart later showing the relationship of the auricular frequency to the variations in conductivity and this rather damages the view that the vagus excitation is responsible for the variations in conductivity and simply throws us back onto some influence affecting auricular frequency ... What a splendid paper on the a-v bundle by Keith. Since then I have dissected a cow's heart and the bundle simply stares you in the face ...

Hay's paper described a case of bradycardia and cardiac arrhythmia, previously reported in the *Lancet* in January. Hay stated: 'The bradycardia was due to heartblock; the block was caused by depression of conductivity.' The patient has since died and an account was given of the course of the illness and points of interest discussed. Charts demonstrating the variations in conductivity and pulse frequency, and the variations in conductivity in relation to the frequency of the auricles and ventricles (referred to in Hay's letter) illustrated the paper, and credit must go to Mackenzie[15] who a year earlier had demonstrated the fact that 'simultaneous tracings of radial and jugular pulses afforded an exceedingly simple and readily demonstrable method' for observing conductivity in man, the method used by Hay[16] to obtain the degree of conductivity. The summary given by Hay and Moore to conclude the paper reads as follows:

> In this communication we have recorded a case of Stokes-Adam disease in its second stage—that is, in the stage of syncopal, apoplectiform, or epileptiform seizures. These seizures were of all grades of severity and tended to occur in groups with periods of comparative comfort intervening. The advent of seizures was usually indicated by definite prodromal symptoms. The necropsy revealed partial obliteration of the a.v. bundle; this would cause a persistent depression of conductivity. An analysis of numerous tracings revealed marked variations in conduc-

[15] Mackenzie, J.: 'New methods of studying affections of the heart', *B.M.J.* 1905, i, 519.
[16] *Lancet* 1906, ii, 273.

tivity, all grades from normal conduction to complete heart-block being in evidence at one or another time. This suggests influences in addition to the organic lesion. Such influences were probably nervous in character and affected conductivity either directly through the vagus or indirectly by altering the auricular frequency.

In the Annus Medicus of 1906,[17] the *Lancet* summed up the position to date with regard to Stokes-Adams disease:

> Few diseases offer such a field for the application of known physiological principles to pathological phenomena as that to which has been given the name of Stokes-Adams disease. The striking character of its symptoms—slow pulse with syncopal, apoplectiform, or epileptiform attacks and the associated phenomena of Cheyne-Stokes breathing, angina pectoris, and cardiac arrest—combine to give it a peculiar interest. Dr A. Keith and Mr M. W. Flack contributed an interesting article to our columns on the auriculo-ventricular bundle of the human heart (August 11th, p. 359).
>
> They minutely described the course and constitution of the bundle and discussed its development. Dr John Hay and Dr Stuart A. Moore have applied these physiological considerations to the pathology of Stokes-Adams disease. Dr Hay made an ingenious and careful comparison of the radial and jugular pulses and his results suggest this would cause a persistent depression of conductivity, all grades from normal conduction to complete heart block being in evidence at one or another time. The phenomenon of heartblock has long been known to physiologists, although their explanation that it arises as the consequence of interference with the normal conduction of the wave of contraction is more recent.

Mackenzie's part in the saga of the a-v bundle (bundle of His) in humans must be acknowledged. His persistence in keeping the matter before Keith—who by his own admission would have turned from it otherwise—and his complete cognizance of the turn of events in Europe, illustrate the compulsion of his search for truth, his conviction that Keith would, in fact, succeed in finding the bundle. Without Mackenzie's earlier researches, Hay could not have made his 'ingenious and careful comparison' of the radial and jugular pulses.

[17] Annus Medicus 1906, *Lancet* 1906, ii, p. 1783. Stokes-Adams disease.

Reference to the medical journals of the period reveals the extent to which Mackenzie's work was openly acknowledged and his views accepted by other clinicians. Professor J. Dreschfeld (Prof. of Medicine, Victoria University of Manchester) wrote thus:

> . . . the important researches[18] of James Mackenzie in this country and of Wenckebach, Kraus, His and Hering and others, based on the researches of Gaskell and Engelmann, have given us new views and a clearer understanding of some of the irregularities of the heart's action in disease . . .

Speaking of paroxysmal tachycardia, Dreschfeld continued:

> the true interpretation of which we are, by the help of Mackenzie's methods and his observations and those of others, beginning to understand . . .

Dr A. M. Gossage, Physician to out-patients at the Westminster Hospital, writing on some aspects of dilatation of the heart, was prolific in his references to Mackenzie's work[19]: ' Mackenzie has discovered '; ' Mackenzie has stated '; ' Mackenzie has noticed '; ' Mackenzie has pointed out '; ' Mackenzie has expressed the opinion ' are only some of the phrases used. Dr S. W. Curl, Physician to the Essex and Colchester Hospital, writes in the same vein[20]: ' Mackenzie thinks '; ' Mackenzie has shown.'

So it was a man of considerable reputation who visited London in May of 1906. He wrote to his brother Will on the 11th of the month: ' I find I am to have a very busy time of it, having appointments with all sorts of people, including one to negotiate the exploiting of my latest invention . . . If you have not sent on the tickets for the theatre keep them till I call on Monday . . . my lecture is fixed for Monday . . .' Mrs Mackenzie and Dorothy accompanied Mackenzie on this visit. His younger daughter, Jean, was now at boarding school in Skipton, an experience which she did not altogether enjoy. The Mackenzies were obviously expected to spend a considerable part of their visit with the Keiths, for Keith had written:

> But my dear fellow—two or three mornings won't suit me— you have to arrange to put in three hours a day with me—you will have your stool and your bench and you sit there and see if

[18] Dreschfeld, J.: A discussion on the diagnosis and treatment of degeneration of the heart apart from valvular disease. *B.M.J.* 1905, ii, 1013.
[19] *Lancet* 1906, ii, 1126, 'On some aspects of dilatation of the heart.' Dr A. M. Gossage.
[20] *Lancet* 1906, i, 1091. 'The Arterial Pulse: Its Physiology and Pathology.' Dr. Sydney Walter Curl.

the atmosphere of thirty years ago does not return. There are 24 hours in the 24, and three of them for work and eight for sleep leaves thirteen for play. I'm sure Mrs and Miss Mackenzie will think that a fair allowance and out of that you have to set aside some hours for us. Mrs Mackenzie must bring her music with her . . .

Sadly, no record remains to show how the Mackenzie family enjoyed this brief London interlude, the forerunner of the life they were to take up permanently the following year, but in his autobiography Sir Arthur Keith described his own visit to Burnley in June of 1906[21]

> . . . In a letter to Celia (Keith's wife) I describe that town as ' a valley of houses and tall chimneys with ranges of green hills rising up round it . . .' Mrs Mackenzie and her two young daughters made me feel at home. ' This is a very comfortable house to live in ', I tell Celia; . . . ' this morning I accompanied Mackenzie into the country to see heart cases; yesterday he assembled his more interesting patients in his surgery.' We played bridge in the evenings.
>
> The chief impression I carried away from Burnley was that of Mackenzie's personality. He was born in 1853 and was thus thirteen years my senior. That gave him an advantage over me. But his chief advantage lay in his bigness—bigness of head, bigness of body, and bigness of spirit. Big men have an unfair advantage over smaller men when they meet face to face to exchange ideas. Ray Lankester (1847–1929) was a big man; his presence always made me feel small. But whereas his personality rather repelled me, that of Mackenzie had an opposite effect; it attracted me mightily. He had that burning zeal which was the hall-mark of the covenanting Scots . . . He was not merely a ' heart man '; he observed and thought about disease in all its aspects. He was a born leader of men . . .

A wider circle of his colleagues was soon to feel the impact of Mackenzie's personality. He was preparing to attend the 74th Annual Meeting of the British Medical Association in Toronto.

[21] *An Autobiography.* Sir Arthur Keith. London. Watts.

Chapter 24

CANADA AND THE CAROTID

Or like stout Cortez when with eager eyes
He stared at the Pacific—and all his men
Look'd at each other with a wild surmise
Silent upon a peak in Darien

KEATS

Unknown to Mackenzie, the path to Canadian Medical circles was being prepared for him. In March, 1906, Osler was writing from Oxford to his friend Dr C. F. Martin in Montreal :

> . . . It would be a very nice thing if a committee was formed among the Montreal men to look after the British Medical Association visitors as they arrive by the steamers at Montreal. It would be an easy matter to show them some little hospitality and take them to the hospitals. A great many will return via New York, so that they will have only the one opportunity of seeing Montreal. If a committee were arranged, mention could be made of it in the *British Medical Journal* about July. James Mackenzie of Burnley, a bully Scot, goes out by the *Ionian* on August 9th. Keep an eye on him . . .

From Groningen, Wenckebach wrote to Mackenzie :

> . . . I don't doubt that you will be successful in Toronto and I hope and wish for you that you will have a jolly good time. Don't be too much impressed by big names and big men. There will be nobody in Toronto who understands this matter half so well as you do . . .

The 74th Annual Meeting of the British Medical Association opened in Toronto on August 21st 1906, under the presidency of Dr R. A. Reeve, Dean of the Medical Faculty of Toronto University. The honour of delivering the Address in Medicine fell to one of Wenckebach's ' big names ', Sir James Barr. At this time Barr was Senior Physician at Liverpool Royal Infirmary and President of the Liverpool Medical Institution. An acknowledged leader of the profession in the North of England, he must have been well-known to Mackenzie, whose reactions to his address are not recorded. The subject chosen by Barr was 'The circulation viewed from the periphery', and Dr Joseph Pratt, writing to Mackenzie from Boston the following October, did not mince his words on the matter :

> . . . I have just been reading with great interest the reprint of your study on the meaning and mechanism of visceral pain[1], which you kindly sent me. I could not help wishing that this had been the oration on medicine instead of Sir James Barr's with its distorted and false view of the circulation obtained from the peripheral standpoint. I am glad that you liked Boston. I know that all of us here were stimulated by your visit . . .

Subsequently Mackenzie had many contacts with this Boston doctor, who became a firm friend to him and his family.

Among the other 'big names' Mackenzie met in Toronto were Sir Victor Horsley, of University College Hospital, London, who read the Address in Surgery; Professor Aschoff of Freiburg (of whom Wenckebach had written somewhat contemptuously : 'I have great doubt about the capacities of Aschoff. You may cut 20 Aschoff's out of one Keith, and the remaining rest will still be Keith . . .'); Professor Erlanger of Wisconsin, Professor Adami of Montreal and Professor Clifford Allbutt of Cambridge. Personal friends attending the Meeting included Professor G. Sims Woodhead of Cambridge, Dr G. A. Gibson of Edinburgh and Dr W. Ewart (whose advice Mackenzie had sought regarding his proposed move to London).

Mackenzie spoke in the first discussion of the Section of Medicine on 21st August. The discussion, on blood pressure in relation to disease, was opened by Dr Percy M. Dawson of Baltimore, and the Lancet[2] reported tersely that :

> . . . Dr J. Mackenzie (Burnley) contributed some remarks illustrated by pulse tracings on some forms of heart failure consequent upon long-continued high arterial pressure. He referred to the five properties of heart muscle described by Gaskell, viz. tonicity, excitability, rhythmicity, contractibility and conductivity—and illustrated his contentions by reference to a series of cases of arrhythmia. He forcibly pointed out the value of the pulse indications in respect of treatment.

At the Section of Medicine meeting on August 23rd, Dr Aschoff spoke on The Pathological Basis of Irregularity and Failure of the

[1] The meaning and mechanism of visceral pain. B.M.J. 1906, 1449.
[2] Lancet 1906, ii, 729.

Heart Muscle, dealing mainly with the His' bundle and Dr Tawara's researches. He was followed by Mackenzie, who spoke on Heart Block. The *Lancet*[3] reported :

> . . . Dr J. Mackenzie (Burnley) said that for many years he had been awaiting an explanation of some of the phenomena of heart block and the researches of Dr Aschoff had supplied an anatomical basis for that explanation. It was to a Canadian, G. T. Romanes, that they were originally indebted for their present knowledge, for his experiments on the neuro-muscular structures of the medusa had started Gaskell on his researches. Dr Mackenzie illustrated by diagrams and tracings the mode of conduction of the contraction wave from auricle to ventricle to explain his contention that in arrhythmia the auricle pre-served its rhythm, while the ventricle failed to respond from time to time to the conduction waves reaching it from the auricle. He registered by a special polygraph the movements in the jugular vein, in the radial pulse and also in the apex beat. In some of his tracings he paid especial attention to the time be-tween the appearance of the auricular systole and the appear-ance of the carotid pulse—this he called the a-c interval, which included the time taken for the impulse to pass to the ventricle and the presphygmic interval (i.e. the time between ventricle systole and the opening of the semi-lunar valves). This interval he regarded as the most useful guide to the condition of the function of conductivity—of the conducting fibres from auricle to ventricle, since the presphygmic interval was fairly constant. Using this as a guide, he showed by means of a series of very interesting tracings various forms of arrhythmia and partial heart block and their dependence upon loss of the conductivity of the conducting fibres. He referred to the action of digitalis and pointed out that its action depended upon the character of the injury which the heart had sustained. He demonstrated some tracings showing the effect of digitalis in producing a mild form of heart block, depressing the conductivity of the conducting fibres. He was of the opinion that no advance would be made unless the various functions of heart muscle worked out by Gaskell were generally considered.

Speaking after Mackenzie, Professor Erlanger described his own investigations into the condition of heart block, stating that he had

[3]*Lancet* 1906, ii, 800.

been able ' to confirm on the mammal every stage of heart block obtained by Gaskell in his epoch-making experiments ', and giving the results of his own researches. The *Lancet*[4] report continued :

> . . . Dr Erlanger also referred to the association of cerebral symptoms with a stoppage of the ventricle in cases of Stokes-Adams disease and regarded the medulla as the probable seat of these changes. Considering cases of heart block in man, it might be stated that, as far as they knew, heart block in man was due to disease of the auriculo-ventricular bundle. In all cases of Stokes-Adams disease which had come to necropsy since the cause of heart block in mammals had been discovered a lesion in that bundle had been found. All grades of partial and complete block had been found in man. In regard to the cerebral symptoms which were preceded by the stoppage of the ventricles. Dr Erlanger was inclined to believe that either the brain or the heart might be the cause of the syncopal attacks . . .

Another speaker at this discussion was W. S. Morrow, Assistant Professor of Physiology at McGill University, who became notable because he hotly disputed several of Mackenzie's views. Morrow described two cases of arrhythmia which he had observed, and concluded his paper thus :

> . . . In the few minutes still left to me I want to draw the attention . . . to the fact that certain publications on the venous pulse in relation to arrhythmia are marred by a faulty interpretation of the normal waves. Mackenzie gives the name ' carotid wave ' to one which had little or nothing to do with the carotid. as is shown by the fact that it is little affected by clamping this artery at its point of origin from the aorta. He gives the name ' ventricular wave ' to one that has absolutely nothing to do with the ventricle in normal cases as is shown by the fact that it is quite as well seen when the ventricle is inhibited by vagus stimulation as when the ventricle is active.
>
> These misconceptions have led some of his followers to gross errors in the interpretation of venous pulse tracings . . . Mackenzie himself has not been entirely free from wrong practical deductions. His conception of the systolic wave as due to the carotid has made him misjudge the auriculo-ventricular interval in a case he reported in the *British Medical Journal* for March 5th, 1904, by assuming a presphygmic interval that does not exist

[4] *Lancet* 1906, ii, 800.

in the venous pulse. His conception of the wave which he calls ventricular—but which should be called the onflow wave or some equivalent term, as it is caused by the onflow of blood from the periphery—has led him to misinterpret a beautiful series of tracings of heart block in his book on the pulse (Figs. 320, 321, 322). It is perhaps not fair to dwell on this latter case, as he must long ago have discovered his slip. In fact, it was his own later teachings that enabled me to detect it.

I have not time here to make good these criticisms by formal proofs, but intend to discuss the causes of the normal waves in detail in a paper before the Physiological Section to-morrow. I mention the matter here in the hope that those interested will glance through the latter paper when published and judge between Dr Mackenzie and me in accordance with the evidence ...

At the Physiology Section meeting the following day Dr Morrow read his paper ' The various forms of the negative or physiological venous pulse.' He stated :

... James Mackenzie of Burnley, England has done more than any other man to diffuse the knowledge of the venous pulse throughout the English-speaking world. His most valuable work has been done from a clinical standpoint, and he has gained a world-wide reputation by the application of his knowledge of the venous pulse to the study of arrhythmia. I feel personally indebted to him for most of what I known about this aspect of the subject. At the same time I do not hesitate to differ from him on many points, to which I will refer as we proceed ...

Morrow traced the six events occurring to make up the ' so-called auricular venous pulse ', and detailed the points on which he differed from Mackenzie and Gibson. Beginning with the auricular wave (called the presystolic wave by Gerhardt) he agreed that both these terms were good. Wave 2, which Mackenzie called the carotid wave, appeared in the jugular pulse, and was ascribed by Mackenzie to the impact of the contiguous carotid artery, hence its name. Morrow continued :

... I do not deny that the neighbouring carotid artery may contribute somewhat to the causation of this wave ... I believe ... that the essential factor in the causation of wave 2 is to be found in a direct action of the ventricle on the auricle, and through the auricle on the veins. I protest against this wave being termed the 'carotid wave', and advocate rather Gerhardt's term 'systolic wave'. I would like to call it the 'ventricular wave' to indicate its origin, but as this term has been used in quite another sense confusion would result, so we must for the present call it the 'systolic wave' . . .

Morrow presented no argument about wave 3, the negative wave, in which he agreed auricular diastole was the preponderant factor. Wave 4, the ventricular wave of Mackenzie, Gibson and others, was one of the most constant waves in the venous pulse:

. . . There is another theory which calls for consideration simply because of the eminence of the men who have advanced it. I refer to Gibson and Mackenzie, who connect this wave with tricuspid regurgitation. Now this is one of the most constant waves in the venous pulse, and is practically universal in dogs and men. I have recorded it from my own neck when in excellent health and most of my audience could do the same from theirs . . . A consideration of Fig. 12 (tracing, dog under morphine and ether) will, I think, convince you that the action of the ventricle is quite unnecessary for the production of this wave, and that it is produced, as Gottwalt claimed, simply from the onflow of blood from the systemic arteries and capillaries which refills the veins just emptied by the auricle diastole . . . This tracing shows that this wave may be more distinct during inhibition of the ventricles than when they are active; I therefore maintain that the essential factor in its production is not the direct action of the ventricle but the onflow of blood from the periphery. The fact that in tricuspid incompetence this wave is obscured by the wave due to the regurgitation of blood from the ventricle, has nothing whatever to do with the interpretation of the normal condition of things.

I therefore protest against this wave being called the 'ventricular wave' by Mackenzie, Gibson and others. I also protest against its being called the 'first diastolic' wave, at it is necessary to distinguish it from wave 6 . . . it may be called the 'first onflow wave', and the other the 'second onflow wave' . . .

Wave 5, said Morrow, did not require prolonged discussion, and wave 6 was 'generally held to be due to the blood flowing into the veins from the periphery during the pause of the heart.' He continued:

. . . It will be noted that two principles have been used in naming the different waves. Some name them after their time relations, and others after their supposed cause. Both methods are widely used, and for the present one must recognize a wave by either of its names. A difficulty in using the names derived from the time relations is that the wave known as the 'first diastolic wave' is partly systolic in time. In a former paper I suggested that it might be called the 'prediastolic wave', although this name is scarcely elegant. In naming the waves after their supposed causation we are met by the difficulty that the name 'ventricular' has been applied by a few eminent writers to a wave that has nothing to do with the ventricle, so that if we use this name for the real ventricular wave confusion may result. This difficulty will only last so long as the term continues to be illogically applied to the onflow wave . . . In closing, I desire to express my indebtedness to professor Karl Hurthle of Breslau, who first drew my attention to the venous pulse, and under whose guidance I carried out my first experiments; to Professor Wesley Mills, my senior colleague at McGill who has assisted and encouraged me in many ways; and to Dr James Mackenzie of Burnley, England, who has taught me so many things, and who, as a fellow general practitioner, has been a constant stimulus to me for many years.

On his return to England, Mackenzie wrote to his friend Dr John Hay of Liverpool:

> . . . When in Toronto I found a physiologist Morrow on the war-path, but by a sweet reasonableness I modified his sting. He read a paper at the physiological section, saying that we were all wrong, and in the enclosed letter and papers you will be able to get an idea of his objections to our view. I want you to read them carefully, say on your journey to Burnley, and we will discuss the different points here. His paper will be appearing bye and bye in the *B.M.J.* and I want you to go for him for different reasons which I shall explain to you when you come to Burnley . . .

The letter from Morrow referred to by Mackenzie was one of several written to him after the Toronto meeting. It was dated September 10th, 1906:

Dear Dr Mackenzie,

I was very pleased, I might even say flattered, at receiving your letter. I am glad to have the opportunity of assuring you that I have for you and also your work the warmest admiration. If it seems presumption in me to criticise certain points in your work I want you to believe that I do not do so hastily but after many years of meditation and experiment. I can also assure you that my personal feelings towards you will not be affected by anything you find it necessary in the cause of truth to say of my arguments . . . It has been a great pleasure to me to meet you and talk with you and I hope some day to meet you again and have a better talk over things in which we are both so much interested . . .

The bulk of this letter was taken up with a further explanation of the points Morrow had raised in his paper before the Physiological Section. The paper was published in the *B.M.J.* in December of 1906, and in the issue of January 12th in 1907[5] Mackenzie replied:

. . . Dr Morrow, in discussing the interpretation of the venous pulse, condemns the interpretation I have given on certain waves obtained from the jugular pulse. As a good number of my papers have been published in the Journal, and as the subject is beginning to be studied in this country, and as many of those who have studied it have accepted my interpretations, I feel obliged to reply to some of Dr Morrow's statements . . . Dr Morrow . . . says I have called a wave a carotid wave when that wave has absolutely nothing to do with the carotid. I was interested to see how he would explain away the reasons I had given for my view, and was somewhat surprised to find that he simply ignored all my facts. I think it a pity that in discussing a scientific subject writers should shut their eyes to all the facts that tell against their argument. I had taken such pains and had gone into such detail to prove my statements, that I certainly thought that Dr Morrow would at least have given them some consideration. He, however, brushes them aside, and to prove me wrong merely gives a tracing where he has clamped the carotid artery and still found the carotid wave to persist. I had already asked Professor Cushny to investigate this subject, and he took tracings from a dog, with the artery and vein lying side by side, and obtained tracings with the carotid wave well marked. He then dissected the vein away from the carotid, and obtained a tracing of the jugular pulse with absolutely no sign of a carotid wave in the tracing. I can only conclude that in Dr Morrow's experi-

[5] *B.M.J.* 1907, i, 112.

ment he had neglected to consider the fact that there might be a recurrent pulsation in the carotid . . .

By watching other cases for years I was able to demonstrate that this wave, which I had called ventricular, increased in size until finally it occupied the whole period of ventricular systole. Every observer recognized the fact that when this wave had attained this size it was due to tricuspid regurgitation; and it was to emphasize the fact that there was a connexion between the small wave appearing at the end of ventricular systole and the wave during the whole of ventricular systole that I called the wave in its rudimental form the ventricular wave. I produced such evidence again in evidence of this fact that many people accepted my interpretation, but here again Dr Morrow simply ignores all the facts I have produced. That the wave may appear in a great many people in whom one can find no evidence of tricuspid regurgitation I readily admit, for the only requisite for its appearance is simply a sufficient engorgement of the right heart and veins with blood, and if the quantity from the periphery is sufficient, one does not need to assume, in the absence of other evidence, any addition back from the ventricle. It may be that I have unduly emphasized the importance of the regurgitant factor, but my reason for this was that previous observers had altogether failed to recognize the effect a slight or moderate tricuspid regurgitation would have upon the venous pulse.

In a personal letter to Mackenzie dated 30th January, 1907 Morrow commented:

> . . . I read your reply with interest and some of my friends are sympathizing with me for the drubbing I have got. I have by no means given up the struggle however, as I think it best to bring the fact as clearly before the profession as possible now that we have started. I have sent a reply to the Journal . . .

Dr Morrow's reply, despite this insistence that he had not given up the struggle, was decidedly defensive in tone:

> . . . In the *British Medical Journal* of January, 12th Dr Mackenzie has done me the honour of replying to my paper on the venous pulse. Dr Mackenzie and I seem to have come to an understanding as to the causation of the wave which he has called the ' ventricular ' and for which I propose the name of ' onflow wave.' We both agree that, as seen in people with

competent valves, it is produced by the blood flowing in from the extremities faster than the heart can receive it. We also agree, I think, that in disease of the tricuspid valves a wave due to regurgitation of blood from the right ventricle blends with this wave, and often completely overshadows it. Our difference is simply one of phraseology . . . I think I appreciate Dr Mackenzie's reasons for using the term ' ventricular ' but I am sure that some have been misled by it.

I consider the question of the ' carotid ' or systolic wave much less important. I am quite prepared to admit that the carotid artery may contribute to its formation. Dr Mackenzie misquotes me when he states that I said it had ' absolutely nothing ' to do with the carotid. I said it had ' little or nothing ' to do with the carotid . . . In my venous pulse paper I admitted that a receiver might be so placed as to get a venous pulse tracing along with the systolic wave from the carotid . . .

Dr Mackenzie finds fault with me for not discussing the arguments advanced in his book. I plead guilty . . .

The real difficulty in the way of an agreement on this (carotid) wave between Dr Mackenzie and me is that he uses preferably, if not exclusively, the internal jugular vein, and tries to include the carotid artery in his receiver. I try to get away from the carotid, and where possible use the external jugular in the hope of getting a pure venous tracing. The result is that there is a larger carotid element in his tracings than in mine . . . If we use Dr Mackenzie's term ' carotid wave ', for the internal jugular, we must call the same wave in the external jugular by the name of the subclavian or some other neighbouring artery. It seems to me that the use of the term ' systolic ' simplifies matters considerably.

Dr Morrow's sting had indeed been modified, and Mackenzie did not reply to this letter. In later years he came to have a very high regard for Morrow's work as is shown by this letter to Dr Martin of Montreal, dated February 1913, when Mackenzie was at the London Hospital :

> . . . This development (the starting of a cardiographic department) is gradually taking place in different parts of the world. Lewis has an excellent department at University College Hospital, and there is another excellent one, on the same lines, at the Rockefeller Institute. It struck me that it would be a great thing for you folks to start one in Montreal.

Morrow was here last week and I saw him several times and discussed cardiac matters with him. It seems a pity that when you have a man with such a profound knowledge of the subject in Montreal, probably the man who knows most about it in the whole of America, that you should not start a department on somewhat similar lines.

The galvanometer will soon be a necessity in every big hospital, but few men will be able to utilize it unless they have a preliminary training with polygraphic work, and Morrow's knowledge of this work is so very extensive that he is peculiarly adapted for directing such a department.

I trust you will forgive me for presuming to dictate upon the subject to you, but as you know, it is the missionary spirit within me desiring to spread the light! . . .

Mackenzie little knew how far his light would spread during the years that followed, though a glimmer of that knowledge touched him at the Toronto meeting. It proved a triumph for the 'obscure general practitioner of Burnley', and his almost incredulous delight and pride are reflected in the letter he wrote on his return to his brother Will:

Burnley, Sept. 18th, 1906.

Dear W.,

I have got back from my sojourn in America, and barring the time on the ocean, I have had nothing but extremely pleasant experiences.

I was entertained right royally wherever I went, for I found to my great surprise that I was known much better in America than I am here. The position I took too in the discussions forced me to the forefront, and I think I can say without vanity that all my remarks were distinctly original and presented new facts in a light that surprised the most intelligent of the audience. My new instrument too excited a good deal of interest and astonishment; I was however startled when I was informed that my name was down for LL.D.[6] from the University of Toronto, and the Dean explained to me that it was only left out because of the numbers of officials in connection with the association who had to be recognized. From a letter I received today from my host in Toronto there is some feeling engendered at my not receiving it, evidently wire-pulling had something to do with it.

[6] LL.D. Doctor of Laws.

At any rate, the fact that some of the folks thought me worthy and that they have stated that it will be given me next year shows that one is not altogether without honour, though for that matter I am not keen after these things. Another testimony of far more value to me was the recognition I received from all the best men in America. Famous men one after another sought an introduction to me, and all were most cordial in their recognition of my work. Perhaps the following incident will show you how helpful such recognition is. I was talking at a bookstall in the exhibition to a publisher telling him I wanted an American publisher for my next edition. He looked at the book and said that of course such a book would be published at the author's risk. I said that the publisher would have to publish it at his own risk and if it were a success he would pay me a royalty. He shook his head when there came up a celebrated Philadelphia physician named Kelly, who is the editor of the leading American Medical Journal. I told Kelly what we were discussing and he exclaimed ' If you publish that in America it will have a splendid sale'. The publisher thereupon said 'Dr Mackenzie, I'll agree to your terms '. I said I would not negotiate with another publisher till I had communicated with him, and he said he would come specially to Burnley to see me next spring.
I went afterwards to Boston and met a lot of smart young doctors and found the same ardent recognition amongst them and I had a very pleasant time.

I am glad of these expressions, because it has reassured me that I am doing the right thing to go to London. Some of my friends, as Woodhead, predict with confidence a very great success, but I do not build on that. I see my way to have an income of about £500 per an., and in addition I will put aside £1,000 to pay rent and taxes for three years. After that is spent and there is no prospect of success, then I'll leave London. In the meantime I shall have completed the work I have set myself to do and Dorothy will have had her training in drawing and music.

What I would like you to do or get your clerk to do is to keep your eye on a likely house somewhere near Harley Street, or in Welbeck Str., Devonshire Place, Weymouth St., etc. I believe certain house brokers keep lists of such places. Perhaps it is too soon yet to bother, but if a likely place offered it might be as well to be on the outlook. I am sort of pledged to stay here till the end of next year, but it is possible I may leave next June.

We have already got a smart young fellow here as my successor and he wants to be married in October of next year and will want this house.

There is just a possibility I may go to America again next year. A San Francisco physician informed me my name was down to give the 'Lane Lectures' in San Francisco. This is a series of lectures given in San Francisco each year by some 'eminent' man. The fee is two thousand dollars (over £400). I said if the offer came next year I would consider it. But that, like many of your briefs, is in the air, and may or may not come to fruition.

I am now in receipt of letters from all parts of the country which promise well for my earning a little in London . . .

The second stage of the Mackenzie saga was about to begin.

Chapter 25

LONDON AT LAST

O wherefore came ye forth,
in triumph from the north

THOS. B. MACAULEY

The last few months of 1906 were busy times travelling from Burnley and house hunting in London. By May 1907 Mackenzie was still in Burnley. Evidently apprehensive of his reception by colleagues in London, he was somewhat relieved, as he wrote to his brother:

Dear W.,

There has been formed a very exclusive association of Physicians of Great Britain and Ireland, limited to 200 Hospital Physicians and lecturers in clinical medicine. A few distinguished outsiders are to be elected and I was the first outsider proposed. I thought of refusing as Associations are a great bore . . .

Nonetheless, it was a great honour and also reflects great magnanimity on the part of leading physicians of his time. So much for the imaginary giants whom McNair Wilson depicted in the *Beloved Physician*. Evidently Mackenzie had arrived with an assurance and confidence which is borne out by his later remarks.

The first meeting is to be held in London and I have been asked if I'll open the leading discussion on the Heart. I replied that if the time was only ten minutes I would not do so, but they said I could take as long as I liked . . .

If he was lacking in confidence in his early years, any such misgivings had deserted him now!

It was November, 1907, when the family took leave of Burnley and set up their new home in 17 Bentinck Street W. This was a rented house, as Mackenzie would have much preferred Harley Street. But the future was still uncertain, and he was not disposed to undertake a long lease. The financial aids were considerable but with dire Scots caution he had budgeted for a period of three years during which, if failure resulted, and his capital had gone, his escape would be back to general practice in a small provincial town.

His total capital amounted, according to Mrs Mackenzie, to about £1700. Three months later a considerable proportion of this investment was to disappear when a big furnishing store called Waring and Gillow went bankrupt. This was a severe blow at a time when financial stringency was paramount and the future was so uncertain.

He was now trying to establish himself as a consultant, but during the first year the signs were anything but promising. In fact, his total income for the first year was only £114. The rent he was prepared to pay for his house was £300! However, leisure, a commodity which he found in so short supply before, was now put to good effect towards the completion of his second book entitled *Diseases of the Heart*.[1] During the next year his income had soared to £1000. When asked to explain this remarkable increase, he replied, ' It was my book '.

However, even with a reputation as a remarkable general practitioner with special interest in cardiology and the author of two text books he still lacked the *sine qua non* of consultant status with entrée to a teaching hospital.

Then one day in 1908 he met Sir James Purves Stewart (1869–1949) the neurologist, who urged Mackenzie to accept an appointment as Physician to the West London Hospital. Later, in 1909, on the invitation of Dr Frederick Price he was also invited to join the staff of the Mount Vernon Hospital in Hampstead.

St. Radegund's
Cambridge.
Sept. 24, 1909.

My Dear Mackenzie,

As a member, however ineffective, of the Mount Vernon Hospital staff I hear with pleasure that we are likely to become colleagues. I am sorry that English people won't get rid of the ' testimonial formality '. For me to write a testimonial for you is an absurdity, as you are the master of a subject—at any rate of a very considerable part of it—in which I have had the advantage of being for many years past, your pupil. I have said already in public, and am repeating it in the next forthcoming volume of my *System of Medicine* that since you published your work on the Pulse (and many subsequent papers) you have made all our ordinary text book knowledge of Heart Diseases seem antiquated. I, like many other physicians, had put aside the sphygmograph as not likely to add very much more to our knowledge, and had turned away to other methods. In your

---

[1] *Diseases of the Heart*. Oxford University Press, 1908 1st edition (1925 4th edition).

hands however—and especially by the use of your more newly invented instruments, a whole range of unexpected and invaluable records have been attained. I may add moreover that we owe to you not merely the records of your own work but the establishment of a far higher standard in cardio-graphical observation than had become customary before the publication of your researches.

Your election to the staff of the Mount Vernon Hospital would be for the very highest interests not of that institution only but also of the science of Medicine.

Pray make any use of this letter you see fit and believe me,

Always very sincerely,
Yours
Clifford Allbutt.

At the same time Dr Price persuaded Mackenzie to move into Harley Street (Magic Name) and offered him a consulting room in the house where he lived. Mackenzie gave up his house in Bentinck Street and moved out to Northwood in Middlesex. For the rent of the consulting room at 133 Harley Street he was to pay the modest sum of £100 per annum. It was a small unimposing room at the back on the ground floor. Unostentatious like his Burnley surroundings, it was, in its way, to acquire a status and reputation no less than 68 Bank Parade.

Despite his growing practice, Mackenzie had leisure time to take Jean on rambles through Hyde Park. The ravages of poliomyelitis on Dorothy had deprived him of this pleasure in Burnley. Patients were now beginning to flow in to his consulting rooms. Life was beautiful, but his joy was shortlived. Jean suddenly developed frontal sinusitis, a virulent infection which was complicated by meningitis, and tragedy of tragedies, she died on 7th April, 1909. How ironic, that a parent who gave so much to medicine should in his domestic life have had so little in return. For today, the first tragedy (Dorothy with poliomyelitis) could, with immunization, have been prevented, while Jean with antibiotics could most likely have been cured. Jean loved horses, and Mackenzie always grieved that financial hardship in those early London days had prevented him from providing her with some riding lessons in Hyde Park. Apart from this it is difficult to discern in his many letters and notes how much these family tragedies had hurt his inner self. If the wounds were deep, the scars were not visible. He would devote himself to his chosen field with even greater vigour.

PLATE 14. Golfing at Northwood.

Before that year was out, two further honours were bestowed on him, the Fellowship of the Royal College of Physicians (F.R.C.P. (London)) and even more illustrious, Fellowship of the Royal Society (F.R.S.London). Seldom, if ever, have such distinctions come so rapidly to such a humble, modest erstwhile general practitioner. The following year, 1910, the University of Aberdeen bestowed on him the honorary degree of Doctor of Laws (LL.D.).

Although he held appointments in two hospitals, both were too specialized for the proper exercise of his skill and ability. One was essentially concerned with diseases of the nervous system, the other with pulmonary tuberculosis. But he could wait.

Still by this time, around 1910/12, although his fees remained surprisingly modest, seldom varying from three guineas per consultation, so many of his clients were of the aristocracy that his diary in those days reads like an edition of Burke's Peerage.

It was already a far cry from 68 Bank Parade to 133 Harley Street.

Chapter 26

DR LINNELL REMEMBERS
(SOME RECOLLECTIONS OF SIR JAMES MACKENZIE BY DR J. W. LINNELL)

In political discussion heat
is in inverse proportion to knowledge

I am now eighty-two years of age—10 years older than he was when he died—but my memory for past events, though not for names is, I think, remarkably good. Or so I'm told.

I first met James Mackenzie in the autumn of 1909. He had only recently been elected to the staff of Mount Vernon Hospital for Diseases of the Chest, which was situated in Hampstead, and as an applicant for the post of Resident Medical Officer (the title was later changed to Medical Superintendent), it was my duty to call on all members of the staff at their consulting rooms. Our interview was brief, for he said that he had hardly found his feet yet. I may say that, at the time, I knew absolutely nothing of the man or his work —as did few medical men in London, whatever their rank and standing. Rather to my surprise, I got the job, and for the next two and a quarter years or so at the end of which time he left Mount Vernon to go on the staff of the London Hospital, I naturally saw a lot of him. The great majority of the 140 patients at Mount Vernon were suffering from pulmonary tuberculosis, but he was granted two or three small four bedded or six bedded rooms for his 12–15 patients which, he always held, were quite sufficient for him or any other clinical research worker.

As Senior Resident, I was responsible for the care of all the patients in the hospital in the absence of the Visiting Staff and of course, for Mackenzie's. So I soon saw that it was incumbent on me to acquaint myself with his work and his methods. He religiously visited his patients at least twice a week, often accompanied by Professor Cushny, the famous pharmacologist, a great personal friend of his, and a man whose special knowledge was, on many occasions, of the greatest value to him. I can still hear him say : ' I wouldna' say that, Jamie. Bide a wee ! Bide a wee !' when he thought James was putting forward some idea or theory too hastily. (I have, indeed, often won-

240

dered whether Cushny's help in those days has been sufficiently recognized; in any case, they were a great pair.)

But he had other helpers. Working for him five days a week and all day long were always two or three, or even more keen young disciples. The most constant of these was Henry Marris, a rich and, in appearance, casual happy-go-lucky fellow, the son of a big Sheffield industrialist. But in spite of his looks he was a first-class clinician (he had the 'Membership', I may say) and full of ideas, many of them most valuable. At first Mackenzie was suspicious of him, as he, with his upbringing and background, had cause to be of such a man; Public School, Cambridge, Barts. etc., a fine tennis-player and skier, and so on; but it wasn't long before he recognized his worth. And in the end he was able to help Mackenzie a lot, and in a rather curious way. Mackenzie, he told me, seemingly the wisest of men in worldly matter, was an absolute child when it came to finance and in consequence persisted in putting his money into all kinds of crack-pot ventures. One day he mournfully told Marris of his losses and the latter, a born financier, said: 'Hadn't you better let me take over the running of your finances? I do happen to know a lot about the game.' Mackenzie gratefully agreed.

Then there were the two Australians, Hume Turnbull and Silberberg, both destined to become leading cardiologists in their native city Melbourne: Schleiter, a pure German from Pittsburg, a very fine pianist; Harry Wiel, almost a genius as a musician and one of the most cultured men I've ever known; Oppenheimer from New York, another highly cultured Jew; Julian McClymonds from Lexington, Kentucky, whose southern type of humour appealed to Mackenzie, himself no humourist, mightily; and there were others; we were in as mixed a crowd as ever one would meet in a hospital anywhere in the world.

Meanwhile he was continually preaching his gospel to the visitors who came from all over the globe to learn from him—save, I would stress, from the British Isles and particularly from the London Teaching Hospitals—the idea of learning about hearts, or for that matter about anything else, from an ex-provincial G.P. couldn't be entertained for the moment by men who accounted themselves—and were at the time accounted—supreme in their different departments of Medicine. Not once nor twice was I asked by senior physicians on the staffs of London Teaching Hospitals (I happened to know quite a number of them personally in those days) 'What's this man Mackenzie doing?' for me to reply: 'Come and see! You'll be very interested, I feel sure—and welcome'. 'We had rather you tell us', they would say; and they never came. Even his colleagues on the staff of Mount Vernon—with one or two exceptions—never seemed to be particularly interested in his activities. Thomas Lewis he kept in touch with always, but he seldom came to Mount Vernon. Lewis was a man who was very kind to me on more than one occasion, but one I found very difficult to know. Wenckebach would come over from Holland from time to time—a great friend of Mackenzie's and a most charming and open-minded man. I remember his telling us how he got the quinine—always accounted his discovery par excellence. It seemed that one day he was consulted (about his heart) by a hard living and hard drinking Dutch sea captain who had spent much of his life in the East Indies. Wenckebach found that he had auricular fibrillation and naturally had it in his mind to order him digitalis, when the mariner said: 'I can stop the irregularity you've been telling me of.' 'How?' said Wenckebach. 'This way' replied the other, and with that, said Wenckebach, he poured into the palm of his left hand what seemed to him an immense amount of a powder which he produced from his pocket (which, later, he found to be quinine), sucked it into his mouth, picked up a glass of water to help him swallow it and—in a comparatively short time the heart rhythm was regular! So are discoveries made, laughed Wenckebach.

Osler, I know, had a great regard and admiration for him (Mackenzie), but I don't remember ever seeing him at Mount Vernon. (This was before the War.)

At the end of an afternoon round he, Cushny, his assistants and various visitors would adjourn to the Residents' Room for tea (I persuaded the Matron to buy for me the biggest tea-pot she could find), and for the next hour, often more, there would be a cut and thrust debate, primarily on cardiological problems, but also on world affairs. And in such a well-informed and international company we learnt more about both, I am persuaded, than we did in any other way.

There is no need for me to describe in detail his many discoveries and his revolutionary doctrines which changed the whole outlook on heart disease throughout the world—they have been written up by him, himself, and others, but a few points come to mind which may interest you. He was a philosopher first and last. One of his basic doctrines was that ' a heart is what a heart can do ', and this in spite of the presence of bruits, irregularities of rhythm etc. He even went to the length on one occasion of saying, as regards hearts, that at times he wondered whether *on the balance* the discovery of the stethoscope had not done as much harm as it had done good, when he thought of the hundreds and thousands of people all over the world who, by its use, had been unnecessarily condemned to lives of invalidism—as of course they had been and were being.

Again, as regards hypertension, at a time when all kinds of restrictions in diet and effort were being advised and all kinds of drug treatment advocated, he would say: 'If—as is unlikely—these various strict regimes are found to add a few months to the length of lives of patients—for they won't do more—is it worth their while submitting to them? Isn't it better for them to go on living their ordinary lives in ignorance and happiness? I think so.' One thing he used to say which is interesting, and this was that he never wanted to be remembered as the inventor of the polygraph. It was, he said, in his eyes essentially an instrument for research. Once an irregularity of rhythm, for instance, had been explained through its use, the G.P. should be in a position to understand its significance. (He, an old G.P., always had the interests of the G.P. in mind.)

What he'd have thought of say, the multiplicity of E.C.G.s esteemed necessary in the examination of all—or practically all— patients sent up to a Cardiac clinic today, I can't imagine.

It has to be realized that in those now far-off Mount Vernon days, the nature of auricular fibrillation was unknown except to a few (I nearly said 'a score') people at most; 'missed beats' might or might not be of serious import, and it was wise therefore to give a very guarded prognosis and advise a curtailment of effort in all cases; sinus irregularity called for prolonged rest; in cardiac failure with oedema *small* doses of digitalis were to be exhibited, to be withdrawn however, immediately the oedema disappeared; large doses in all cases were strictly forbidden (an old physician on the Senior Staff of the London Hospital taught his students that any dose of tincture of digitalis exceeding m3 was dangerous) and the prolonged exhibition of the drug was almost regarded as malpractice!

Then, as regards angina pectoris, patients were in practically all cases kept in bed for long periods and only gradually allowed to crawl about, their lives henceforward a burden. In this connection it may interest you to know that one of his stock questions to any newcomer was what he'd do in a case of angina, expecting of course to get the usual answer—and practically always getting it. Without boasting may I say that I shook him badly when, soon after we first met, he asked *me* what I would do. 'One thing I'd practically never do', I replied, 'would be to put the patient to bed—and then only under dire necessity. I'd tell him to carry on with his ordinary work, as far as he found possible, refraining, however from doing anything likely to bring on an attack of pain, e.g. running to catch a 'bus or train, and so on. Apart from aught else, such a regime would prevent his becoming utterly miserable, a nuisance not only to himself but to his family.' He stared hard at me and then said : ' Laddie, you've been reading my book.' ' I'm sorry, sir, but I didn't know that you'd written one ', I replied. ' Then who was it taught you that?' he asked. 'A physician on the staff of the " London "—now unfortunately dead —named Schorstein ', I told him. 'Ay, I'd have loved to meet that man, I've heard a lot about him ', he said, ' I thought I was the only man who taught that.' (He was ever a humble man at heart.) But, I assure you, there were few physicians like Schorstein; he died, by the way from diabetes when he was still in his forties.

Mackenzie was downright to the point of being rude at times, in his manner of teaching. I well remember his asking a bevy of well-known American physicians, who had come over for a visit, to listen to the heart of a fat, emphysematous type of patient. When they'd finished their examination, he asked each in turn, starting with the most famous, what he'd found. ' Waal, Dr Mackenzie ', said the first, ' all I can say is that the heart sounds seem to me very weak '—and with this opinion all his companions agreed. ' So that is your opinion ', said Mackenzie, ' the action of the heart is weak?' ' I guess so ', said the leader, and once again all his companions agreed with him (at that time a good deal of emphasis was put on the loudness of heart sounds). ' Well ', said Mackenzie, ' if you put a pillow or an air cushion over the chest of the healthiest man you know, wouldn't you expect to hear weak heart sounds?' ' Why certainly ', was the answer. ' Here gentlemen ', said Mackenzie, ' is a man who has a pillow of fat over his chest-wall and beneath it, an air cushion of emphysematous lung. Will any one of you raise his right hand above his head, in the ancient Scots manner, and swear in the presence of God and his Maker that, judging from the evidence so far put forward, there is anything whatever the matter with the heart? No? Then why in Heaven's name suggest that there is?'

' You say my heart isn't 100 per cent normal, Dr Mackenzie? What then in the way of exercise shall I be allowed to take when I go home?' a patient would ask. ' How old are you, man?' (or it might be ' woman ') would be the answer. ' Fifty five? Well, if you don't know, at that age, what you can do or can't do, you're a fool ! Neither I nor any other doctor can tell you. You alone know, or will know. If you become unduly short of breath or get pain in the chest on effort, you'll leave off doing what you happen to be doing at the time, and in the future, without anyone telling you. Otherwise, carry on living as normal a life as you can manage. Don't let anyone make an invalid out of you if you can possibly help it!'

It was a time when it was a cardinal belief throughout the profession that a healthy heart could be ' strained ' by overmuch exertion. In consequence, ' athlete's heart ', ' rowing man's heart ' and so on and so on was being diagnosed daily, especially by school doctors and doctors practising in University towns. Mackenzie, literally, stormed against such a belief. 'When I was in private practice in Burnley', he would say, ' working-class boys would leave school at 14 or earlier and start swinging heavy hammers in the works in the town all day and every day, and I never saw any harm come of it, so long as the heart was healthy.' And once, at any rate, he said to me: ' I've never been sure that boys with rheumatic heart disease ever did themselves any real harm either—they soon found they couldn't do such work and gave up.'

One well-known doctor at Cambridge who was continually diagnosing ' athlete's heart ', ' rowing man's heart ', etc. he used to make great fun of. ' I'm a Scot ', he'd say, ' and as fond o' the siller as any other Scot, but some years ago I wrote to this gentleman and offered him £5 for every case he'd send to me of a healthy heart which had been injured by over-exertion. I've kept my money so far.'

An interesting fact he divulged to us one day, I remember, and that was that in practically every case sent to him in which a runner or rower or the like had collapsed—genuinely collapsed—in the course of a race, he had discovered that there was another factor involved, usually an active infection, a mild attack of influenza etc.

He disliked the word ' neurasthenia ' exceedingly. ' I don't know what it is ', he'd say. And he never had much use for neurasthenics. Once, I remember, we had a soldier in one of his beds—this was, of course, before the First World War—who had persistent tachycardia, was markedly tremulous and sweated profusely; and he, for once, was completely foxed for a diagnosis and, in consequence, irritated to a most unusual degree. Looking back, I'm not sure that the man may not have been suffering from acute Graves' Disease without any obvious thyroid enlargement or eye signs—not uncommon, as you know, in men—but he didn't know this, nor did any of us; nor did anyone else, I think, in those days. Finally, an American—I think Schleiter (who, no doubt, had read of many cases in the American Civil War) suggested ' Soldier's Heart ', as a possible diagnosis. Mackenzie came down on him like a ton of bricks. ' Soldier's Heart? Soldier's Heart?' he almost snorted, ' and what's Soldier's Heart?' In a moment of inspiration, I think, I said boldly, ' Soldier's Heart is

Railway Spine.' Whereat he became more wrathful than ever. 'And what's Railway Spine. I'd like to know?' he asked scornfully. ' I don't know ', I replied, ' but this I do know; it's a reality.' (I hadn't been Casualty Officer at Poplar Hospital for Accidents for nothing.) He looked at me witheringly and moved on to the next bed.

This episode had a rather curious sequel. When I was with the 20th (Guards) Brigade in France in 1914–15, I wrote and told him that I was absolutely convinced that the so-called ' D.A.H.' was, in almost every case, ' Railway Spine.' But for once he didn't reply. Instead he and Thomas Lewis took the line that ' D.A.H.' was due to some unknown type of infection, and this time, I feel sure he went off the rails.

In spite of his dislike of the word ' neurasthenia ', he would warn his hearers of the fact that ' a cardiopath so easily becomes a neuropath ' and, as regards angina pectoris (about which he, alas, knew all there was to know at that time) he insisted that there were always two cardinal factors to be taken into consideration :

(1) The actual pathological state of the heart; and

(2) The nervous make-up of the patient.

A highly-sensitive man with angina, he would say, may suffer the torments of the damned and yet live far longer than the far-from sensitive man, say of the navvy class, who makes little of his aches and pains—a fact still, I feel sure, not sufficiently recognized by cardiologists. In spite of his ever-searching mind it never, seemingly, occurred to him that 'status anginosus' was due to coronary occlusion. Still, the marvel is that as a hard-working general practitioner in an industrial town he made the world-famous discoveries he did.

I'm proud to have taught him two things :

(1) he had an idea that all patients with pneumonia who developed auricular fibrillation died; I didn't believe it, and on my own initiative over a period of some months, visited a number of big Poor Law Hospitals and brought back to him radial pulse records (one couldn't take tracings from the neck in pneumonia) which, he agreed, proved my point.

(2) I taught him the value of applying one's own ear to the chest-wall and listening for highly pitched aortic diastolic bruits. It happened in this wise : one afternoon, accompanied by a bevy of famous American physicians, he found one of his assistants examining a man's heart. ' What's wrong with the heart?' asked Mackenzie. ' Well, it ought to be a case of aortic regurgitation ', said the assistant, ' but for the life of me, I can't hear

246

any diastolic murmur.' ' Maybe you, gentlemen ', he said to the Americans, ' will be able to find it ?' They listened with their (to us) strange-looking stethoscopes, but all drew blank. ' Let me listen with my old wooden stethoscope,' said Mackenzie, ' if it's there I'll find it.' But he too drew blank. 'And yet it's there, and quite easy to hear ', I said, ' if you apply an ear to the chest-wall.' Always willing to try anything, he did so and immediately said ' He's quite correct—I can hear it plainly.' When later he went on to the ' London ', there was always a small table-napkin, they tell me, placed on his table in the Out-Patients' Cardiac Department.

He was in politics the fiercest of Radicals: I was given to understand that his father—or maybe it was an uncle—was quite unjustly turned out of his farm by a Scottish nobleman, and he never forgot it. In any case, if anyone at tea started a political argument, he, the most scientifically-minded of men at his work, immediately got hot under the collar and would make the most unwarranted statements imaginable, accusing the Conservatives and the House of Lords of every conceivable wickedness. Cushny, meanwhile, would sit silent and unmoved like an old Sphinx, but in all probability enjoying it all immensely—he possessed a sardonic humour which was always a joy to me. After one of Mackenzie's best performances one afternoon, I walked with Cushny down to the tube station and in the course of conversation said to him : ' It's queer how Dr Mackenzie—when at work a cold scientist—throws scientific thinking to the winds when he touches politics.' ' James Mackenzie ', said Cushny, ' often says, and says rightly, that the general outlook in medicine is completely crystallized. His political outlook Linnell, became crystallized in the 70's !' (I concluded that Cushny was a Conservative.)

His work was his life; he was in other words a ' dedicated ' man. When he lay dead on his bed, John Parkinson and I found on his bedside table a new edition of Haliburton's physiology (I feel sure it was Haliburton's). Outside interests he had none—save golf. He was a widely educated man; but in what one today calls ' culture ' he had no interest. He loved old English and Scots ballads, especially the latter, as one would expect to be the case, and he used to say that nothing gave him more enjoyment than the singing of 'Caller Herrin' ' by the daughter of an old Northern Ireland friend of his, who was being trained for light opera in London—she had indeed a charming soprano voice and sang it delightfully.

His courage was superb. How many years he suffered from angina I forget, but I seem to remember it was 12 or more. In any case, I

247

never heard him once complain, and he went on playing golf, accompanied by tabs trinitrini, till the last year of his life, I believe. When I used to visit him in his last days, he would sometimes say: 'Go into the drawing room and talk to Lady Mackenzie: I'm going to have an attack—but not a word to her, mind ye!' I'd do as he said, and a few minutes later he'd stroll into the room smiling and to all appearances, free from any pain or anxiety.

As to religion, he never—or almost never—mentioned it in my hearing; I think he was a complete agnostic.

He died undoubtedly from an attack of coronary occlusion. John Parkinson and I, I learned later, were rung up early in the morning for one of us to go at once and see him. He left written instructions regarding the procedure that should be adopted on his decease, and among them was one which directed that his heart should be removed and sent up to St Andrews for pathological examination. This John Parkinson and I did, but for several years—I don't know why—we received no report on the findings. Finally John was, I believe, fully informed, and he, I know, would be only too willing to give you the report, if so desired, but I have little doubt but that you have already obtained it from the St Andrews Pathological Department. Neither John nor I attended the Cremation Service. We were both invited, I may say, by Lady and Miss Mackenzie, but since, in the directions I have mentioned, he expressed the wish that only members of the family should be present, we thought it our duty to obey him—regretfully.

And that's where I will end.

J.W.L.

Addendum

A few words regarding his attitude to the First World War;

He consistently refused to believe that there could be a war between Britain and Germany—' great, kindly Germany '. It was after all, the attitude generally adopted by the Radical wing of the Liberal Party then in power; so he, as I have said, a fierce Radical, could take no other. Me, who had good information through sources there is no need for me to describe, he would jeer at—in the friendliest fashion I hasten to say—' Laddie, you're daft, utterly daft! This war you keep havering about—there'll be no war!'

But the war came, and I crossed to France in August, 1914. Though I hadn't seen him for a considerable time, his was one of the early letters I received. ' You were right, laddie, and I was wrong ', he wrote. It was just like him!

248

A not inappropriate postscript to this addendum would be to add that John Linnell was awarded the Military Cross (M.C.) for distinguished bravery. He died in 1967.

Chapter 27

THE LONDON HOSPITAL

Veni, vidi, vici

Julius Caesar 37

The Honourable Sidney Holland, later Lord Knutsford, now enters into the story. The son of a Cabinet Minister, he had studied Law at Cambridge. Possessed of considerable wealth and with proved organizational ability, he became a member of the London Dock Board. The following story may be apocryphal, but it is worth recounting. He was invited to serve on the Board of the Poplar Hospital at a time when there were immense medical staffing difficulties. These he studied and remedied, it is said, by sacking the entire staff! Be that as it may, his ability in such matters attracted the attention of the Governors of the London Hospital on which he was invited to serve. This was a general teaching hospital with a great reputation. Knutsford was restless and dynamic, and his influence was to be writ large on the fortunes of the ' London ' at that time.

Knutsford had never met Mackenzie, but he had heard about him!

There is some confusion about the appointment of Mackenzie to this famous hospital and one of the reasons for this may lie in the complexities of its organization at that time. This is not without interest.

There were essentially two elements of administration; firstly the University, concerned with teaching and secondly the Hospital itself, concerned with patient care. Diagrammatically the academic component can be as shown in diagram on facing page.

The ' London ' as it was affectionately called, was the property of the Governors, a Governor being one who subscribed five guineas per year. A life Governorship cost 30 guineas. The system, Knutsford's biographer writes[1], had revealed the possibility of abuse ' since the body of Governors is responsible for professional staff appointments and a packed court of one-year subscribers could secure the appointments of individual candidates. The system had therefore been altered to prevent such abuse before Sydney (Lord Knutsford) took office ' (as Chairman).

[1] Memoirs of Sydney Holland Lord Knutsford by J. Gore.

THE LONDON HOSPITAL

University of London
|
London Hospital Medical College
|
College Board

The hospital administration was much more complex:

London hospital

Court of Governors

House Committee   Medical Council
(30 Life Governors)   (Consultants)
No Medical representation.

Medical   Surgical
Committee   Committee

The House Committee (entirely lay members) was concerned with finance and with the conduct of the hospital ' in every sphere of activity '. It met weekly and appointed its chairman each year. The entire medical and surgical staff had to be re-elected annually.

Sydney's attitude to the Honorary Medical Staff is worth noting here also.

> He regarded them with caution, though with a deal of sympathy and intense interest. Because he had foreseen the danger of allowing the medical staff too much say in matters of administration and policy, he was vigilant in preserving the overriding powers of the lay committee. With him, too, patients came first and all other interests were subordinate to theirs. If an operation were postponed after a patient had been prepared for it, he must know the reason why, and if it were not sufficient he struck and struck hard. In a famous instance, he once rocked the medical profession by forcing the resignation of a distinguished surgeon who had forsaken a patient on his operation list to attend a private case in the West End. His acute judgement of character sometimes caused him to differ from the recommendations of the Medical Council to his medical (house) staff, and there are instances of young men of unproved ability whose feet were set on the ladder by Sydney's choice of them against the verdict of the medical profession.

This then was the man who was to be such an influence in Mackenzie's time at the ' London.'

251

Years later in 1930 Lord Knutsford wrote to Lady Mackenzie about a photograph of Sir James.

> The picture has arrived. It is charming. Your daughter has made him too tidy. A lawnmower cannot go over a craggy mountain ! I loved the carelessness of his personal appearance.

The mountain was to prove a little too craggy for the senior consultant staff, but they had not bargained for the determination of the new Chairman. Mr Morris was secretary to the Hospital at that time.

94 Portland Place,
10/12/1910.

Dear Mr Morris,

The Medical Council have carefully considered Mr Sydney Holland's letter with reference to Dr James Mackenzie, and are in entire sympathy with it and will do all in their power to meet Mr Holland in this matter. *At the same time, the Council is most strongly of opinion that no exception should be made to the ordinary and customary method of election to the Staff of the London Hospital* and therefore Dr James Mackenzie can in no way be regarded as a member of the Staff. The Council feel that it is desirable that Dr James Mackenzie should be invited to become a Lecturer on Cardiac Research at the London Hospital Medical College. The Council also wishes to inform the House Committee that certain members of the Senior Medical Staff (Drs Kidd, F. J. Smith and Dawson) are willing to place a certain number of their own beds (limited to six) at the disposal of Dr Jas. Mack. for the purpose of Cardiac Research, for a period not exceeding three years, provided that the House Committee are willing to allow them to do so.

I remain,
Yours sincerely,
Theodore Thompson.

Among the physicians on the ' London ', then were Sir Bertrand Dawson, Robert Hutchison and Henry Head. But Mackenzie had no easy passage. Three weeks before Knutsford's letter telling him of his appointment the hounds were in full cry.

RE THE MEDICAL COLLEGE[2]

The secretary reported that the Board of Education had asked that a set of Standing Orders be drawn up for the Medical College which should embody the old Agreement between the Hospital and the College with certain new rules and conditions which it had been decided to incorporate. These had been submitted to the meeting of the Medical Council on Friday last and approved. The secretary read such part of these Standing Orders as were new, and these were approved and referred to the Quarterly court on 7th December. Such Standing Orders are herewith inserted.

STANDING ORDERS FOR THE MEDICAL COLLEGE AS TO MANAGEMENT

The Medical College shall be managed by a College Board in trust for the Governors of the Hospital.

The college Board shall consist of 12 members of whom 6 shall be elected by the House Committee from amongst its members; the Chairman of the House Committee for the time being, being always one of such six members; the remaining six shall be elected by the Medical Council (For Constitution of Medical Council. See clause 1, Page 4 of Indenture) from amongst its members.

The College Board where in their opinion it would be for the benefit of the college may elect to be members of the Board not more than 4 gentlemen, either *honoris causa* or for services rendered or to be rendered to the college etc.

As to lecturers

Members of the Staff, fully qualified, shall have the preference for any vacant lectureship, provided nevertheless that this law does not bind the Governors to appoint any lecturer who although he may be legally qualified, is not in other respects suited to the position.

Obviously, Lord Kuntsford had set the cat amongst the pigeons. New Standing Orders were rushed through Medical College in the previous few weeks and although the ranks of the Consultants had been breached, in technical terms, they were apparently determined to have no more of it. Preference for a vacant lectureship should go to an existing member of the staff (presumably Consultant Staff). In normal circumstances this would have precluded Mackenzie. Moreover, did the Minutes mean that while Mackenzie was legally qualified, he might in other respects be unsuited for the post? On the face of it, the 'London' Consultants were giving way, but only grudgingly.

[2] Minutes of the London Hospital, Nov. 28, 1910.

The battle now won, Knutsford hurried to welcome Mackenzie, albeit with a display of eagerness to say how unanimous it had been!

Kneesworth Hall,
Royston,
Herts.
22.12.10.

Dear Dr James Mackenzie,

I have been hoping to make your acquaintance. That will come in time. But I cannot let another day go by without extending to you a Chairman's hand of welcome to the London Hospital. You do us honour by joining us. You come by the unanimous wish and invitation of the Lay Committee, Staff and Teachers, and yet in so inviting you they are breaking every precedent of the last 140 years.

Mr Henry Fenwick, the Chairman of the Medical Council, has written most generously offering to defray the cost of any apparatus or fittings you need. True, you start with only 6 beds of your own, but all the Staff will give you the heart cases—I am happy because this means progress, and the biggest Hospital in England must never stand still and now your work and your methods will be still further spread abroad.

Thus began a fruitful association and friendship between two men, so alike in their unity of purpose and so different in background and upbringing. This warm affection lasted throughout their lives, as this later episode relates.

Kneesworth Hall,
Royston,
Herts.
25.4.21

Knutsford to J.M.
My dear Friend,

I had a call from Lord Devonport last week. He said he had been told that I was a friend of yours. 'Is, yes, thank God' 'Well then, can you ask Sir James to see me. I will gladly go to St Andrews to see him.'

I hesitated to ask you telling him you had given up seeing private patients but ...

Yours ever,
Knutsford.

MINUTES : RE DR JAMES MACKENZIE[3]

On Jan. 4, 1911, a letter was read from the Medical College stating that Dr James Mackenzie had been unanimously appointed lecturer in Cardiac Research at the College.

Dr R. (later Sir Alun) Rowlands became his first house physician (1911–12). The limitation of beds and lack of entry to the out-patients department irritated Mackenzie. Later, by arrangement, it was decided to allow every other cardiac case to come to him. Mackenzie was still dissatisfied.

It was nearly two years since Mackenzie had been appointed Lecturer in Cardiac Research at the Medical College. His private consultant work was rapidly increasing, but he was still no closer to the Promised Land—appointment to the Consultant Staff of the Associated Hospital—the London. Mackenzie was now anxious to withdraw, and here began the second chapter of the confused story of the London Hospital.

By the end of 1912, the restrictions of clinical access through limited allocation of beds seemed to have been becoming too much for Mackenzie and he began to look for a successor.

MINUTES RE THE CARDIAC DEPT.

The Secretary reported that he had heard that Dr (later Sir Thomas) Lewis had expressed his willingness to take up this appointment at this hospital as successor to Dr James Mackenzie on the following conditions:

(1) That he be a Member of Staff of the Hospital as Physician in charge of the Cardiographic Department.

(2) That he be a Member of the Medical Council.

(3) That he have six to eight beds allotted to him.

It will be noted that he was to be appointed *not* as Lecturer in Cardiac Research, but as Physician to the Hospital. If the Medical Committee were keen to have Lewis, The Medical Council were more reluctant. They added further conditions.

(1) That while holding the office of Physician of the Cardiographic Department, Dr Lewis should not hold any post in connection with any other Medical School.

(2) That Dr Lewis attend not less than three days a week, and give not less than 12 lectures or demonstrations a year.

and (3) That at the end of 7 years, the record of work and usefulness

---

[3] Minutes of the London Hospital, Jan. 4, 1911.

of the Cardiographic Department shall be considered by the Medical Council, who shall then advise as to the continuance of the Department.

Whether it was the evident paucity of beds, the lack of out-patient facilities or the evident caution and reluctance of the established hierarchy of consultants, Lewis wrote to Professor Wright to say he had been appointed Assistant Physician at University College Hospital. The Council 'learned with regret that its efforts to meet the requirements of Lewis had been of no avail.' This digression is not without importance historically, as it will be seen later that it was to Lewis that Mackenzie was to hand over the torch of cardiological research which was to shine so brightly in British medicine during the next twenty years.

Mackenzie was then reported to be willing to continue his position until a successor could be found. He would be willing to continue his work and indeed very much increase it, if the Committee could see their way to allow him 20 beds, an out-patient department on one afternoon a week and the laboratory in which to do his research work.

The Committee considered the offer a most generous one, and the Secretary was instructed to inform Dr Mackenzie that the Committee were giving it their most careful consideration and would communicate with him later.

If the senior consultants of the Medical Council were reluctant and uncertain of the viability of this venture in cardiology, Knutsford would seek advice elsewhere.

Dr John Linnell[4] resident Medical Officer (later Medical Superintendent) of Mount Vernon Hospital, first met Mackenzie when the latter was appointed to the staff in 1909 and was 85 when he wrote a vivid account of his association with him.

> One day, to my great surprise, I was invited to lunch at the London Hospital by the Chairman, Lord Knutsford, and the Secretary, Sir Henry Morris (I'm not quite sure whether they had these titles at the time). Wondering what was in the wind, I went, and after lunch the Chairman said to me: 'There was a reason, Linnell, for our asking you to lunch. It is this: we understand that you've worked under a heart specialist named James Mackenzie for a considerable time?' 'For over two years', I replied. 'Well we'd very much like to know not only what *your* opinion of him is, but what his reputation is in the

[4] Dr J. W. Linnell, 1878–1967.

medical world, speaking generally.' 'Outside Britain', I said, 'He is looked on by some of the best-known physicians in the world as the greatest heart specialist in the country and, many would say, in the world, at the present time. In Britain, his own country, he is a prophet without honour.' 'I can't believe he is as famous as you make out', said Lord Knutsford. 'You've only got to ask the leading physicians in America, Germany, France, our colonies, Japan and other countries for their personal opinions, sir, and you'll find I'm correct', I replied. 'This is very interesting to us, Linnell', he said, 'for strictly *entre nous*, we are being urged by certain people, whose names I won't mention, to put him on the staff of this hospital.'

I naturally said nothing to Dr Mackenzie, but one afternoon a few weeks later he took me aside and said: 'I've been asked if I'm willing to go on the staff of the "London." You're a "Londoner": what would you advise.' 'I find it a very difficult question to answer', I replied. 'I look on things like this: the "London" people will think they are conferring a very great honour on you, supposing you agree to go on their staff. In my opinion you will be conferring a great honour on the "London" You're world famous already, and further honours mean nothing to you. And there are other things to think of. Here you've got all the beds you need and in addition, you have a team of exceptionally able youngsters willing to work full-time for you. You won't be allowed to have them at the "London." Things will be very different, and this I can tell you in all sincerity as an old "Londoner" who knows the "London": you are not going to be happy there.'

He went there, as you know, and one evening shortly before he died he said to me: 'You told me I shouldn't be happy at the "London", Linnell. You were right—you were right!' No, I knew he wouldn't be, and when in 1920 I became one of the two Medical Registrars there (in those days there were two Medical and three Surgical Registrars only) on two occasions senior members of the staff showed their bitter hostility towards him by traducing his ability and reputation (probably purposely) in my presence, and I don't suppose I did myself any good by fiercely defending him. As I did, I'm glad to say.

Lord Knutsford was cultivating the ground very assiduously. This second battle on behalf of Mackenzie was two-fold :—
(1) To establish a new and separate Cardiac Department
and (2) To have Mackenzie appointed to the Staff (of Consultants).

Who better to advise him than Sir William Osler, the Regius Professor of Medicine at Oxford.

From the Regius Professor of Medicine, Oxford.

3rd January, 1913.

Dear Holland,

Yes, undoubtedly—good for the hospital, good for the patients, and good for the profession. It is not an entirely new departure for at the St Antoine in Paris, Vaquez has such a department. Mackenzie could get about him a group of young fellows. It would be particularly helpful to have the laboratory side well developed. In preventive medicine there is nothing more urgently needed than the study of the relation of these rheumatic affections (particularly in childhood) to heart disease. It is simply appalling the amount of damage done in an incipient way, and a special department for the study of the whole subject would be most helpful.

Sincerely yours,
W. OSLER.

Sydney Holland, the layman, was not to be deflected by the influence of Harley Street. He was now displaying his big guns!

Mr Holland, the Minutes[5] state, also read a letter from Sir Clifford Allbutt on the subject.

The Committee unanimously decided that a department of 20 beds under the care of Dr Mackenzie, with an out-patient department, should sit one day a week and that Dr Mackenzie should have the use of one of the hospital laboratories (Dr Bulloch's had been offered), and the Secretary was instructed to report this to the Medical Council asking the Council to consider the matter, which was urgent.

It was ratified by the Medical Council on 20th January, 1913, adding that Mackenzie's title should be ' Physician in Charge of the Department for Cardiac Research '. A compromise of 15 instead of 20 beds was proposed. Mackenzie, his aims achieved at last, was delighted. Later, he agreed to reduce the 15 to 12 beds, on the understanding that Sir Bernard Dawson and Dr Percy Kidd allowed him to see any heart cases he might wish to, in their beds. On July 14th, 1913, he was appointed a member of the Medical Council. He had now, indeed, arrived!

Proposals were then drawn up and approved for the appointment of First Assistant to Mackenzie in the Cardiac Department. He was also given a House Physician and Laboratory Technician. Dr (later

[5] Minutes. London Hospital, Jan. 6, 1913.

4 JAN 1913

3rd January, 1913.

Dear Holland,

Yes, undoubtedly - good for the hospital, good for the patients, and good for the profession. It is not an entirely new departure, for at the St. Antoine in Paris Vacuez has just such a department. Mackenzie could get about him a group of excellent young fellows. It would be particularly helpful to have the laboratory side well developed. In preventive medicine there is nothing more urgently needed that the study of the relation of those rheumatic affections (particularly in childhood) to heart disease. It is simply appalling the amount of damage done in an incipient way, and a special department for the study of the whole subject would be most helpful.

Sincerely yours,

W Osler

13. Norham Gardens.

Greetings for 1913

PLATE. 15. Letter from Osler to Knutsford.

Sir) John Parkinson was appointed First (Chief) Assistant on 3rd September, 1913.

Practical evidence of the intuitive wisdom of Knutsford and his support for Mackenzie was soon to follow.

GIFT TO HEART DEPARTMENT[6]

A letter was read which had been sent to Dr Mackenzie. A patient of his, Miss E. S. Paterson, an old lady of between 70 and 80 had made a promise that about £20,000 would be left by her to be invested, the income to be used for the investigation of problems connected with the heart's working and relief. The money was not to be spent for building purposes . . .

The committee heard of this letter with the greatest gratification and thanked Dr Mackenzie.

When the war came in August, 1914, the staff dispersed and the department was closed ' some of the officers of the Department had joined the Army. Dr Mackenzie himself had given up his Heart Beds for use of the wounded . . .' However, ' the Committee very thankfully accepted Sir James Mackenzie's most generous offer of his services on Tuesday afternoons in the Out-patient Department '.

Soon visitors from all over the world came to visit Mackenzie and talk about his work. He attended the department twice a week, and one always had the impression, says Parkinson, his First Assistant, that he expected more of us than we were physically or mentally able to give. It was not that he implied we were not working; he merely expected us, as indeed he expected other people, to work harder than they did in research. He expected, and in fact demanded more and more observations to that end, that is Medical Research. His interest in the establishment of a cardiac department was primarily as a research tool, rather than a clinical service.

' This must not be misconstrued ', added Parkinson. ' Mackenzie, while eager and anxious to further medical research, did not lose sight of the need for human sympathy. He was in fact a very human and humane man. There was nothing essentially wrong about his emphasis on research.'

In April, 1918, Mackenzie resigned his post as Physician to Cardiac Department of the Hospital as ' he was retiring from all medical work and going to live in Scotland '.

The following month, the Committee decided to appoint Sir James Mackenzie, M.D., F.R.S., a Consulting Physician of the Hospital, while

[6] Minutes of H.C. June 15, 1914.

the following week, Sir Bernard Dawson attended the Committee and spoke of the proposal to have a picture of Sir James Mackenzie painted and presented to the National Portrait Gallery. The long legged boy from Picstonhill had come a long way.

In 1919, the Cardiac Department, which eight years previously had set out in a determined manner to systematize and standardize diagnosis and treatment of heart affections as influenced by modern methods, still remained closed and without a director.

In 1920,[7] the appointment of Dr John Parkinson as assistant Physician to the Hospital and Physician in charge of the Cardiac Department marked its renaissance.

After long legal delays the Paterson Bequest amounting to some £11,000 became available, providing *inter alia*, a sum of £1200 towards building the Special Department, the first investigator to be Mackenzie (if he be then on the Staff). The Investigator was to be called ' the Paterson Medical Officer ', later ' Paterson Research Scholar '.

The list of incumbents provide a distinguished roll of British cardiologists

Parkinson, Dr John	1923–1924
Scott, Dr Kenneth	1925–1926
Bradford, Dr D. Ewen	1926–1928
Cookson, Dr S. Harold	1928–1930
Evans, Dr William	1930–1948[8]

In parallel with these events before the First World War, Einthoven[9] had in 1903 published his classic, ' Die galvanometrische Registrirung des manschlichen Elektrokardiogramms, zugleich eine Beurtheilung der Anwendung des Capillar-Elektrometers in der Physiologie '.[10] The adaption by him of the string galvanometer for the recording of electro-currents produced by the activity of the heart was to revolutionize cardiology. Compared to Mackenzie's clinical polygraph, this was an instrument of great precision, as a motor car is to a horse and cart.

It was said that Mackenzie resisted this new contraption. On the contrary, an E.C.G. was obtained in the early days of the Cardiac

---

[7] Evans, *London Hospital Gazette* 1931, 35, 14.
[8] After 1948, with the advent of the National Health Service the Paterson Bequest was merged with the general hospital endowments fund.
[9] Willem Einthoven, 1860–1927.
[10] *Archiv für die gesamte Physiologie des Menschen und der Tiere*, vol. 99, Bonn, 1903.

Department. As Parkinson says, if Mackenzie was not in favour of it he would not have bought it. Instead he used to send his private patients to Parkinson and was interested in the interpretation and value of the E.C.G. machine, but not deeply. In other words, he knew that it added considerable information beyond that of his own techniques which he had perfected in Burnley with the use of a polygraph, but he was not prepared to start anew and learn all over again that which would become a new chapter in his life.

He, however, resisted X-rays in the diagnosis of heart disease, despite the fact that Parkinson was very keen on developing the technique. Mackenzie thought it would be of very little help even in the determination of cardiac enlargement. Mackenzie admitted the value of the E.C.G. but he was afraid, ' as were all of us at that time ', says Parkinson, that doctors would get too fond of instruments and allow their clinical senses to atrophy. Dependence on instruments would replace the powers of questioning and observation.

Nonetheless, this was an important milestone for Mackenzie. In a sense it was his watershed, on one side of which lay the past with the limitation of diagnostic aids and the need for developing to the highest degree, one's clinical sense, and on the other side a future bringing new and complicated instruments which lent precision to diagnosis. If that vista did not include heart transplantation and the complexities of immuno-suppressive drugs, it certainly looked forbidding to the general practitioner of Burnley. Lewis said that all Mackenzie's fundamental work ended with Burnley but this obviously was not true although the pace slowed and his diagnostic methods in London were rapidly being overtaken by events.

Despite these difficulties in trying to establish a firm foothold at the London Hospital, recognition of his worth was coming in other ways. He was invited to give the Oliver Sharpey Lectures[11] before the Royal College of Physicians of London in 1911. Later, in that year he delivered the Schorstein Lectures on Auricular Fibrillation at the London Hospital. In March 1915, he was elected a Fellow of the Royal Society (F.R.S.). If scientific recognition in being invited to join the ranks of such distinguished past and present company as Newton, Davy, Huxley and Sherrington, was not enough, then the bestowal of knighthood upon Dr James Mackenzie in June of that same year was surely the acme of achievement and honour.

Recognition of a more intimate and personal kind was to result from a chance meeting with an old fellow student, Professor Matthew

[11] *British Medical Journal* 1911, i, 793, 858; *Lancet* 1911, i, 919, 986; *Abst. Medical Times* London, 1911, XXXIX, 278.

18

Hay[12] of Aberdeen, with whom he was to renew an old and warm friendship.

> Marischal College,
> Aberdeen.
> 30, May, 1914.

My dear Mackenzie,

I don't think I ever felt for the moment so put out as when I met you in Oxford on Thursday and failed to recall your surname. It looked as if I had almost forgotten one of the most valued of my old fellow-students whose work is now known throughout the whole medical world. I am not often guilty of such lapses of memory, but somehow for the moment the thing escaped me, and I was not helped by feeling the position very keenly. As a matter of fact, there is no-one of my own year whose career I have followed with keener interest or greater appreciation, and have directed many of my medical friends to a perusal of your papers. And several times have I, within my own mind, been wondering when you would come to your rightful position in a professorial chair in some important seat of learning. But memory plays me a curious trick once in a while, specially at the fag end of a very busy session such as I have had this summer.

I am sorry that as I had to return here on Thursday evening I had not another opportunity of seeing you, though I went specially to the Medicine Section to look for you.

I would like very much if you could spare the time when you are in the north to come and see me and spend a few days under my roof. There is no-one whom I should more greatly welcome.

> With kindest regards,
> MATTHEW HAY.

From Matthew Hay, the most distinguished Graduate of Mackenzie's year, and reputedly the most brilliant Medical Officer of Health of this century, this indeed, was no mean tribute.

[12] Professor Matthew Hay, 1855-1932, Chair of Public Health, University of Aberdeen.

Chapter 28

MOUNT VERNON HOSPITAL AND THE
SOLDIER'S HEART

Lo now, what hearts have men !

ALFRED, LORD TENNYSON

Dr John Parkinson, First Assistant to Mackenzie at the London, had
joined the R.A.M.C. and was at the front somewhere in France.

133 Harley Street,
3 December, 1915.

My dear Parkinson,

I was very glad to hear from you and to learn that you are
alive and well . . .

I went down to the London Hospital yesterday for the first
time since the War broke out . . . I asked (Morris) whether he
had heard anything of that legacy of £11,000 which Miss
Paterson promised us. The good lady has died but she did not
manage to alter her will in our favour, so the Department is
again on the rocks.

The nature of Soldier's Heart, at all events of those invalided
home—is coming out very clearly. We have examined over 300
cases and we find that over 90% have got no cardiac disease
although there are symptoms such as dilatation and murmurs,
but I find that these are simply part of the general condition of
weakness affecting chiefly the vaso-motor system and the brain.
. . . I therefore drew up a memorandum and submitted it to
Clifford Allbutt and Osler with the suggestion that as over 90%
of the so-called heart cases were of this description, they should
be treated upon different lines. It would be advisable to get a
hospital especially devoted to this purpose. Both of them are
strongly supporting me and the War Office is being approached
officially by the Insurance Committee to ask them to adopt my
suggestion. If this is done, I shall make a request for you to be
sent home to help me . . .

Mackenzie was not too hopeful about the outcome of either of
these proposals, but he was able to write Parkinson again . . .

133 Harley Street,
13 Jan., 1916.

My Dear Parkinson,

I got Osler and Clifford Allbutt to accompany me to Keogh and we had an interview with regard to the Heart Hospital idea, and after a considerable amount of discussion, it was granted to us. We are to have 400 beds at Mount Vernon Hospital at Hampstead . . .

I was asked to take charge of the whole affair but . . . I thought it was better that younger men should have the opportunity. So four men are going to be given charge, each one to have 100 beds and under each consultant, two assistants. Osler, Clifford Allbutt and I will act as consultants and will advise in regard to the lines of treatment, although a free hand will be given to the four physicians.

Lewis will take charge of 100 and probably keep his eye on the laboratory: Meakins will have charge of another 100, and probably Hume of Newcastle will have charge of the third 100. If you care you will have charge of the fourth 100 and also the electrocardiographic department . . .

If you know of any man such as Batchelor[1] who would like to work as your assistant you might let me know and I will try and get him released as well.

Yours very sincerely,
J. Mackenzie.

Had Mackenzie aspired to personal ambition, he would have undertaken sole charge of the unit, but this he declined. The Hospital Unit, started in 1917, was arranged in three instead of four ' firms ',

Drs Lewis and Cotton (Assistant and later Chief Assistant)
Dr Meakins and Dr   ?
Drs Parkinson and Allan Drury (Physiologist)

Dr Thomas Cotton, a Canadian, arrived in Europe to do postgraduate study. Here his Dean introduced him to Osler, who had always been his idol in medicine. Like others all over the world, he revered the great man and his acute assessment given with North American candour adds piquancy to our understanding of these men, at that time and in relation to each other. In a personal interview with Cotton, he said :

[1] Dr H. W. Batchelor, Mackenzie's House Physician at the ' London ', was later killed in action.

Osler and Allbutt could talk the same language, but not Osler and Mackenzie. Mackenzie was not a great physician in the clinical sense. He was a pioneer in the rough-shod manner. Osler was a classicist. At the London his colleagues, consultants, (and competitors), did not think highly of him, particularly since he came from general practice. Maybe they did, as they asserted, know the difference between innocent murmurs and those which were not. They held that it was only because it was put over in such a way by Mackenzie that it mattered to the rest of the clinical world ...

Much of what Lewis has done has been undone, as with Mackenzie. Someone wrote about medicine that anything which has lasted for 25 years in medicine is pretty good.

This could be said of both Mackenzie and Lewis. Obviously Dr Cotton did not rate Mackenzie very highly.

Parkinson writes,[2]

... these (Osler, Allbutt and Mackenzie) were great men, and how different they were. Allbutt was dignified and delightful, but never condescending ... Osler arrived before we breakfasted and added some joviality to the gathering there and information in the wards afterwards. Mackenzie took it more seriously and entered into each phase of projected research ...

If Dr Cotton was forthright in his views about Mackenzie, he was even more candid about Lewis!

Long before the establishment of the special unit at Mount Vernon Hospital, Mackenzie was writing about 'The Recruit's Heart'.[3] The functional efficiency of the heart can best be assessed from a knowledge of the amount of exertion that can be undertaken without distress. Emphasizing the importance of the life history of actual patients, he goes on to say it is too often assumed that the presence of a murmur or irregularity must of necessity indicate heart failure or liability to failure.[4]

As if to anticipate the conclusions of research and treatment in the new Hospital Unit about to be established, he now directed his attention to 'the Soldier's Heart'. The first accounts given of the 'Soldier's Heart' were those during and after the American Civil War. During the First World War Mackenzie had examined over 400 cases certified and treated as heart affections, and in his view

[2] British Heart Journal 1954, XV, January.
[3] British Medical Journal 1915, ii, 563; ibid. 1915, ii, 807.
[4] British Medical Journal 1916, i, 117.

the majority of these were not in fact heart disease at all. These heart manifestations were more in the nature of indications of general illness. (Incidentally this work was done with the assistance of Dr McNair Wilson at the instigation of the Medical Research Council.)

In 1920, in giving a lecture at the Institute in St Andrews on symptomatology,[5] he was to return to this theme. The condition went under a variety of names, Da Costa's Syndrome, the Soldier's Heart, the Irritable Heart of Soldiers, Disordered Action of the Heart (or D.A.H.), Effort Syndrome and Neuro-Muscular Asthenia. This is not peculiar to soldiers, he said, but of frequent occurrence in civil life.

The main symptoms of which the soldiers complained were shortness of breath, exhaustion or palpitation coming on in response to effort or when at rest. Occasionally there was slight enlargement of the heart. He held that while overexcitability of the heart is brought about mainly by a disturbance affecting its nervous mechanism, in all probability the same injurious influence affects the myocardium itself so the efficiency of the heart may be impaired.

> While the foregoing are essentially the features of D.A.H., if the patient be more carefully ' scrutinised ' other symptoms will be found. His face is often lined and drawn; he is often nervous in manner and occasionally he shows fine tremors in his hands and fingers. Inquiry reveals a varying degree of mental disturbance, apathy, disinclination for exertion, mental depression and irritability of temper . . . In many cases other phenomena are detected, but these are sufficient to show that in nearly all these cases there is a mental side to the ill health as well as cardiac . . .

Mackenzie went on to emphasize a favourite theme of the ' law of associated phenomena ', whereby in most, if not all diseases, other systems or organs were invariably involved. In short, this was a plea for a general or holistic approach to the patients, and Mackenzie saw the imminent and inherent dangers in the trends towards specialization in one organ or system of the body. The general practitioner was speaking.

[5] *British Medical Journal* 1920, i, Apr. 10 & 17.

Chapter 29

ENVY AND MALICE

All fame is dangerous : good bringeth
envy, bad shame

Gnomologia, 1932

Sir John Parkinson referred to a rumour about Mackenzie which was prevalent among certain colleagues in London during the First World War and which unfortunately has lasted to the present day. This was to the effect that Mackenzie was party to providing medical certificates on the basis of cardiac irregularity and disease to enable men to avoid military service. Sir John strongly repudiated this allegation. Parkinson knew about the rumours then, but they were such that there was no evidence to prove, and therefore no reason why it should be disproved. He reiterated 'I just didn't believe it, as Mackenzie was such a transparently honest man, but like all successful men, he readily created enmity. His colleagues and consultants in London were extremely jealous of his success—naturally so because he was taking not only practice from them but prestige and much of the limelight. It is so easy to make up such stories; it is quite another matter to contradict them and know how this can be done without creating undue publicity.' Indeed in 1917, there is written evidence that Mackenzie refused to assist a relative who sought to have his case presented sympathetically to the recruiting authorities.

It is obvious that Mackenzie, despite all the honours which then came his way, had a difficult furrow to plough during his sojourn in London.

No biography has been written about Sir Thomas Lewis (1881–1945). Few letters[1] exist unfortunately to tell of the long and fruitful association between Lewis and Mackenzie. Literary license may permit the author to peep behind the veil which surrounds the enigmatic personality of this Welshman, and the relationship between these two great men.

[1] Two from Lewis to Mackenzie and a reply from Mackenzie dated 1924 and in present possession of the author. One from Mackenzie to Lewis was presented to the Library of the New York Academy of Medicine by Mrs William P. St. Lawrence and reprinted by permission of the New York Academy of Medicine, from *Academy Bookman* 1961, 14, 6. See also *American Heart Journal* 1961, 62, 716.

Twenty-eight years younger than Mackenzie, Lewis was born in 1881, the son of a wealthy and influential mining engineer of Cardiff. He had a sheltered background, being tutored at home before attending Clifton College. His was a distinguished career at University College, Cardiff. In 1910, he became the first Beit Memorial Fellow which started him on the long series of investigations in experimental and clinical research which made him famous. As stated earlier, he became consulting physician to the University College Hospital in London, gave up private practice in 1916 to devote his whole time as a research physician on the Staff of the Medical Research Council, with a ward and laboratories placed at his disposal.

Although with the aid of the new electrocardiographic studies, much of his important work centred on auricular fibrillation and flutter, his researches were protean in nature and extended to Raynaud's Disease and acrocyanosis, intermittent claudication, angina pectoris and the phenomenon of pain. That he should produce 230 scientific papers, and twelve monographs and textbooks, is testimony to his output and scientific worth.

Mackenzie always praised and complemented Lewis on his work, but it becomes obvious, although the gap in their ages placed them more in the category of father and son, or master and student, there existed on Lewis's part a love-hate relationship which is perhaps understandable in the context of medicine at that time. Moreover there was for a time an unhappy estrangement between them, the cause of which cannot be discovered. One suggestion was that Lewis, editor of *Heart* journal, refused to accept a certain contribution from Mackenzie while another unfair allegation was that the latter used some of Lewis's original work in a textbook without acknowledging it. In any case, this difficulty was later overcome and certainly Mackenzie held no malice towards Lewis for it. There is, however, no doubt that Lewis was an awkward and difficult personality as the following comments will show. ' Lewis did not inspire affection.' ' Lewis did not accept Dr Cotton for several weeks until he discovered Cotton knew something which he did not. Similarly he treated Dr Paul Dudley White,[2] an American from Boston, with the same cold indifference. However, he began to notice Paul White was using a slide rule for doing certain complicated measurements. This was new to him and it meant skill and power which he did not possess. Paul White was then acceptable!' Another colleague wrote ' Lewis looked very strongly for his own affairs and was so difficult.' Others would

[2] Cardiologist who attended President Eisenhower during his first and subsequent attacks of coronary thrombosis.

describe him as a lonely, sad man, but ruthlessly ambitious. What is remarkable is that despite his well founded scientific reputation in the very heart of London, he should find it personally difficult to raise money for such a worthy cause.

> 10 Chesterford Gardens,
> Hampstead, N.W.3.
> April 9th, 1924.

Dear Mackenzie,

I am anxious to place the journal *Heart* on a more secure basis. We have about 400 subscribers and the costs are about £700 a year. This means we cannot sell under about 38/6d a volume. That is very clear. I am contemplating an arrangement under which some body like the Royal Society shall have the appointing of the Editor and shall stand as godfather to the Journal.

What I should most like to see is an endowment of about £5,000 for the Journal, to be used purely for reducing the cost of the volume. It would be a great thing if we could reduce the cost to a really reasonable figure. My idea is that if an endowment could be obtained, it should be controlled by the body appointing the Editor, and that Shaw and Sons would return audited accounts each year, and receive the income from the fund for use in reducing cost to readers.

Do you know of anyone who could be approached from this point of view?

> Yours sincerely,
> (Sgd.) THOMAS LEWIS.

In 1923, Mackenzie's nephew Basil Sholto Mackenzie, the present Lord Amulree, was a medical student at University College Hospital and the following is an extraordinary record.

> New Park,
> St. Andrews, Fife.
> 5 Nov., 1923.

Dear Basil,

. . . I was amused at your description of Lewis as it fits him exactly. He always takes himself very seriously, and wears an air of solemnity which seems to cover a great mass of profound wisdom, whereas it is but a lid over an empty pot! This is between ourselves, and when you come under him you can ask questions and see what sort of answers you get . . .

This statement is extraordinary because it is so out of character with the temperament and attitude of Mackenzie. It is the only derogatory remark which exists in all the masses of private correspondence about any individual, professional or other. It was dictated, of course. He was also by this time a very ill man suffering frequent attacks of anginal pain. He was getting near the end and some of the bitterness of the early estrangement may have momentarily flitted across his memory. More likely, perhaps, the answer lay in the last sentence and may mean that Lewis, although a great technical cardiologist, was not in the real sense of the word, a clinical cardiologist. Verbosa et grandis epistola !

' Thomas Lewis,'[3] wrote Parkinson, ' had his own physiological path to follow and was much more than a disciple: Mackenzie claimed no more than that he won his interest for cardiology: he had great affection for him and often expressed admiration for his achievements in research.'

[3] *British Health Journal* 1954 XV, Dec./Jan.

Chapter 30

CLAMBAKE

Interpone tuis interdum
guadia curis

Dyonisuis, Cato

New Park,
St. Andrews, N.B.
20th Feby., 1919.

My Dear Old Friend,

I am sorry my letter describing my American experience did not reach you, as it was written when the events were fresh in my mind, so that I am only able to give you a somewhat imperfect description. The contrast with my visit to America this time with that first expedition in 1885, when I wandered alone an unfriended figure over the Continent, was very great.

After I had been settled here for three weeks, beginning for the first time in my life to rejoice that I had no duties to compel me anywhere, a request came from Lord Beaverbrook, the Minister of Information, to say that a request had come from the American Medical Association, a body of 80,000 doctors, wishing certain representatives of the Government to attend their meeting in Chicago, in the middle of June, adding to their request that I might be one of the representatives. I replied that I was willing at this time to do anything for the good of my country, but as a mission would require men who would be able to address large audiences, I had not only no experience of public speaking, but I was convinced that I did not possess the ability to do so. Notwithstanding this, Lord Beaverbrook replied that the request was so earnest that I should go, that the Government would take it as a great favour if I could accede. So I journeyed up to London, and got our instructions, and went down to Liverpool to sail in some mysterious ship, at some time which they would not tell us, and which they wanted to be kept secret. Next morning, the whole thing was in 'The Times', stating that Sir Arbuthnot Lane (1856–1943. Surgeon, London), of London and Colonel Bruce (Surgeon, Toronto) of Toronto, and myself, were sailing to America upon a Government mission.

271

We arrived at Liverpool and found our berths on the huge *Aquitania*, a vessel of over 50,000 tons, and each of us had a splendid State-room with our own private bath attached. We sailed at the end of May and made for Halifax. We were escorted by a Man-of-War for the first day, then after that, we had to depend upon our own speed, nearly 30 knots per hour, so we went zig-zagging all the way across the ocean to defeat any attempt to torpedo us. We were compelled to wear life-belts nearly all the way. Arrived at Nova Scotia, we disembarked a great number of Canadian soldiers' wives and their children. About a mile up the bay we saw the results of that terrific explosion which had occurred two years before, when a munition ship collided with another and blew up, and the force of the explosion was such that it levelled all the houses on the shore for nearly half a mile square. We had spent five days in coming across, and we ran down to New York in 24 hours. Here, on landing, a deputation met us, and for the next month we had no more control of our movements, but were sent from one part of the country to another, having no rest. Fortunately, I was hoarse and I was excused. From New York we went to Washington, in order to be received by the ambassador, the Earl of Reading. We had tea with him. I asked him ' What on earth had I come to America for ', and he said ' he did not know '. I asked him ' What I was going to do '. He said ' I could do as I liked '. He was very nice and said, before we went he would get up a banquet for us at Washington. ' Have I come purposely from New York to Washington for a banquet? ' ' Yes ', he replied, and I said, ' You are a busy man, and don't want to be bothered with too many people, and for my part, a banquet, even with him, would not tempt me from New York '. So he laughed and said that it would be all right. But my Canadian colleague, . . . was very wroth. From Washington we went to Cincinnatti and had a great reception there. A big dinner was got up for us, after which we had to make an oration. The next day we were most hospitably entertained. In fact, the hospitality of the Americans, like everything else in that country, is too big. We were never left alone, everybody thinking they must do something for us, with the result that we were utterly wearied every day in body and mind, with the incessant entertainment during the whole time we were in America. From Cincinnatti we went to Baltimore, and were shown over the Johns Hopkins School. It was reckoned to be in the very forefront of medical schools, having enormous endowments, so that medicine is broken up into a great number of specialities, and the students have to learn an enormous number of different methods, but in conversation with the authorities, I never was more surprised to find such a stupid outlook as they possessed. I could say with confidence, that we were far better taught in Edinburgh in our student days than the men are today in such places. (vide Osler[1].) But what struck me above all, was their absolute conceit and complacence, and when we discussed certain phases of medicine in which they pretended to being the most up-to-date, I found them extraordinarily superficial. So far as my own work is concerned, they had not even realised the elementary principles necessary to guide them in understanding the meaning of the symptoms which their numerous methods revealed. From Baltimore we went on to Chicago. I had a most bewildering time there. We had to attend banquets, and address numerous meetings. The first evening we went, there was an enormous audience, to which we were introduced, and we had to stand up and make our bow. We had not to speak that night. There was a Senator there who made a speech, a regular barnstormer, who thumped the table and bellowed like a bull-of-Bashun, and I thought to myself, 'What a ridiculous object you are.' Next night there was another enormous meeting in a theatre, with 5000 of an audience, and another 1000 who were turned away. A number of short addresses were given by the representatives of all the different Allies, and I was the first to speak, and I found myself bellowing and thumping the table in the same ridiculous manner as the orator of the night before! I addressed one or two medical meetings on subjects with which I was familiar. Here I had the nicest incident of the whole visit. There is a golf association of doctors, who hold their annual meetings always at the same time as the association meets, and I was asked to participate in the competition, which I did and played badly. Afterwards we had a banquet at the Club, and I sat by the Chairman. In front of us there were the prizes, a number of very ordinary-looking cups, but there was a very dainty little clock in a morocco case, and as I sat at dinner I admired this clock beyond all the other prizes. After dinner the Chairman distributed the different prizes, all except this little clock. Then he stated that there was a prize to be given to the most successful player amongst the Allies, and that I had

[1] Author's comment!

273

succeeded in winning it. I think I made my best speech there of anywhere! They were all doctors, mostly general practitioners, and I just talked to them of my experiences in Burnley, and they relished it immensely. From Chicago we travelled 14 hours further west to Minnesota. In a small village or town called Rochester, some 35 years ago, a doctor there had started a small hospital during some epidemic. After the epidemic had subsided, the Roman Catholic Sisters, who run the hospital, suggested to the doctor that they might continue the hospital with the treatment of other complaints. This he did, and practised mainly surgery, so that there gradually grew up a surgical hospital to which the patients came from a considerable distance. His name was Dr Mayo. He had two sons, Willie and Charlie Mayo, and after graduation, they joined him and developed the surgical practice to such an extent that Rochester is now probably the greatest surgical centre in the world. These brothers organised the hospital in such a way that the patients all pay one-tenth of their income, and so successful were they that people came from all parts of the world, and now, they have not only a great big hospital, but they have got an institute for the examination of patients with some 60 or 70 specialists who employ every conceivable means for the investigation of the patient's complaints. There are about ten or a dozen operating surgeons and they begin at 7.30 in the morning and operate continuously till one 'oclock. The Monday of the week on which I went there, there were no less than 305 new patients from all parts of the world, who had arrived for treatment. The Mayos are splendid fellows, very simple and they have made as much money as they want. They have endowed their institute with funds that yield 250,000 dollars per annum. I stayed with them and although men of enormous wealth, they live in a simple way, but everything in their house is of the most perfect kind. They were very anxious for me to make a long visit, but I could only put in one day. I tried when there, with some of the younger men, to inculcate a different conception from what they had, but found it was simply impossible for them to realise what I was driving at. There was one fellow in particular, who had devised a very pretty way of finding out the amount of CO_2 given off by the lungs in exophthalmic goitre. I tried to show to him that such a discovery did not carry us far, and that what he ought to try to do was to find out why his patient developed this complaint, as it was really a secondary complaint. The amusing part, however, was that I could not get them to see what I was driving at, and as I did not value his discovery very much, he informed the Mayos that I was too old to appreciate a new method! In the evening we had a Levée after the style of Martin Chuzzlewit. It was a warm summer evening and I stood bareheaded in the garden and shook hands with a great crowd of doctors and their wives and friends. Unfortunately there were mosquitoes about, and the next morning I discovered a great many bumps on the top of my bald head. From here I went back to Toledo in Ohio, and spent a day with a disciple of mine who had come to see my methods in Burnley in 1905. It is a manufacturing town and beautifully situated upon Lake Erie. From here I went away back to Boston. There we had a great reception. There was a big medical meeting in session, and at the half hour we were marched up to a closed door, then the doors were thrown open. There were about 700 or 800 people present and as we entered they all stood up and the band played 'God Save The King', and we got on the platform and bowed as though we were Royalty. That evening we went away to a small village twenty or thirty miles north of Boston for the night. The day before we had been sweltering in heat; this day it was as cold as mid-winter. We stayed with the surgeon there in a big house and he gave one of the most remarkable entertainments called a 'Clambake'. I understand that a proper Clambake is a picnic on the Sea-Shore, where there is a fantastic meal made in a great big pot. His was a picnic inside, and out of his great big cistern in which he had cooked the food, he produced clams, lobsters, chickens and other dishes. From Boston we went away west again to Detroit, where we were entertained in the usual sumptuous fashion, and taken over Henry Ford's Works, an enormous place which turned out over 3000 motor cars per day. At that time the whole place was given up to making munitions, chiefly aeroplane engines, small ships and small tanks. When I saw what was being done there and in another huge workshop I realised that the Germans could not long stand against the terrific armaments that were being made for their destruction. From Detroit we sailed at night across the Lake to Cleveland, where the usual performance was gone through, always with the big meeting addressed at night. Some seven years ago, a partner of Andrew Carnegie had consulted me in London being at that time supposed to be very ill because of his blood pressure. He was living upon a vegetarian diet and was very depressed and miserable, when I told him that there was nothing the matter with the blood pressure but to go and live a normal life and just take in moderation any kind of food that he found agreed with him. He came back to see me a year later a totally different man. He had seen that I was in America and wrote that he wanted to consult me, so I wrote and said that if he would get up a meeting we would come to Pittsburg; so from Cleveland we travelled all the way to Pittsburg. He gave us a good reception, and I found him at the age of 81 wonderfully well, and we addressed another huge audience. He had sent round to all the churches the fact that we were coming, and the congregations had, most of them, either adjourned or stopped the services so that we had a great many parsons there, and after our orations we were surrounded, congratulated and encouraged. From there we went to Philadelphia, where the Mayor had arranged a reception for us. We got there early in the morning, having travelled all night. Put into a motor car, taken to an hotel, breakfasted, put into another motor car, driven down to the docks, where a motor launch was waiting for us then we were taken away down the river for about an hour, when we came to a place called Hog Island. In the month of October this island was little better than a swamp. When we saw it, it was a huge building yard employing 30,000 men with 50 Slipways in each of which was a large steamer being built. From there we went to the Remington Factory where an enormous number of rifles were being made and tested. We motored back to Philadelphia, stopping to have a sandwich on the way, as we were faint from hunger and it was getting towards 3 o'clock in the afternoon. In Philadelphia we were shown some new hospital buildings, and then in the evening were entertained by the municipal authorities to a banquet. In my speech I told them that I had visited their City in 1885, and wandered about it, not knowing a single individual, and I contrasted that visit with the position that I was in this night. We had again a great big audience to address, and this was the last, and I felt greatly relieved. Next day we came to New York and two days later sailed for home in a ship the *Lapland*, of 25,000 tons. We were one of a convoy. There were 13 ships altogether and for a day out of New York we were accompanied by cruisers and torpedo destroyers. After the first day the torpedo destroyers left us and the cruiser took us across the Atlantic. It was a strange sight; all the ships were camouflaged with those peculiar patterns which renders the ship's course impossible to recognise through a periscope. Each ship had its station and they maintained their relative positions in a most wonderful way all the time. It took us eleven days to cross but where we went to, I don't know. One day we were away south in tropical weather, possibly near the Azores, then we were away north off the coast of Ireland. Two days before landing we were told there would be a number of British torpedo destroyers to protect us, and in the morning we looked all about and could see nothing of them, but our attention was diverted, and somebody suddenly said, 'There they are', and we looked and there were 20 or 30 of these boats all about us, and for two days they kept this position until we reached the north of Ireland, which was the most dangerous part, and we then sailed between Scotland and Ireland down into the Mersey.

Arbuthnot Lane tells a delightful story of this tour. To escape from the remorseless demand on their time, and the overwhelming hospitality, they repaired one evening to a cinema. Pathos was the theme and Mackenzie, unfamiliar with this form of entertainment was enthralled. In the semi-darkness Lane turned to find Mackenzie sobbing and the tears running down his cheeks. Asked what was wrong he replied "The puir Lassie, the puir lassie."

Bruce gave an equally amusing sidelight on Mackenzie. There was an agreed protocol at these many meetings, in that Bruce would address the audience followed by Lane, both surgeons, then by Mackenzie on Medicine and Cardiology. They had listened to each other *ad nauseam*. At their last meeting in New York/Boston no sooner had the chairman sat down when Mackenzie got up and gave a verbatim speech of that which belonged to Bruce!

Whatever misgivings he had about the purpose of the visit, there is no doubt that Mackenzie enjoyed himself immensely.

> Ministry of Information,
> London.
> 17th July, 1918.

Dear Sir James,

I have read your report on your visit to America with the utmost gratification . . .

It now remains for me to thank you for your patriotic devotion in undertaking this delicate and important task amid the pressure of your other work.

SIR JAMES MACKENZIE, M.D., 1853-1925

The consciousness that your mission has been so successfully accomplished must in itself be a matter of profound personal gratification to yourself and your colleagues.

Beaverbrook.

For this whistle stop tour, no three ambassadors, Scot, Englishman and Canadian, could be so different in outlook and approach. But Beaverbrook obviously chose well. No pot boiler this, but as a medical menu, it was obviously to the American taste.
Clambake indeed!

Chapter 31

DRAMATIS PERSONAE

Power is founded on Public Opinion
NAPOLEON

The Memoirs[1] of Mr Cecil King, which have appeared recently in the *Sunday Times* entitled *The Shabby Millionaire* add medical interest to the Mackenzie story. Alfred Harmsworth, Junior, (later Lord Northcliffe[2]) was born near Dublin, the eldest of 14 children. He became one of the richest and most powerful of British Press Barons, owning or controlling at various times: *Answers, The Sunday Companion, Horner's Penny Stories, London Evening News, Daily Mail, Weekly* (later *Sunday*) *Despatch, Daily Mirror, The Observer, The Times,* Associated Newspapers and the Amalgamated Press.

> Northcliffe often seemed a great hypochondriac, often travelled with a doctor and was always fuming about his health. But then Stanley Morrison who wrote the history of *The Times,* said he was being treated in Germany from 1911 onwards for syphilis. Certainly his symptoms towards the end were those of G.P.I., which is tertiary syphilis.

Cecil King, his favourite nephew, writes that the biographies of Northcliffe, Pound and Harmsworth, make the story difficult to understand because they leave out the sexual side of his life. According to King, Northcliffe had various 'affairs' and it is alleged that he had a number of children born in France whose births were not registered.

Northcliffe was noted for the frequency with which he made out new Wills... Excerpts from one of his biographies[3]:

> *1917.* Lord Northcliffe was advised by a Bournemouth doctor, A. E. Blackburn, to consult Sir James Mackenzie. Mackenzie later wrote to Blackburn: 'I saw Lord Northcliffe and found the condition you describe. The systolic bruit is one of those

[1] *Sunday Times* Weekly Review 1969, 16 Feb., p. 49.
[2] Lord Northcliffe (1865–1922).
[3] *Northcliffe.* Biography by Reginald Pound and Geoffrey Harmsworth.

which I find occurring not infrequently in men who are over 45 years of age'. The patient was 'out of tone', and Sir James advised a more hygienic life.

1919. Northcliffe was suffering from a non-malignant growth in his throat which caused a troublesome cough. He had no faith in the Harley Street doctors and let them know that their medicine was no good. He reserved the greatest respect for Sir James Mackenzie, to whom he was taken by MacNair Wilson of *The Times*, who had been Mackenzie's assistant. Wilson said that the interview was the most nerve-racking of his life. Northcliffe had complained of heart pain and feared angina pectoris. 'I want a frank opinion', he said to Mackenzie. There was a snap in his tone which the physician did not like. 'This is a place of science, not a newspaper office', the great consultant replied with quiet firmness. From that time, when Northcliffe spoke of him, Mackenzie was 'that grand old Scotsman'.

1919. Mackenzie wrote to Northcliffe at Nairn: 'Allow me to congratulate you on your recovery from the operation. As one who has appreciated your work during the war and who is grateful for what you have done, I read with concern the reference to your illness in the newspapers, while I was interested in you personally as one who had consulted me.'

Northcliffe saw Mackenzie in August 1919: 'the great heart man who, though retired, has taken great interest in my case'. Later he wrote that he had seen Mackenzie: ' a fine old leonine Scot who used vigorous and profane language about the quacks of Harley Street and district.' Mackenzie said to him: ' You are 54 years of age. You have overworked all your life. If you were a manufacturer with two or three businesses I would tell you to sell all but one. It is obvious that you cannot do that, therefore it would be well if you began work slowly and gradually and go *up to about three days a week.*'

1919. Northcliffe wrote to Twells Brex, a young *Daily Mail* writer suffering from undiagnosed pains: ' The only safeguard is several opinions. If you will read Sir James Mackenzie's book, which I send you herewith, you will find that he, the greatest of his kind, practically knows nothing.' (Brex was, in fact, suffering from inoperable cancer).

Mackenzie had warned Northcliffe to be sensible and rest: ' He stripped me to the skin and examined me very vigorously indeed.'

1919. In September of this year his (Northcliffe's) principal secretary wrote: ' Sir James Mackenzie had started an Institution for investigation into the early stages of disease and the conditions that favour its origin. The Chief has promised to help him with £500 a year for five years. The Chief has sent the £500 for this year direct to Sir James, who replied: "I thank you very sincerely for your cheque, which I have received. Your generosity has been of the greatest encouragement and help to me in tackling a very difficult problem.'

To another London consultant Mackenzie sent a medical report. This was 3 years before Northcliffe died.

133 Harley Street, W.
17th May, 1919.

Dear Dr Seymour Price,

With regard to my medical examination of Lord Northcliffe two days ago, the following is what I found: Pulse 92 per minute, of normal volume, and regular in rhythm; no evidence of thickening of vessel wall; systolic blood-pressure rather raised for his age, being 162 mm; on percussion left border of heart about in nipple-line; a well marked systolic murmur audible over the whole precordium and in the axilla, its point of maximum intensity being at the apex.

X-ray examination of heart shows the organ to be very horizontally placed, left border ¼″ outside nipple-line, and transverse measurement at least 7″ — thus, considerably enlarged; considering the age and build, the aortic shadow is normal, transverse measurement being 2¾″ to 3″. The electrocardiogram shows left-sided preponderance, poor T deflections, and inverted P's in lead III.

The poorness of the T waves indicates that the end of the ventricular contraction is not strong.

Considering how very horizontally the heart is placed, I do not think the inversion of the P deflections is of any pathological significance.

As I have stated, the systolic blood-pressure is rather above the normal, which is not surprising in view of the very strenuous life that Lord Northcliffe has led, and the heart is considerably enlarged.

In my opinion, the organ is somewhat impaired, and the affection is myocardial, in all probability the result of the attack of pneumonia during youth. But I see no reason with regard to the heart, why the operation should not be performed —providing the matter of the anaesthesia is satisfactory. The last point is of great importance, and instead of discussing the matter with you by letter, I should be much obliged if you would be so good as to come and see me or failing this I will come and see you.

Perhaps you would be so good as to allow me to see his Lordship about once a year.

Yours sincerely,
J. Mackenzie.

From Nairn where Northcliffe was on a golfing holiday, he wrote to Mackenzie promising to contribute the £500 a year for five years towards the St Andrews Institute. This was in no way a fee for services rendered but an overt token of his high personal regard for Mackenzie and his pioneering work. Each instalment, be it from Edinburgh, London or Bangkok, carried with it a message of goodwill and encouragement. Northcliffe set off on a famous world trip in 1920 (did Mackenzie advise it?) when messages by letter, postcard or telegram would bring cryptic accounts of his progress.

Grand Hotel de Pekin.
November, 13th 1921.

My dear Sir James,

The six months holiday I am getting — a real holiday — has made me feel twenty-five, though I am fifty-six and a half. I attribute it to the complete change of life and interest, the hot and cold sea baths on the very long voyages I am having, plenty of deck chair (perhaps a little too much) and the intense interest I feel in all there is about me. Few people have had a more interesting tour of the world. I see every place worth seeing on my route and everybody worth knowing.

I don't think that I have been to a place yet where Scots are not numerous; bank and insurance directors, railway men, diplomats, they are everywhere.

As to golf, I have played it in very strange places. As I write I am just off to play on the golf course at Pekin.

Yours very sincerely,
NORTHCLIFFE.

Postcard to Sir James Mackenzie at St. Andrews, Scotland.
Picture of Golf Links, Nuwara Eliya, Ceylon (6300 feet up)

Message reads: I hope they sent that cheque. Man, but I'm feeling fine!

Sgd. Northcliffe.

(Postcard undated, postmark illegible)

Telegram to Sir James Mackenzie, New Park, St Andrews, 21.12.1921.

Message reads: Lord Northcliffe cable from Bangkok greetings and best wishes.

Price, *The Times*.

Mackenzie himself an old and very ill man had obviously travelled down to London to see his former patient and generous benefactor, several weeks before the terminal event. Lady Northcliffe writes:

1 Carlton Gardens,
S.W.1.
July 26th, 1922.

Dear Sir James,

You will forgive me for not having written before, and believe me it is not that I was insensible to the very great kindness you did. I cannot tell you how truly grateful I was to you. Your visit gave my poor Northcliffe not only pleasure, but confidence, and you helped me — and his Doctors more perhaps than you realised — he listened to you and was more content to remain where he was. I grieve to tell you that there is no improvement, although it is marvellous that he holds out as he does against the disease — but he is weaker than he was and there have been kidney complications since you saw him.

Still we all cling to that tenth chance — and go on hoping.

Please believe in my very real gratitude to you for taking that long journey — and coming to him as you did — as a friend — and may I say a friend to me also?

Yours sincerely,
(Sgd.) Molly Northcliffe.

Northcliffe died at 10.12 a.m. on Monday, August 14th, 1922.

41 Sloane Gardens,
S.W.1.

Dear Sir James,

Thank you so much for your letter of sympathy. I am more than glad to have your approval of my statement, for it had to be given an hour after his death when I was in no mood to

283

grant any interview. Your visit was of very great help to us and in particular to me, much of your advice was invaluable to me in managing a situation that teemed with difficulty. The question of another and recent will made without my knowledge or in my absence has arisen; would you mind sending me your opinion in writing as to his testamentary capacity at the time of your visit — it would strengthen my hand greatly.

Yours gratefully,
P. SEYMOUR PRICE.

Mackenzie, asked to give an opinion as to Northcliffe's sanity wrote:

The St. Andrews Institute for
Clinical Research,
St. Andrews,
Fife.
Aug. 25th, 1922.

Dear Dr Price,

I have been thinking over the state of Lord N's mind, and recalling the incidents when I saw him. At times he was quite rational and then he would wander off and say most absurd things. Whether he had sufficiently long periods of sanity to make a Will I am unable to say with that fulness of knowledge which would be expected in a Law Court — for instance.

I hope that the worry of having to decide that question is not to be added to your burden.

I have been having communications about 'Cures', all wanting to get into touch with you. I have tried to protect you, but I suppose you are still being persecuted.

Yours sincerely,
(Sgd.) J. MACKENZIE.

Did Northcliffe have Tertiary Syphilis? Yet another recent biography[1], followed by an article[2] by the same author entitled 'What *was* wrong with Northcliffe?' resurrected, yet again, the question —'As far as Northcliffe's health was concerned: did he have syphilis, and what was his mental condition? The two might or might not be connected. The second was the one that really matter-

[1] *The House of Northcliffe* by Paul Ferris. London: Weidenfeld and Nicolson, 1972.
[2] *World Medicine*, February 2nd 1971, page 17.

curiosity, but in the case of a literary man whose private life is almost as obscure as his writing is famous, any small light which may be thrown upon his private life is not only of interest but of value to the literary student. It is well known that there are three rather sharply demarcated phases in James' writing and it would be of interest to know whether or not at the age of sixty-six he was depressed by the fear of sudden death and whether such a feeling is manifested in his literary work.

While I myself am not intimately acquainted with James' brief hints of his private life, I very much doubt whether so reticent a man would confess to such fears.

You may be interested to note that in the preface to the definitive New York edition of James' work he devotes several most interesting pages of his conception of the way the mystery in *The Turn of the Screw* must be most strongly veiled and implied but never concretely described or explained.

> I am, Sir, with highest esteem,
> Very respectfully yours,
> HAROLD RYPINS, M.D.

There is no record of Mackenzie's reply but like Sophocles, he may have said ' to its author, everything is dear!'

Continuing the American theme is an amusing letter from Dr Fred Shattuck of Boston:

Boston, September 21, 1922.

Dear Sir James,

This is to introduce to you Dr Dwight O'Hara whom I do not know personally but whom I know about. He, recognizing that they don't know everything down in 'Judee', is crossing the water bent on blood-sucking — the blood of the spirit, not that of the flesh. You are more plethoric with medico-spirituality governed by Scottish sense than any man I know or know of, and I hope you can spare Dr O'Hara some of your surplus.

Believe me,

> Yours very truly,
> F. C. SHATTUCK.

Sir James Mackenzie, M.D., etc.
St. Andrews, Scotland.

Also from Dr Abraham Flexner of New York writing from Amsterdam:

11 June, 1922.

Dear Sir James,

I have come to Europe once more for the purpose of seeing medical schools, and I want very much to see the work which you are now doing at St. Andrews . . .

and from Dr. Simon Flexner:

> The Rockefeller Institute for
> Medical Research,
> New York.
> 6 June, 1921.

Dear Sir James,

As I wrote you I would do on April 18, I have now taken up again your proposal to send a man (or men) from this side to your Institute, and have presented the matter to our Board of Scientific Directors.

The general view is the one I presented to you, namely that it seems scarcely feasible to find just the right person intentionally. On the other hand, we will be on the alert for such a man, and if he appears put before him the attractive offer for training that you make. I suppose it would take several years for such a man to become really trained, and hence in looking ahead he would have to feel that a real opportunity was available for him afterwards. Even with our Institute we do not make long commitments until we feel reasonably sure a man will make good.

Again with many thanks and warm regards.

Yours sincerely,
FLEXNER.

Few students of Medicine will be unaware of the epoch-making discovery of Ross in regard to the missing link in the cycle of transmission of malaria. The discovery of *Plasmodia* in *Anopheles* is a story of triumph, of the incessant battle of man against disease. It is also the story of a great man, pitting himself against the obstacles of disbelief and military indifference.

Ross, although born in India, was of Scots extraction and there is much of individual character, perseverance, single mindedness and devotion to research in the two men to account for the high regard which they came to hold for each other.

In his memoirs[1] where one can almost hear Mackenzie's *cri du coeur*, Ross writes:

[1] Sir Ronald Ross, *Memoirs*, p. 239.

Owing to no fault of mine, two long years were to elapse before I was to see again in another continent, that wonderful revelation of human malaria in mosquitos. During that time, all my work was to be pirated by foreigners, and the same maladministration which now drove me into the wilderness was to force me finally out of India when my discovery might have been of real help to her swarming and dying millions.

Mackenzie immersed with his polygraph and tracings in Burnley, also found time for literary pursuits, to write *Mary Helm* and that series in the School Magazine and much else, but he could never aspire to the poetic powers of Sir Ronald Ross. On that very evening of his famous discovery, 21st August, 1897, Ross sat down and wrote:[2]

> This day everlasting God
>   Hath placed within my hand
> A wondrous thing; and God
>   Be praised. At His command.
> Seeking His secret deeds
>   With tears and toiling breath
> I find the cunning seeds,
>   O million — murmuring Death.
> I know this little thing
>   A myriad men will save
> O Death, where is thy sting?
>   Thy victory, O Grave?

In 1902 Ross received that most coveted of all honours, the Nobel Prize in Medicine[3]. Their first meeting appears to have been in 1918, and it is apparent from the correspondence that a warm and personal friendship ensued. Ross, like Mackenzie, was so critical of much that was happening in medicine and medical research ' There is a lot of laboratory tinkering going on . . . it is often extremely ignorant and quite worthless, and the workers do not seem to know yet what the word proof means . . .' and later . . . ' pathology divorced from clinical work tends to become absolute rot . . .' and in 1921 . . .

I have been very busy for two months over my mathematics, having been engaged in writing a book on a new kind of algebra, invented by myself in 1885. I do not expect to finish the book or possibly even to publish it; but must do the work

[2] J. O. Dobson, *Ronald Ross*, 1934. London: Student Christian Movement Press.
[3] R. L. Megroz, *Ronald Ross*, 1931. London: Allen and Unwin.

whether I like it or not; by some occult influence! I suppose it is a form of lunacy . . .

His admiration for Mackenzie's work was only equalled by that of Mackenzie for Ross. Writing to Mackenzie in 1923, he said:

> You had indeed a rough road to travel and I am sure that nothing greater than your auricular fibrillation has been done. It is fundamental and I well remember the rubbish we were taught before . . . As for comparative statures I put J. M. and R.R.

This was no idle compliment. Sir Ronald Ross, himself a recipient of the coveted honour, submitted Mackenzie's name for the Nobel Prize in 1920. But who was to recognize a general practitioner, even so remarkable a one as James Mackenzie? Perhaps, like Shakespeare, he could now say:

> I have touched the highest point of all my greatness
> And from that full meridian of my glory
> I haste now to my setting . . .

> King Henry VIII — Venus and Adonis.

Chapter 32

FAREWELL TO HARLEY STREET

All men think all men mortal, but themselves
YOUNG: *Thoughts of Life, Death and Immortality*, 1742

Apart from careful records in his notebook of fees there is little relevant information about his eleven years of private consultant work in Harley Street. Suffice it to say that even by present day standards his income in 1916, 1917 and 1918 was immense and had been increasing year by year. In July, 1917 in a postscript to Will, he added ' I have had a " corking " month.' His fees were seldom more than three guineas, occasionally five, but he was seeing as many as 12 to 15 patients a day. Why then, at the very zenith of his career, and while riding high on a professional wave of consultant prestige, should he in October, 1917 decide to throw it all up, and retire to the relative isolation and obscurity of St Andrews? Money and the accumulation of wealth certainly did not rank high in his aspirations. He had already sacrificed financial security in leaving Burnley. He was generous, and there is ample evidence that he was ever ready to help medical colleagues in financial straits.

Parkinson feels that the primary reason was his health. Dr Orr, who was his doctor in St Andrews gives a very full account of Mackenzie's medical history. Apart from his attack of typhoid fever in Burnley, and his troublesome migraine and attacks of renal colic in later years, he had no other illnesses. Occasional extra-systoles commenced at the age of 40, but the first evidence of real cardiac involvement was in 1901 at the age of 47. This was a heart attack with irregularity of the pulse which occurred after running 300-400 yards. The earliest symptom of distress occurred in 1907, the year he came to London, but it was the following year that Mackenzie experienced his first severe attack of cardiac pain. By 1911, there was definite limitation of effort but by 1918 when he came to St Andrews he was still able to walk at any pace without discomfort for a distance of two miles. He played a round of golf regularly; he was given to attacks of intermittent claudication on continuous

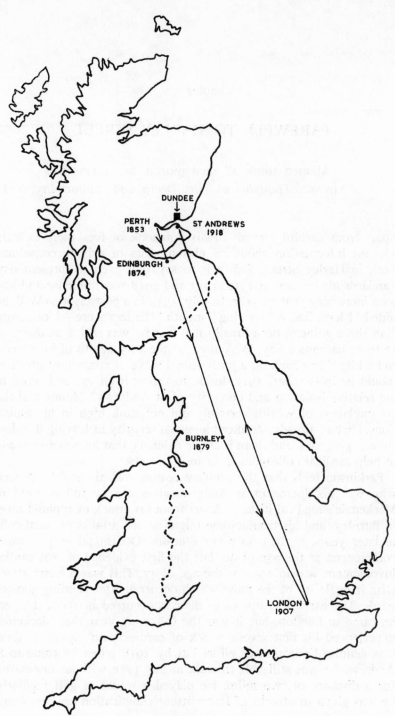

FIG. 5. Historical Milestones in Mackenzie's career.

walking, but this understandably became less pronounced as time went on owing to the increasing frequency of chest pain which was already placing limits on his physical activity.

To Mackenzie these omens must have been perfectly clear. Yet, despite the increasing burden of private consultant practice, the previous year 1916, saw the publication of yet another text book entitled *Principles of Diagnosis and Treatment in Heart Affections*. It went to three editions, five later impressions, and was soon to be translated into German, Italian, Russian and Polish. His pen was never idle, more publications were in process.

Dr MacNair Wilson opens his biography of the St Andrews period, by stating simply that 'Mackenzie returned to general practice, in order to study the early symptoms of disease'. Was it not that Mackenzie, aware of the significance of his own symptoms, would seem to have left London to escape from his own reputation as a consultant cardiologist! The inexorable demands on his time and practice were inimical to one with increasing evidence of heart disease and early arterio-sclerosis. He was comfortably well off. He needed more leisure time to devote to writing and the dissemination of the medical knowledge and principles he had acquired. He held definite and distinct views on the existing defects of medicine and medical education. St Andrews with its library and nearby medical school in Dundee would provide him with the necessary stimulus for study and writing. This leisure had been denied him in Burnley and (because of the demands of a private practice) to a lesser extent in London. It is in this context that his later endeavours in St Andrews must be viewed and the success or failure of the Institute assessed. In March, 1918, he rented and moved into a house called New Park, St Andrews.

There are no precise details of the actual date when he conceived the idea of establishing the Institute in St Andrews. In his tour through the States in June 1918 he was obviously impressed by the success of the Mayo Clinic which he referred to as an ' Institute for the examination of patients' in 'a small village or town called Rochester'. The method of endowment of the Mayo Clinic, achieved by patients donating each according to his means, and its medical and financial success from small beginnings must have left its mark on Mackenzie. Here, perhaps, were novel ideas which might succeed in Scotland.

In the autumn of that year he wrote to his young relative, Dr Andrew Garvie, then a general practitioner in Halifax:

New Park,
St. Andrews.
7 Sept., 1918.

Dear Andrew,

. . . We got settled here in April . . . Do you think you could send me a classification of 1000 cases? Not a minute one, but grouped: (1) old age (2) premature birth, (3) genito-urinary system, (4) diseases of digestive system, (5) diarrhoea and enteritis, (6) pneumonia, (7) other disease of the respiratory system, (8) bronchitis, (9) organic disease of the heart, (10) other disease of the circulatory system, (11) disease of the nervous system, (12) cancer, (13) phthisis, (14) other forms of tuberculosis, (15) measles, (16) whooping cough, (17) diphtheria, (18) influenza, (19) scarlet fever, (20) violence, (21) other causes.

This would be of great assistance to me. I think you said you would keep such a record. If anything comes out of my attempt I will let you know.

Give my very kind regards to your wife, I trust she and the family keep well.

Yours sincerely,
J. MACKENZIE.

(Garvie[1] was a remarkable character, to whom we shall return in a later chapter.)

Mackenzie was evidently turning his thoughts again to general practice and the mass of unsolved medical problems which it presented. In the event he anticipated what has now been realized by the Royal College of General Practitioners that morbidity in family medicine, to be meaningful would require its own distinctive classification.

With evident pride, he now wrote:

New Park,
St. Andrews,
12/7/1918.

Dear Sir William,

Many apologies . . . I didn't see the Birthday Honours in America . . .

This honour of a knighthood conferred upon his younger brother gave him great joy. With some feeling, he could write at this time

[1] Dr A. Garvie died on August 20, 1969 at Bradford. Aged 84.

about Sir William's son Sholto (the present Lord Amulree, then a Medical Student).

> He has been differently brought up from you and me. We had to fight with our backs to the wall. What would be privation to him, was nearly luxury to us . . .

How true!

But to return to the idea of an Institute. In a letter on the day before his death, he wrote:

> When I left London, I dared not tell anyone the real reason of my leaving, for it would have been looked upon as a piece of folly. For years, I had been gradually convinced that the whole tendency of research was on wrong lines; it was devoid of fundamental principles, was haphazard and could not supply the kind of knowledge which would enable us to solve medical problems. It was with the object of searching for this principle that I undertook at the age of 65, the burden and responsibility which were very heavy, of starting an Institute for the purpose of this quest.

But old men forget. It may seem ungracious in retrospect to question the accuracy of such memories and milestones, but this is essential to any objective appraisal of the Institute and its subsequent closure. Did he choose St Andrews for retirement, to establish an Institute, or both?

If Mackenzie feared the ridicule of his professional colleagues, it is surprising he did not confide in his brother Will. Whether it was the drawing up of a practice contract, the question of wills or house leases, his uncertainties of moving to Manchester, Edinburgh or London, Will was always his confidante and adviser. The correspondence in the Burnley years was voluminous. Naturally, due to their nearness to each other in London, only two letters exist for the period from 1907 to 1917. When he moved to St Andrews, the correspondence was in full flood again.

To Will:

New Park,
St. Andrews,
27 Nov., 1919.

Dear President,

> . . . It is a curious reflection that you are the first head at a new departure in politics and economics, that is bound to have a profound effect upon the industrial history of the nation and

I am the first head of a new departure in medicine. If my scheme is intelligently carried out it is bound to influence the history of medicine, and although it seems conceit to compare very humble beginnings with the lustre that surrounds yours still it has in it the germ of great things. What do you think of my letter in yesterday's *Times*? It is the first shot in what is going to be a long fight. It is indirectly intended for the present Ministry of Health who are going to legislate in utter ignorance of the problems and I have a faint hope they may realise the significance of an Institute. The letter is also the first step towards an appeal for help . . .

and later

Dec. 7, 1919.

. . . You will see how the *Times* is booming the Institute. It has made such an impression that the Medical head of the Ministry of Health is making a special visit to inspect it before advising legislation and I am hoping to get it officially recognised and subsidised if we fail in getting funds. The fact that I have struck out on independent lines and shown how things should be done which the enormous sums of money spent by the Government for their kind of work (about £70,000 p.a.) has proved futile . . .

Three months after the Preliminary Meeting to launch the Institute, he writes:

New Park,
St. Andrews,
Decr. 29, 1919.

Dear Will,

. . . There is a small cloud on the horizon the size of a pin-head, which may herald the oncoming of a great success to our scheme. The scheme is essentially intended to make good the defects in the practice of medicine and especially as practised by the Panel Doctors. I have at various times placed my ideas and my labours at the service of the Government, to have them quietly ignored. I knew they were hatching an ambitious scheme, and I warned Sir G. Newman and Dr John Robertson of Birmingham (who were the chief Hatchers) that they were blind men leading one another and for certain would find the ditch.

Two days ago, I received a letter from Sir Robert Morant, the Permanent Head Official, confessing that they had completely failed to get a workable scheme for recording the Diseases which the Panel Doctors would treat, that he had made enquiries at all sorts of people and they one and all said I was the only person who could guide them in this matter. Would I undertake the Chairmanship of the Committee and they assured me everything would be done as I wished and that the meetings would be arranged to suit my convenience and all expenses paid.

I have replied that I will help all I can but an interview would be required to show to them the nature of the task they had set themselves. I intend to show that this is a matter that can't be done unless through some Institute like ours and that no one but myself has had the experience and to lead them gently to see that in place of wasting £100,000 they had better endow us.

What think you?

There was no mention in Mackenzie's scribbled notes which served as an agenda at the preliminary meeting of the Institute that the development of a system of medical records was to be an important part of the Institute's activities at the outset. Indeed, his notes read ' a few panel patients ' and ' so the cases should be few.' And again, somewhat impatiently, he writes:

21. Jan., 1920.

Dear W.,

I have not yet heard of a date for my interview with Morant and his colleagues. If I do not hear today I'll write M. as this uncertainty is keeping me from other affairs. We are prepared to launch out a call for funds, but I have a hope the Government may like the Scheme . . .

The scheme is rapidly developing and its possibilities are now becoming so evident that it looks as if it might be the beginnings of the biggest revolution medicine has ever seen!

Whether at the advanced age of sixty-seven, Mackenzie, on this apparent crest of elation, was wise or prudent, the following events will show.

Chapter 33

ST ANDREWS—THE VISIONARY

Ars longa, vita brevis
HIPPOCRATES

Reference has already been made to the absence of any point in time when Mackenzie conceived the idea to establish the Institute of Clinical Research. In any case, it was born some 18 months after his arrival in St Andrews.

> Castlemark,
> St. Andrews,
> 2, Sept., 1919.

The James Mackenzie Institute for Medical Research

Sir,

A preliminary meeting of the Staff will be held on Friday 5th September at 4.30 p.m. in Harlow (Professor Waterston's) to discuss general arrangements.

You are urgently requested to be present.

> Yours truly,
> J. HUNTER P. PATON,
> *Honorary Secretary.*

There was no agenda as such, but on Mackenzie's notice of invitation were the following scribbles in pencil:

Agenda.

Naming the Institute.

Materials — A few panel patients.
— Consider first what we mean to do.

Early — *Early stages and cause.*
— The early stage important as it gets us nearer the cause.

We have first to train ourselves in the detection of symptoms. If we begin straight off we'll get on wrong lines and waste much valuable time.

So the cases should be few and scrutinised together.

PLATE 16. The building which housed the St Andrews Institute for Clinical Research.

Hours — Two a day at first with discussion from 1 till
2 p.m.

Furnishing and Management of Institute
Caretaker.

Next meeting I'll give an introduction how symptoms might be
perceived.

It is rather curious that finance did not loom large on Mackenzie's
provisional agenda because then, as later, it was to absorb a great
deal of his time and effort. Indeed its spectre was to haunt the
activities of the Institute long after his death. Mackenzie, as mentioned earlier, did not display great skill in handling his own financial affairs; it is a moot point whether he showed any greater talent at
the outset in establishing the Institute on a sound financial basis. It
may be, influenced by the history and origins of the Mayo Clinic,
he had greater confidence in the generosity of future patients, than,
in fact, transpired.

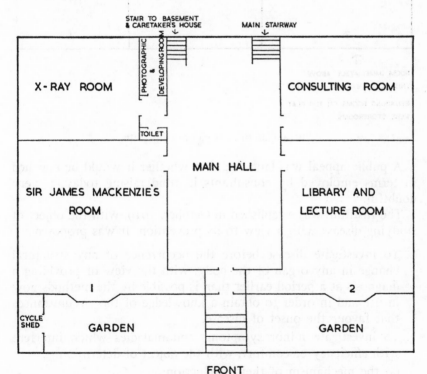

FRONT

FIG. 3. Plan of Ground Floor of Institute.

299

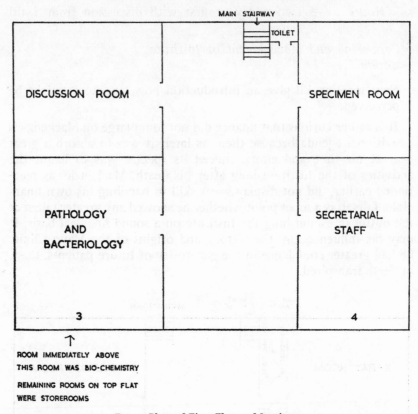

FIG. 4. Plan of First Floor of Institute.

A public appeal was launched, but whether it would be couched in terms employed by consultants in fund raising today, is very doubtful.

The Institute was established in October, 1919, with the object of studying disease with a view to its prevention. It was proposed:

1. To investigate disease before the occurrence of any structural change in any organ of the body, with the view of providing a diagnosis at a period earlier than is possible by the methods now in use and in order to obtain a knowledge of the circumstances that favour the onset of disease.

2. To investigate minor symptoms and maladies which interfere with efficiency or comfort, with the object of determining:
   (a) the mechanism of their production;
   (b) their bearing upon the future health of the patient.

3. To study the conditions under which the patient lives (food, work, surroundings, etc.)
4. To record all cases and keep in touch with the patients who have been seen, with the aim of discovering the relation between environment, ailments and subsequent disease.
5. To follow up patients in order to observe the outcome of complaints.
6. To conduct research into the early symptoms and predisposing causes of consumption.
7. To conduct research into the early symptoms of ill-health in children.
8. To provide post-graduate courses of instruction for the training of general practitioners in methods of clinical research, which they may employ in their private practices.
9. That trained general practitioners should undertake the research, associated with specialists in charge of departments for Bacteriology, Chemistry, Radiology, etc.

It went on to say:

> St Andrews has been selected as a suitable place for the Institute. Its size permits of a knowledge of the circumstances of each patient; and, as many of the inhabitants are non-migratory, individuals can be observed for years and records of the development and progress of their maladies kept.
>
> Sir James Mackenzie, who has devoted so much attention to Clinical Research, and who, in Burnley, and later in the London Hospital, by his own discoveries, has demonstrated the value of the new methods, is the Director of the Institute.
>
> Under his direction a staff of qualified medical and scientific men are now engaged in work.
>
> The Institute has been recognized by the Carnegie Trustees, among whom are the representatives of the four Scottish Universities, and a grant of £1000 per annum for five years has been given to St Andrews University for the direct purpose of assisting the Institute.
>
> A suitable building has been secured in lease, with the option of purchase, for the Institute. For its full equipment and purchase a sum of £6000 is required.
>
> The annual expenditure is estimated at £5000.
>
> The Council of the Institute, being convinced after a year's working of the extreme value of this Research, earnestly appeal for further financial support.

Mackenzie was naïve to think it would have the desired effect. There was no doubt about his own popular image and appeal, but did the wider public get his message? Moreover, Scotland traditionally thrifty and tight-fisted, was not London, where habitually wealth tends to accumulate and the opportunities for persuasion in fund raising would have been so much more promising. Why did he not, while still in London, button-hole his many wealthy patients, including millionaires like Northcliffe and Gulbenkian? It would also be naïve to think that Scotland, so soon after the ravages of war, could even emulate the vast wealth of America in giving such general support to the Mayo Clinic. But to Mackenzie such difficulties were not insuperable. He had, time and again, succeeded where lesser men had failed. To the task ahead.

Although novel in itself, the establishment of the Research Institute was, in effect, an extension of the clinical work and philosophy so patiently pursued during his days as a general practitioner in Burnley. What *was* novel in the objectives of the Institute was the need to study disease *with a view to its prevention*. Much of his earlier efforts had been devoted to diagnosis and cure; now he would devote his time to the study of early signs and symptoms and endeavour to assess their significance before disease became manifest. Items one, two and three of the objectives displayed Mackenzie's techniques in general practice. Could he inspire in the local practitioners that same infectious enthusiasm and fervour which characterized his own labours in Burnley? Enthusiasm yes, but can one impart genius and that unique quality for clinical research which he displayed so convincingly in his early years. After all, the practitioners were in St Andrews before he came. They were not selected by reason of qualities which were essential for the pursuit of research. In retrospect, the remarkable feature is that with such apparent shortcomings, they achieved so much.

The activities of the Institute during its existence have been recorded in two ways.

(1) Annual Reports,[1] giving the names of

    (a) the Council of Management,

    (b) the Staff of the Institute,

    (c) the Director's Report, and

    (d) the Treasurer's Report.

and

[1] James Mackenzie Institute. Reports 1–26.

(2) Clinical Reports[2] Volumes I to III giving an account of original work or of papers presented at the Institute.

The Council of Management consisted of a number of businessmen from St Andrews and Dundee together with Sir James Irvine, F.R.S., Principal of the University. The Honorary Secretary for many years was Dr J. Hunter Paton.

The staff of the Institute with Sir James as Honorary Director, consisted originally of

Dr Leonard Bryson, M.D., M.R.C.P.E.

Dr W. B. MacTier, M.B., C.M.

Dr James Orr, M.B., Ch.B.

Dr J. Hunter P. Paton, M.B., Ch.B.

Dr Andrew Rowland, M.D.

with the assistance of:

Percy Herring, M.D., F.R.C.P.E., Chandos Professor of Physiology, The University, St. Andrews.

and

David Waterston, M.D., F.R.C.S.E., Bute Professor of Anatomy, The University, St. Andrews.

In addition, there were a number of *Honorary Medical Staff*

Colonel R. J. Geddes, C.B., D.S.O., late A.M.S.

R. L. Girdwood, M.B., Ch.B.

H. W. Laing, M.D.

A. R. C. McKerrow, M.D., Ch.B.

later Professor A. Patrick, M.A., M.D., F.R.C.P., from Dundee.

Consulting Surgeon.

W. Huntington, L.R.C.P., M.R.C.S.

later Professor L. Turton Price from Dundee.

Consulting Ophthalmologist

A. Maitland Ramsay, M.D., F.R.F.P.S.

Over the years others joined the Institute notably Drs W. F. Mair, C. S. McEwan and Norman MacLeod.

The Laboratory Staff consisted of a Chemist and Bacteriologist both on the Staff of the University, while Dr Paton and Mr W. Smith acted as Radiologist and Radiographer respectively.

Apart from the Office Staff, consisting of three Assistant Secretaries, all seemed to be part-time with the Institute, and devoted considerable effort, additional to that demanded by their own particular practices. This is a remarkable testimony not only to the

[2] Reports of the St Andrews Institute for Clinical Research Vols. I, II and III.

selfless devotion of these many practitioners but to the man who inspired them.

In the first Annual Report, it is stated that the entire staff were constantly engaged in work on the following lines:

1. The investigation of diseases before the occurrence of any structural change in any organ of the body with a view to providing a diagnosis at a period earlier than is possible by the methods now in use.
2. The investigation of minor symptoms and maladies which interfere with efficiency or comfort, with the object of determining
   (a) the mechanism of their production.
   (b) their bearing upon the future health of the patient.
3. The study of the conditions under which the patient lives (food, work, surroundings etc.)
4. The recording of all cases and keeping in touch with the patients who have been seen, with the aim of discovering the relation between environment, ailments and subsequent disease.
5. The follow up of patients in order to observe the outcome of complaints.

Five areas of research were their concern during the first year, the diagnosis of disease, the investigation of pain, glandular enlargement, diseases of children and consumption. Would it be unkind to say, that one tiny fragment of any one of those subjects would, in itself, be task enough for any band of part-time workers effectively to devote time to, in any one year? The ideas were certainly original but were the plans and organization realistic?

The building which they managed to rent with an option to buy (later given effect to) was a substantial three storey dwellinghouse with basement,[3] situated on the Scores, looking out over the Old Golf Course and the East Sands. Not entirely ideal for the purpose, nonetheless it was put to very good use.

The building obviously is still in very good condition and will stand up for many years to come. Alas! all or nearly all the Institute Staff have passed on. To Mackenzie and his valiant band of Research workers, we might well with Wordsworth, enshrine these words on the front of that old Institute building

> Methinks their names shine still and bright,
> Apart, like glow-worms on a summer's night.

[3] When the War broke out, the building was taken over by the Military Authorities and reverting to civilian use is now in Annexe to the Scores Hotel. See communicating corridor.

Chapter 34

CIVIL SERVANTS AND CIVILITY

Nitor in adversum

OVID

Items 4 and 5 of the aforementioned objectives concerned the keeping of records of all cases and the follow up of patients in order to observe the outcome, an idea which may have emanated from the influence of Lord Knutsford at the London Hospital. Mackenzie's notes at the preliminary meeting of the Institute were towards the close and intensive study of a *few patients*, ' so the cases should be few and scrutinized together.' No such proviso was included in the objectives, and it may be that he was prevailed upon to extend the records to *large numbers* of *patients* by the then current plans of the Ministry of Health. If so, it was to present him with problems of numerical size and magnitude demanding methods of statistical analysis and correlation which were quite beyond his ability to handle or even comprehend.

Mackenzie's previous encounters with Government departments were, acording to his own remarks, anything but pleasurable and rewarding. With some impatience, he now sought the help and interest in his scheme of the Medical Research Council, whose hard-pressed and kindly secretary was Sir Walter Morley Fletcher. The response was to be cautiously sympathetic if not critical.

Medical Research Committee,
15 Buckingham Street,
Strand, W.C.2.
March 25th, 1920.

Private

Dear Sir James Mackenzie,

I am extremely sorry not to have written earlier in answer to your interesting letter and the memorandum on the Medical Aspects of the National Health Insurance Act which you kindly sent. To my dismay I have only just become aware that you have a meeting about this on Friday.

The fact is that both your letter and memorandum needed a good deal of thought on my own part, and Sir Robert Morant

305

wanted to talk to me about your proposals from his different point of view. This was put off day by day in the rush of business, and then as you know he was taken suddenly ill on March 8th and died on the 13th. This dreadful blow, and some business I have had to do for his family, put many other things out of my mind, including, I am afraid, your letter. In the last day or two moreover I have been prostrate with a cold.

As to your memorandum, I need hardly say that I agree most cordially with the whole line of argument. As you know, I greatly hoped that you would take the Chair of the Committee here as I understand Morant invited you to do. I am greatly interested in the last pages upon the methods used at the St Andrews Institute. I think that the methods here suggested will not only give invaluable opportunities for research but will also help greatly the adoption of a proper system of recording in the medical services that have to be set up throughout the country, by the practical experience and demonstration they will give.

As to your letter, whilst I am most grateful for the kindness it shows, I am a little uncertain as to what immediate reply will be most useful. As I said last month when we met, I cannot conceive that my Committee could fail to give all the help in their power to your work at St Andrews, and to take advantage of the opportunities you are making there. We agreed that I should have to come and discuss this with you on the spot while seeing the actual work, and I understood you wanted me rather later in the year. If you are ready for this now, however, I will gladly come at almost any time if you will kindly tell me what dates would suit you. I am greatly looking forward to coming as soon as possible. I should like to avoid Easter week itself.

Nothing you said in our talk, and nothing in your letter, suggests that any definite financial arrangement could have been reached before you told us that you were ready for a visit, but you speak of wishing to say at your meeting that you are "in alliance" with us. That I am sure you could say with truth so far as we are concerned; so far as I know the whole Committee are with you in your main ideas and, so far as I know them, in all your methods. We owe a great deal to you; we have followed your lead in several notable instances and I think only the War has for the time being prevented our going further in other directions you desire. You on your part do not think so warmly of us. I am less disturbed by that than I should be if I were not perfectly convinced that your coldness springs in large part from your not knowing many of our difficulties and from not realising the actual nature of much of the work being done. I sympathise keenly with you in your desire to get ahead on the new lines you are laying down, and shall do all I can to get my Committee to co-operate in the best way. We have been forced from the beginning to recognise that much of the best research work cannot be done at once because the workers fit for it have to be first found and trained. Yet we could not (we think) have abstained from supporting meanwhile not only what good work was being done but much other work and many other workers who are not, from our point of view or from yours, ideal. I do not think any of the work being done now for us, even if some of it be on old and unfruitful lines, will be wasted so long as it is honest and thorough. It may not all make advance, but it will find its place and be useful when advances shall have been made in due course by the right pioneers. On these grounds — though I hope very soon to discuss these much more fully with you—I do not see how you can be, or feel yourself to be, in any kind of "opposition" even to the least useful of the work now being done with support from us.

With kind regards,
Yours sincerely,
WALTER D. FLETCHER.

New Park,
March 29th, 1920.

My Dear Fletcher,

These two great objects I have in front of me (1) the establishment of rational and systematic Research in Medicine, and (2) the conversion of Walter D. Fletcher to my views, for I recognise that (1) would be greatly facilitated by (2).

My objection to your present attitude is not due to antagonism to laboratory work. If you really understood my point of view, you would realise that I am desirous to make laboratory work of far greater use than it is at present. Your view is, I think, that laboratory trained men are better trained and more scientific. This I readily admit, so long as they confine themselves to these particular spheres. When, however, they attempt to deal with matters connected with the human body, they go beyond their sphere and are unable to understand the phenomena, or the manner in which research should be pursued. It takes a far longer time for a worker to become a competent research worker in clinical medicine than in mere laboratory matters. The chief reason being that to understand the significance of clinical phenomena the patient has to be watched often for many years.

The fundamental, and guiding principle in research is to understand the nature of the problem in all its phases before you attempt research. In the case of diseases the first stop is to study the disease in all its phases in the human body, and when this is done the real difficulty will be revealed, and then the aid of the laboratory worker can be sought and applied far more intelligently than at present when the laboratory worker starts an investigation indifferent to or ignorant of the fundamental principles I have enunciated. This is where I see a distinction between rational systematic research and the haphazard of today.

I have had a curious and interesting experience of the conception of research held by authorities, and it has revealed to me the nature of the difficulties Sir R. Morant and you have to contend with in dealing with committees. The Scottish Consultative Committee appointed a Sub-committee in Research and appointed 3 Medical Officers of Health, a Statistician and myself. Two of the M.O.H. were appointed as authorities in Research because they had served on the Medical Research Committee, to wit, M. Hay and Chalmers of Glasgow. We had two meetings with a fourth M.O.H. Leslie Mackenzie of Edinburgh. They could not evolve a single idea, beyond vaguely hinting at a flying squad of experts to investigate epidemics, or the providing of more laboratories up and down the country. I took the opportunity to point out that as M.O.H. they were supposed to be familiar with the diseases that afflicted the people in their towns[1], and asked if they had any idea what was the nature of the diseases. They hummed and hawed and supposed they did. I then showed them that they could not know the great bulk. Thus I said to Matthew Hay, in Aberdeen there are 170,000 inhabitants. At least 40,000 would be ill every year. Of this number 10,000 would suffer from trivial ailments, and 30,000 more or less severe. Of these, probably not more than 5000 would be correctly diagnosed, so that left 25,000

[1] See later chapter *The New Epidemiology*.

people suffering from diseases which impaired their health and of which many died, and yet no one had any idea of what their trouble was. I suggested, did they not think that there was an urgent demand to face this huge problem, and not fritter away their time investigating little epidemics. Their reply was that that was a matter which concerned the Medical Research Committee. I asked them to join in, making strong representation on the need for such a research, but they wouldn't! The work of this Consultative Committee is bound to be futile, and no issue of value will come out of it.

Another point I look upon as being peculiarly the function of your Committee — the prevention of hasty legislation. When a scheme is propounded, the question should arise — does the knowledge exist to carry out this scheme? There is no authority to turn to but you. When for instance, Morant's fine conception for statistics of disease was incorporated in the Insurance Act, he was told the thing could be done, and was greatly taken aback when I demonstrated to him that medical knowledge did not permit of its being done. So, in regard to the provision of Sanatoria for Consumptives — he was assured that the early stages could be recognised, and legislative proposals were based on the assumption that the knowledge existed, with the result that the conception has failed. Newman is preparing to dash on the same rock. This scheme of his to keep records of people before they are born till their death, is bound to fail for reasons so obvious that I can only conclude he is wilfully shutting his eyes to the danger. When you come here I will demonstrate to you the difficulties, for we are attempting similar work and find the greatest difficulties in dealing with a far simpler problem.

In wishing you to be associated with us, I am not wanting any financial assistance. I realised long ago your Committee either would not help such an enterprise, or only do so grudgingly and inefficiently. I realise you must be bombarded with fantastic schemes, and this of mine could not be differentiated from the futile ones. So having the strength of my convictions I ventured on the scheme, depending on its merits to commend itself to sensible people, and so in any appeal for help, I have been met most generously. We still want a lot, but I am prepared myself to give a goodly portion of my savings to get it going, and until it is going, and doing good work, I do not wish you to take any responsibility. But I feel that, if you see what it is doing, and watch its progress, you will see that it has the

claims I make for it, and in a few years time you can then slip in
and take charge of its further development. I can only look forward to guiding it for a few years.

These letters are being quoted at length, not because they represent the lines on which the Institute was to develop, but because it
illustrates the minds of two great men giving thought to issues of
great national import, which were to become the central issues of
medicine of today. Of course, Mackenzie was right about the extent
of non-infectious diseases in the community and of which Medical
Officers of Health were largely ignorant. No doubt, in the conditions
then prevailing, there was justification for their primary concern
with epidemics of infectious disease including pulmonary tuberculosis. Today, fifty years later, there has come into being the new
epidemiology of non-infectious disease, of coronary thrombosis,
chronic bronchitis and diabetes. But then Mackenzie was a prophet,
not without honour, a visionary, impatient for action and even
becoming a little truculent with the impassivity of the Civil Service.

> Medical Research Council,
> 15 Buckingham Street,
> Strand, W.C.2.
> April 1st, 1920.

Dear Sir James,

I am very grateful for your long letter of the 29th March and
all the more so because it shows me even more clearly that there
is no real differences of opinion that I can see. I believe I
honestly agree with every word you say.

I agree that a very large part of the laboratory work being
done is inefficient or even useless because of its divorce from
genuine clinical work. Much of it is sterile also for another
reason, namely its divorce from biochemistry, and from the
experimental work of physiologists. We have to breed men
with real knowledge of chemistry and physics to come into
pathology, and we have to break down all the partitions between physiology and pathology.

But what has forced itself upon me more than anything else
in these years is exactly the cleavage you point to, namely the
pathologists working so to speak in mid air, out of touch with
any clinical work really worth the name. I believe we agree
wholly with you that that is the primary problem, and that
new men have got to be bred to do clinical research work. My
Committee agreed about this long ago; there are really hardly

more than three men in the whole of London adequately trained, and perhaps you would put it even lower. What we pointed out to Fisher and Newman two years ago has been almost laughably fulfilled by the failure to find men for these new so called ' clinical units ' in the London Hospitals. What is true even of the hospital work as done now is of course even more true of the systematic study you are forwarding upon the beginnings of disease.

I am much interested in what you say of your Committee meetings in Edinburgh. Your experience exactly fits with what I suffered from here in exactly the directions you name.

I will not say more now, because I hope to come in the second half of this month to see you at St Andrews as you so kindly suggested, and I shall look forward not only to seeing the work you are doing, but to having a long talk about our past and present difficulties and the prospects of the future. I would only say one word more now, and that is in protest against your saying you ' realised long ago ' that my Committee would not help your work or would only do it ' grudgingly ', and that they would not be able to differentiate yours from other ' fantastic schemes.' Really we have not deserved this! We did adopt one small practical part of your suggestions early in the War, and it was the War only that suspended that for a time. You were not prepared then as you are now to take a hand in it yourself, and that makes the whole difference.

Believe me,
Yours sincerely,
WALTER M. FLETCHER.

Mackenzie's attitude to Fletcher was rather curious. He did not wish immediate financial assistance but hoped at a later date that the Medical Research Council would move in and seemingly in some carte-blanche manner take over when the Research Institute had become firmly established and productive. Surely, in this he was being unrealistic. By his own admission funds were all-important. Had he presented his case on a narrow front and sought M.R.C. support on *one* of his many objectives his case would have been much more convincing. That this, in fact, did emerge it is true, but one begins to perceive the shortcomings of Mackenzie when fishing in unfamiliar waters. In Fletcher, he was up against an acute discerning brain, ready to question McNair Wilson's contributions to *The Times* and gently but incisively drawing the inference that

311

medical research can not be held to be the sole prerogative of general practitioners, and indeed unselected ones at that.

Medical Research Council,
15 Buckingham Street,
Strand, W.C.2.

Private

Dear Sir James,

I returned from my delightful visit to you to find some heavy arrears of business here, and much to be done in preparation for the first meeting of the new Medical Research Council next week. This has delayed my writing to you. I was very grateful for your letter of April 22nd and the accompanying Memorandum. I have thought much both about our talks and now about this Memorandum, and even now am hardly ready to write fully about either.

I am sorry you still fear my ' backsliding.' I daresay it is good for me that you should regard me as a heretic from your point of view, needing conversion. I can only say that, however poor my ability and methods may be, I still believe that I have consistently worked and fought, ever since I came to London in 1914, for the same objects that you have in view, and against the traditional spirit of mediaeval bunkum in present professional practice and education. The imperfections of our present work come, I think not as you suppose, from vicious intention, but only from the very absence of scientific clinical work which you deplore, and which I think we recognise as clearly as you do. We agree with you that men have to be trained for this clinical work, and that hardly any are at present ready for it. But while much (by no means all) of our present work suffers for want of marriage with clinical work of the right kind, it is not in itself to be condemned, or the men in it to be discouraged. It is not the laboratory men who have wished to be kept away from the patients in bed; it is the wrongly educated physician who has kept them away. All this I think you admit, but what I want you to see is that we are on your side in this matter. I daresay some of us may differ from you here and there in this or that direction, and on questions of detail. But that matters nothing; the great thing is that we have a common fight for a common cause.

Your work at St Andrews, with a view to practical results,

still as the days pass, groups itself in my mind under the same four headings.

(1) The aspect that chiefly strikes me both for novelty and germinal importance is your Institute as a *training school* for practitioners. There is nothing like it, I think, elsewhere, and I hope from this seed will spring a training system all over the country. I think that is your best gospel — that present medical education does not educate practitioners. This is a matter for the Ministry of Health and Board of Education, and not primarily for us, but it affects us closely, and I look forward to seeing your work having an immense influence.

(2) The next thing that appeals to me is on the research side — the study of the beginnings of disease. This, as you rightly say, can only be done in general practice. Where I think you have erred, if I may say so, is in supposing or giving the impression that you suppose, that any, or many, practitioners (under present conditions) can do this work. Wilson, of *The Times*, is always making a parrot cry that research work can only be done ' by general practitioners '. He takes this from you, but without the qualifications you would give it, and he does harm to the good cause, because men only laugh at what he says without seeing the principle that lies behind.

Your system at St Andrews does allow the work to be done, and it can be done by selected men (we have three selected on your own advice at work already). My mind is not yet clear how we should proceed to develop and organise this work more widely through the country; I am thinking a good deal about it.

Do you know, by the way, anything of a proposed Association of General Practitioners for Collective Research, started at Stockton-on-Tees? I have papers about it that Osler sent me.

As an immediate practical step, I am asking the M.R. Council next week to make a whole-time grant to Rowland for work in your Institute on the early beginnings and diagnosis of tuberculosis in young people, which would be part of our general tuberculosis scheme. (You did not give me Rowland's initials, and I do not find him in the Directory). Will you kindly send me particulars of him on a postcard?

(3) Next comes, I think, the work of following up and recording the onset and the after-histories of disease. No man can do this, even in a long life-time, for enough cases; Hippocrates meant this when he said ' ars longa, vita brevis.' Only an

institution can do the work on a wide enough scale, or with enough continuity. I think this needs much thought. We do not even know the best methods to use. I value your work as an earnest exploration of methods. I have long seen that the Ministry of Pensions will by a kind of accident give us valuable help under this head, and we are already trying to use that to the full. It is almost a scandal that hospital staffs have not regarded this kind of work as a necessary duty, if the advice for which they are asked and paid is to have an honest basis.

I think the M.R. Council would be ready to make a grant for the clerical expenses of this side of your work, and if you agree, I will bring that before them.

(4) Then there is the study of treatment, and here especially there is the study of the honest, i.e. the scientific, use of drugs or other remedies. I want to work towards the Drugs of Pharmacopoeia Committee of which we spoke. I missed Cushny at Edinburgh, but hope to see him soon. I have had a long talk with Dale, who cordially sympathises. He will think more, and we are to have another talk. I hope to write soon again about this.

I was very glad to see Dr Paton here, and I can understand how useful he is to you on the organising side. I told him I looked forward to coming to St Andrews again, if I may in the autumn. I want to get T. R. Elliott to come and see you presently. I talked to Thomas Lewis about my visit, and found him keenly sympathetic with what you are doing.

This would be a very hopeful time but for the deplorable outlook at the Ministry of Health. Morant's loss seems more and more irreparable, and in any case the proper work of the Ministry is sorely hampered by dreadful irrelevancies like housing, arrears, insurance business, poor law and bad legacies of panel practice.

Believe me,
Yours sincerely,
p.p. Walter M. Fletcher.
A.D.T.

This last letter from Fletcher, post hoc, ergo propter hoc, so incisive and so discerning, could well find a place in the final analysis of the Institute. He could also see one important area of the Institute's activity, viz. morbidity as distinct from mortality, the latter which for far too long has remained the favourite field of measurement of both medical officers of health and epidemiologists alike.

These exchanges have surely a claim to an important place in the history of medicine in this country.

> Medical Research Council,
> 15 Buckingham Street,
> STRAND, W.C.2.
> May, 6th, 1920.

Dear Sir James,

Thanks for your note of the 3rd May about Rowand. I hope to write after the Council meeting tomorrow.

I look forward to hearing further from you about the drugs question, or on any of the other points in my letter of April 29th.

I had to write that letter in a hurry, and it occurs to me that I omitted one large aspect of the subject, namely, the great desirability of our estimating, if we can, the immense amount of ' morbidity ' in the country among the people, as contrasted with ' mortality ' of which we do have direct measurements. This of course is wrapped up with the administrative question of medical records at which the Minstry of Health Committee (which you refused to join) is now working. I mention this now, not to discuss it, but only to name it with other points as a big thing we must keep definitely in view and take early action upon.

> With kind regards,
> Believe me,
> Yours sincerely,
> W. M. FLETCHER.

Medical Records, their use and value and the problems inherent in their collection, their value for patient care on the one hand and long term research on the other, were to become an important and central theme of research by the Institute. The Medical Research Council had relented.

> Many of the conditions of ill health that weakens adults can be traced back to infancy or childhood . . . We have appointed a Committee to investigate the question of the origin of ill health in children and the M.R.C. has granted a sum to one member of that Committee for the purpose of investigation . . .[1]

In the Report of the following year it states that the M.R.C. have generously given a sum of £1300 annually to the Institute, £800

[1] St Andrews Institute for Clinical Research, 2nd Annual Report, 1921.

being paid to Dr Rowand, Professors Herring and Waterston, while the remainder of £500 is contributed directly ' towards our friends for the keeping up of Institute Records, clinical and other expenses.' It would be difficult in the conditions prevailing in general practice in 1919 to ignore the importance of tuberculosis as an important community problem. In the event, and judging by the publications, suprisingly little time was devoted to it.

In the provision of post-graduate courses for general practitioners, Mackenzie was far ahead of his time. Yet it is only within recent years that it has become established practice in which the respective Ministries of Health in England and Scotland have seen fit to offer financial incentives for practitioners to do so.

There is some ambiguity in the proposal that ' trained ' general practitioners should undertake research. Did training mean in general practice or in research methods? Certainly Fletcher had distinct views on this. Moreover, in showing willingness to accept the skills of radiology, Mackenzie had travelled far from the London Hospital where he had little or no use for the value of X-rays, fearing, so he thought, that it might blunt the senses and the acute perception of the clinical observer. In addition, there is no evidence that he was not enamoured of the help to be had from either Chemist or Bacteriologist, divorced as they were from contact with the patient.

Was St Andrews the most suitable place for the Institute? It is true that its size would enable practitioners to possess a knowledge of the circumstances of each patient, but only in a general way, little different from a single-handed practitioner operating in a village of some 1000 or 1500 population. In a sense St Andrews could be likened to a large village, physically isolated but with some knowledge of the inter-relationship and relative familiarity of groups, families and their antecedents. It would also be true that, in the main, the population would be non-migratory and that individuals could be followed up, or at least traced, many years later, a fact which the author was able to demonstrate in a later study.[2] To some extent the same could be said of many communities in the North East of Scotland, including the larger cities of Aberdeen and Dundee. There were other and more compelling reasons why St Andrews might be considered unsuitable, a criticism to which reference will be made in a later chapter.

Above all, Mackenzie was to be the Director of the Institute. How could such a venture fail when led and inspired by a man with such

[2] *Further Studies in Hospital and Community.* Nuffield Provincial Hospital Trust, 1962.

an international reputation. Had he not decided to come amongst the local practitioners to inspire and teach and create a new approach to family medicine and in the process begin yet another phase in a remarkable career?

Nor was he idle during this early period of planning the Institute. In 1919 he published yet another book *The Future of Medicine*[3] and dedicated it to the Right Honourable Viscount Knutsford, a zealous friend of Medical Science. In a sense, this book was to be an epitome of his current philosophy and embodies much of what he incorporated into the origins and plan of the Institute. While recognising the great contributions which pathology, especially at postmortem, had made to the greater accuracy of clinical diagnosis, he was sceptical.

> Most subjects can best be studied by starting at the beginning and continuing to the end. The gradual evolution of Medicine he said somewhat cynically, has shown that disease can best be studied by starting at the end!

He developed the theme that although gastro-intestinal diseases form an unusually high proportion of those affecting the community during life, this was not reflected in the death rates. In other words 'morbidity' did not lead to 'mortality', but these less serious diseases were nevertheless important, as they might debilitate the individual and so make him susceptible to more serious and mortal disease. The only medical person, poised to avail himself of these early signs and symptoms, was the general practitioner. Events, however, have superseded Mackenzie's adherence to the importance of signs and symptoms. He classified disease into four stages:

(1) The predisposing stage — individual free from disease but liable to be attacked from some inherent weakness or an outside source.

(2) The early stage — signs, many subjective.

(3) The advanced stage — disease progressed to point where its presence is revealed by a physical sign.

(4) The final stage — when individual has died.

Mackenzie had the irritating habit of using the terms signs and symptoms synonymously. It is doubtful if it was his intention to study the First Stage, rather was he endeavouring to refine the elements of Stage (2) of signs and symptoms before the manifestation

[3] *The Future of Medicine* 1919. Oxford Medical Publications, London.

of overt disease. In classifying a predisposing stage, he was intuitively foreseeing the development today of techniques of multiple screening, or pre-symptomatic diagnosis, e.g. mass radiography, diabetic surveys and screening for phenylketonuria etc., etc., but then this was 1919. Mackenzie's restless mind was forever groping and who can say what developments in the pre-disposing stage would have resulted had the early momentum continued? But events were to prove otherwise.

Chapter 35

ST ANDREWS—PROSPECT AND RETROSPECT

If I don't succeed, I *have* succeeded.
And that's enough.

LORD BYRON

In starting a scheme of this kind (the Institute of Clinical Research) Mackenzie wrote in the first Annual Report.

> We wish our supporters to recognise that we are attempting a very big task, and the difficulties to be surmounted are great.

It is doubtful if Mackenzie really understood the magnitude of the task he had undertaken. He was now 67 years old, at an age when most individuals are retired. He was already experiencing attacks of coronary insufficiency (angina). He must have known that his expectation of life was very limited, and yet he chose to launch this great venture when ultimate success or failure he almost certainly would never live to see. In trying to assess the value of the Institute the author will try to judge its prospects objectively as it were seen through the eyes of a medical practitioner of that time. This will be difficult. With greater assurance one can look back and assess how and where things went wrong. For in doing so, it will in some ways, depict the man himself with all his strengths and weaknesses.

A. *Was St Andrews the right environment for a longitudinal study of this kind?*

(1) It is true the town had a largely non-migratory population, but it is doubtful if the distribution of its population according to the Registrar General's Social Classes would have been comparable to that of Scotland itself.

(2) It had a University and Library, but no medical school. It is true that pre-clinical teaching was given at St Andrews, but the Institute was concerned with clinical (indeed post-graduate) medicine.

(3) Although clinical teachers from Dundee did take part on occasion, in joint clinical case conferences at the Institute no evident enthusiasm was displayed. It is a moot point whether it might have been wiser to have established it in Dundee, or at least in some of the villages on the North of the Tay in closer proximity to the

319

Medical School. There is no doubt that despite the existence of a ferry and railway, the River Tay (until the road bridge was completed a few years ago) constituted then a real physical barrier to intellectual and cultural links between the two halves of St Andrews University.

(4) It is tempting to state that in choosing St Andrews, Mackenzie was choosing the wrong place and for the wrong reasons. One interpretation, if not too unkind, was that St Andrews offered Mackenzie everything that he could have wished in his retirement — golf, quietude, a University Library, nearness to Perth and his farming roots, and onto this he decided, somewhat artificially, to graft something entirely novel, if not alien, to the medical atmosphere then prevailing.

B. *Was it sound judgement to assume that because a group of general practitioners of all ages had chosen St Andrews as the place for their life's work, then ipso facto, they were by some token the kind of men who would naturally take to clinical research and to long term methods of clinical observation and study?*

(1) The answer is obvious and yet it is a testimony to them, inspired no doubt by the enthusiasm of the great man himself, that they achieved so much during the existence of the Institute. The various Annual Reports bear witness to this.

(2) Mackenzie wrote in the preface to the First Annual Report.

' I therefore selected the general practitioners of the town to be my helpers because they had, one and all, realised the importance of the problem of the early stages of disease, having each been confronted with it in his daily work.'

There was *no selection* of practitioners as such. *All* (except perhaps one) took part in the work of the Institute. Mackenzie was surely being naïve.

C. *The patients' private medical attendant shall supply us with records not only of the symptoms of his cases but also of their progress . . . In this way we hope that the early symptoms may be correlated with the eventual outcome of the illness.*

(1) Here again, Mackenzie was displaying a weakness which seems to afflict the majority of clinicians even today. They assume wrongly that descriptive data relating to one patient can be correlated with similar data from large numbers of other patients, with-

out departing from the descriptive or qualitative methods with which they are daily familiar.

(2) Without 'quantifying' the 'descriptive' data being collected by the practitioners then any lessons learned could only be termed 'clinical hunches.'

(3) Without computer facilities, these lessons would not become quickly obvious unless in the course of a lifetime, some more obvious correlation would become apparent between childhood symptoms and adult morbidity. The author, using the Institute Records did just this in comparing catarrh in childhood with chronic bronchitis in middle age[1].

(4) Mackenzie's clinical research in Burnley was individual and personal. In the collection of his research data, he was at one and the same time clinical observer, physician, pharmacologist, pathologist and epidemiologist all in one. In St Andrews his role was so different. Here he was trying to lead a clinical orchestra without fully understanding the score. Enthusiasm was not enough.

D. *Did he foresee the value and importance of medical records in clinical research?*

(1) He did indeed. Mackenzie was meticulous and painstakingly thorough in the recording of medical and clinical data while in Burnley. Prodigious memory though he had, he committed the important and essential details to paper.

(2) He failed, however, to perceive that while these kinds of data were sufficient for *one* observer, they were inadequate for several interpreters.

(3) Mackenzie did not seem to appreciate the importance of what is now commonly understood today as 'observer error' in medical as in other forms of research. One observer may see the same object differently *at different times*, while two observers may fail to agree about something *at the same time*.

(4) As it was, the records of young infants were collected, added to in subsequent years and stored away. Looking back and taking out case notes at random they would seem to differ little from those one would expect in a good Maternity and Child Welfare Department of a Local Authority. In short, while he had the vision to see the place of medical records in longitudinal research, he had not

[1] Harnett and Mair (1963). Chronic bronchitis and the catarrhal child. Scottish Medical Journal 8, 175

yet perceived that *descriptive* data, so beloved of the clinician, had to be sacrificed for *quantitative* data which are the raw materials of the epidemiologist.

It is easy, in retrospect, to criticize Mackenzie and, with hindsight, to point to where he went wrong at St Andrews. It is idle to speculate where Britain would stand in relation to its National Health Service today, if Sir William Morant and Sir Morley Fletcher, sympathetic to Mackenzie's ideas and ideals, had been able to persuade the Civil Service to act differently and certainly more imaginatively. When computers have been given their rightful and important place in recording medical data of all kinds, then the planner and historian would do well to ponder the thoughts, the hopes and frustrations of these three men Morant, Fletcher and Mackenzie.

E. *The final question is: Was the Institute at St Andrews a success or a failure?*

In the sense that as an active force in clinical research it was gradually losing momentum long before the outbreak of the War in 1939, then it could be said to have failed. Success, it could be argued, would be manifest in its survival to the present day, and seen in efforts to break new ground in clinical research. By these criteria, it was a failure.

But to measure its place in medical history in this way is to do less than justice to the man himself and to the ideas he conceived.

> The general practitioners[2] of the district gathered round him and week after week, they sat down together to discuss medical problems that were to initiate a new movement in medical knowledge . . . His influence over his disciples was largely due to his wonderful power of sowing seed in the minds of other men . . .

That was it — yet a further opportunity for 'sowing seeds' of medical knowledge. His presence could only have been effective during the first five years of its existence, yet his influence prevails — the Institute was yet another medium not necessarily for the pursuit of research alone, but for portraying in a new situation another facet of this remarkable man.

[2] *Reports of the St Andrews Institute of Clinical Research*, Vol. III, Page 12.

Chapter 36

THE NEW EPIDEMIOLOGY

But he that prophesieth, speaketh unto men to
edification and exhortation and comfort

1 Corinthians 14, 3

It is amusing to speculate on the lone gold prospector of olden
days who, digging and scraping through endless soil and rock,
suddenly chances upon a seam of great potential wealth! Should
he let it be known to other prospectors around him? How to
capitalize on his discovery?

Division of Medical History,
University of . . .
Medical Centre,
U.S.A.

Dear Professor Mair,

In a recent lecture presented to our department by . . . .
on the general subject of Sir James Mackenzie, it was disclosed
that the term Epidemiology was first applied to non-infectious
diseases in a letter from Mackenzie to Morant.

In a recent publication *Epidemiologic Methods* B. McMahon,
T. Pugh, J. Ipsen Boston 1960, it is stated the term ' epidemic '
has ' until quite recently ' been entirely restricted to the description of acute outbreaks of infectious diseases and cites the
acceptable definition of epidemic (from the American Public
Health Association, 1960) as ' the occurrence in a community
of a group of illnesses of similar nature, clearly in excess of
normal expectation.' This would, of course, include the non-
infectious diseases, especially heart disease and lung cancer. No
one would now object to state that the United States and Great
Britain are now experiencing epidemics of these diseases. As
Mackenzie suggested this possibility in ca. 1920–21 I find it
quite anticipatory and most interesting . . .

It is hoped that my reply has done nothing to harm Anglo-
American relationships!

Dundee,
Novr., 1961.

Dear Dr ....

The reference by Sir James Mackenzie on the epidemiology of non-infectious disease was found in a letter by Mackenzie to a young doctor starting off in life as a general practitioner or physician. The information came to us through researches and explorations into the documents and literature in the hands of Mackenzie's relatives.

I find myself in some difficulty over this issue, (1) because, in a sense, it is still copyright until I obtain permission from the general practitioner to use it in the biography I am writing on Mackenzie, and (2) my own view is that, for the moment it should be held in reserve, so to speak, by those of us who are interested in this subject, and then referred to publicly when the book reaches print.

I am sorry not to be more helpful and forthcoming, but I hope you will appreciate my position.

Yours sincerely,
Alex Mair.

This young general practitioner was Dr Andrew Garvie, a cousin of Mackenzie.

Garvie (1885–1969) had retired to Blairgowrie, where I interviewed him in 1960. An engineer, or rather an engineer draughtsman, ' for the firm I was apprenticed to, had taken me in the drawing office.' He decided later to enter medicine and qualified in Glasgow. He was a character! Of independent mind, Garvie was obviously influenced, but not overawed, by the reputation of his famous cousin. His student politics in his student days were distinctly left — Socialism, to which he was to cling throughout life although, in some ways, he was prepared to resist its crusading fervour when the State began to intrude with the Panel Doctor System.

133 Harley Street, W.
22nd April, 1914.

Dear Andrew,

I have sent on to you a couple of books that I have written, and I want you particularly to read and study *Symptoms and their Interpretation*. If you will apply the moral that I try to inculcate there I think you will find it of very great use to yourself in future life.

Don't set out to practice simply with the idea that you are going to make sufficient to live upon, but try, if possible, to advance medicine by your own observations.

The line that I would suggest for you would be to make short and concise notes of all your patients, and try to understand very thoroughly the cause of their complaints. This will lead you to investigate your patient with more interest, and you will by-and-by discover things which you do not at present suspect.

The general practitioner has a very great field before him which is unexplored, and which nobody fully appreciates. I forget whether I gave you a copy of my article on 'The teaching of clinical medicine.' If you will read it you will see what I am driving at.

If you stay in Halifax in partnership you might be able to do a great deal of preliminary work which would help you in the future to get a much better position. I know from my own experience that in the kind of work that you will have, you will have great opportunities. But before entering into partnership you must clearly recognise the limitations of what a partnership means, and before you decide you had better send me all particulars, because I have had a great deal of experience in the arrangements of partnerships, and some young fellows make dreadful mistakes in binding themselves wrongly.

In your spare moments you might also take up the study of French and German, and when you have a holiday I would suggest that you should go to Paris or to some German town, but there is no use of your doing this unless you are familiar with the language.

Let me know later how you like your work, and in the meantime I shall be keeping my eyes open if anything better happens here. I think if you are to enter general practice amongst a working class people, where the best field for observation is obtained, you are far better in the North than in the South.

> With kind regards,
> Believe me,
> Yours sincerely,
> J. MACKENZIE.

Good advice this to the aspiring physician. There was more to follow.

133 Harley Street, W.
18th January, 1915.

Dear Andrew,

. . . It might also be as well that if your income would permit, you should have, not only a motor-bicycle, but also a small car, as you would find that it would be so easy to make extra visits that it would soon pay for itself. At present do not be niggardly but rather launch out a little as the appearance of success often makes success possible . . .

With kind regards,
Yours sincerely,
J. MACKENZIE.

There followed several letters from Mackenzie to Garvie, advising and guiding the young man, about house purchase, rent, rates, practice contracts, partnership and much else. Garvie valued this advice and was grateful too for help about his own health, but on Mackenzie's medical pronouncements, he was not so sure.

133 Harley Street,
Mar. 1915.

Dear Andrew,

. . . In the meantime, just pay attention to your patients and note the conditions you are ignorant of and after a year's observations take a holiday and come up to London and perhaps work out a plan of campaign for the future . . .

Three years later Mackenzie had retired to St Andrews but the correspondence continued.

New Park,
St Andrews,
23rd April, 1918.

Dear Andrew,

Let me have your records, imperfect as they are, as soon as you can. I'll compare them with mine; I want the facts broadly. You should continue your observation, and try to compare your results with those of the Hospital statistics and death statistics with much greater minuteness than I am doing; the object is to call attention to the great differences between the statistics of death and of those of diseases that impair the community.

There is to be an attempt, I suspect, to get up clinics in the state medical service with ' consultants ' reared in Hospitals and laboratories. I want to point out from these statistics that the 'consultant' should come from the general practitioners, and if you get in with this work I can foresee a great field for you.

Yours sincerely,
J. MACKENZIE.

Guidance, encouragement, exhortation were to follow in quick succession. Time was running out. Did he see in Garvie another Scot, a young clansman to whom he could hand over the Fiery Cross inveighing him to arms in the cause of research in general practice?

New Park,
St Andrews.
2nd February, 1919.

Dear Andrew,

I have been reading over your long letter again, and I want you now to carefully map out yourself a line of inquiry which you should steadily pursue. Having got a right outlook upon the different diseases that afflict your community, select one or two for special inquiry. Suppose you should take up kidney affections. Take a careful note of all your cases with albuminuria, not only making an analysis of the urine to find out the more common features, but of all associated symptoms, such as the sense of well-being, presence or absence of headache, the condition of the arteries, with the blood pressure, systolic and diastolic, and the condition of the heart, and any other phenomena you may detect. When you see a sign or symptom, get to know how it is produced and what happens to the patient who shows it. You might also begin to pay more attention to your intestinal cases. Get to know Arbuthnot Lane's views upon intestinal stasis. Read up my book upon the interpretation of symptoms. Look out for areas of hyperalgesia and for resistant muscles. Cultivate the method of observation in regard to these symptoms. Never put down a note of a symptom such as pain or tenderness, stating that it is in the organ until you have excluded the possibility of its being in the skin or in the muscles. Be extremely exact and concise in your description of every symptom. And you might just make a note of your mental condition this year and this time next year, read it over and see what a different outlook you take upon symptoms, if you follow these simple directions.

327

I have just finished my book dealing with this matter, and I will send you a copy when it is published. I am hoping that it will inspire a few general practitioners with a spirit of inquiry, and certainly I will strengthen their hands in this understanding.

We are fairly well here, although my wife suffers a good deal from her headaches at times. Give my regards to your wife and believe me,

Yours sincerely,
J. MACKENZIE.

and again,

New Park,
St Andrews.
6th March, 1919.

Dear Andrew,

You are perfectly right to carry on your research work upon those lines which you yourself have discovered. That is one of the rules I advise all young men entering upon research, to find out the problem for themselves. My suggestion in regard to albuminuria was merely to give a definite object until you had discovered a specific problem for yourself. Moreover, I found it of great use to have always a central object, because if you get to understand thoroughly the principles of the manifestation of disease in one, you will find that they can be applied to others, so that a profound familiarity with kidney disease would probably lead to the great extension of knowledge of this organ conforming to what I was able to do for the heart. However, you are far better to follow your own line. There is only one thing I would say; cultivate the critical spirit, and be very chary of generalisation. The accurate perception of facts will lead to an advance in knowledge far more than any big generalisation. When you say that your views are corroborated by Leonard Hill, you do not convey to me an impression of much value. I know Leonard Hill too well to expect that he will ever contribute anything of value to the study of disease. He is profoundly ignorant of the elements of Symptomatology, and no man can ever make any progress with the study of disease until he has a fundamental knowledge of symptoms.

With kind regards,
Believe me,
Yours sincerely,
J. MACKENZIE.

Mackenzie was evidently trying to inculcate into the young general practitioner the necessity to concentrate on *one distinct area or system*, believing that the acquisition of fundamental knowledge of the principles of clinical physiology which this would give, was an invaluable, nay indispensible, prerequisite to clinical research. But it was to be clinical research in the image of Mackenzie. Garvie saw it differently.

New Park,
St Andrews.
19th May, 1919.

Dear Andrew,

In regard to the quietness after influenza, such experience is nothing unusual in one's life in the past. Our influenza of 1892 was even worse than this last attack, and a very curious thing was that, busy as we were in those times, the yearly average of deaths, and of sickness, was not much greater than at other times. The quietness after an epidemic is quite a common feature. Of course, any person can find out some explanation. We all know that in an epidemic, for instance, of measles, the people are not as liable to measles again, though, as you state, it is due to the production of antibodies; you don't get a bit further forward.

With kind regards,
Believe me,
Yours sincerely,
J. MACKENZIE.

Garvie by this time, had been working for an M.D. Thesis on his work in general practice[1], but before submitting, had referred it to Mackenzie for comment. As it happened, Mackenzie's assessment of the Thesis was apparently higher than that of the examiners. Garvie was not awarded honours, indeed he failed, and had to resit the clinical examination. Of greater importance, perhaps, was the reference in the remaining parts of the letter to epidemiology.

New Park,
St Andrews.
March, 15th, 1920.

Dear Andrew,

I have read your thesis with much pleasure and have just one word of criticism to offer. Naturally, here and there one . . .

[1] A. Garvie (1921) M.D. Thesis University of Glasgow. Pandemic of Influenza 1918–1919 and as it affected an industrial area.

might discuss certain propositions, but it is doubtful if any conclusion better than yours could be arrived at.

I shall be very much surprised if it does not get a gold medal, for it is seldom a subject of such importance is handled in such a masterly manner . . .

Moreover it has put you upon a line of observation which is much required, and by similar observations on other diseases you will throw a flood of light in dark fields.

If you continue this line of work, in five years' time you will have done more for epidemiology than any other living man, *and you need not limit your observations to epidemic diseases* (author's italics).

Do you know my latest craze? The creation of Panel Doctor Specialists! The hospital specialist sees disease only when it has damaged the body — the Panel Specialist sees it through its whole life history. *You will become the first Panel Epidemiological Specialist if you care* (author's italics). Say nothing but quietly go on at it.

Do not get the notes printed — this typed copy is excellent and just get the local printer to bind or stick it to plain boards. The title is quite good.

Yours sincerely,
J. MACKENZIE.

'You need not limit your observations to epidemic diseases.' Infections or communicable diseases were then rife, and it is evident from the frequent correspondence between them that when Mackenzie referred to epidemic diseases, he meant measles, scarlet fever, chickenpox etc. He was, in fact, referring to the epidemiology of *non-infectious* disease and that in this field the general practitioner had unrivalled opportunities.

New Park,
St Andrews.

Dear Andrew,

I am not surprised you should fail — some examiners try to find out where a man's knowledge is deficient — not, as he ought, how much he knows . . .

and returning to a familiar theme, he continued

Your experience should make you realise the doctrine I have been preaching for years, (against) the divorce of teaching from the practice of medicine . . .

And here, Garvie began to show discernment of an unusual kind. He was interested in mathematics in simple (and later complicated) methods of numerical analysis and to realize the inherent weakness of the philosophy behind the St Andrews Institute. How could a heterogeneous group of general practitioners collect masses of recorded signs and symptoms, unless and until some means could be found to handle group data. The observations of one man important in a different age, had now to be sacrificed for a different technique which we now realize as the epidemiological method.

Huddersfield,
Nov. 1920.

Dear Sir James,

. . . When I started on my investigations as you suggested, when I came back from London, I saw it was absolutely necessary to discover a system for the co-relation of symptoms. I think you will agree with me that all men who have made big advances in medicine have had the brilliant faculty of co-relating their past experiences with fresh cases and thus to single out diseases. It is brilliant but it is not scientific. During this time I have been gradually accumulating a fair amount of information but I could not see how I was going to analyse that information and it is strange that it is only this week I believe I have discovered the clue . . .

Garvie had acquired a new confidence and was prepared to stand up to Mackenzie. He saw the need to devise a system whereby symptoms could be correlated with symptoms, and patients with similar symptoms grouped. The system must be built up on facts, while allowing for opinions which might be subjective and so on.

Garvie thought he had found a solution to this problem.

I have been testing it in every way and it appears to be mathematically correct . . . Unfortunately I do not think I can be able to explain it without you seeing the actual working of the calculations . . .

Mackenzie returned to the challenge.

New Park,
St Andrews.
Nov. 1920.

Dear Andrew,

. . . In Soldier's Heart, we began with a definition of disease = the reaction of the tissue to a noxious agent. We rarely can

331

detect the noxious agent by direct observation and so must seek him by the reaction i.e. the symptom it produces. Only a few diseases are fully diagnosed and we represent them with the diagram:

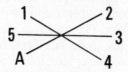

'A' being the noxious agent and 1 2 3 4 5 the reaction or symptoms. A number of diseases can be recognised by the peculiar group of symptoms or syndrome, but the noxious agents is not yet recognised and we represent them diagrammatically thus:

as in measles etc. Most ailments have a number of symptoms as yet not differentiated with sufficient clearness to permit their being grouped =

$$\left(\begin{array}{c} (\quad) \\ (1\quad) - \\ \overline{(\quad 5} \end{array}\right.$$

There we are engaged in separating into different groups. You will see we are going much on your lines and I point this out lest you think we have taken your ideas . . .

Garvie replied, that in many ways, they had both been thinking along similar lines and on similar problems, but

so far as I can see the system you have adopted is one which I tried to follow up for about six months but found it failed to reveal the necessary co-relation which was a first essential.

Here was where Mackenzie failed, and Garvie almost succeeded. Mackenzie believed that by drawing on his own experiences and observations in heart disease, where the parameters were fairly well defined, one could apply similar techniques to other diseases where the evidence was multi-factorial. Moreover he was relying not on his own single minded genius, but on a group of observers — the general practitioners whom he had 'selected.'

Had he sensed this when he replied to Garvie?

New Park,
St Andrews,
June, 1921.

. . . What we are doing here is to watch the progress of such illnesses as yours in the hope, that bye and bye we may be able to say what is the matter. As we are only at the beginning of the attempt, we would not help you, and your coming here would be a disappointment . . .

Garvie replied that as soon as he had the calculating machine ready, it was his intention to go back over his past records and place them in the system. What this machine purported to do is not quite clear. What was clear was that Mackenzie had, in his latest endeavour in the Institute at St Andrews reached his high water mark. New kinds of statistical and epidemiological skills were needed to handle, analyse and interpret the masses of data and information he and the practitioners were collecting.

Mackenzie impatient at Garvie's persistence ended his next letter.

It simply means that we must each pursue our research upon the lines which seem good to us. Your experience bids you to take one view; my experience bids me to another and there's an end o't.

Writing in 1959 to Dr Clifford Parsons, Garvie with delightful frankness and modesty, when asked if he (Garvie) was difficult to get on with, he admitted of hostility with the local Insurance Committee, the Ministry of Health, the local General Practitioner Hospital Staff and the local Public Health Authorities! Perhaps this brittleness may explain a little of the difficulties he had in having his original views accepted. Later in the same letter, he adds,

There is no doubt that Mackenzie would have been famous without emphasising the methods by which he gained his experience. Looked at in the light of modern methods of measuring the significance of data, I doubt very much if Mackenzie's work and data would have stood up to statistical tests, for, with a much larger practice and almost double the length of time (in my practice) I am convinced that the number of heart cases he had, could not have been very considerable . . .

But to go back again in time, in this difficulty of trying to group together, or to plot on a graph, a multiplicity of related or unrelated observations (symptoms), both Mackenzie and Garvie were then facing seemingly intractable problems. Mackenzie believed implicitly that by careful clinical study and observation, these facts could be committed to memory. Later, when occasions of diagnosis demanded it, he could depend on his own memory store, to reproduce the information to show correlations where they existed, and with clinical judgement to arrive at a correct diagnosis. Garvie disagreed. In his view, this form of differential diagnosis had only been possible and successful, where observations or variables were *few in number*. Beyond a certain limit, large numbers of symptoms, physical signs, social, pyschological and environmental data relating to many patients could only be handled successfully by resort to a different and more impersonal method of numerical analysis. Garvie with his engineering and mathematical bent was quick to realize this, but he too, was a man before his time. Refinement of statistical methods and their application to human biology was a postwar (1939-1945) phenomenon. The electronic or digital computer was an even more recent development. Nowadays, statisticians, aware of the potential inherent in these two developments, have introduced a new technique which is referred to as numerical taxonomy. Already, this method has been used successfully in clinical research to unravel and so identify two or three distinct pathological entities, e.g. in liver disease where, with overlapping of biochemical data, only one condition seemed hitherto to exist. If this statistical approach has a place in clinical research, then its future in the epidemiology of general practice is bright indeed. Moreover if this prospect is fulfilled, then future leaders of general practice should not forget the stimulus and leadership of Mackenzie and Garvie. They looked outwards, pointed upwards and failed. But then, Everest was not conquered by courage and determination alone. With hindsight, in medicine as in so many other forms of human endeavour, man must always seek that appropriate blend which is both Art and Science.

So in an age of statistical theory and electronic computers Dr Garvie lived to pass judgement on Mackenzie, on his success but also on the reasons for his failure at St Andrews. This, however, is not to decry the prophetic vision of his great cousin, who pointed the way to the new epidemiology.

Moreover some future Mackenzie Lecturer might well find it profitable to give further study to the relationship between these two men, and to ascertain to what extent Garvie formed the bridge between two distinct eras in general practice, the one clinical research and the other epidemiology.

Chapter 37

REMINISCENCES

Professor Davd R. Dow, Emeritus Professor of Anatomy, Queens College, Dundee, then within St Andrews University, writes in August, 1963:

I recall the occasion over forty years ago when the late Professor Waterston informed me with enthusiasm that Sir James Mackenzie intended to retire and reside in St Andrews, and I was soon to learn that his stay there would be marked by great activity.

My first contact with him took place one morning in the Anatomy Department as I prepared a lecture — demonstration on the nerves of the abdominal wall. In a flash he cross-examined me about their segmental connections and their importance in the mechanism of referred pain from the viscera.

Did I explain that aspect of their significance to our students? His bearing that morning was forceful and kindly. I was surprised indeed to meet a physician with such detailed knowledge of the precise areas of skin supplied by the nerves in question.

Along with medical practitioners in St Andrews I was invited to attend weekly meetings at the Cottage Hospital. Mackenzie presided, when the history of the patient's illness was accurately recorded and an analysis of symptoms discussed.

Every comment had to be most carefully measured. There was no room for surmise or loose deduction, and certainly guess work was out of count. Mackenzie did not suffer fools gladly and deplored the casual examination of a patient or an exploratory laparotomy without previous exhaustive scientific examination. He told me that while he valued the X-ray as an adjunct in diagnosis he was afraid of its wholesale use as an easy method and warned against too much reliance on the machine to the detriment of the human faculty.

When the Clinical Institute was opened Mackenzie held the weekly meetings there and presided over them with the same penetrating critical mind. It was evident that he had a very sound knowledge of certain aspects of Physiology and Anatomy and this he brought to bear on many of the cases whose symptoms were being analysed. These meetings more and more

336

revealed the strength of Mackenzie and the depth of his clinical knowledge. Like most men who are great, he was modest and did not make any attempt to impress. Indeed it was no surprise to find him talk of his ignorance of disease.

He had a profound regard for some general practitioners whom he felt were in the most favourable position to detect and understand the early symptoms associated with the onset of disease. Indeed the work at the Institute included the recording with meticulous care these early symptoms, their mechanism of production, and the full application of their prognostic significance.

In cases of heart disease Mackenzie had by that time (1918–1924) spent at least twenty years in finding out which are the essential symptoms. For example, he was able to point out that the symptom that mattered most in early heart failure was pain on effort, others perhaps looked for a definite sign.

Anginal Pain was one of the subjects which received much attention at the Institute and it was to the Anatomy Department that Mackenzie brought hearts of those who had suffered in this way and died suddenly. He suspected that the condition was associated with Coronary occlusion and directed me to make a detailed dissection of the Coronary Arteries in their entirety, pointing out that inspection of the orifices of the arteries was not enough. Our knowledge of Coronary Thrombosis today tends to dwarf such observations, but forty years ago its cause was obscure and Mackenzie was drawing attention to a possible explanation.

Alas! I was soon to ask him to see my father who at the age of sixty was suffering from cardiac failure. He told me then that he thought the changes in the heart had probably begun thirty years before the onset of symptoms.

While perhaps we appreciate more fully today that a proper understanding of function can guide us in the understanding of disease processes, it was not so generally acknowledged in Mackenzie's life time. He established that a great many symptoms owe their origin to variations in normal functional activity.

He thought that in a place like St Andrews where the native population was not, on the whole migratory, records could be made of illness throughout the lifetime of the individual and he showed how clinical medicine should be studied as he had done it through long continued observation of symptoms before there were clinical signs of disease.

An illustrative case comes to mind — that of a ploughman who lived near Boarhills—He said he was ' unable to work ', yet he presented no signs of disease — his heart sounds continued to be clear for years, but his story did not change. The label of neurosis was attached to him. He had passed through the hands of a few medical practitioners. Ultimately Mackenzie was asked to see him and diagnosed heart disease, confirmed later by the patient's sudden death.

While the Reports from the Institute give the names of the St Andrews Practitioners and the Professors of Anatomy and Physiology who were active on its staff, it was also a place of pilgrimage for doctors, young and old, and from overseas. On all Mackenzie made a lasting impression of his genius and greatness.

As in the case of John Hunter, Observation and Simple Experiment ran through the core of his work.

Like other men of greatness his work received early recognition in Germany, U.S.A., Canada, and other foreign countries long before it did in our own. Hurst wrote in *Guy's Hospital Gazette* after a visit abroad that the best known and most frequently quoted English Physician in Germany was probably Dr Mackenzie of Burnley.

While he enjoyed world-wide repute he evidently impressed equally the ancient city of his adoption. In the words of an old St Andrean who saw Sir James passing with one of the doctors:

' There's the auld doctor frae London wha has garred the doctors here ken that they ken naethin.'

We must not regard Mackenzie as only a Heart Specialist, or think of him as one who worked within narrow confines. His vision was broad; his range extensive. He said to me, ' Mark my words — the big advances in Medicine in the next twenty five years will be on the Sympathetic Nervous System and on the Capillary Circulation.'

Time has shown the correctness of his prophecy.

D'Arcy Thomson was an impressive figure on the streets of St Andrews — so was Mackenzie — tall, broad shoulders, strong face with a burly beard. He had a forceful personality, was a doctor who inspired much confidence, and was always willing to sit down and impart knowledge and explain phenomena. To this day I recall vividly the instruction he gave me about the movements of the heart.

I can measure his diagnostic ability with that of Specialists with whom I worked in London and the Provinces, and he stood

338

alone as a Master. Like many others I benefitted greatly by my contact with him and am grateful for the privilege of having known him.

Criticism could be made about Mackenzie's apparent failure to recognize coronary occlusion as a separate and distinct clinical and pathological entity. But now, again, he was obviously on the scent! Unfortunately, prolix though he was in writing upon everything medical even to the very end of his life, his interests had become more general and philosophical and no reference can be found in his letters and correspondence relating to coronary thrombosis or myocardal infarction.

Another outstanding world figure in the field of cardiology was Dr Paul Dudley White, of Boston, Mass. who wrote in 1961.

Dear Professor Mair,

I am writing in answer to your recent letter to say that I doubt if I can put my hand on any correspondence of mine with Sir James Mackenzie.

I worked primarily with Thomas Lewis but I did see a fair amount of Mackenzie when John Parkinson was his house physician. I did visit St Andrews in 1922 a year or so before his death. And so I can give you only reminiscences.

My first learning about Mackenzie was through Dr Joseph Hersey Pratt, the originator of the Pratt Hospital of the New England Medical Center of Tufts Medical School in Boston. He was Instructor in the Harvard Medical School when I was a student. He had and used a Mackenzie ink polygraph. That would have been about 1911 or 1912. My first study of cardiac arrhythmia and the jugular pulse was with a Mackenzie ink polygraph under the wing of Dr Pratt, who incidentally was an old friend of Mackenzie and had seen him at work in his home in the north of England before he moved to London. In fact, I think Dr Pratt actually called on Mackenzie's watchmaker in order to expedite one of these instruments for himself since at that time there was great demand from all over the world and a very long waiting list for these handmade instruments.

In 1913 when I started work with Sir Thomas Lewis at the University College Hospital Medical School I called on Sir James with a letter from Professor Richard C. Cabot, one of my clinical professors of medicine here at Harvard University. He was very gracious to me and I attended a number of his clinics when I could escape from Lewis' laboratory. My lifelong acquaintanceship with John Parkinson; with whom I spent a night only last November in London, stems from that period of 1913-14. My next view of Mackenzie was at the Hampstead Heart Hospital before it moved to Colchester. Mackenzie, Allbutt, and Osler were the visiting physicians and Lewis was their house man. I made rounds with Mackenzie and Lewis and attended their lively debate during rounds as to the etiology of neurocirculatory asthenia, which was later called the irritable heart of soldiers or effort syndrome. Mackenzie vigorously supported the idea that this syndrome was the result of thyrotoxicosis too early to diagnose otherwise. Lewis would have none of it and claimed that it was the result of low grade infection. His idea was based on contaminated blood and urine cultures, one of the few mistakes he ever made.

Then several years elapsed before Dr Joseph Aub and I visited Mackenzie at St Andrews in 1922 where we visited him at home, walked around his garden, and had luncheon or tea, with him and his wife, I have forgotten which. Incidentally, on that occasion, Joe Aub and I played on the famous golf links at St Andrew's, not very well I am sure, on a cold August day when our aged caddy said that it was one of the best summer days they had ever had. At that point I had great respect for the rugged constitution of the Scotsman. Mackenzie, although I am sure always fond of Thomas Lewis and cognizant of his great ability, was having an out with him at the moment and we argued about his clinical ability, Later, of course, Lewis wrote a wonderful tribute at the time of Mackenzie's death.

Mackenzie was a great pioneer, really the initiator of modern cardiology in English speaking countries.

Sincerely,
Paul D. White.

Chapter 38

THE LAMP IN THE GABLE WINDOW

Looking back over these pages, how inadequate, one feels, has been the attempt to portray this remarkable man.

Much of his personal letters, his output of published work (which was quite prodigious), anecdotes and individual comment have been pieced together in order, if not to obtrude, at least to enable the story to unfold, to tell itself. In the event, the story may have lost in the telling.

Knutsford, it will be recalled, when referring to Dorothy's picture of her father, wrote, ' a lawn mower cannot go over a craggy mountain.' How vivid! And yet how true.! This story may have attempted the impossible. It may well have fallen far short of the expectations of Mackenzie's disciples and admirers throughout the world. But not having had the privilege of meeting the great man (like so many still alive who so kindly and with pride, described him to me). I must surely have set out to climb this mountain all too poorly equipped.

How could one adequately portray the man, even through the kaleidoscope of such a colourful career — his drives, ambition, determination, his will to serve, perchance to succeed, to dominate lesser mortals, his motivation, the dedication to a cause, that missionary zeal, the quality of living life to the full, his very simplicity . . .

. . . And then, the mist cleared, I had reached the top of Ben Lawers. Windswept and alone, I rested. Then the descent . . .

Squelching through wet moss and sparse, sodden grass, the rarefied atmosphere seemed to give wings to my thoughts and quests. A tiny pool lipping over slowly into a silent trickle, winding its way cautiously towards the crest. Was this the beginning? I followed on. Other trickles joined together moving to form a larger pool, onwards over the edge, faster, quite sizeable now — moving onwards.

Farther down, it dripped over the hanging ledge, acquiring soon an individuality of its own, and in the ripples of the larger pool below, reflecting the blue and white of the sky above. Restless to get on, it emerged as a stream, audible and impatient. Reaching the lower slopes, it disappeared, to re-appear in the dense and tangled heather beneath. In the process, it would refresh itself from the sparse and

Fig. 1. Engraving by Dorothy Mackenzie.

hungry subsoil, on and on. Accepting other tributaries, it had now grown to a larger stream, still restless and turbulent, taking short cuts — here over a raging waterfall — there losing itself in a deep and rocky cleft, to emerge in the glen below, a sizeable river. Narrow at first, its course was now more powerful and direct. Huge rocks, it ignored. Eddies disappeared to reappear in endless flow. Miles beyond it had acquired depth and breadth. There was a new momentum, undeterred by obstacles and nature's effort to deflect its course. Narrows gave rise to rapids, cascading brown water by white, broken rushes and bubbling froth. On and on, widening towards its end, it seemed to tire, to resume its peace and quietude, to merge in the vast expanse of Loch Tay. A mountain is huge, impassive, remote. But here was a living product of that mountain, something that had both life and purpose. It had an identity of its own. Was this not the true Mackenzie?

Looking back over these 72 years, it has been for me an exciting and exhilarating experience. How refreshing to follow that great river from the uncertain beginnings to the torrents beyond. And here one would wish to join with the reader in trying to remember the outstanding impressions of that remarkable story.

One recalls his early upbringing, his home life, and above all, the unswerving support of his mother, which had such a profound influence on his career. Having missed out in his early years, by leaving school so early, he seemed impatient to make good with the opportunity that a University education now afforded him. To him as to so many poverty-stricken youths from Scotland in those days, University education was accepted not as a right, but as a great privilege. In some ways, but perhaps with greater sensitivity towards human situations, he had so much in common with that other great Scotsman, Andrew Carnegie. Both were haunted by stark poverty, both were influenced and supported by dominating mothers, both set forth to slay giants and having succeeded and been acclaimed by the world, they could not resist the call to come home again. Scotland can indeed be proud of such sons.

In intellectual and academic terms, Mackenzie in later years, no doubt with tongue in cheek, was apt to overplay the log-cabin to white house philosophy: that he had no brains; he was a dunce at school and yet he succeeded where, with his mental equipment he should surely have failed. Study of his academic performance gives the lie to this.

There is no doubt, however, that in medical terms, the Burnley period was the acme of his career, where against unbelievable odds, whether of time or resources, he applied himself to clinical research and succeeded in a way which, for ever, will be writ large in the annals of British medicine. Not only did he carry out the exhausting work of a busy general practitioner, live, love and laugh the life of a family man, but by his perspicacity and single-minded devotion to the task, he has forever placed the medical world in his debt.

In his move from Bank Parade to Harley Street, there was something of the David and Goliath about him. Or was he tilting at windmills, at imaginary enemies who refused to recognize his worth? Or rather, like his countryman, David Livingstone, did he have a gospel to proclaim to an unbelieving profession, as he once quoted in an aside to his cousin, the Reverend David Keir? Whatever it was that drove him on from Pictstonhill to Perth, Perth to Edinburgh, then from Burnley to Harley Street and finally St Andrews, he seemed always to be seeking yet a new challenge, a new world to conquer, and determined in the process to enjoy it.

In his clinical work, he was indefatigable, his interest in clinical research inexhaustible. It would be idle for one who is not a clinician, to speculate on the real place and contribution of Mackenzie to the history and evolution of cardiology. On this, even today, no doubt, cardiologists may differ. Suffice it to say that his work on irregular action of the heart, the action of digitalis and the studies on auricular fibrillation were fundamental contributions to the clinical understanding of heart disease at that time, conspicuous only by the failure by him and others of his era to recognize the significance, even the presence, of that condition so important and so prevalent today, coronary thrombosis or myocardial infarction. In so doing, one is conscious of falling into the same trap of viewing events in the light of history and forgetting the situation and circumstances obtaining at the time of the events of which we write.

All this is not to overlook much else which flowed from his fertile and inquiring mind: heart disease in pregnancy, visceral reflexes, principles of drug therapy, the significance of signs and symptoms, and much else (see Bibliography). To the end, he remained a general practitioner. By any standards, he succeeded in packing into one lifetime an amount and output sufficient to fill three. How this was achieved we shall never know, but certainly Dorothy maintained that much of the credit and success in her father's professional career he ungrudgingly attributed to the dedicated help he received from his wife. No small tribute this, and appropriate too that this sweet, delicate, devoted lady should live and be entitled to be addressed as ' Lady ' Mackenzie.

APPENDIX

I. Material formerly in the possession of Sir James Mackenzie. Presented to the Wellcome Historical Medical Museum by Lady Mackenzie

Polygraph, prototype made by Mr Shaw, a watchmaker of Padiham, Surrey for Sir James Mackenzie	R 28057
Spare tambour and arm for polygraph	R 27647
Tambour—probably an experiment specimen	R 27646
Dudgeon's Sphygmograph	R 27649
Small case of anatomical dissection instruments by Gardner, Edinburgh	R 27651
Pair of Spencer Wells' forceps	R 27906
Monaural stethoscope, metal and vulcanite (for the pocket)	R 27648
Monaural stethoscope of wood	R 27650
Fountain pen inscribed ' J. Mackenzie ' (Waterman) in case	R 28054
Bronze medal (University of Edinburgh) for practical physiology to James Mackenzie, 1877	R 28055
Bronze medal (University of Edinburgh) for Forensic Medicine to James Mackenzie, 1878	R 28056
An original photograph. Three-quarter view, with beard, in late life	

List of doctors whose photographs adorn 68 Bank Parade, Burnley:

1. Dr Samual Howarth
2. Stephen L. White (died 6/6/1858 at 57)
3. Dr Brims
4. Dr Briggs
5. Dr Brown
6. Dr Mackenzie

II. Post-Mortem Report on Heart of Mrs Ashworth (undated)
BY
Dr (later Sir) Arthur Keith

1. Also show great dilat. of auricles with atrophy of musculature post-mortem close in right auricle.
2. Tricuspid (18 × 9 mm) Mitral (12 × 5) Stenosis.

3. Sup. vena cava not cert (heart in L.H. Museum Collection).

4. A.V. bundle. The central fibrous body is atheromatous and at point of perforation the bundle (there $1\cdot5 \times 0\cdot3$ mm) is affected and fibrous with a certain cellular change. This is also seen in the node at the commencement of the bundle and I think is due to proliferation of the cells of the capillary walls. The artery to the bundle is greatly thickened (wall $0\cdot5$ mm thick, lumen 1 mm) and here and there one can see very minute vessels quite closed by cellular proliferation of its wall.

Thus the node and the commencement of the bundle are certainly pathological and I should expect conduction to be delayed. Further forwards, the bundle becomes healthy, of average size, the subendo-cardial tissue is thickened. The apical part of the left ventricle is dilated and the trabeculae atrophied.

III. Mackenzie Family Tree

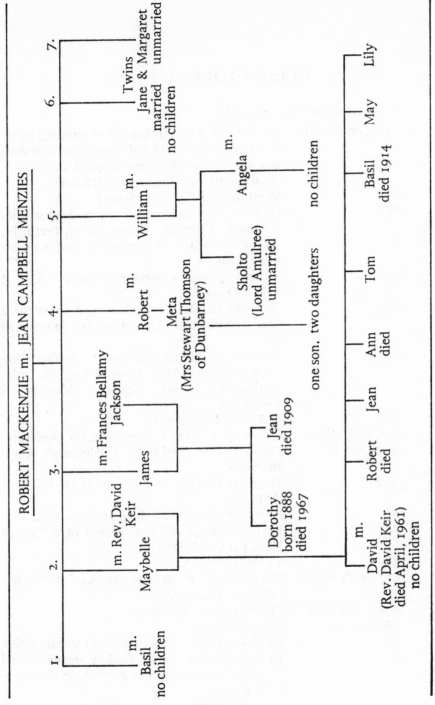

CHRONOLOGICAL EVENTS

Sir James Mackenzie, 1853-1925

1853 (4th April)	James Mackenzie was born at Pictstonhill Farm, Scone, the third child and second son of Robert and Jean Mackenzie (Jean Campbell Menzies) He attended the village school at Scone
1865	Went to Perth Grammar School
1868	He left school and became apprenticed to Reid & Donald, Chemists, George Street, Perth. He served four years' apprenticeship, and one year as assistant
1873	He was offered a partnership in the firm of Reid & Donald
1873	He went to Glasgow and worked there for a year as a chemist (Alex. Ross, 251 Sauchiehall St)
1874	Entered Edinburgh University, passing University Prelim. (April 1874) in English, Latin, Arithmetic, Euclid, Algebra, Elements of Mechanics
1878	M.B. & C.M. Edinburgh
1878 (July–Nov.)	Colliery practice at Spennymoor, Co. Durham
1878 (Nov.)	House doctor (Resident) at Edinburgh Royal Infirmary
1879	Went to Burnley as assistant to Dr Briggs & Dr Brown
1880	He was offered a third share in the practice
1882	M.D. Edinburgh (Clinical Report of a Case of Hemi-paraplegia Spinalis)
1885	Visited the U.S.A.
1887 (13th Sept.)	Married Frances Bellamy Jackson at Shottermill, near Haslemere
1888 (11th Dec)	Dorothy Mackenzie born
1889/90	Polygraph in use
1890	He discovered extra-systoles, an event which passed unnoticed until Cushny demonstrated the occurrence of the extra-systole in the mammalian heart

1892	Mackenzie contemplated going to Manchester as a consultant (letter to W. Mackenzie 8.12.92)
1893	Jean Mackenzie born
1902	Published *The Study of the Pulse*
1902	Correspondence with Wenckebach began
1903	Association with Arthur Keith began
1904	Visited Wenckebach in Groningen
1904	Visited Dr Schott's Polyclinic at Bad Nauhiem
1904 (Dec.)	Decided to leave Burnley for Edinburgh; influenced in this decision by Wenckebach
1905	Decided against Edinburgh in favour of London
1905	Henry Head advised strongly against Mackenzie's going to London, though Dr Ewart was confident of his success. Mackenzie reverted to the idea of going to Edinburgh
1906	He attended the B.M.A. Meeting in Toronto
1907 (May)	Formation of 'Association of Physicians of Great Britain and Ireland'; limited to 200 hospital physicians and lecturers in clinical medicine. Mackenzie was elected and opened the leading discussion on the heart in London
1907 (Nov.)	Moved from Burnley to London (17 Bentinck Street)
1908	At West End Hospital for Nervous Diseases (Physician to the Hospital) Sir James Purves-Stewart at this hospital
1908	Published *Diseases of the Heart*
1909	On staff of Mount Vernon Hospital, Hampstead
1909	Death of Jean Mackenzie
1909	Elected F.R.C.P.
1909	Moved from Bentinck Street to Northwood and rented consulting room at 133 Harley Street
1909	Published *Symptoms and their Interpretation*
1910	Hon. Dr of Laws (Ll.D.) Aberdeen University
1911 (Jan. 4th)	Appointed Lecturer in Cardiac Research to the London Hospital
1911 (July)	Delivered the Oliver Sharpey Lectures on Heart Failure before the Royal College of Physicians
1911	Delivered the Schorstein Lectures on Auricular Fibrillation at the London Hospital

1912 (July)	Mackenzie proposed to relinquish his position at London Hospital; the position was to be taken over by Lewis who, however, was appointed to University College Hospital
1913 (Jan.)	Mackenzie proposed Cardiac Dept. at London Hospital. Appointed ' Physician in Charge ' of Cardiac Dept.
1913 (July)	Appointed member of the Medical Council
1914	Formation of Military Cardiac Dept. at Mount Vernon
1915 (March)	Fellow of the Royal Society
1915 (June)	Knighthood
1916	Published *Principles of Diagnosis and Treatment in Heart Affections*
1917 (Oct.)	Decided to leave London for St Andrews
1918 (March)	Moved into New Park, St Andrews
1918 (June–July)	Visited U.S.A. to attend Medical Congress in Chicago (at request of Lord Beaverbrook)
1918	Sir James's brother William knighted
1919	Published *The Future of Medicine*
1919 (Oct.)	Establishment of the St Andrews Institute
1919	Sir Robert Morant (Medical Research Council) asks Mackenzie to be Chairman of Committee
1920	Appointed Hon. Physician to the King
1920	Proposals put forward for a post-graduate school for training of panel doctors
1922	Correspondence with Sir W. Robertson and the Carnegie U.K. Trust re funds for the Institute
1922 (June)	His speech to Perth Academy
1923	Published *Heart Disease and Pregnancy*
1923	Published *Angina Pectoris*
1924 (Nov.)	Awarded Charles Mickle Fellowship, Toronto University
1924	Left St Andrews for London (53 Albert Hall Mansions, Kensington, S.W.7)
1925 (Jan.)	Mackenzie proposes that money from the Paterson Bequest (London Hospital) be used for a Research Student
1925 (25th Jan.)	Death of Sir James Mackenzie
1926	Publication of *The Basis of Vital Activity*
1926	Publication of *The Beloved Physician*

BIBLIOGRAPHY

IN

DECENNIAL PERIODS

Pre-1890

A case of hemiparaplegia spinalis with remarks on muscular sense. *Lancet* 1883, I, 995 and 1040.

A case of spinal injury exhibiting the phenomenon named paradoxical contraction. *Lancet* 1883, II, 942.

A Trip to Yellowstone Park. Burnley Literary and Scientific Club, 13th Oct. 1885.

On a case of herpes zoster. *Manchester Medical Chronicle* 1889, X, 288.

The Necessity for a Hospital for Infections Diseases in Burnley. Burnley Literary and Scientific Club, 5th March, 1889.

1890-1899

A case of multiple symmetrical herpes zoster. *Manchester Medical Chronicle* 1890–91, XIII, 356.

Notes of the influenza epidemic of 1891. *Manchester Medical Chronicle* 1891, XIV, 331.

Associated pain of visceral disease. *Caledonian Medical Journal* 1891.

The significance of the pulsations in the veins. *Caledonian Medical Journal* I, 1891.

A case of aneurysm of the heart with symptoms of angina pectoris during life. *Manchester Medical Chronicle* 1891–2, XV, 302.

A contribution to the study of sensory symptoms associated with visceral disease. *Manchester Medical Chronicle* 1892, XVI, 293; *Medical Press and Circular* 1892, n.s. LIV, 210.

Some points bearing on the association of sensory disorders and visceral disease. *Brain* 1893, XVI, 321.

The pilomotor or goose skin reflex. *Brain* 1893, XVI, 515.

The Real and the Imaginary. Burnley Literary and Scientific Club, Nov. 21, 1893.

353

Pulsations in the veins with a description of the method for graphically recording them. *Journal of Pathology and Bacteriology* 1893, I, 53.

Herpes zoster and the limb plexuses of nerves. *Journal of Pathology and Bacteriology* 1893, I, 332.

The treatment of aseptic wounds without bandages or dressings. *Caledonian Medical Journal* 1893–4, I.

The venous and liver pulses and the arrhythmic contraction of the cardiac cavities. (Part I) *Journal of Pathology and Bacteriology* 1894, II, 84; (Part II) *Journal of Pathology and Bacteriology* 1894, II, 273.

On tricuspid and so-called pulmonary systolic murmurs. *Caledonian Medical Journal* n.s. I, 1894.

The significance of the venous pulse. *Edinburgh Medical Journal* 1893–4, XXXIX, 1106; *Transactions of the Medico-Chirurgical Society of Edinburgh* 1894, n.s. XIII, 69.

Tricuspid stenosis. *Edinburgh Hospital Reports* 1894, II, 304.

Heart pain and sensory disorders associated with heart failure. *Lancet* 1895, I, 16.

The treatment of aseptic wounds without bandages or dressings. *British Medical Journal* 1896, I, 267.

A probable diagnostic sign of tricuspid stenosis. *British Medical Journal* 1897, I, 1143.

The site of pain in gastric ulcer. *Edinburgh Medical Journal* 1897, n.s. II, 154.

A case of gastric ulcer with characteristic seat of pain. *Edinburgh Medical Journal* 1897, n.s. II, 591.

The movements of the heart in health and disease. *Edinburgh Medical Journal* 1898, n.s. IV, 213.

The alleged retardation of the pulse in aortic regurgitation. *Edinburgh Medical Journal* 1898, n.s. IV, 349.

A note on peritonitis. *Caledonian Medical Journal* 1898, III.

Migraine—Chapter in *A System of Medicine* C. Allbutt, 1899, VIII, Macmillan.

1900–1909

Pain: a paper read before the neurological society of London. *Brain* 1902, 99.

The cause of heart irregularity in influenza with a demonstration of the clinical polygraph. *British Medical Journal* 1902, II, 1411.

Hyperdicrotism. *Edinburgh Medical Journal* 1903, n.s. XIV, 527.

The nature of symptoms in appendicitis. *British Medical Journal* 1903, II, 66.

The sensibility of the peritoneum and abdominal organs. *British Medical Journal* 1903, II, 1497.

A plea for more accurate clinical observation. *Caledonian Medical Journal* 1904, VI.

Observations on the inception of the rhythm of the heart by the ventricle as the cause of continuous irregularity of the heart. *British Medical Journal* 1904, I, 529.

Ein Fall von Störung der Reizleitung im Herzmuskel. *Deutsche Medizinische Wochenschrift* 1904, XXX, 875.

Blood pressure instruments. *British Medical Journal* 1904, I, 987.

The maternal heart in pregnancy and the management of pregnancy complicated by heart disease. *British Medical Journal* 1904, II, 918.

A discussion on certain changes in the circulation due to pregnancy, auricular paralysis, paroxysmal tachycardia and affections of conductivity. *British Medical Association* July, 1904.

A suggestion for the observation of new paths in the spinal chord. *Caledonian Medical Journal* 1904–05, VI, 134; *Medical Press and Circular* 1905, n.s. LXXIX, 558.

Über an der Atrio-ventriculargrenze Ausgelösten Systolen beim Menschen. *Archiv für Physiologie* S. 230, 1905.

Ovarian pain. A plea for more accurate clinical observation. *British Medical Journal* 1905, I, 387.

Journal 1905, II, 845.
tions of the function of conductivity. *British Medical*
human heart. *British Medical Journal* 1905, I, 587; (3) The
Journal 1905, I, 519; (2) The action of digitalis on the
(4) The action of digitalis on the human heart in cases
A new method of studying affections of the heart: (1) Affec-
ception of the rhythm of the heart by the ventricle.
where the inception of the rhythm of the heart is due to
An inquiry into the cause of angina pectoris. *British Medical*
British Medical Journal 1905, I, 812.
the ventricle. *British Medical Journal* 1905, I, 759; (5) In-
actions of digitalis. *British Medical Journal* 1905, I, 702;

Preliminary enquiry into the tonicity of the muscle fibres of the heart. *British Medical Journal* 1905, II, 1689.

Clinical methods for recognising heart block. *British Medical Journal* 1906.

Arterio-sclerosis. *British Medical Journal* 1906, I, 319.

The meaning and mechanism of visceral pain. (Part I) *British Medical Journal* 1906, I, 1449; (Part II) *British Medical Journal* 1906, I, 1523.

The nature of some forms of heart failure in consequence of long continued high arterial pressure. *British Medical Journal* 1906, II, 1007.

Definition of the term ' heart block '. *British Medical Journal* 1906, II, 1107.

The role of the general practitioner in the advancement of medical science. *Caledonian Medical Journal* 1907, V, 83; *West Canada Medical Journal* 1907, I, 281.

Two cases of Cheyne-Stokes respiration (with A. R. Cushny). *Journal of Physiology* XXXVI, 1907.

The interpretation of the pulsations in the jugular veins. *American Journal of Medical Services* 1907, n.s. CXXXIV, 12.

Die Bedeutung der Ventricularen Form des Venenpulses. *Medizin Klinik* 1398, 1907.

The extra-systole: a contribution to the functional pathology of the primitive cardiac tissue. *Quarterly Journal of Medicine* 1907, I, 131.

Abnormal inception of the cardiac rhythm. *Quarterly Journal of Medicine* 1907-8, I, 39.

The action of digitalis on the human subject. *Proceedings of the Royal Society of Medicine, Therapeutical and Pharmacological Section* 1907-8, I, 29.

Spa treatment of affections of the heart. *Practitioner* 1908, LXXXI, 34.

Counter-irritation. *Proceedings of the Royal Society of Medicine, Therapeutical and Pharmacological Section* 1908-9, II, 75.

Methods for recording and interpreting graphic records of the movements of the circulation. *Proceedings of the Royal Society of Medicine, Clinical Section* 1908-9, II, 87.

Nodal bradycardia *Heart* I, No. 1, July, 1909.

1910–20

A discussion on the effects of digitalis on the human heart. *British Medical Journal* 1910, II, 1600; *Heart* 1910-11, II, 9.

A case of angina pectoris associated with great excitability of the vaso constrictor mechanism. *Heart* 1910–11, III, No. 3.

The Oliver Sharpey Lectures on Heart Failure. *British Medical Journal* 1911, I, 793, 858; *Lancet* 1911, I, 919, 986; Abstr. *Medical Times*, London, 1911, XXXIX, 278.

Digitalis. *Heart* 1911, II, 273.

Auricular fibrillation. Shorstein Lectures delivered at the London Hospital, 1911.

Some manifestations of a healthy heart in the young frequently taken as indications for treatment. *British Medical Journal* 1912, II, 1697; *Proceedings of the Royal Society of Medicine* 1912–13, VI.

Rheumatic affections of the myocardium. *Proceedings of the Royal Society of Medicine, Balneological and Climatological Section* 1912, VI, 35.

Prognosis of Heart Affections from the Life Assurance Aspect. An address delivered to the Life Assurance Medical Officers' Association, March, 1913.

On the teaching of clinical medicine. *British Medical Journal* 1914, I, 17.

George Alexander Gibson: an appreciation of the man and his work. *Edinburgh Medical Journal* 1914, n.s. XII, 484; Abstr. *British Medical Journal* 1914, I, 1053.

The recruit's heart. *British Medical Journal* 1915, II, 563; *British Medical Journal* 1915, II, 807.

The soldier's heart. *British Medical Journal* 1916, I, 117.

The Lumleian Lectures and medical research (a letter). *Lancet* 1917, I, 820.

The Lumleian Lectures and medical research (a letter). *Lancet* 1917, II, 61.

The Renaissance of Medicine: The Lumleian Lectures and medical research (a letter). *Lancet* 1917, II, 255.

Principles of diagnosis and treatment in heart affections 1917. The spirit of English medicine. *New York Medical Journal* 1918, CVIII, 115.

The aim of medical education. *Edinburgh Medical Journal* 1918, n.s. XX, 31.

Assessing the value of symptoms. *Medical Standard* 1918, XLI, 377; Medical Insurance and Health Conservation, Dallas, 1918, XXVII, 445; *Dominion Medical Monthly, Toronto,* 1918, LI, 65.

Heart failure and pregnancy. *Lancet* 1918, I, 50.

The aim of medical education. *Midland Medical Journal* 1919, XVIII, 43.

The future of medicine. *The Contemporary Review* April, 1919.

Assessing the value of symptoms. *Canadian Practitioner and Review* 1919, XLIV, 34.

The cardiac complications of influenza. *The Practitioner* 1919, CII, 19.

Disease of the arteries: aneurysm of the aorta (With R. L. Girdwood). *The Oxford Medicine* Chap. XIV, 1919.

Medical research: defects due to want of knowledge of preliminary conditions. *Times.* November, 1919.

1920–

The soldier's heart and war neurosis: a study in symptomatology. *British Medical Journal* 1920, I, 491.

The importance of symptoms in medical practice and research. *Edinburgh Medical Journal* 1920, XXV, 156.

An address on clinical research. *British Medical Journal* 1920, I, 105.

The defects of medical practice, education and research. *Glasgow Medical Journal* 1920, XCIV, 257.

An investigation into the idioventricular rhythm and the theory of disturbed reflexes. *Lancet* 1921, I, 679.

The relation of heart disease and pregnancy. (Part I) *Lancet* 1921, I, 1163; (Part II) *Lancet* 1921, I, 1230; (Part III) *Lancet* 1921, I, 1281; (Part IV) *Lancet* 1921, I, 1342.

Quinidine in auricular fibrillation (a letter). *British Medical Journal* 1921, II, 576.

The theory of disturbed reflexes in the production of the symptoms of disease. *British Medical Journal* 1921, I, 147.

A letter: on the occasion of his election as honorary member of the Brooklyn Cardiological Society. *Long Island Medical Journal* 1921, V, 15.

The opportunities of the general practitioner are essential for the investigation of disease and the progress of medicine. *British Medical Journal* 1921, I, 797.

The theory of disturbed reflexes in the production of the symptoms of disease. *Reports of the St Andrews Institute for Clinical Research* 1922, I, 49.

An address on clinical research. *Reports of the St Andrews Institute for Clinical Research* 1922, I, II.

The position of medicine at the beginning of the Twentieth Century, illustrated by the state of cardiology. *New York Medical Journal* 1922, CXV, 61.

The nature and significance of heart symptoms. (I) *British Medical Journal* 1922, I, 505; (II) *British Medical Journal* 1922, I, 551; (III) *British Medical Journal* 1922, I, 590.

Observations on the process which results in auricular fibrillation. *British Medical Journal* 1922, II, 71.

Fifty Years Ago–The Young Barbarian. *Perth Academy Magazine* 1922.

The principles of symptomatology: an introduction to a new outlook in medicine. (I) *Lancet* 1923, II, 963; (II) *Lancet* 1923, II, 1020; (III) *Lancet* 1923, II, 1069.

Some reasons for failure in solving problems connected with tuberculosis. *British Journal of Tuberculosis* 1923, XVII, 12.

A plea for clinical physiology. *British Medical Journal* 1924, I, 1122; *Therapeutic Gazette, Detroit, Michigan* 1924, n.s. XL, 533.

A new outlook in cardiology. (I) *British Medical Journal* 1924, I, 5; (II) *British Medical Journal* 1924, I, 57; (III) *British Medical Journal* 1924, I, 104.

The application of the principle of the reflex arc to the interpretation of cardiac signs. *Reports of the St Andrews Institute for Clinical Research* 1924, II, 9.

Preliminary enquiry into the nature of the cell impulse. *British Medical Journal* 1924, I, 361.

Some general principles of cellular and organic activity in relation to symptoms. Reports of the St Andrews Institute for Clinical Research 1924, II, 21.

The real value of strophanthus as a cardiac remedy. *Therapeutic Gazette, Detroit, Michigan* 1924, XLVIII, 153.

A critique of the surgical treatment of angina pectoris. *Lancet* 1924, II, 695.

Clinical research in general practice. *Correspondence in British Medical Journal* 1924, various.

Cardiology and the General Practitioner (a letter to an editor from William J. Cruickshank, M. D. Brooklyn, relating to the first cardiological society having been established in America). Memorandum on the proposed Alteration of the Rules of the College to enable Fellows to participate in Private Clinics. John Bale, Sons & Danielsson.

BOOKS

The Study of the Pulse. Young J. Pentland, 1902.

Diseases of the Heart. Henry Frowde, Hodder & Stoughton, 1908.

Symptoms and their Interpretation. Shaw & Sons, 1909.

Principles of Diagnosis and Treatment of Heart Affections. Henry Frowde, Hodder & Stoughton, 1916.

Angina Pectoris. Bale, Sons & Danielsson, 1918.

Auricular Fibrillation. Bale, Sons & Danielsson, 1918.

The Future of Medicine. Henry Frowde, Hodder & Stoughton, 1919.

Heart Disease and Pregnancy. Henry Frowde, Hodder & Stoughton, 1921.

Angina Pectoris. Henry Frowde, Hodder & Stoughton, 1923.

The Basis of Vital Activity. Faber & Gwyer, 1926.

INDEX

The Central Press (Aberdeen) Ltd